INDONESIA

Bill Dalton was born in Waltham, Massachusetts. After a stint as a paramedic in the street battles of Santo Domingo and four years as a student of philosophy at the University of Copenhagen on the GI Bill, Dalton embarked on a seven-year journey through 81 countries, working as a letter sorter in Scandinavia, an apple-picker in Israel, a rum-runner in India, an English teacher in war-torn Cambodia, and a gardener in Australia. Dalton founded Moon Publications in a youth hostel in Queensland, Australia, in 1973, and has worked writing and publishing travel guides ever since. Though his travels have taken him around the world, he has a special interest in Southeast Asia. During the past 26 years, Dalton has explored over 100 of Indonesia's 17,000 islands, visiting the country at least 30 times and amassing a total of more than six years in the islands.

INDONESIA

Bill Dalton

Photography by Kal Muller

Odyssey Guides, an imprint of The Guidebook Company Ltd, Hong Kong
G/F 2 Lower Kai Yuen Lane, North Point, Hong Kong
T 852 2856 3896 F 852 2565 8004 E-mail odyssey@asiaonline.net

Distribution in the United Kingdom, Ireland and Europe by
Hi Marketing Ltd, 38 Carver Road, London SE24 9LT, United Kingdom
ISBN: 962-217-303-9

Although the publisher and author of this book have made every effort to ensure that the
information was correct at the time of going to press, the publisher and author do not
assume and hereby disclaim any liability to any party for any loss or damage caused by
errors, omissions or misleading information.

Grateful acknowledgement is made to the following authors and publishers for permissions
granted:

Michael Joseph Ltd. and A P Watt Ltd. for *Poisoned Arrows*, © 1988 George Monbiot;
Lutterworth Press for *Zoo Quest for a Dragon* by Sir David Attenborough © 1957; Aitken &
Stone Ltd. for *Among the Believers*, © 1981 V S Naipaul; Curtis Brown & John Farquharson
for *Six Moons in Sulawesi*, © 1949 Harry Wilcox; Longman Group (UK) Ltd. for *Flowering
Lotus*, © 1958 Harold Forster.

Grateful acknowledgement is made to the following authors:

Madelon Lulofs for *Rubber* © 1933; Mochtar Lubis for *Twilight in Jakarta* © 1968.

Editor: Taran March
Designer: David Hurst
Maps: Chris Folks
Cover Concept: Aubrey Tse

Front cover photography: Ted Carroll
Photography by Kal Muller, except for: Bill Dalton 166, 167, 180, 185, 247; Patrick Lucero
37, 66, 133, 169, 208; Gilles Massot 13, 34, 70-71, 75, 102, 103, 121, 140, 141, 146, 151,
196, 197, 230, 231, 235, 244.

Production by Twin Age Limited, Hong Kong
Printed in Hong Kong

Contents

St Francis Xavier

Facts for the Traveler   49

Dutch trading post at Bandaneira

(*above*) *Lagoon near Manokwari, Irian Jaya;*
(*below*) *Ballet based on the epic Indian poem "The Ramayana"*

(above) Paradisaea raggina, *or Birds of Paradise;*
(below) Mount Sambung, Java

Nusatenggara

Kalimantan

(above) Early steamboat exploration of Borneo

Dutch missionaries with New Guinea natives

Excerpts

Maps

Balinese girl at festival, Munduk, northern Bali

Introduction

The Physical Environment

This 5,200-km stretch of islands embraces a total area of five million square kilometers, about one million square kilometers more than the total land area of the United States. The surrounding sea area is three times larger than the land, and Indonesians are one of the few peoples in the world who include water within the boundaries of their territory, calling their country *Tanah Air Kita,* literally "Our Land and Water."

Of the country's 17,110 islands, Indonesia claims the better part of three of the world's largest—New Guinea, Borneo, and Sumatra. Only 6,000 are named and 992 permanently settled. The massive island of New Guinea consists of Papua New Guinea on the east and Irian Jaya to the west, only the latter an Indonesian territory. The northern one-quarter of the island of Borneo belongs to Eastern Malaysia and Brunei, while the southern three-quarters comprises the Indonesian provinces of Kalimantan.

VOLCANOES

Inhabiting a portion of the intensely volcanic Ring of Fire, most Indonesians live and die within sight of a volcano. The islands are the site of the earth's two greatest historic volcanic cataclysms, Krakatoa and Tambora, and each year brings an average of 10 major eruptions. This activity not only destroys, but provides great benefits. The Hindu monuments constructed for over 750 years on Java were for the most part built from cooled lava rock, ideal for carving. The chemical-rich ash produced by an eruption covers a wide area of surrounding land; rivers carry ash even farther by way of irrigation canals. Thus Indonesia enjoys some of the most fertile land on the planet. In places it's said you can shove a stick in the ground and it'll sprout leaves.

Indonesia is the place to see volcanic craters seething with bubbling, steaming gray mud, rocks covered in bright yellow sulphur, and vast rivers of black gaseous lava. The trapped heat under the earth is an almost limitless source of alternative energy. It's estimated there are at least 217 geothermal locations in Indonesia with a total potential of 16,035 megawatts.

CLIMATE

Indonesia straddles the equator and days are all roughly the same length. The sun rises promptly at 0600 and sets just as predictably at 1800. The country has a typical monsoonal equatorial climate with only two seasons: wet (Nov.-April) and hot

(May-Oct.). In reality it's always hot and always humid, with the temperature changing very little; the wettest places are in the mountains of all the main islands.

Locales east of Solo in Central Java have sharply defined dry seasons, the duration increasing the closer the area is to Australia. The Palu Valley in Central Sulawesi receives less than 50 cm of rain per year. In the far southeastern islands of Timor and Roti, the dry season can last up to seven months. Sumatra and Kalimantan have no dry season.

Indonesians look upon climate differently than people in the West. Warmth is associated with "hard work, pain, terror, bad," while in the West most think "pleasant, cozy, secure, healthy." Indonesians prefer to socialize and promenade in the cool evenings. Because the hard winters of North America and Europe never occur here, there isn't the drive to finish tasks before the season changes. This explains in part the Indonesian concept of *jam karet* or "rubber time."

FAUNA AND FLORA

Although covering only one percent of the earth's surface, Indonesia is amazingly rich in animal and plant life. Contained within its land and water territory are 17% of the world's bird species, 16% of the world's amphibians and reptiles, 12% of the world's mammals, and 10% of the world's flora. Spanning 4,800 kilometers across two biogeographic zones—the Oriental and the Australian—and with landforms ranging from mangrove swamps to glaciers, Indonesia is no doubt the most diverse natural wildlife repository on earth.

Hundreds of different species of mammals are scattered throughout the archipelago. These include the orangutan, with its blazing orange shaggy coat; deep-black wild cattle weighing up to two tons; 35 cm-high miniature deer; clouded leopards; mountain goats; wild warthogs; the Asian sun bear, with a large white circle on its chest; and long-snouted tapirs which gallop like stallions, tossing their heads and whinnying. The fauna of Irian Jaya resembles that of Australia: vividly colored birds of paradise, spiny anteaters, mouse-like flying possums, bandicoots. In northern Sulawesi lives the world's smallest species of monkey, which can easily sit in the palm of the hand. Reptiles include the giant Komodo dragon, the reticulated python, and deep-croaking geckos. Two hundred mammal species, of the 500 in the world, are found only in Indonesia.

Of approximately 1,500 bird species worldwide, 430 are found only in Indonesia. There are peacocks, pheasants, partridges, turkey-sized pigeons, and jungle fowl who incubate their eggs in volcanic steam. Black ibis fly in V-formations, the blue-crowned hanging parrot of the Riaus emits sharp penetrating notes, the glossy black talking mynah of Nias mimics gibbons, and the rhinoceros hornbill of the Kalimantan jungle cackles gleefully with human-like laughter.

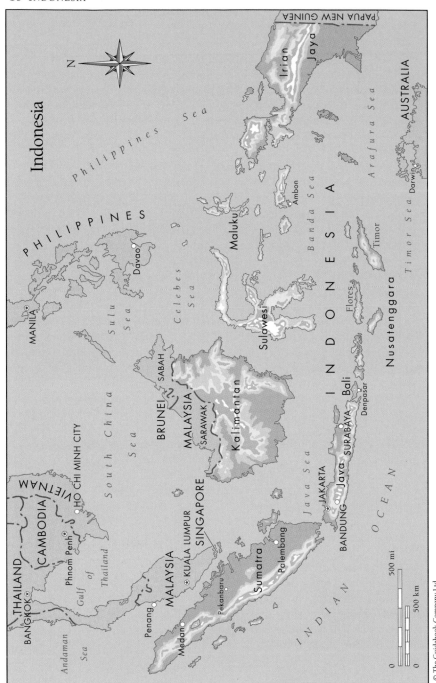

Insect and arachnid forms number in the hundreds of thousands: aquatic cockroaches, praying mantises like bright green banana leaves, beetles in the shape of violins, submarine-diving grasshoppers, and the world's most extraordinary moth, the Atlas, with a wingspan of 25 cm. There are spiders that catch and devour small birds in giant webs, and scorpions with bites like bee stings. The fabulously colored butterflies are world famous.

In Indonesia's seas are found the world's rarest shell, the Glory of the Seas; crabs who clip down coconuts and open them on the ground; bony-tongued and luminous fish; freshwater dolphins; fish that climb mangrove trees looking for insects; seaweed that reaches lengths of 75 meters; and the world's only poisonous fish.

Due to its extreme geographic fragmentation, Indonesia is richer in plant species than either the American or African tropics. There are 250 species of bamboo and 150 species of palm. In the more fertile areas flowers are rampant—hibiscus, jasmine, allamanda, frangipani, bougainvillea, lotus lilies one-half meter wide. Java alone has 5,000 plant species; there are twice as many species on Borneo as in all of Africa. Sumatra is home to the insectivorous corpse plant, which smells like putrefying animal flesh to lure insects, and the world's largest bloom, the one-meter-wide rafflesia. The luxurious vegetation of Borneo hosts seductive orchids which glow in the perpetual twilight of the jungle. Here is found the world's only black orchid, *Coelogyne pandurata*.

History

When you read Indonesian history, you read world history. This country is a subtle blend of every culture that ever landed here—Chinese, Indian, Melanesian, Portuguese, Polynesian, Arabian, English, Dutch, American—wave after wave of invaders and migrants who either absorbed earlier arrivals, killed them off, or pushed them into more remote regions. This ongoing and unending process explains Indonesia's astounding ethnic diversity.

THE ANCIENT PEOPLES

Java was one of the earliest homes of human beings. In 1891 the fossil skull of Java Man (*Homo erectus*) was discovered at Trinil in Central Java. This erect near-man thrived some 500,000 years ago at the very beginning of the Pleistocene epoch. Charcoal and charred bones indicate these people used fire. *Homo erectus* was not an ancestor of present-day Indonesians but a vanished race all its own; the species either couldn't adapt or was wiped out by more advanced beings. In 1931, 11 skullcaps were found at Ngandong, belonging to a more advanced race than *Homo erectus*—the so-called Solo Man. All 11 skullcaps had been deliberately cracked open: it is assumed Solo Man was a brain-eating cannibal.

Starting about 40,000 years ago, early Australoids entered New Guinea and the Lesser Sunda Islands. Negritos, a pygmy people who began to radiate through the islands about this time, were some of the first known fully human migrants into Indonesia. There are still genetic traces of these short, woolly-haired, round-headed people in eastern Sumatra, the Lesser Sundas, and the deep interior of Irian Jaya.

More advanced than the Negritos were the two humans whose skulls were found at Wajak in East Java. The true ancestor of present-day Indonesians, the Wajak Man is the earliest known Homo sapiens found on Java, living about 10,000-12,000 years ago. These groups seeped and percolated into the archipelago from many directions over the span of centuries, rather than arriving in a series of coherent, monolithic, and coordinated mass migrations.

THE HINDU/BUDDHIST PERIOD

Indian chroniclers wrote of Java as early as 600 B.C., and the ancient Hindu epic the *Ramayana* also mentions Indonesia. By the 2nd century A.D. Indian traders had arrived in Sulawesi, Sumatra, and Java. Bronze Age Indonesians had many similar cultural traits that made the Indian culture easy to absorb. Indonesian feudal rulers most likely invited high-caste and learned Brahmans to migrate and work as a literate bureaucracy. Indian influences, including Hinduism, touched only the ruling classes; there was no significant impact on the rural people, who have always leaned more toward animism. By the 5th century, Indonesians were using southern Indian script to carve Hindu inscriptions.

Sanskrit words found in the Indonesian language today indicate the specific contributions Indians made during their period of influence in the islands, which lasted 1,400 years, from A.D. 200 to 1600. The most far-reaching and significant Indian exports were metaphysics, philosophy, and the Hindu concept of a divine ruler with unchecked powers. Indians practiced a more integrated religious system than the Indonesians, featuring a heirarchy of gods with specific roles to play. By the 5th century, Brahmanist cults worshipping Shiva had sprung up on Java and temples confirmed the authority of Hindu religious beliefs.

The Sriwijaya Buddhist kingdom rose in southern Sumatra during the 7th century and exercised a wide sphere of influence over all of Southeast Asia. On Java, early Hindu states rose and fell—Pajajaran, Sailendra, Kediri, Singosari. Most, though very rich and powerful, were mainly coastal empires.

THE MAJAPAHIT EMPIRE

The Indonesian-Indian era reached its apogee in the 14th century East Javanese Majapahit Empire, considered the Golden Age of Indonesia. Though it thrived for barely 100 years (1294-1398), Majapahit was Indonesia's greatest state. During this last mighty Java-Hindu kingdom, Indonesian sculpture and architecture suddenly veered away from Indian prototypes and a revitalized native folk art emerged. When Islamic traders arrived in the 15th and 16th centuries, they found a complex of well-established Indianized kingdoms on Java and Sumatra. Borneo was still only marginally Indianized, Sulawesi barely at all.

Even though Islam ostensibly erased Indian cultural traditions from Java by the 16th century, much is still visible from Buddhist-Hindu times. The *kraton* courts of Solo and Yogyakarta are today enclaves of Java-Hindu culture. The religion and culture of Bali, the *gamelan* orchestra, and the five-note scale were also inherited from India. Many motifs and styles of the earlier Hindu culture permeate Indonesian art: all over Java you can see Hindu-style gates leading to mosques and the cemeteries of the Islamic high saints. Indian epic poems have been adapted into living Indonesian theater and Indian mythic heroes dominate the plots. Place-names of Indian derivation are found all over Indonesia, and Indian scripts persisted until Indonesian was latinized in the 20th century.

ISLAM

Arabs started arriving in Indonesia as early as the 4th century, engaged in trade with the great civilizations of the Mediterranean, India, Southeast Asia, and China. In the 14th century the Mohammedans consolidated their hold on Gujerat in India and began to expand their trade considerably in Indonesia. This was the beginning of the archipelago's Islamic period.

Islam caught on in far northern Sumatra first, then spread to Java. The religion took hold most solidly in those areas of Indonesia least affected by the earlier Hindu civilizations: the north-central Java coast, Banten in West Java, and the Aceh and Minangkabau regions of northern Sumatra. Demak was the first important Javanese city to turn Muslim, in 1477, followed by Cirebon in 1480. In 1478, a coalition of Muslim princes attacked what was left of the Hindu Majapahit Empire, and Islam was here to stay.

Islam exerted a democratizing, modernizing, civilizing influence over the peoples of the archipelago. Islam also had a great political attraction, serving in the early 16th century as a force against Portuguese colonial domination, and 100 years later against the Dutch. Java's Hindu princes were probably first converted to Islam by a desire for trade, wealth, valuable alliances, and power; then the people took up the faith of their ruler en masse. Pre-Islamic signal towers became Muslim minarets, and the native Indonesian meeting hall was transformed into a mosque.

THE PORTUGUESE PERIOD

The Portuguese were the first Europeans to enter Indonesia. Carrying their God before them, these vigorous and bold traders arrived in Indonesia 87 years before the Dutch. The Portuguese period lasted only about 150 years, from about 1512.

Portuguese was the lingua franca of the archipelago in the 16th century, and initially even Dutch merchants had to learn it. Portuguese involvement was largely commercial and did not involve territorial expansion; the period was of small significance economically and had little effect on the great intra-Asian trade artery stretching from Arabia to Nagasaki. In 1570, the Portuguese murdered the sultan of Ternate in hopes they'd gain favor with his successor. The inhabitants revolted and threw them off the island, the beginning of Portuguese decline in Indonesia. The sun set permanently on Portuguese possessions in the area when Portugal decolonized East Timor in 1974.

For their small numbers and the brevity of their tenure, the Portuguese had a deep impact on Indonesia. Much musical influence is evident, and Indonesian is sprinkled with hundreds of Portuguese loan words. Tobacco was introduced by these medieval adventurers. Por-

Portuguese ships were the first bearers of European civilization, arriving 100 years before the Dutch

tuguese shipbuilding techniques and designs are still followed in Sulawesi and Nusatenggara. Old Portuguese helmets and spears are kept as family heirlooms, and scores of Portuguese forts are scattered around Maluku and other eastern islands.

THE ENGLISH PERIOD

Early in the 17th century the English were direct rivals to the Dutch in the exploitation of the East Indies. Although treaties dictated the two chartered companies would peacefully cooperate, they were far from amicable partners. Underlying enmity erupted at last on Ambon in 1623, when the personnel of an English factory were tortured and executed, accused of conspiring to seize the local Dutch fort. Vivid woodcut illustrations of the Amboyna Massacre printed in the popular press enraged the English public.

Almost 200 years later, during the Napoleonic Wars, Java was occupied by English forces, and the sultan's *kraton* in Yogyakarta was stormed and subdued. The young and energetic Sir Stamford Raffles (1781-1826), an official of the English East India Company and founder of Singapore, was appointed governor. He immersed himself enthusiastically in the history, culture, and customs of Indonesia, uncovering the famous Borobudur temple. But because England wanted to prepare Holland against attack by France and Prussia, most of the Indies were handed back to the Dutch in 1816. By 1824 the English had shifted their attention to Singapore and eventually abandoned Indonesia altogether.

The English made another brief and ignominious appearance on Java in 1945 to accept the official Japanese surrender of the islands and to keep order, but within several months they were accused (accurately) by the Indonesians and the world of being pawns of the Dutch. By 1946, they had extricated themselves from their awkward role. The most long-lasting result of British rule in Indonesia is left-hand driving.

THE DUTCH ERA

By the time European traders reached the East Indies in the early 16th century, the islands had government, cities, monumental temples, irrigation systems, handicrafts, orchestras, shipping, art, literature, cannon-fire, and astronomy. The Dutch started their involvement here as traders, first entering Indonesia at Banten in 1596 with just four ships. When these ships returned safely to Holland with their valuable cargoes of spices, the result was wild speculation. Backed by private companies, 12 expeditions totaling over 65 ships were sent to the East Indies between 1598 and 1605. The Vereenigde Oost-Indische Compagnie (VOC) was chartered in 1602, a private stock company empowered to trade, make treaties, build forts, maintain troops, and operate courts of law throughout the East Indies.

The Dutch did everything they could to isolate the islands from outside contact. They gained their first foothold in Batavia in the early 17th century and within 10 years were sinking all foreign vessels found in Indonesian waters. They opened strategic fortified "factories," or trading posts, over the length of the archipelago. Using a combination of arms, treaties, perfidy, and puppets, they became increasingly involved in the internal affairs of Indonesian states.

An infamous forced cultivation system, the Culture System, was instituted in 1830. Virtually all of Java was turned into a vast state-owned labor camp, run somewhat like the antebellum slave plantations of the United States. Javanese farmers were starved to produce cash crops: in 1849-50 serious rice famines occurred in the great rice-producing area of Cirebon. By 1938 the Dutch owned and controlled over 2,400 estates, equally divided between Java and the Outer Islands.

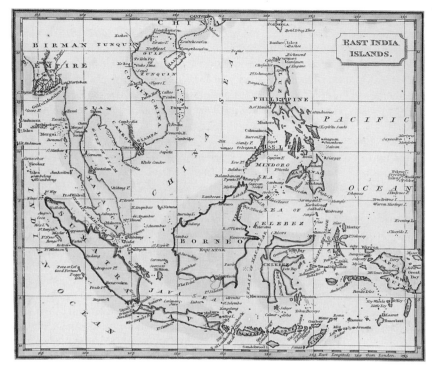

East India Islands, Tyrer 1821

COLONIAL RULE

The history of Dutch colonial rule was based on a racial caste structure perpetrated by emigrant Dutchmen, who ran an efficient, immense island empire with just 30,000 government officials. Under Dutch rule no higher education was available to Indonesians until the 1920s. In 1940, about 90% of the people were illiterate, only two million children were in school, and just 630 Indonesians had graduated from Dutch tertiary institutions.

The imperiousness of Dutch administration began to soften in the early 20th century, with the implementation of the Ethical Policy, which indicated a desire to begin a true partnership with the Indonesian people. But the colonialists never really considered handing these regions over to the island's indigenous peoples.

NATIONALISM

Intellectuals and aristocrats were the earliest nationalists. Diponegoro, the eldest son of a Javanese sultan, was the country's first nationalist leader. In 1825, after the

Dutch built a road across his estate and committed various other abuses, Diponegoro embarked on a holy war against them. He was a masterful guerrilla tactician, and both sides waged a costly war of attrition in which 15,000 Dutchmen and 250,000 Indonesians died, mostly from disease. At one point the Dutch even considered pulling out of Java. Diponegoro fought for five years until treacherously lured into negotiations and arrested; he lived a life of exile until his death in 1855.

Indonesians were intrigued when little Japan defeated mighty Russia in 1905. Indonesia didn't pass completely into Dutch hands until 1911, and that's when these foreigners started to lose it. Guided by the mistaken notion of to-know-us-is-to-love-us, the Dutch sent gifted Indonesians to Holland for higher education. Many of these same Western-educated Indonesians later became fiery nationalists; by providing education to Indonesians, the Dutch made themselves redundant. By the time WW I arrived, a number of nationalist organizations had sprung up, revealing the extreme dissatisfaction and impatience the Javanese masses felt for colonial rule. The Javanese were waiting for a Ratu Adil, a Righteous Prince, who would free them from their oppressors.

The Indonesian National Party (PNI) was founded in 1927. PNI sought complete independence through Gandhi-style noncooperation, and an ex-engineer named Sukarno emerged as its chairman. With his oratorical power and dominating, charismatic style, Sukarno soon became Indonesia's most forceful political personality.

Grappling with the world depression of 1929, the Dutch were in no mood to bargain, determined to make up for their losses by increasing the exploitation of Indonesia's natural resources. A ruthlessly efficient secret police force imposed order throughout the islands. Increasingly repressive measures were enforced against nationalist leaders—Sukarno and his compatriots Hatta and Sjahrir were rounded up, exiled, released, rearrested. The Dutch broke up political parties and waived petitions. Anti-Dutch feelings grew. In 1940, when the Germans invaded the Low Countries, the capitulation of Holland had a shocking, sobering effect on the Dutch community in Indonesia. To the Indonesians the Dutch suddenly didn't seem so powerful. But instead of seeking to improve relations with Indonesians to form a united front against a possible Japanese invasion, the Dutch continued their repression.

WORLD WAR II

The Japanese brought the war to the doorstep of the Dutch East Indies. In January 1942 Japanese troops landed on Sulawesi and Borneo, and by February the Japanese launched a full-scale invasion of Sumatra. The crucial battle for Java was joined on 27 February when 14 Allied ships met a superior Japanese invasion fleet in the Sunda Strait and were blown out of the water. On 1 March 1942, Japanese forces landed in Batavia; the Dutch forces surrendered on 9 March.

A Wartime Encounter

At the age of six Sitor was sent to the Dutch boarding school. It was a Christian school, but he wasn't required to be a Christian. He was, however, required to speak in Dutch, in class and out of it. The longest school holiday lasted a month. He went back then to his village. He would be greeted warmly by his father (then over eighty) and his mother, but there would be no conversation. He would simply sleep in one of the houses of the village, and eat from the common pot. There was always food, prepared by some distant relative.

He was at his last year at the secondary school in Jakarta when the Japanese came. They landed first in south Sumatra, in the middle of February 1942. Two weeks later, Sumatra overrun, they landed in western Java. The Dutch Army retreated. The streets of Jakarta were empty; people stayed indoors. But one day Sitor and some of his friends went out on their bicycles. And it was near the big Dutch colonial monument, near the present site of the Borobudur Intercontinental hotel, that Sitor saw the first Japanese soldier.

The soldier was on a bicycle, one of the famous fold-up bicycles of the Japanese army. The soldier was tired and sweating; his uniform was thin and cheap, and he smelled of sweat. He stopped the boys. He made it clear—though he spoke only Japanese—that he wanted the bicycle Sitor was riding.

The Japanese fold-up bicycle was shoddily made and hard to pedal. Sitor's bicycle was British, a sturdy Humber or Raleigh or Phillips. But this bicycle, which was a little too big for Sitor, was far too big for the Japanese. He tried to ride it but decided he couldn't. Sitor was five feet three inches; the Japanese was some inches shorter.

The Dutch monument, near where this meeting took place (replaced today by a gigantic bronze statue of an exultant man breaking chains), was of an early Dutch colonizer pointing down, as Sitor said, to the conquered land of Indonesia. And Sitor reflected even then—having kept his bicycle—on how strange it was that a man as small as that Japanese soldier should have defeated the very big Dutchman.

~ V S Naipaul, Among The Believers, 1981

The Japanese immediately backed the nationalists and orthodox Muslims, the two groups most opposed to Dutch rule. The new masters even spoke of one day granting Indonesia its independence. But the Japanese soon proved themselves more ruthless than the Dutch. Indonesia was included in Japan's mythical "Greater Southeast Asia Co-Prosperity Sphere," which in reality meant the country would be exploited of every possible resource, whether material or human.

Sukarno, who was retained by the Japanese to help them govern, cleverly used every opportunity to educate the masses, inculcating in them a nationalist consciousness. Bahasa Indonesia, the language the Japanese used to spread their propoganda out to the smallest villages, became a gigantic symbol of nationalism. The Japanese also created an armed home guard, later to become the core of a revolutionary militia that would fight the Dutch. As the war progressed and the Japanese began losing, greater real power began passing into the hands of Indonesians.

THE REVOLUTION

Eleven days after Hiroshima, on 17 August 1945, Sukarno and Hatta declared independence in Jakarta and the Republic of Indonesia was born. The British, who arrived in Jakarta in September 1945, were charged with the thankless task of rounding up Japanese troops and maintaining order. Duped into fighting for the Dutch, they got more than they bargained for in bloody street battles with Indonesian fighters, culminating in the furious month-long Battle of Surabaya in November 1945. Convinced the republic was supported wholeheartedly by the Indonesian masses, the British informed the Republican government it was responsible for law and order in the interior. This constituted de facto recognition of the new Indonesian government.

The Dutch intended to start up where they'd left off, but they were mistaken. During the internal revolution against the Dutch (1945-49), communications were nonexistent and the provinces were on their own, administratively and militarily. Bands of politically passionate young people (*laskar*) emerged. The total strength of these irregular armed troops far surpassed the official Republican army. Internationally, in the early years of the struggle, the Indonesians were almost alone in their fight against the Dutch. It was the independent Asian states, the Soviet Union, Poland, and the Arab states who first gave the new republic their support.

In 1948 an ultraconservative government was voted into power in Holland, one that considered further negotiations futile. In December, Yogyakarta was bombed and strafed, then occupied by Dutch paratroopers. Sukarno and most of the members of his revolutionary cabinet were taken into "protective" custody. But Indonesian Republicans controlled the highways, the food supply, and the villages. What they didn't control, they burned or blew up. *"Merdeka!"* ("Freedom!") was on everybody's lips.

Outraged world opinion eventually rallied behind the new Republic and the UN applied real pressure. It was also pointed out that the amount the Dutch were spending to regain the islands was embarrassingly close to the sum the U.S. had granted Holland for war reconstruction aid under the Marshall Plan. The U.S. Congress rebelled, and in 1948 withdrew its support of the Dutch.

Finally, the Dutch transferred sovereignty to a free Indonesia on 27 December 1949. On that day, all over Indonesia the Dutch flag was hauled down and the red and white flag of Indonesia hoisted in its place. Not turned over to the Indonesians was the western portion of the island of New Guinea (Dutch New Guinea), an unsettled issue which was to remain a festering sore between the two countries for the next 15 years.

POST-INDEPENDENCE

On 16 December 1949, the Indonesian House and Senate unanimously elected Sukarno president of the new Federal State of Indonesia. The country was quickly recognized by most nations, and the UN admitted it as its 60th member in September 1950. "It was not enough to have won the war," Hatta said. "Now we must take care not to lose the peace."

It would not be easy. When the Dutch left, the Indonesians had nothing—no teachers, no higher-level civil service class, no national income. The new Republic turned over cabinets every six months, and there was chaotic bickering and dissension among the military, religious, left-wing, and conservative factions in the embryonic government. In 1955, 169 different political parties fought for 257 seats. To stop the chaos, Sukarno declared in 1956 his policy of "Guided Democracy," involving the creation of a National Council made up of members handpicked by himself. Sukarno reinstituted the age-old Indonesian tradition of *mufakat,* or decision through consensus. Political parties and legislative bodies were abolished.

The Outer Islands claimed, rightfully, that the central government was neglecting them and that Jakarta was too lenient toward communists. In February 1958, West Sumatra and North Celebes revolted, demanding more Outer Island, Muslim-oriented autonomy. Seventy army battalions were mobilized to suppress the insurgents. Sukarno ordered the landing of troops on the eastern coast of Sumatra, and by 17 April 1958 central government troops took Padang. On 5 May Bukittinggi fell. In 1962, Sukarno ordered amphibious landings and paratroop drops into the Dutch-controlled territory of West New Guinea. These forays stirred the U.S. to put relentless pressure on the Dutch to capitulate. The Netherlands turned the territory over to UN administration in 1962, which in turn handed it to the Indonesians in 1963 under the stipulation that an Act of Free Choice occur within five years. Tribal leaders agreed without a vote to integrate with the Indonesian Republic in 1969.

"Pariah Among Nations"

By the late 1950s, Sukarno was accumulating ever more power, press censorship had appeared, and the jails were filling with politicians and intellectuals. During the early 1960s Indonesia left the UN and became militantly anti-Western. To prevent Sabah and Sarawak, the British-controlled sections of Borneo, from joining the proposed Malaysian federation, Sukarno initiated an aggressive *konfrontasi* military campaign. Raiders attacked the Malaysian peninsula and skirmishes broke out in northern Borneo between Indonesian, British, and Australian troops. Sukarno aligned himself with Communist China, parroting its official anti-imperialist line.

For 20 years this visionary and mesmerizing leader welded the islands together by adroitly playing off powerful groups against one another, his government a hectic marriage of widely disparate political ideologies. When he told his people that Marxism, nationalism, and Islam were all reconciled in one political philosophy, "Sukarnoism," they embraced it. Sukarno squandered billions on colossal stadiums, conference halls, and grandiose Soviet-style statuary. The inflation rate was running at 650% per year; mammoth foreign debts had accumulated; opposed factions of the military, communists, Muslims, and other groups were grappling for control of the government. The political polarization between Army generals on the one side and the Indonesian Communist Party (PKI) on the other was nearing the breaking point.

The 1965 Coup

On the night of 30 September 1965, six top generals and their aides were abducted and brutally murdered. What followed was one of the most massive retaliatory bloodbaths in modern history. An unknown general named Suharto mobilized the army strategic reserve (KOSTRAD) against "communist conspirators." The Indonesian army had never forgiven the communists for an attempted coup in 1948. While the armed forces stood aside, fanatical Muslim youths burned the PKI headquarters in Jakarta to the ground.

Over the following months all of Java ran amok, resulting in the mass political murders of as many as half a million people. The Communist Party was obliterated, the government bureaucracy purged of sympathizers, and the army assumed control of the country. In 1966, Indonesia's militant *konfrontasi* campaign with Malaysia was called off and the Jakarta-Peking axis abruptly ended. Suharto opened the country to Western investment, and the Indonesian congress announced plans to rejoin the UN. Although his role in the plot was never made clear, Sukarno's power was systematically undermined by the new regime until his death in June 1970.

The Ascent of Suharto

A mild-mannered speaker, quiet, pragmatic, and a shrewd professional soldier,

Suharto is today Indonesia's head of state. Born of humble parents in 1921 in a village near Yogyakarta in Central Java, the second president's personal style stands in stark contrast to his flamboyant and magnetic predecessor. Suharto was put in charge of the military campaign to wrest control of Irian Jaya from the Dutch but happened to be in Jakarta at the time of the 1965 coup. In the right place at the right time, Suharto's troops played a decisive role in the turmoil of October. After dismantling Sukarno's Guided Democracy, Suharto installed a patrimonial regime which soon became popularly known as the *Ordu Baru* ("New Order").

TODAY'S ECONOMY

Following the crises of the 1960s, Suharto's New Order changed a badly managed economy into a liberal market economy backed by foreign investment and state planning. By balancing the budget and controlling the money supply, Suharto brought down inflation from a staggering 639% in 1966 to under 15% in 1969. Resources were redirected from wasteful prestige projects to producing food and clothing and building roads and harbors. The new administration wholeheartedly adopted Western development strategies and encouraged foreign investment. When Suharto took office in 1967, the average per capita income was just over $70 a year; today, it's over $600.

By the early 1990s manufactured goods accounted for 27.7% of total Indonesian exports, overtaking agriculture. Indonesia eventually took its place as a major oil producer as well, joining OPEC in 1962. When oil prices quadrupled in 1973, Indonesia's export earnings doubled, though this period of abundance ended with the global recession. Though oil continues to be a source of government revenue and foreign exchange, natural gas is playing an important role as an alternative energy source. Indonesian production rose dramatically with the discovery of huge reserves in northern Sumatra and East Kalimantan; today Indonesia is the world's largest exporter of natural gas. And with proven coal reserves of at least 1,730 million tons, production is expected to reach 40 million tons by the year 2000.

But Indonesia is still very much an agricultural nation. Agriculture employs more than half the workforce and contributes about 25% of the gross domestic product. Rice is Indonesia's most important crop, grown virtually everywhere. Indonesia ranks among the world's top five producers in rubber, coffee, cocoa, and soybeans and is currently the third biggest coffee exporter after Brazil and Colombia.

Fishing employs directly or indirectly about 1.5 million people. Dominating the industry today are large mechanized commercial fleets owned by Chinese or Indonesians who've entered into joint ventures with the Japanese and Taiwanese. They account for up to a quarter of the catch yet make up only two percent of the total fleet.

Over 2.5 million visitors arrived in Indonesia in 1991, the highest in the Asociation of South East Asian Nations (ASEAN) despite the Persian Gulf War. Backpackers and surfies, who spearheaded the tourism boom of the 1970s and '80s, are now being replaced by leisure visitors. Tourism is the highest foreign exchange earner in the non-oil and gas sector after textiles and wood-based industries.

The People

The country is an ethnological gold mine, the variety of its human geography—336 ethnic groups—without parallel on earth. Shades of skin vary from yellow to coal black. Welded together by a unifying lingua franca and intermarrying freely, Indonesians represent all the Asian cultures, races, and religions. They worship Allah, Buddha, Shiva, and Jesus—in some places an amalgam of all four. Living in a collection of local archipelagic nations, many Indonesians identify themselves in local terms: Orang Toraja, Orang Sawu, Orang Mentawai. This sense of local identity with one's tribe and clan has fostered an attitude of tolerance toward other cultures summed up in the Indonesian expression *lain desa, lain adat* or "other villages, other customs."

Due to the archipelago's size and terrain, many of Indonesia's ethnic pockets have remained extremely isolated. You can find ways of life separated by some 5,000 years; people live in the Neolithic, Bronze, Middle, and Nuclear ages. Some Indonesians wear rings and rat ribs in their noses; others read the *Asian Wall Street Journal* and mimic Western rap.

Indonesia has the fourth largest population in the world, some 180 million, which equals the population of all other Southeast Asian nations combined. Better health care, decreasing infant mortality, and longer life expectancy keep more people alive. The population of Java, which comprises only seven percent of Indonesia's total land area, has tripled this century, reaching 110 million, 60 percent of Indonesia's total. Despite the government's best efforts at family planning, the Asian Institute of Management projects that by the year 2020 the country's population will be 253.7 million, 52% comprising a huge, urban middle class. Over the next 30 years Jakarta will double in size, from 10 million to 20 million people. Indonesia has probably the world's largest collection of cities with populations over 200,000—26 at last count. Around 20% of Indonesia's population now lives in urban areas.

THE INDONESIAN FAMILY

Ever since nomadic Malay hunter-gatherers began cultivating rice in the fertile ashes of burned forests some 4,500 years ago, rice has been at the very center of Indonesian culture. The structure and pressure of this grain's intensive cultivation has given rise to very close-knit, cooperative families, especially on Java, the island that supports the bulk of the population.

(following pages) Children of Lembaka Island

The heart and soul of Indonesia is the village. About 80% of the people still live in 60,000 agricultural communities throughout the archipelago. The village council of elders is the foundation of Indonesian democracy, and village and family loyalties come before all others. The extended family is a sophisticated structure that makes alliances and friendships, keeps people happy, and offers a superbly supportive environment for children and elders. Children must forever honor and respect their parents. A young adult working outside the home turns over wages to the family, submits to opening of personal mail, is expected to help in the cost of sending younger siblings to school, and must contribute to the expenses of supporting mature members of the family. The nation as a whole is looked upon as a family. Both the president and schoolmasters are referred to as *bapak* or *pak* (father). A schoolmistress or *warung* proprietor is addressed as *ibu* (mother).

ADAT

Meaning indigenous customary law, this is the word Indonesians utter when you ask about a custom with obscure origins. This unwritten, unspoken traditional village law governs the actions and behavior of every person in every village and city *kampung*. Evolving from a time when villages were largely collectivist and self-governing, *adat* dictates what foods are eaten and when, ceremonies for the ill or dead, ownership of land and irrigation systems, architecture of family houses and granaries, criminal and civil law covering theft and inheritance, relations between siblings, marriage, the treatment of guests—the total way of life.

Most of the more elaborate and cultic manifestations of *adat* have been forgotten; it now covers only the basic necessities and social obligations of life. Though the original meaning of many acts and gestures may be lost, they are rigorously performed without question. *Adat* is not in the law books; it's in the genes. Some say *adat* strangles the people because it encourages superstition instead of reasoning, that it stifles progress because all actions are based on precedent. Change from within Indonesian society is very slow.

Language

Such is the diversity of tongues in Indonesia—200 indigenous speech forms, each with its own regional dialects—that often inhabitants of the same island don't speak the same native language. Irian Jaya is home to an astounding 10% of the world's languages. Fortunately, one language, *Bahasa Indonesia*, is taught in all schools; it's estimated about 70 percent of the population is literate in this language, the only cultural element unifying the entire geographically splintered population.

First used as a political tool in 1927 with the cry "One Nation, One Country, One

Koran *lesson at a home in Nusatenggara*

Language!" it's the only language used in radio and TV broadcasting, in official and popular publications, in advertisements and on traffic signs. Films shown in Indonesia are required by law to be dubbed in standardized, modern Indonesian. Most of the country's regional languages change forms and endings to show deference to the person addressed; *Bahasa Indonesia* does not. Thus, Indonesian has been a force for the democratization and unification of the different races and classes of Indonesia.

Although Indonesian derives from Old Malay, the proliferation of acronyms and infusion of foreign words makes Indonesian reading material barely comprehensible to Malaysians. Known for economy of vocabulary and simple, even childish phrases, Bahasa Indonesia is actually an elaborate, subtle, and ambiguous speech form for expressing complex thought.

Initially, this nontonal language is sublimely easy to learn. It's written in the familiar Roman alphabet, words are pronounced the way they're spelled, the morphology is very simple. Nouns and verbs lack cases, genders, declensions, confusing conjugations—no verb "to be." Perhaps the most difficult aspect of the language is its use of prefixes and affixes to turn roots into nouns and verbs.

Arts and Crafts

With its giddy variety, competitive prices, and unique motifs and themes, Indonesia is one of the world's great shopping adventures. You'll find here a vast array of fashionable clothing, inexpensive leather goods, exquisite textiles, and stunning jewelry.

Tradition and superb craftsmanship are exemplified in the simplest domestic crafts: the mats, sunhats and bamboo implements of Java; the basketry of Roti; the flute-making of the Torajans; the bamboo *angklung* of Sumba. Unfortunately, there are also quantities of mass-produced souvenirs, repetitive carvings, and dreary bric-a-brac. Because of the country's tropical climate, stone temples and megaliths are the only remnants of ancient Indonesian art; works by the common people, rendered in cloth, papyrus, palm leaf, and wood, long ago disintegrated. But the motifs and symbols survive. Designs and techniques of prehistoric painters and sculptors are still widely used in textiles, metalwork, and woodcarvings on houses and ships.

TEXTILES

Indonesia's scattered isles offer probably the world's greatest collection of traditional handmade textiles. You'll find many regional and island specialties, with unique patterns, designs, and colors. Similar to tie-dying, *ikat* textiles are created by tying off already dyed weft or warp threads to retain various designs and colors while the rest of the fabric is dyed. Most of these tribal fabrics survive only in the more remote parts of the archipelago, particularly in the eastern islands. *Ikat* dyes are made from local plants and minerals, and the woven textiles are used as *sarung,* head cloths, *selendang,* banners, or as ceremonial shrouds.

Batik

Indonesia's most renowned textile craft, *batik,* where wax is applied to the cloth to resist the dye, produces beautiful works of art on cotton. The wax can be applied by hand (*tulis*) or with a metal stamp (*cap*). In *batik tulis,* hot wax is poured into a small bamboo instrument called a *canting,* used like a pencil to apply a wax pattern. The material is then dipped in one color, and all parts of the cloth not covered in wax take up

A batik *market in Solo, Java*

the dye. This labor-intensive waxing and dyeing process is repeated until the desired colors and shades appear on the cloth. One completed cloth can incorporate hundreds of different patterns.

Cap, or stamped *batik,* where the same motifs are repeated over one side of the entire cloth, is by far the most widely used method. The majority of *sarung* sold in Indonesia are actually not *batik* but "*batik* motif," also known as "hand-print *batik*". It takes experience and keen observation to identify *batik* produced with the print/*cap/ tulis* combination. Sellers can be very unhelpful; sometimes it seems everything is "*halus*" (finest quality). Always ask where your *batik* was made; today the main *batik*-producing centers are Cirebon, Yogyakarta, Solo, and Pekalongan on Java. *Batik* is also produced as far north as Jambi in South Sumatra.

ANTIQUES

In Indonesia you'll find Ming china, old coins, bottles and inkwells, embroidery, 300-year-old trading beads, chandeliers, brass lamps, delft ware, pewter ware, canopied beds, old chests and carved doors, *wayang* puppets, vintage tools, clocks, walking canes, and Indonesian tribal masks. There's still a lot of traditional art here, despite the onslaught of ruthless collectors who've turned to Indonesia after plundering West Africa.

The best antique flea markets are on Java, particularly in Solo, Jakarta, Cirebon, Semarang, and Surabaya. Don't miss Solo's **Pasar Antik**, one of the largest and most colorful antique markets in Indonesia, especially for period artifacts from the Dutch years. Learn as much as you can beforehand so you can separate the gems from the junk. Visit museums, take tours. Attend cultural lectures sponsored by Jakarta's **Ganesha Society** and run by the American Women's Association. These events are usually publicized well in advance in the special-interest sections of the local press. Jakarta's **City Museum** and **National Museum** offer excellent examples of the various antiques and regional styles found in Indonesia.

In a large city like Surabaya or Bandung, antique shops are frequently located close to one another on one or two streets. Java's most famous row of antique shops is along Jakarta's **Jl. Surabaya**, dominated by shrewd Minang merchants. Other antique haunts include the shops along **Jl. Kebon Sirih Timur Dalang, Jl. Majapahit,** and **Jl. Kamang Bangka.** In Yogyakarta, check out the shops in **Kota Gede** and along **Jl. Malioboro** and **Jl. Taman Garuda.** Shops are usually cluttered and disorganized, so you really have to dig. Sometimes you have to travel a bit to find the genuine stuff. Timor and Flores are known for antique ivory, Medan for old Batak tribal artifacts, Maluku and Kalimantan for old china. Banda Aceh, in far northern Sumatra, is famous for its antique gold, old knives and swords, Dutch porcelain, and rare woven textiles.

Maloh Dayal beadwork, Kalimantan

CARVING

Indonesia's hundreds of ethnic groups produce some of the world's most sought-after and exciting primitive art. Here are fascinating forms of woodcarving: *si gale gale,* life-sized wooden puppets the Bataks of North Sumatra jerk to life when a child dies; eerie two-meter-high ancestor figures from the Leti Islands in Maluku; the menacing demons, *naga,* and human-like fish of Java; the handsomely grained ebony animal figures and mythical birds of the Balinese; the posts, house gables, and window shutters of the Sumbanese and Alorese; frightening masks, war shields, arrowheads, stone axes, and spears from Irian; attractive shields from the Dayaks of Kalimantan.

Woodcarving

The woodcarving center of Java is Jepara, famous for its ornately carved furniture and panels. Torajaland and Asmat are the carving centers for the eastern islands. On Lake Toba in North Sumatra, the Bataks skillfully carve ancestor figures, masks, magic augury books, and wands. Traditionally, Mas is the woodcarving center of Bali, though the work occurs all over the island. Bare teak or mahogany are favored by some Balinese carvers, but many use bright pastel oils to paint feathers or scales on wooden objects.

Perhaps the most spectacular example of ethnographic carving are the magnificent phallic ancestor *bisj* poles of the Asmat of southern Irian Jaya. Some artifacts, such as a Dani digit chopper, are hung with dog hair, chicken feathers, and pig scrotums, and would tend to clash with typical Western decor. Other carved pieces, such as a marvelous carved Batak door resplendent with mysterious lizard motifs, would fit into a Western home perfectly.

Other Carving Media

The detail on buffalo horn, bone, ivory, or hornbill beak can be so extreme you need a magnifying glass to truly take in the work. For the best and cheapest carved tortoiseshell, seashells, and other sea ornaments, go to Ambon and Ternate in Maluku and Manado in North Sulawesi. In Maluku clove stems are used to create tiny figures of sailors on the decks of miniature sailing ships. For stonework, using smooth lava rock, visit Magelang on Java. Batubulan is Bali's stonecarving center.

Leatherwork is prepared mainly on a crude grade of buff-colored buffalo hide. On Jl. Malioboro in Yogyakarta, Indonesia's leather-carving capital, sidewalk vendors sell luggage, briefcases, lampshades, pendants, belts, purses, and sandals. The workmanship is amateurish and the styles old-fashioned, but the prices are incredibly cheap. Another major leather carving center is Bandung in West Java. The best-known carvings in hide are the gilded shadow puppets used in the *wayang kulit* of Central and East Java. These flat puppets, representing different characters from the Hindu epics,

Wooden wayang golek *puppets, West Java*

make excellent decorative wall pieces, particularly if backlit. Rows of wooden pup-pets-in-the-round (*wayang golek*), also depicting Hindu characters, make striking displays.

METALWORK

Metalworking in bronze, brass, tin, and iron still thrives in areas where Hindu influence was once strongest—the prosperous seaports of Java, Bali, South Sulawesi, coastal Borneo, and West Sumatra. The most praised examples of ancient Dongson-derived artifacts are the remarkable bronze kettle drums (*moko*) of the Pantar and Alor islands of eastern Nusatenggara. Students of contemporary metallurgy can see percussion-type *gamelan* instruments made at **Pak Sukarna's Foundry** in Bogor, and in Blahbatu, Tihingan and Sawan villages on Bali. Brasswork is the specialty of the Makassarese of southwestern Sulawesi. Probably the most popular metal souvenir is the legendary *kris*, the ceremonial dagger worn by Javanese and Balinese. Antique bejeweled specimens can cost well over Rp21 million, though keepsake varieties with wooden handles are available for less than Rp21,000.

JEWELRY

Indonesian artists excel in such precious metal crafts as silversmithing and the setting of semiprecious stones in silver and gold. Gold is quite cheap in Indonesia; try the gold shops along Jl. **Hasanuddin** in Denpasar on Bali. Silver is also inexpensive, especially the way it's cut in Indonesia. Some workshops cut the stuff by as much as 50percent; good quality work is 92.5 percent pure. No matter what the silversmiths of Bali, Yogyakarta, and Bukittinggi tell you about the excruciating handtooled work they poured into pieces, don't pay more than Rp8000 for a ring, brooch, or small pendant. The silver centers of Indonesia are Ujung Pandang in South Sulawesi, Kota Gadang in West Sumatra, Kota Gede in Central Java, and Celuk, Mas, and Denpasar on Bali. It's usually quite easy to see artisans working in the shops and factories of Kota Gede and Celuk.

PLAITING

Indonesia's oldest craft. Woven containers are still made where rural people are unwilling to spend precious cash on tin or plastics. Bamboo, rattan, *sisal,* nipa, and *lon-tar* palm are ingeniously utilized all over Indonesia, probably most creatively by the Sundanese of West Java, the Dayaks of Kalimantan, the Sasaks of Lombok, and the Balinese. The palm-leaf offerings set outside the houses and temples of Bali are greater works of art than the island's world-famous copycat paintings and carvings.

Since sophisticated "modern" tools like iron hatchets, axes, machetes, small planes, and knives are needed to gather bamboo and to work it, the plaiting crafts are associated with the more advanced cultures of western Indonesia. Split bamboo is made into nets, hats, wickerwork, mats, and umbrella frames. Indonesians turn out ingenious tables, comfortable chairs, chests, standing closets, four-poster beds, and cabinets from wood and vegetable fibers. They're extremely adept at refurbishing antique furniture or creating new antique-looking pieces.

CERAMICS

Since plentiful bamboo is so easily made into vessels, ceramic firing techniques have never developed into an advanced craft in these islands. Glazed earthenware is crafted in Kasongan village near Yogyakarta, Plered in West Java, Kediri on Lombok, and Pejetan on Bali.

Indonesia was once a trading center for ceramics, and today contains the largest, most comprehensive collection of Chinese ceramics outside China. Well-preserved pieces are found throughout the archipelago: dug from old graves on Sumba, in the Dayak longhouses of Borneo, on the shelves of dusty souvenir shops of Ambon. Though traces of exquisite Han dynasty ceramics have been unearthed, more common is "Kitchen Ming," so-called because they were items of everyday use by the Chinese from A.D. 1400 to 1800. Celadon ware, known for its heaviness and subdued decoration, is encountered all over Indonesia. The farther you travel from the tourist haunts, the cheaper the pottery. Giant Tang vases cost Rp500,000 in Ambon, and whole sets of Kitchen Ming will run as little as Rp250,000 in Samarinda. Porcelain from Japan, Thailand, Vietnam, and Burma also turns up in Indonesia. Arabian and European earthenware is quite scarce. Jakarta's **National Museum** on Medan Merdeka and the **Adam Malik Museum** in Jakarta Pusat feature Indonesia's most stunning collections of antique Chinese ceramics and porcelain.

PAINTING

Not until the late 19th century did an Indonesian painter, the Javanese Raden Saleh, attain fame in the European art world. Most of the Indonesian art of this period merely imitated Western styles and was devoid of originality in concept or design. Just before WW II, artists in associations such as **Pelukis Rakyat** and **Seniman Indonesian Muda** began working with genuine Indonesian expression through the adaptation of Western techniques in oil and *batik*. The impressionist **Affandi**, the "Picasso of Indonesia," was one of the leaders of that early effort. Direx Gallery, across the road from his old studio on Jl. Solo just west of the Ambarrukmo Palace Hotel in Yogyakarta, sells Affandi's work. Also check out the *batik* paintings in the shops along Jl. Tirtodipuran. Concentrations of talented contemporary artists display work in galleries in Jakarta, Yogyakarta, and in and around the busy art center of Ubud on Bali.

Primitive Art

There is a whole world of difference between an artist like Munu or Tambai and our Western conception of an artist. We think of an artist as one who creates, who makes an individual contribution to the beauty in the world by expressing his personal vision of the world. But a Toraja artist is no individualist, no originator. He is totally objective, concerned only to pass on the traditional forms of his art as pure as he received them.

I suppose "craftsman" would be a better name for most savage artists. They are not concerned with winning personal reputations. They serve their art as a priest serves his religion, safeguarding the continuity of tradition, celebrating truths and forms already expressed.

In Bori I had an artist friend, Tambai. It was pleasant to sit on a corner of a granary platform, watching his cunning left hand carving the panels for the new house he had been commissioned to decorate. He was a strangely dedicated figure as he sat at work, his waist-long hair coiled around his head and bound with a narrow fillet, never uttering a word while the short knife in his left hand first sketched and then carved in relief the lovely designs on the black-painted panels at extraordinary speed. His inseparable friend Bulan often sat with him in silence, leaning drowsily against a pillar as he watched.

Detail of ceiling mural from the Court of Justice at Klungkung, Bali

Tambai had no notion of himself as belonging to a class exalted above other skilled workers. He had no inkling of my conception of the artist and aesthetics. When I said his panels were melo he was pleased that I agreed with him, but we were using the word differently. I meant that the designs on the panels were to me things of beauty; he meant that the panels were pieces of good and faithful workmanship.

Nor did old So' Kadoya, whose house they were to adorn, see them as melo in my sense. To him they expressed power. I don't mean that he saw them as crude symbols of his wealth, though they were that in so far as only men of substance could afford the services of fine artists; I mean that the intangible quality about the designs was for him not aesthetic but strength and invigoration, a virtue something akin to the strong soul and magical strength of the red tabang plants growing round the house.

It seemed to me that most Torajas had considerable feeling for form. The mud balls modelled for me by the small children of La'bo were instinct with energy. But Western influences may well corrupt their gift.

One morning after a small crowd of Bori men had spent the evening at the bungalow there I found a cock carved in one of the roof posts, a vivid sketch of fewer than twenty careless knife-strokes. I inquired who had done it; for I wanted to see whether he could work with paint and paper, and, if so, commission him to do end-papers for this book; but they were afraid I was angry at the defacement of the roof post and the artist would not reveal himself.

The Ampulembang of Tikala, appealed to, assured me that there was a fine artist in one of his villages who could work on the cartridge paper I offered and he would order him to paint me the conventional cock and rising sun, as appear on the gable of most rice-barns. Alas, the artist had been school-trained, and I was brought, not the leaping vitality of the Toraja cock and the sun he brings back each morning with his song, but a pathetic daub, a realistic drawing of a cock with a pale lemon sun, the whole thing so anaemic that it repelled.

It was shocking to realise how quickly and completely a vigorous talent could be depraved.

~ Harry Wilcox, Six Moons In Sulawesi, 1949

Holidays and Events

Indonesians take their festivals and holidays seriously. Colorful spectacles celebrating religious, patriotic, or tribal holidays are so frequent and elaborate it's a wonder people have time for anything else. On holidays, Indonesians dress in resplendent white clothes or appear in bright new *sarung* and *kebaya,* immaculately groomed. Because of the incessant Indonesian heat, celebrations are usually scheduled early in the morning or late at night.

For events on Java and Bali, consult the free, full-color, and very detailed *Calendar of Events* booklet available at Garuda offices, Indonesian consulates or embassies, and tourist offices in Jakarta or Denpasar. Some regional tourist offices might also provide lists of annual local events.

Islamic religious holidays are predominant in Indonesia. The Islamic calendar is based on the lunar year (354 days), so festivals move backward through the solar months, the dates varying from one year to the next. Hindu Bali has its own festivals, reckoned with a calendar of 210 days per year. Indonesia's Christian population uses the Gregorian calendar of the West but put their own spin on Christian holidays.

RAMADAN

A monthlong fast in the ninth month of the Javanese calendar. Islamic fasting is less drastic than the Hindu custom of total abstinence from all food and drink. During *Ramadan (puasa)* Muslims visit family graves and royal cemeteries, reciting prayers and burning incense. Special prayers are chanted at mosques and at home. Brand-new velvet *peci* (caps) are everywhere. Each day begins with the whole family rising at 0300 or 0400 and gorging themselves on as much food as they can. The fast is broken each day at sunset, usually in groups. The fasting month ends when the crescent of the new moon is sighted with the naked eye.

LEBARAN

Also called *Hari Raya* (or, in Arabic, *Idul Fitri*). The first day of the 10th month of the Arabic calendar, marking the end of the monthlong Muslim fast. No matter what the obstacles or cost, millions of Indonesians return to their villages to feast and celebrate with their families. Tom-tomming and firecrackers all night long precede 0700 festivities, when everyone turns out for an open-air service and mass prayers in the village square. This is followed by two days of continuous feasting and public holidays. It's a joyous time of mutual forgiveness, with pardon asked and received for the wrongs of the past year.

OTHER HOLIDAYS

Christmas *(Hari Natal)* is a national public holiday, ardently celebrated among the Minahasans of North Sulawesi, the Irianese of Irian Jaya, the Batak of North Sumatra, and the Catholics of Flores. Wafat Isa Almasih (Good Friday) is observed in the traditional manner. Easter is known as Kenaikan Isa Al-Masih; businesses usually remain open.

Nyepi, the Balinese New Year, is an enthusiastically celebrated holiday. Following a night of noisemaking and merriment, the Lord of Hell, Yama, rids Bali of devils. Nyepi usually falls during the spring equinox at the end of March or beginning of April.

Waicak Day draws Buddhist visitors the world over to participate in mass prayers and ceremonies at the massive Borobudur monument in Central Java. Art, musical, and theater performances, wayang kulit, and other Javanese theater presentations feature the history of this great 9th century Buddhist sanctuary.

Imlek is the Chinese New Year; Indonesian Chinese visit temples and elders, attend family reunions, gamble, eat special foods. While Imlek is not an official state holiday, you'll realize how much Indonesia's economy depends on the Chinese when you see the number of shops and businesses closed for the festivities.

Independence Day, or **Hari Proklamasi Kemerdekaan,** marks the anniversary of Indonesia's declaration of independence from Holland on 17 August 1945.

PERFORMING ARTS

In addition to the religious, national, and regional holidays and festivals there are also regular performing arts presentations—the graceful dances of Java, the dynamic martial arts of Sumatra, the mesmerizing dance dramas and operas of Bali. In the **Batak Cultural Center** of Prapat, visitors are enthralled by Batak songs. Wayang puppet shows, for both tourists and Indonesians, often accompany holiday celebrations. The dazzling court dances of Java are staged at open-air theaters in Prambanan and Pandaan each May during the dry season. On Lombok, the popular cupak gerantang dance is omnipresent. Upscale hotels are likely venues for regional dance performances; ask your hotel or check schedules at tourist offices.

ARTS AND CRAFTS FAIRS

Usually organized by the government or the community, these fairs promote the arts and crafts of a particular area. Among the regular annual events are the **Jakarta Festival** in the third week in May; the Bali Arts Festival in June and July; the June **Lake Toba Festival** in North Sumatra; North Sulawesi's **Bunaken Festival,** held in July; the **Krakatoa Festival** in July in West Java; the August **Lake Poso Festival** in Central Sulawesi; and East Kalimantan's September **Erau Festival**. These fairs are a time for processions, boat races, songs, dances, and fairs.

HOLIDAY TRAVEL ADVISORY

Religious and secular holidays can seriously inconvenience travelers. Many of Java's resort towns and hill stations are crowded with domestic tourists during major public holidays like Independence Day; transportation facilities are overwhelmed during

Lebaran. Make accommodation and train or bus reservations at least a week in advance. During holidays prices go up; accommodations throughout Indonesia fill to capacity. Although the holy fasting month of *Ramadan* is a slow travel period, it's not always easy to find something to eat in orthodox Islamic areas.

Food

Indonesia has one of the world's great cuisines, drawing on influences from around the world. From India came curries, cucumber, eggplant, and cowpeas. From the Americas, chili, pepper, vanilla, soursop, pawpaw, and pineapple. The Chinese brought the wok and stir-fry, Chinese mustard, and brassicas. From Arabia arrived kebab and flavorful goat stews. Peanuts, avocado, pineapple, guava, papaya, tomato, squash, pumpkin, cacao, and soybeans were all introduced by Europeans.

Staples

The basic diet on most of the islands is rice (*nasi*), supplemented with vegetables, fish, and occasionally meat and eggs. The soybean is the vegetable cow of Asia. Rural people feast on such hearty and organic soybean-based foods as *tahu* (beancurd), *tempe* (fermented soybeans), and *kecap* (soy sauce).

Indonesia offers a staggering amount of fresh seafood: tuna, shrimp, lobster, crab, anchovies, carp, prawns, and sea slugs. Try succulent baked fish (*ikan bakar*), or a huge plate of perfectly prepared prawns in butter and garlic sauce. *Baronang* is a fat fish with a great taste and very few bones. *Belut* (eel) are caught at night in the rice-fields; buy a good-sized bunch of this crisp delicacy wrapped in newspaper.

Spices

Indonesia, known for its deliberate combination of contrasting flavors and textures, taught the world the use of exotic spices and herbs. Surprisingly, you seldom come across the spices—nutmeg, pepper, mace, and cloves—that gave the "Spice Islands" their name. Indonesian saffron (*kunyit*) is used to color rice dishes an intense yellow. *Terasi*, a red-brown fermented shrimp paste with a potent aroma, is used in most sauces. Salty soy sauce (*kecap asin*) is a necessary adjunct to many Indonesian meals. There are many kinds of hot chili pastes (*sambal*) made from red chilies, shallots, and tomatoes; the *sambals* from Padang in West Sumatra are some of the hottest in Indonesia. When in doubt as to whether a dish is spicy-hot, inquire of the waiter or cook *"Pedas atau tidak?"* ("Hot or not?"). If the dish is too hot, squeeze a little lemon with salt over it.

A traditional dance, Madura, Java

NATIONAL DISHES

Fried rice (*nasi goreng*) and fried noodles (*mie goreng*) are fried in coconut oil with eggs, meat, tomato, cucumber, shrimp paste, spices, and chilies. Sold at roadside stalls for Rp750-1500, these are among the most popular everyday foods in Indonesia. If *istimewa* (special) is written after either dish, it means it comes with egg on top.

Sate consists of bite-sized bits of marinated or basted chicken, beef, mutton, shrimp, or pork skewered on veins of coconut palm, grilled over charcoal, then dipped into a hot sauce made of chilies, spices, and peanuts. The *sate* man comes with his whole kitchen on his shoulders. He squats in the gutter and fans the embers of his charcoal brazier until it glows red hot, then turns out sizzling kebab.

Served from pushcarts, *warung, rumah makan,* and restaurants everywhere, *nasi campur* is a filling plate of steamed rice with flavorful beef, chicken, mutton, and/or fish, plus a mixture of eggs and/or vegetables, roasted peanuts, and shredded coconut heaped on top. A thin sauce covers it all. *Nasi campur* will set you back a mere Rp1500-4000; it's the best deal in Indonesia.

Soto ayam is a delicious chicken soup flavored with lemongrass and other herbs and spices; this soup is often eaten as a main meal with a side plate of *nasi*. A very filling staple in Chinese eateries is *mie kuah,* noodle soup in broth. Vegetarians can order a meatless *mie kuah sayur.*

Rijstaffel (rice table), a sort of Indonesian smorgasbord, is a legacy of the Dutch. In colonial days, a ceremonial *rijstaffel* could include as many as 350 courses, all served with rice. Today, 10-15 courses is the norm. You can experience a *rijstaffel* at the Oasis (Jl. Raden Saleh 47) in Jakarta as well as in upscale hotels like the Bali Hyatt. Poor man's *rijstaffel* can be sampled in any *nasi padang* restaurant.

Krupuk is the Indonesian pretzel, a crispy, oversized cracker made from fish flakes, crab claws, shrimp paste, or fruit mixed with rice, dough, or sago flour. Indonesians use *krupuk* for bread or as scoop for curry or *gado-gado,* a warm salad combining potatoes and other boiled vegetables in a rich peanut sauce.

EATING VEGETARIAN

Bali and Java are the easiest places to secure vegetarian dishes. There are tasty, cheap, and clean vegetarian restaurants in Jakarta (Paradiso 2001, Jl. H. Agus Salim 30) and Medan (Restaurant Vegetarian Indonesia, Jl. Gandhi 63A). On Bali's rural roadsides, you can buy freshly steamed vegetables and *lontong* for pennies. To make sure you get your point across, say *"Saya senang sekali makan sayur-sayuran"* ("I like vegetables very much"); in Padang restaurants point to each dish and ask *"Tanpa daging?"* ("Without meat?").

FRUITS

Discovering the new tastes of inexpensive local fruits is one of the delights of Indonesian travel. Stands selling fruits and/or juice stay open long after most other stalls close down. Prices depend on season. To deflect disease, all fresh fruit should be washed and peeled before eating.

There are pineapples (*nanas*), pomelo, melons, and guavas. The delicious mango tastes different on every island. Jackfruit (*nangka*), weighing up to 20 kg, is used in cooking *nasi gudeg*. Sweet *jeruk* (oranges) run about Rp1500 per kilo. Lemonade is *air jeruk sitrun*. *Jeruk Bali* is a large pomelo-like grapefruit and *jeruk Garut* are sweet tangerines. Also sold everywhere in season are *salak, rambutan,* litchis, breadfruit (*campedak*), papaya, and avocados. But pride of place among all Indonesian fruits must go to the cheap and ubiquitous banana (*pisang*). Indonesia boasts 42 varieties in every shape, flavor, texture, and size.

Try local fruit like mangosteen (*manggis*), round and purple, the inside like a creamy orange. The smelly, infamous *durian,* spiked like a gladiator's weapon, tastes simultaneously like onions and caramel. Within the litchi-like *rambutan* is a dark green transparent jelly, tasting something like a grape but far more luscious. *Salak* is called snake-fruit because of the remarkable pattern of its skin. Carefully peel and enjoy; it's similar in taste to an apple.

Drinks

Thirsty foreigners are provided, in most cases, with boiled water at their *losmen*, homestay, or hotel. About 20 brands of commercial "mountain spring water" are available in plastic containers. Or quench your thirst at ice juice stands (*warung es jus*) or carts along the street. They sell natural, if overly sweetened, drinks like citrus juice (*air jeruk*), *es zirzak,* or the incredible avocado drink *es pokat* (*es avocad* on Bali), made with coffee essence, palm sugar, and condensed milk.

About the only drink Indonesians themselves take with meals is China tea. For sweetened tea, say "*teh gula*"; for unsweetened tea say, "*teh pahit*" or "*teh tawar.*" Powerful coffee, introduced by the Dutch in 1699, is grown widely on Java, Bali, and Sumatra.

Heineken of Holland taught Indonesians how to brew the country's ubiquitous pilsner-style Bintang lager. Drinks such as whiskey and soda are known here by their English names. Mildly alcoholic *tuak* (palm toddy) is brewed from various palm sugars a month before consumption. *Brem,* usually home-produced, is rice wine made from glutinous rice and coconut milk.

Desserts

Most desserts derive from sticky or glutinous rice. *Ketan* is rice pudding cooked in coconut milk and sugar syrup; *kue lapis* is a layered pudding of rice or mung bean flour. *Lontong,* a main ingredient in *gado-gado,* is rice cooked in banana leaves; *bubur santen* is rice porridge cooked with palm sugar and coconut milk. A common *kampung* dessert is *es campur,* typically consisting of sweet syrup, milk, gelatin, sweet bread cubes, *tape* (tapioca), colored bright green.

WARUNG

When hunger strikes, follow your nose to the rows of glowing, hissing gas lamps illuminating Indonesia's night markets (*pasar malam*), located on the perimeters of bus, minibus, and train stations. Here you'll discover a collection of ramshackle mobile *warung*. By far the best food for the money is served in these makeshift foodstalls, which also do a brisk business at midday. Many specialize in *soto, sate, nasi goreng, mie goreng,* or *lontong*. Also available are such snacks as *krupuk, pisang goreng* (fried bananas), thinly sliced sweet potatoes, and fried *tempe*.

If sitting in one *warung,* you can still order from others nearby. Choose one with good food and a friendly atmosphere, then walk around to the various neighboring *warung* and order different food items, all the while pointing back toward your table.

RUMAH MAKAN

Meaning "eating house," a *rumah makan* is a full-service Indonesian restaurant offering a complete menu of dishes cooked to order as well as precooked foods wrapped to go. Menus can number 12 or more pages, but this only means the staff can cook the dishes if the ingredients are available. Rather than listen to interminable replies of *"Ma'af, tidak ada"* ("Sorry, we're out"), just ask outright *"Sedia makanan apa?"* ("What do you have?"), or *"Apa keistimewaan di rumah makan ini?"* ("What's the specialty of the house?").

NASI PADANG

The Minangkabau region of West Sumatra produces some of the best cooks in Indonesia, and it is in their *nasi padang* restaurants that the visitor will find the tastiest, spiciest Indonesian food. *Nasi padang* restaurants offer the quickest service of any eatery; they're also some of the most expensive. As soon as you're seated, waiters bring cold napkins, free glasses of hot tea, a lit candle to keep the flies away, and semi-sterilized utensils in a gass of hot water. No menu is needed. Simply utter the word *"nasi"* while pointing to the window filled with basins and platters of spicy-hot food, and waiters will then set up to10 small dishes on the table. You pay only for what you eat, so get the prices right before diving in. The sauce from each is free so you can order a lot of rice, eat a couple of dishes, and use the sauce from the rest; this is what the Indonesians do.

Facts for the Traveler

Tourist Offices And Tourist Literature

Overseas, the Indonesian government maintains Indonesian Tourist Promotion Offices (ITPO) where brochures, maps, and timetables are available. There are ITPOs, for example, in Los Angeles, San Francisco, Singapore, Tokyo, and Frankfurt. Many have tourist promotion offices attached, as well as a Garuda office. In Indonesia itself, tourist offices usually go by the name **Bapparda, Diparda, Kanwil Depparposte,** or **Kantor Pariwisata.** Or you can simply ask for the *kantor pariwisata.* In large provincial capitals, these offices are usually found in or near the governor's office. Although tourist offices in big tourist centers like Jakarta, Bandung, Yogyakarta, Solo, Bali, and Ambon are quite efficient, providing good information and brochures, others may not be as helpful. Woefully underfunded, the staff could be uninformed, not conversant in English, their files neglected. In the smaller cities, the best hotel or biggest travel agency often takes the place of the *kantor pariwisata.* Many tourist offices are inconveniently located out of town to take advantage of cheap rents.

Some regional offices publish excellent booklets and pamphlets. Obtain a *"Calendar of Events"* listing all major religious and public holidays and annual cultural events. One of the best information centers on things Indonesian is the **Directorate General of Tourism,** Jl. Kramat Raya 81 (P.O. Box 409), Jakarta, which publishes literature and maps on all 27 Indonesian provinces. Also well informed and fluent in English are the people at the **Visitor Information Center,** Jakarta Theatre Building, Jl. Thamrin 9, which boasts a wide selection of publications and maps. Here's where you can pick up the really useful **Jakarta Bus Routes** and **Train Services** and **Jakarta General Information.**

The local **Garuda, Merpati,** or **Bouraq** airlines offices, although not strictly in the tourist information business, may employ personnel more knowledgeable than those in official government tourist offices. Garuda staff often dispens informative, full-color brochures on each Indonesian province. Travel agency personnel can also be extremely helpful. In small towns, the **Department of Education and Culture** (Kantor Pendidikan dan Kebudayaan, or PDK) is the best place to go for inquiries of a historical or cultural nature. PDK people can sometimes provide the exact locations of old ruins, or distribute maps and literature on sites, art forms, architectural attractions, and dance venues.

Visas

For many nationalities, tourist visas are no longer required to enter Indonesia. Tourists and those delegates attending conventions and conferences receive a "tourist pass" or "entry stamp" upon arrival. As long as they exit and enter through certain air- and seaports, nationals of 37 countries do not need a visa. Visitors from other countries can obtain a tourist visa from any Indonesian embassy or consulate; two photos are required, together with a small fee. All visitors must possess a passport valid for at least six months after arriving in Indonesia.

A tourist must possess an onward ticket by plane or boat out of Indonesia, or a letter from an air carrier, shipping or cruise company, or travel agency confirming the purchase of those tickets. If you fly into Kupang without a return air ticket to Australia, the Indonesian authorities want to see A$1000 dollars. Don't lose the white arrival/departure card you receive with your entry stamp. If you do lose it, go to the nearest immigration office and obtain a replacement. Don't wait until your departure date to inform immigration officials it's lost. The two-month tourist pass cannot be extended. If you want to stay longer you must leave Indonesia, then reenter.

Tourists entering through designated sea- and airports do not need visas, but if you enter Indonesia at any other point, you're required to obtain a proper visa beforehand and will receive 28 days upon arrival. If you enter Indonesia overland from Papua New Guinea, or take a boat from the southern Philippines to East Kalimantan, you're entering Indonesia illegally. However, policies change. For example, every Indonesian embassy and consulate in the world insists you need a permit from Jakarta to travel in the interior of Irian Jaya. This is a myth. At Jayapura's police station, permits (*surat jalan*) for the interior are issued routinely while you wait. Or your guide can secure a *surat jalan* for you and your party if you give him money for the fee (Rp2000) and four passport photos per person.

Customs Regulations

Customs procedures have become even more relaxed with the installation of green and red routes at international airports. Tourists with nothing to declare use the green route with no baggage inspection.

Duty-free items acceptable for import are: 200 cigarettes or 50 cigars and .9 kg of tobacco; cameras (no limit) and reasonable amounts of film; two liters of liquor; and a reasonable amount of perfume for personal use. All weapons and ammunition, narcotics, anything considered pornographic (read: *Playboy*), books with Chinese characters, and Chinese medicines are forbidden entry into Indonesia, though customs officials may be relaxed about enforcement or take your *Playboy* as a "tax."

Technically, photographic equipment, computers, radios, typewriters, cassette recorders, TV sets, cordless telephones, and transceivers should be listed on your passport, declared to customs, and displayed upon departure, but officials don't check. All movie films, videocassettes, laser discs, records, and computer software should first be screened by the Film Censor Board. You must clear printed matter using Indonesian languages with the minister of culture. If you need to carry prescription medication, get a letter from your doctor. The import of pets, plants, and fresh fruit is strictly controlled.

Be mindful that importation into other countries of souvenirs bought in Indonesia can be problematic. Be sure any souvenir you buy can legally enter your home country, as some items are confiscated and destroyed. Anything purchased with feathers or furs or made in part with organic matter is also high risk.

What to Take

DOCUMENTS

You need a passport to cross borders, exchange currency, cash traveler's checks, pick up mail, rent a room, and satisfy, immigration, and bank officials. Write down your passport number, traveler's check numbers, credit card numbers, vital contact addresses, and any other pertinent information. Make two copies. One copy you should carry with your luggage; leave the other with a friend or family member back home. Register all valuables such as cameras and tape recorders in your passport. If these items are insured before you leave your home country and are registered in your passport, that's vital proof if the items are stolen.

It would also be wise to jot down your plane ticket numbers, place and date of issue, and how tickets were paid for (credit card number, cash, personal check); this information is invaluable if the ticket is lost or stolen, and could save you enormous hassles. It's advisable to travel with a copy of your birth certificate in case you lose your passport.

An International Student Identification Card (ISIC) could be useful in obtaining discounts of up to 25 percent on rail and flight tickets. To apply, write CIEE Student Travel, 205 East 42nd St., New York, NY 10017, U.S.A., tel. (212) 661-1414. Obtain an International Driver's License, valid for a year, from your local automobile association. You never know when you'll want to rent a car or van; an Indonesian license on Bali costs Rp63,000.

CLOTHING

Choose patterned or dark-colored fabrics that won't show wear or soil quickly. In a tropical climate, cotton clothes are most comfortable. But since 100 percent cotton requires ironing, bring along a few half-cotton, half-synthetic, wrinkle-free garments for special occasions and visits to bureaucratic offices. Indonesia is too hot for Western-style sportcoats, so either buy a light *batik* sportcoat or an attractive batik long-sleeved shirt for dress-up—quite acceptable and very fashionable.

Except in the mountains, denim is too hot for Indonesia. Light summer trousers are better suited for this climate. Take along a warm light sweater or cardigan. A water-resistant jacket packs light and if worn over sweaters keeps you warm. It's generally considered inappropriate for men to wear shorts for anything but the roughest manual work, long-distance cycling, or trips to and from the bathroom or beach. Recommended also is a cloth or khaki fishing hat deep enough to stay on your head in heavy winds and with a brim to protect you from rain and sun. Spray with water repellent.

Women should take long-sleeved blouses and longish skirts. Skimpy clothing, backless dresses, shorts, and even slacks can be offensive in this Muslim country, especially if worn in mosques, temples, churches, or on formal occasions. A bikini will pass provided it's worn only at the swimming pool or in Kuta or Sanur Beach on Bali. Bathing suits can double as underwear; they're easy to wash, quick-drying, light, and comfortable. Take one wrinkle-proof dress that's easy to wash. Scarves are stylish, lightweight, and compact, and can be used as belts, shawls, or temple sashes.

You need one pair of hiking shoes, one pair of sandals, and one pair of dress shoes. Strap-on sandals you can wear anywhere—everyday traveling, hiking, snorkeling, coral walking, dancing, motorcycle riding, even to the immigration office. Dress shoes come in handy for meetings with officials. Although flip-flops almost always come with your hotel or *losmen,* they're invariably too small for Westerners. Don't expect to buy good quality footwear in Indonesia. The international chain Bata sells inexpensive shoes in leather, canvas, or plastic, but a U.S. size nine is about the largest size they make. It's extremely hard to find size nine shoes for women.

Money

The Indonesian monetary unit is called the *rupiah,* issued in notes of Rp100, Rp500, Rp1000, Rp5000, Rp10,000, Rp20,000, and Rp50,000. If heading into the countryside or to remote places like the interior of Irian Jaya, take lots of small denomination notes—it's nearly impossible for people out there to make change for Rp20,000 (and up) notes. Always keep on hand lots of Rp500 and Rp1,000 notes: taxi drivers and small vendors are invariably "out of change" and you'll need small change for public WCs and snacks.

In Indonesia a price is attached to everything "extra"—a better seat on the bus, extra sugar or ice in your drink, to urinate at the market, for the use of a fan, for each and every application form at a government office. There's even a per-letter fee just to pick up poste restante letters.

MONEYCHANGING

The U.S. dollar, accepted all over Indonesia since WW II, is still the most useful foreign currency here; the rupiah is based on it. Though the U.S. dollar will probably bring the most favorable exchange rate, it's possible to cash other well-known currencies like Australian dollars, German Deutsche marks, Netherlands florins, and French and Swiss francs. Canadian dollars are more difficult.

Though you can change traveler's checks in most places, cash is sometimes a different matter. Many smaller banks frown on the good old British pound.

EXCHANGE RATES AS OF MARCH 1998

US$1 USA	Rp7,736
UK£1 United Kingdom	Rp12,660
¥100 Japan	Rp6,008
A$1 Australia	Rp5,160
C$1 Canada	Rp5,445
NZ$1 New Zealand	Rp4,470
S$1 Singapore	Rp4,742
HK$1 Hong Kong	Rp1,000

"STOP PRESS"

The rupiah has been experiencing wild fluctuations around the time of going to press. Travelers should check the current exchange rate before leaving home.

Large denomination U.S. notes ($100s as opposed to $20s) fetch a higher rate of exchange. Indonesian banks, even on Bali, refuse to touch foreign banknotes that are soiled, worn, or physically damaged. Banks also won't exchange foreign coins.

Exchange rates for various currencies vary. In many cases, the headquarters bank changes money, but city branches do not. **Bank Bumi Daya** consistently gives good rates. **BNI** is usually at least as good. **Bank Expor Impor** always changes foreign checks or cash. All have branches throughout the country. The best rates tend to be in tourist areas. Bank hours are generally Mon.-Fri. 0800-1200, Saturday 0800-1100; get to the bank early to avoid lines. You'll need your passport and tourist entry card for each transaction.

In the far reaches of Indonesia the exchange rates could be downright criminal, or there could be no banks at all. Venture to such outlying areas only with stacks of Indonesian cash, with no denomination higher than Rp20,000. Avoid, if you can, exchanging money at hotel front desks, where you'll receive at least five percent below the rate offered by state banks. Airports usually offer very competitive rates.

Moneychangers generally don't charge a fee for their services, so you can change money as often as you want. They also offer quicker service and better exchange rates. They're open both earlier and later than banks.

The main roads of Kuta and Sanur on Bali and Jalan Jaksa in Jakarta are literally choked with moneychangers.

TRAVELER'S CHECKS

There's no black market in Indonesia, so for safety's sake bring only a small portion of your funds in cash. Though rates are often better for traveler's checks than for cash, always carry some $5, $10, and $20 bills in case you need quick money when banks are closed or refusing traveler's checks. The bulk of your traveling funds should come in the form of a widely accepted brand of traveler's checks such as American Express. Some places do not use the Indonesian phrase *(trapel cek)* for traveler's checks. *Cek jalanan turis* is probably a more widely understood term.

Bank Bumi Daya, Bank Expor Impor, Bank Rakyat Indonesia, and **Bank Negara Indonesia** accept most Australian and better-known TCs. Upon presentation of your passport, it usually takes about 20 minutes to cash TCs at a bank. If the clerks won't accept your brand of TCs, ask for the manager. Major hotels, department stores, and many pricey shops will also take TCs, at poor rates.

CREDIT CARDS

Indonesia is very much a cash-oriented society. **Visa, MasterCard,** and **AmEx** credit cards can be utilized only in the major tourist and business centers equipped to process charges—Medan, Lake Toba, Palembang, Jakarta, Yogyakarta, Solo, Bali, and Lombok. Midrange to upscale hotels, tourist-oriented souvenir shops, domestic and international airline offices, and the more expensive restaurants accept them, as will travel agencies. Most Java and Bali merchants can't authorize your limit, so you can only purchase goods equal to a total value of around Rp250,000. Also, it's common for Indonesians to add a two to five percent "commission."

Your passport and credit card are needed for all transactions. Be sure to verify the total amount charged. Ask the retailer or service provider to convert the total amount into dollars and cents, then write the amount on the charge slip. That way, in spite of currency fluctuations, you'll know exactly what you owe your credit card company. Maintain a list of your card numbers so you can cancel your cards if you lose them. Leave a duplicate list with a friend back home. Don't discard charge slips until charges have been paid. Later, if you discover you've been cheated by a merchant, write your credit card company to resolve the matter. Always keep your credit cards in sight when making a purchase.

You can also use your Visa, MasterCard, or AmEx (but not Diner's Club) credit card to obtain cash advances (normally up to $500) from moneychangers, though they'll charge a steep six percent commission. On Bali, **BNI** doesn't charge a fee if you use your credit card to get cash. Other banks may charge three percent. **Bank Duta** does not charge a commission on cash advances in Medan, Palembang, Jakarta,

Yogyakarta, Solo, Legian, Ubud, Cakranegara, Ambon, or Jayapura. Neither does **Bank Central Asia** (BCA), with branches all over Indonesia. In other banks you may give the clerks apoplexy if you hand over your Visa card for cash.

BARGAINING

In Indonesia, bargaining is most critical in open markets, with anyone who quotes you a ridiculous price, when taking *becak*, and with vendors of tourist souvenirs. Always ask for a lower rate for your hotel room. Bargain for transportation on *bemo* and buses only if you know you're being overcharged. Prices for tailors and hairdressers are standardized and fixed, but bargain with your mechanic and tire-fixer.

Buying and bargaining in Indonesia can be good-humored or infuriating—your choice. It's a social vehicle by which one requests and receives favors, a means to solidify one's status in the local economy. An item has many prices, each reflecting the correct charge for a particular customer from the shopkeeper's point of view.

Bargaining should be leisurely, light-hearted, and friendly. Never get angry. Bargaining is a game won by technique and strategy, not distemper and threats. The process can be a prolonged exchange lasting days and even weeks. It's challenging to try to obtain the same price as the locals. There's a second, higher price for out-of-town Indonesians, and a third and even higher price for Chinese, *orang besar* (big men), Jakartans, Indonesians from other islands, and foreigners like you.

All verbally stated prices are merely starting points from which you should receive anything from a 10 percent to 50 percent discount. Shops selling goods at only fixed prices *(harga pas)* are becoming more common, offering a shopping environment Western consumers will feel immediately comfortable in. In these stores, the price is set, with no discounts or reductions. If you see a price posted or attached to an item, it's a fixed-price shop. If no fixed price sign is posted or no prices are attached to merchandise, there's room for haggling.

Postal Services

SENDING LETTERS

You can drop letters, aerograms, and postcards into mailboxes on the street or mail them at hotel reception desks, regardless of whether or not you're a guest. Aerograms are the cheapest and fastest way to send a letter abroad from Indonesia. You can purchase stamps at hotel front desks, and sometimes in shops selling postcards. Very useful on Bali are the postal agents of Kuta, Sanur, and Ubud, who sell stamps, postcards, and stationery. These agents also send telegrams and offer poste restante pickup.

Less conveniently, you can buy stamps at the post offices found in any midsized Indonesian town. Go to a window with a scale, as your letter must first be weighed and assigned a stamp value. Next, proceed to another window for the actual stamps. Wedge yourself politely but persistently into the clump of people and push your letter as far as possible through the barred window, to gain the attention of the postal clerk. After securing your stamps, take them over to the glue stands and apply glue to the back; the glue on Indonesian stamps is weak. If possible, watch the stamps until they're cancelled to assure they're not stolen. Register anything of value. If you want to be 100 percent sure of delivery, use a reputable courier service like **Elteha**, **Usaha Express** or **DHL**, which have offices in all major Indonesian cities.

Two forms of express service are available: blue envelopes marked *Kilat* ensure air mail service, while yellow envelopes reading *Kilat Khusus* are the equivalent of air mail/special delivery. These envelopes are available at all post offices. Express service costs an extra Rp65 and usually saves at least one or two days. **Kilat** letters, like ordinary letters, may be put into any mailbox along the street. Always use *Kilat* service for international mail; letters sent to the Americas, Europe, or Australia will arrive in five to seven days. Bring strong envelopes to Indonesia to make sure your exposed film or important papers arrive safely.

PACKET POST

It's always best to ship a small parcel from the post office yourself; if you use a professional shipper, pay all the money up front. Include your name and address on a slip of paper inside the package as well as on the outside. To mail packages surface post to foreign destinations, you'll need form CP2, an expedition document, and C2/CP3, a customs declaration form. Since you'll need five copies of C2/CP3, bring spare carbon paper; post offices often fail to stock carbon paper. A customs officer will check your parcel to confirm you're not mailing antiques. After the inspection, pack and seal the parcel in front of him. Be sure to secure proper documentation for any statue or antiquity to show to customs officials at the airport or docks. A receipt with a certified dealer's registration number should suffice.

To Europe or North America, international seamail can take up to six months, though the average is two to three. If you don't have much to send back, surface post is less expensive than a shipping company, which charges a minimum of $175 for a portion of a container.

There are specialized air-express companies on Bali, so if you're buying crafts in the Outer Islands, wait until you get back to Bali to airfreight them. These companies are expensive, charging about Rp16,800-21,000 per kilo (five-kilo minimum), and taking 7-10 days. **PT Golden Bali Express**, Jl. Kartini 52, Denpasar, is one of the most competent companies on the island.

RECEIVING MAIL

It's more reliable to have letters sent and receive them at your hotel rather than rely on poste restante. If you must use the latter, have your mail sent to one of Jakarta's two main post offices: **Central Post Office** (Kantor Pos Pusat), Jl. Pos Utara, open Mon.-Sat. 0800-1600; or Jl. Kapt. Tendean 43, open Mon.-Thurs. 0800-1600, Friday 0800-1100, and Saturday 0800-1230. Bali's main post office is in the administrative district of Denpasar called Renon; you can also have your mail sent to post offices in Kuta, Ubud, or Singaraja. A fee of Rp50 is charged to retrieve a poste restante letter.

All mail should include your last name underlined and in caps, with only your first and middle initials, or letters could get missorted under your first name. Follow your name with your address, the town name, the island name, then Republik Indonesia. Receiving goods in Indonesia is still risky, especially medicine, books, and magazines. Don't send anything valuable in letters mailed to Indonesia; 30 percent of all letters never arrive. Aerograms and postcards, however, almost always get through.

Phone Service

Though it still requires a bit of persistence, you can now routinely place both domestic and international calls in Indonesia. Both domestic and international calls can be placed from hotel rooms, pay phones, the local telephone office, or in a WARTEL, a privately run, retail telephone service shop.

You'll find yellow-and-gray public pay phones here and there, but they're sometimes out of order. You can also make local calls from pay phones in hotel lobbies and airport terminals. To continue talking, you must plug in Rp100 coins every two minutes. Oftentimes tourists can use phones at reception counters in hotels and restaurants. Ask. Indonesians, however, will prefer to dial the number for you. Phone books are difficult to come by and don't always list all businesses and residences. On Bali, where the system is computerized, dial 108 for information.

Place long-distance calls within Indonesia by dialing direct. Dial first the city code number, then the local number. The archipelago is divided into five zones; calls are priced according to zone. Indonesia's country code is 62. When calling Indonesia internationally, dial 011, then the country code, then the city code without the zero, then the phone number. For example, the city code for Jakarta is 021, but when calling from a foreign country you dial 011-62-21 plus the number.

Twenty cities offer International Direct Dialing (IDD) service to 127 countries. IDD phones are standard in upscale hotels in all the main tourist areas of Indonesia. For IDD calls, just dial 00-801 plus the country code, then the local number. Where direct-dialing is unavailable, obtain quick operator assistance by dialing 104 in

Jakarta, 108 on Bali, and 101 in the rest of Indonesia. Your time starts as soon as you start talking to the home country operator. Hotels levy a preposterously high surcharge on calls. Take a *becak* to the nearest **WARTEL** or city telephone office instead; in the larger cities, these offices are open 24 hours a day, seven days a week.

Credit card calls are extremely convenient, especially for intercity calls, and much cheaper and faster than WARTEL offices. With **Kartu Telpon** cards, you can phone for about one-third the hotel price, with no minimum duration. Nearly all towns in Indonesia now have card phones; you purchase different denominations or units (Rp5000 minimum).

Special **Home Country Phones** are available at major airports, some WARTEL offices, in big hotels and at big shopping centers. These phones connect you with an operator in your home country by simply pushing a button adjacent to the name of the nation you wish to reach. The charge is billed to your home phone in your home country. Once you get through to a home-country operator, you can reverse the charges, generally cheaper than dialing direct from Indonesia. If there's no answer or the receiving party refuses to accept your call, there's no charge. Collect calls are accepted only between Indonesia and Europe, North America, and Australia.

Any **WARTEL** and many hotels' reception desks will send faxes for you; Rp10,000 to Rp15,000. You can receive a fax at any WARTEL for Rp1000-2000. For overseas cables, allow 36 hours. A 15-word full-rate cable to the U.S. runs Rp8050, telexes Rp10,000-15,000. Cables sent to points within Indonesia are much cheaper.

Time

There are three time zones in Indonesia. West Indonesia Standard Time (Sumatra, Java, the western half of Kalimantan, Bali, Lombok) is Greenwich Mean Time plus seven hours; Central Indonesia Standard Time (eastern Kalimantan, Sulawesi, Nusatenggara) is G.M.T. plus eight hours; East Indonesia Standard Time (Maluku, Irian Jaya) is G.M.T. plus nine hours. For the correct time in Jakarta, dial 103. Most of Indonesia is on or so close to the equator that the days and nights are about the same length. On Bali, about midpoint in the archipelago, the sun rises at 0600 and sets at 1800 with only a few minutes variation throughout the year.

BUSINESS HOURS

Hours vary from one business to another, from city to city, and from season to season. Even more complicated is the convolution of the Indonesian work week due to the mixing and simultaneous use of two religious calendars, the Islamic and Gregorian. Banks, offices, and schools close early on Friday because it's the Sabbath, but in order to fit in with the world at large, Sunday is also observed as a day of rest. Saturday, meanwhile, is a partial work day, so the Indonesian work week consists of four full days and two partial days.

In the small towns, restaurants and *warung* usually close several hours after sunset. Expect businesses to take midday lunch breaks of an hour or more, during which time no one answers the phone. During major religious holidays such as the month-long Muslim fast *(puasa)*, restaurants in Islamic areas are closed during daylight hours.

Generally speaking, government offices open at 0800 Mon.-Sat., closing at 1500 or 1600 Mon.-Thurs., 1130 on Friday, and 1400 on Saturday. Always get an early start for government offices, before the lines get too long and the day too hot. Banks are open 0800 or 0830 to 1200 or 1300 Mon.- Fri., and 0800-1100 on Saturday. Bank branches in hotels often remain open into the afternoon, and moneychangers in tourist centers stay open at night. Shopping centers, supermarkets and department stores operate from 0900 to 2100 or even later, seven days a week.

Electricity

Electrical service is gradually spreading into the most remote corners of the archipelago. Still, electricity in the *kampung* and even in some larger towns can be minimal, so get used to solitary dim bulbs and oil lamps. Power is fairly reliable, but brownouts are not uncommon. Streetlighting is haphazard. Since the sidewalks and streets of Indonesia are full of pitfalls and debris, always carry a flashlight. The country's drainage ditches are really treacherous, particularly at night.

In the past, current has run 110 volts, 50 cycles AC, but most areas are changing over to 220-240 volts, 50 cycles AC. Check to make sure which current is running before plugging in expensive electrical appliances. Transformers are readily available and reasonably priced, as are 220-volt appliances. If you carry a computer or hair dryer, bring a stabilizer and adapter if your plugs are not of the round, slim, European two-pronged type. Power surges at night mean the current can fluctuate between 180 and 220 volts, so unplug that razor.

Media

The government-operated TV network, connected with Jakarta via domestic satellite and microwave, is called Televisi Republic Indonesia, or TVRI. This station is a tool of the state, and programming is dominated by Indonesian-language, paternalistic, nationalistic local and international news, speeches, welcoming addresses, and endless coverage of handshaking ceremonies between Suharto and his ministers or other heads of state. There are also pro-government educational and Islamic religious programs, Indonesian music and drama, soccer and badminton matches, Taiwanese *kung fu* movies, and American programs dubbed in English and subtitled in Indonesian.

Cable News Network (CNN) began broadcasting via Indonesian satellite in 1991 and today its signal is accessible by two-meter dish. News, music, films, and other entertainment emanate from Hong Kong's Asiasat and are now available 24 hours a day throughout Indonesia.

The government radio network, Radio Republik Indonesia (RRI), with 45 stations, comprises the national system. RRI broadcasts news and commentary in English about an hour each day. In addition, many private radio stations broadcast RRI news and Indonesian and Western music on AM and FM. About 20 foreign radio stations broadcast programs in Indonesian. Shortwave reception takes in English-language programs such as BBC, Voice of America, and American Top 40.

ENGLISH-LANGUAGE NEWSPAPERS AND MAGAZINES

English-language dailies published in Jakarta include the *Indonesian Times* (morning), the *Indonesian Observer* (afternoon), and the *Jakarta Post.* Singapore's *Straits Times* also frequently publishes stories on Indonesia. Other English-language papers include the *Surabaya Post* and the *Bali Post,* newspapers providing limited world coverage. Local newsstands also sell overseas editions of the *Asian Wall Street Journal, London Times, Bangkok Post, International Herald Tribune,* and *The Australian. Time* and *Newsweek* are readily available.

Specialized magazines serving the business community include the weeklies *Review Indonesia* and *Asiaweek.* Both magazines are excellent sources of news on Indonesia, with an emphasis on the economy, and both are available from newsstands in the metropolitan and tourist areas. *Inside Indonesia* is an incisive Australian magazine with brilliant insights on Indonesian politics, new technologies, lifestyles, culture, and the business community. *Indonesia News Service* digests current news stories about Indonesia from leading magazines and newspapers.

MAPS

It's hard to get good maps in Indonesia. Indonesian tourist offices dispense national, regional, and local maps free, but you can't always rely on their accuracy. Try to get hold of the *Indonesia Tourist Map,* a handy, full-color booklet of maps and facts that should last about as long as your two-month pass. Regional tourist offices also give away town plans of the main cities of Sumatra, Java, and Bali. The *Falk City Map,* available for Rp9500 at any major hotel or bookstore in Jakarta, is the best map to Indonesia's capitol.

The best folded maps are produced by Nelles Verlag GmbH, Schleibheimer Str. 371 b, D 80935, Munich 45, Germany, tel. (089) 351-5084, fax 354-2544. These beautiful creations feature vivid color printing, topographic features in realistic relief, and major city plans in margin inserts. Widely available in U.S. bookstores for $6.95; cheaper in Indonesia (around Rp5000). Periplus Editions publishes a three-map series with a focus on Java. Another high-quality folded map is *Hildebrand's Travel Map* of Western Indonesia, which covers Sumatra, Java, and Sulawesi.

Transportation

The most important thing to understand about travel in Indonesia is the concept of *jam karet,* or "rubber time." Departure times are stretched or contracted depending on the whim of the driver, pilot, or captain and how full or empty the vehicle is. Don't be in a hurry—no one else is. For physical comfort, the best time of the day for travel is from 0600 to about noon, and after the sun goes down.

In the peak tourist seasons (June-Aug. and Dec.-Jan.) it's sometimes impossible to get a ticket, confirmations disappear at the drop of a bribe. Everything is full; you might have to wait several days, particularly for extraordinarily busy connections like Ujung Pandang to Denpasar. Avoid traveling during religious holidays such as *Idul Fitri* (the end of *Ramadan*), when millions of Indonesians hit the road to visit relatives. On Friday, the Muslim holy day, most offices and many businesses are closed and transportation almost stops at 1100 or so when Muslims go to pray. Tourists who don't speak *Bahasa Indonesia* will have difficulty communicating with drivers/operators. Some train and bus stations, airports, and Pelni shipping offices feature special *loket turis* (tourist ticket windows) with English-speaking ticket clerks. In a big city, always ask for the *loket turis* if you want to buy tickets or make reservations. Tourist offices in the cities dispense info, brochures, and maps, and can also be useful in booking hotels and arranging tours, transport and boat charter, and train tickets.

PAPERWORK AND PERMITS

Always carry your passport anywhere outside Bali; police will often ask to see it. **International Student ID** cards can sometimes secure discounts on flights, ferries, or trains. An International Driver's License is available from your local motorist's association. When hiring a bicycle, you can use your license as a deposit rather than your passport.

Permits are required to visit many of the country's reserves and national parks. They're available for around Rp2000 from the **Dinas Perlindungan dan Pengawetan Alam** (PHPA) office in the park itself, or at a PHPA office in the town nearest the reserve. You can also apply at an Indonesian consulate before leaving for Indonesia. Stays of five days are permitted. Anyone wishing to stay longer should apply directly to PHPA's main office in Bogor, West Java at Jl. Ir. H. Juanda 9; open 0730-1100. Include date of planned visit, length of stay, number of participants, nationality, and passport information.

A *surat jalan* is a letter travelers may be required to carry while traveling in restricted areas of the Outer Islands like areas of East Timor and some of the far valleys of Irian Jaya's highlands. Obtainable only from local/regional police stations, this advance permit is sometimes necessary to secure connecting transportation: requires two to three passport photos, and takes at most an hour to obtain.

TRAVEL BY AIR

Most big towns in Indonesia are connected to Jakarta by air. Indonesia's three main air gateways are the **Sukarno/Hatta International** in Jakarta, the **Polonia** in Medan, and **Ngurah Rai** in Bali. A good number of Indonesia's provincial airfields—particularly in the eastern islands—are served only by Skyvans and consist of nothing but a grassy strip. There are 45 private or semiprivate airlines operating a zany collection of aircraft. State-run **Garuda Indonesia Airways** (GIA), offering both domestic and international services, is the largest and slickest. Their head office is at Wisma Dharmala Sakti, Jl. Jend. Sudirman 32, Hotel Borobudur Intercontinental, tel. (021) 360-033. At the Jakarta airport, the number is 550-500. **Merpati**, swallowed up by Garuda in 1989, is the second-largest airline; the head office is located on Jl. Angkasa 2, Kemayoran, Jakarta, tel. (021) 417-404, 413-608.

Other airlines, flying mainly domestic routes, include **Mandala** (head office: Jl. Garuda 76, P.O. Box 3706, Jakarta Pusat, tel. [021] 420-6645); Bouraq (Jl. Angkasa 1-3, Kemayoran, Jakarta, tel. (021) 629-5150 or 659-5179); Sempati (Ground Floor Terminal Bldg., Halim Perdana Kusuma Airport, Jakarta, tel. 809-4407, fax 809-4420); and **Pelita**, (Jl. Abdul Muis 52-54, tel. 375-908). These alternative airlines concentrate on the low-traffic outer-fringe areas not covered by Garuda, and their fares average 15-25 percent less. You can obtain the various nationwide timetables from each airline at the main airline offices or tourist information centers. Routes, fares, and airlines change frequently, so call to find out what's available. Always confirm flight availability and book a seat as far in advance as possible at the local airline office in your city of departure. Charter aircraft cost US$300-800 per hour, depending on the type of aircraft. You can rent helicopters in Irian Jaya for around Rp2.1 million per day.

Airport tax ranges from Rp4000 to Rp6000 for internal flights and should be included in the price of your ticket. For international flights the tax is Rp20,000. Baggage allowances range from 10 kg on smaller planes such as the 18 seat DHC Twin Otter up to the normal allowance of 20 kg.

TRAVEL BY SEA

Interisland passage on large seagoing passenger/cargo ships (kapal laut) is still seriously deficient for an archipelagic nation of this size; smaller boats are required to reach the more remote attractions. On these craft you'll meet a fascinating cross-section of locals and travelers. The most reliable oceangoing shipping company is state-owned **Pelayaran Nasional Indonesia** (Pelni), with over 70 cargo and passenger ships connecting the country's major and provincial harbors. Obtain a schedule from the Pelni head office at Jl. Angkasa 18, Jakarta, tel. (021) 421-1921, fax 421-1929. You can purchase Pelni tickets through travel agencies or direct through a Pelni office in one of 32 ports. If you pay a bit more and go second or first class, the Indonesian archipelago is a place where you can experience leisurely travel in the stateroom style of Joseph Conrad and Somerset Maugham. First Class fare includes two single beds, a/c, TV, day and night videos, a table, comfortable beds, bathroom with hot showers, and palatable meals on white tablecloths.

Other shipping lines, such as **Samudra** and **Trikora Lloyd,** also have vessels working the archipelago, but they're principally cargo carriers, carry few passengers, and don't sail according to fixed schedules.

Check with the *syahbandar* (harbormaster) in the ports about the comings and goings of boats and their prices. A port may be no more than a copra shed on an isolated beach, or a rickety pier along a marshy riverbank, but you'll always find the *syahbandar* office somewhere on the waterfront.

Still one of the best deals in Indonesia is a 6-8 day voyage on the smaller motorized vessels, or *kapal motor.* Highlights of these informal tours are the islands of Komodo and Rinca, but you also stop at islets and beaches along the way. The price includes transport, accommodations (sleep on deck), food, and equipment. The return trip is cheaper—Rp100,000 pp—as there aren't as many people heading west as east. Pack like you're going on a camping trip.

Inexpensive **ferries** connect Sumatra and Java, Java and Bali, Bali and Lombok, and all the islands of eastern and western Nusatenggara. These ferries can transport motorcycles and bicycles; some are designed to carry cars and trucks. Ferries run once or twice a day or several times a week. Some ferries, like the one that runs from Sumbawa to Komodo and on to Flores, travel both ways, passing each other en route. The rivers of Kalimantan—the island's highways—are served by large, sluggish river ferries chugging up- and downriver carrying people, purchases, and merchandise, stopping frequently in innumerable small port towns for an hour or so.

TRAVEL BY TRAIN

Sadly, Indonesia's unique state railway system (PJKA) has been neglected, while stinking, noisy *bemo, oplet,* and minibuses proliferate. Indonesian railways date back to the late 19th century; at one time, the Java State Railway held the world record for the longest nonstop narrow gauge, running between Batavia and Surabaya. There are now 7,891 kilometer of track, all on Java, Madura, and parts of Sumatra. Java's rail system, the most extensive, runs the whole length of the island, connecting the east coast with the ferry for Bali and the west coast with the ferry to Sumatra. In Sumatra, trains operate around Padang, Medan, South Sumatra, and Lampung.

Both fares and schedules are posted at most train stations. Fares range from Rp35,700 to Rp105,000 for the Jakarta-Yogyakarta-Semarang-Surabaya journey, depending on the train and class. The *Bima* and the *Mutiara Utara* on Java are luxury trains, linking Jakarta and Surabaya. The *Bima* is the only one with sleepers. An executive class seat on the air-conditioned *Mutiara Utara* or the Bima train from Jakarta to Surabaya costs Rp51,000-58,000, while a business class seat runs Rp31,000-36,000. The *Bima* passes through Yogyakarta and Solo, while the *Mutiara* runs on the northern route through Semarang. The *Senja Utama Solo* is an express service, with reclining seats but no air-conditioning, from Jakarta to Yogyakarta and Solo. The fare is Rp46,000 executive class, Rp24,000 business class. The *Senja Utama Semarang* runs Rp40,000 executive class and Rp18,000 business class from Jakarta to Semarang. If your ticket costs Rp200-400 more than the fare you see listed, a "station fee" *(bea stasiun)* has been added. The amount of the fee depends on the ticket price.

In Jakarta, you can order tickets as long as a week in advance, at least for the express trains. In other cities, tickets are available only on the day of departure. Double-check schedules. If you board a train without a reserved seat, you'll stand and sway the whole way. You can't book a roundtrip by train; you must make return reservations at the point of departure. To save the hassle of getting to a station and waiting in line, for a small fee you can make reservations one to three days in advance through a travel agency.

TRAVEL BY BUS

Daytime bus travel on congested roads is slow, hot and exhausting; buses move much faster in the cool of the night. Many big cities are connected by *bis malam* (night buses). These custom-built nonstop buses usually leave in the late afternoon or early evening and arrive the next morning or afternoon, with a limited number of stops, about once every two or three hours. Generally *bis malam* are safer, cooler, faster, and more expensive than regular day buses—the Indonesian equivalent of the U.S. Greyhound system. Long-distance buses require about an hour to cover 40-45 km.

Local buses offer slow but frequent service between and around most small towns and cities. Destinations are posted above the front windshield. Big city bus stations usually feature a row of buses, engines running, ready to pull out. If the first bus is full, just climb on the one behind. It will leave within minutes. Once these local buses hit the road, wherever a passenger awaits is a bus stop. Often there's standing room only. Be extra careful with your money and valuables—lots of pickpockets.

Fares for short distances, especially on Java and Bali, are extraordinarily cheap. Few local 20-km-plus rides ever cost more than Rp2000 and more than Rp20,000 worth of bus travel in one day can be exhausting. With minibuses you can often haggle the price, but on the big express buses there's usually a standard fare—fixed and inarguably cheap. The price of intraisland ferry crossings is often included in the bus ticket price. Children ages 4-11 are usually charged half the adult ticket; children under four ride free. For local buses, fares are almost always posted over the ticket window (loket) at the bus station.

BECAK

A *becak* (pronounced "BEH-jack") is best described as a man-powered tricycle-taxi, an enjoyable form of transport for up to two passengers. Passengers sit side by side in front of the driver, a canvas or cloth canopy providing some measure of protection from the sun, fumes, and dust. When it rains, a large flap of transparent plastic is brought down over the passengers in front. No other form of conveyance combines all the viewing advantages of walking-pace travel with the comforts of a city taxi. But unlike taxis, *becak* are slowly being legislated out of the larger cities because of the disruption they cause to the flow of traffic.

Few work harder for their bowl of rice than the *tukang becak*, who usually chooses this hot, heavy work because he has few other choices. Though he speaks rudimentary English, you won't find a better guide. He knows where to change money, the location of the best crafts shops and entertainment districts, where to find the cheapest hotels. He'll walk up hills, pushing you from behind, though if it's too steep, please get out and walk to give the guy a break.

Costing Rp500-2000 for a one- to five-km ride, *becak* are considered by Indonesians slightly extravagant. Always agree on the fare before climbing in. Don't try to bargain with "tourist" *becak* drivers in and around popular tourist sites. Just walk a block away in any direction and look for another one. On occasion, drivers may refuse to take the money agreed upon; if that happens, just put it on the seat and walk away. Don't argue.

TAXIS

Taxis—licensed and metered, as we know them in the West—are available only in Jakarta, Bandung, Yogyakarta, Solo, Semarang, Surabaya, and on Bali. In the rest of Indonesia you'll find private cars or unmetered taxis, for which you pay an agreed-upon or fixed amount. You can usually find taxis on certain streets in inner areas of the city, in a special taxi stand beside the *alun-alun,* outside the larger hotels, or cruising the streets looking for fares. Taxi drivers speak little English, often know only the names of major streets, drive on both sides of the road, and do not heed speed limits.

With the notable exception of Jakarta, highly trafficked, profitable routes, such as between airports and major cities, are seldom serviced by buses or other modes of transport. However, it is often possible to walk 500 meters or so outside the airport gate to a main highway and flag down a public *bemo*, minibus, or hitch a private car. When heading from cities out to the airport, it's cheaper to hire local transport like a *bemo* or minibus, not a taxi—but allow plenty of time.

If you have friends to share the fare with, taxis can be a better value than public transport. Licensed taxis (yellow number plates) equipped with a meter usually charge Rp800 for the first kilometer plus Rp500 for each additional kilometer. It's your responsibility to have the exact fare because the driver will never be able to make change. You can charter taxis at about Rp6500-8000 per hour, or by the day or week. In Outer Island areas, like Biak on Irian Jaya or Palopo in Central Sulawesi, where vehicles are scarce, taxis won't take you for less than Rp10,000 per hour. Most drivers expect a small tip.

HELICAK

A cheap alternative to taxis, these motorized three-wheeled vehicles consist of a cabin mounted on a motorcycle, sheltered from the sun and rain by a tinted plastic

The Welcome Statue, central Jakarta

The National Monument by night

bubble. A *helicak* can fit two passengers, who sit in the bubble in front of the driver. Quite common in Jakarta, they run Rp2000-3000 for short distances.

BAJAJ

Making deep inroads into the traditional *becak* (pedicab) market in many cities is the *bajaj*, a two-seat, three-wheeled vehicle that is essentially a motorized version of the *becak*. Built more for Asians than for larger Western frames, the chugging *bajaj* look like a cross between a pickup truck and a golf cart. Over-revved, loud, dirty, and dangerously unstable, *bajaj* can pack six to eight passengers and are quicker than taxis because of their ability to squeeze between trucks and buses. *Bajaj* drivers charge a negotiable fare on a trip-by-trip basis and can be hired in almost all large towns except Denpasar, Bali.

BEMO, OPLET, MICROLET

Bemo is short for *becak motor*. This is an open-backed canopied pickup truck running on a regular route. Made in several sizes, a *bemo* is outfitted with two rows of low, wooden passenger benches down the sides. Large four-wheeled *bemo* can carry 12-16 people sitting knee-to-knee. There are three ways you can die in a *bemo*—a head-on collision, suffocation, or fright.

An *oplet* generally operates on specific routes and between cities and nearby suburbs. The word comes from the Dutch verb *opletten* (to watch out for), from the days when servants were ordered to *oplet* for a taxi scheduled to pull up in front of the house. In Sumatra, an *oplet* could be a rainbow-colored Chevrolet bus or minibus, reminiscent of the Filipino jeepney, while on Java it's a canopied pickup truck with seats. In bigger cities such as Jakarta, *microlet* are replacing the *oplet*. These light blue vehicles charge the same fares and run the same routes. Actually, all the fine distinctions between different types of small public vehicles are becoming redundant now as old-style vehicles are gradually giving way to Japanese-made minibuses.

MINIBUSES

Also called *colt* (pronounced "koll"). Assembled in Mitsubishi's Surabaya plant and from there spewed out all over Indonesia, these minibuses feature 11 seats holding up to 20 people with one conductor hanging out the side. Operating on the shorter, heavily trafficked routes more frequently than the big public buses, minibuses have in fact replaced buses on many transport routes. Minibuses are generally Rp400-1000 more expensive than buses but are considerably faster and more convenient and comfortable. They're also more prone to accidents.

Ask officials at bus and minibus stations for the correct fare. In many cases the fares are also posted, although the actual fares asked by the drivers and their assistants are invariably higher. Before taking off, your minibus driver might circle around the town or city for 20 minutes soliciting passengers to fill all remaining seats, only departing once they're full. Midway through the journey you might be asked to board another minibus to take you the rest of the way; be sure the new driver doesn't charge you again.

Minibus companies specialize in city-to-city, door-to-door service. For example, if you want to go from Cirebon to Jakarta, phone the **4848 Bus Co.** in Cirebon. They'll ask where you are and where you want to go and at what time; buses leave almost every hour to Jakarta for a fare of Rp20,000.

CAR RENTALS

The local tourist office can suggest people or businesses who rent vehicles; someone in the office might even have one or know of one to rent. Before sealing a deal for a long-term rental, take your driver on a day outing to plumb his character and personality and determine how well he drives. Also make sure the a/c works before settling on a per diem rate. The cost of hiring a car varies wildly, depending upon where you are. In the Baliem Valley of Irian Jaya it can cost Rp150,000 per day; in Jakarta, Rp100,000 per day; in Bali as little as Rp40,000 per day. Also expect a lot of parking and entrance fees. Anywhere but Bali, the rental automatically comes with a dependable driver. You're expected to pay for the driver's meals and accommodations in special rooms hotels provide for drivers (around Rp15,000 pp per night).

There are numerous car rental agencies, including **Avis**, Jl. Diponegoro 25, Jakarta 10310, tel. (021) 334-495. Daily rates are around Rp147,000 per day. **National Car Rental** Kartika Plaza Hotel, Jl. Thamrin 10, Jakarta 10320, tel. 333-423, offers competitive rates. Another rental agency is **Bluebird**, Jl. HOS. Cokroaminoto 107, Jakarta 10310, tel. 332-064, 333-000, fax 332-175. It's also possible to rent by the hour. Avis in Jakarta and Bali offers chauffeur-driven cars starting at Rp21,000 per hour for a Toyota. There's usually no tax, and gasoline is included. You must be at least 25 years old, 19 for National. An International Driver's License is also necessary. **Nitour**, Jl. Majapahit 2, Jakarta 10160, tel. 346-347, 346-344, 340-955 and **Pacto Ltd.**, Jl. Taman Kemang II/Blok D-2, Jakarta Selatan, tel. 797-5874, 797-5879, are trustworthy, long-established Indonesian-based companies found in all the bigger towns.

If you're renting a car or *bemo* with driver, be sure it's understood who'll pay for the gas (usually you). It's not necessary to carry extra gasoline while motoring in Java, but since the distances between stations are sometimes great, fill your tank when you have the chance. Called bensin or premium in Indonesia, gas costs around Rp750 per liter. Only the state-owned Pertamina oil company may sell gasoline from *pompa bensin*, or filling stations. Look for the famous seahorse emblem.

MOTORCYCLES

Motorcycling is a fast and inexpensive way of getting around, and often the only way to negotiate dirt roads in the rainy season. An International Driver's License (endorsed for motorcycles) is required to rent a bike. Rent motorcycles in Yogyakarta, Solo, and Pangandaranon on Java, and Kuta Beach, Candidasa, Sanur, and Denpasar on Bali for around Rp10,000-12,000 per day; rates are cheaper by the week. Most motorbikes are rented by private parties, usually young men hoping to make the bike pay for itself. Before sealing the deal, carefully check the battery, oil, brakes, cables, and clutch before you agree to a rental fee. Leave your passport or student ID as collateral and take the bike for a test drive. You should possess at least a crude knowledge of motorcycle mechanics if you plan to rent a bike here. It's also advisable to bring a few simple tools—screwdriver, wrench, pliers, and the like.

Another type of motorcycle transport is called *ojek* or *honda sikap*. Here you pay the motorcycle driver for the privilege of riding on the back of his bike. The *ojek* driver, for both motorcycles and bicycles, is called a *pengojek*. *Ojek* drivers usually cluster at road junctions with infrequent *bemo* service or none at all. Pushbike riders can be approached for *ojek* rides as well. When riding double, females are expected to sit sidesaddle while holding onto the packrack—a real trick. When dismounting from the back of a motorbike, be careful not to touch the hot exhaust pipe.

(following pages) Tanjung Pinang, Riau Islands, Sumatra

TRAVEL BY BICYCLE

Cycling in Indonesia is rewarding but demanding. At the places where it's most pleasant to ride a bicycle—Yogyakarta and Solo on Java, Candidasa and Ubud on Bali, Senggigi Beach on Lombok—rentals are plentiful and cheap. Elsewhere it takes some searching, and you may never find a bike that really works. Most rentals are sturdy black machines that resemble two-wheeled tanks. For rentals, count on a rate of Rp3500-4000 per day or Rp8000-12,000 per week. Mountain bikes rent for Rp10,000-15,000 per day. A critical bike accessory is a horn or very loud bell; a good helmet is also essential. Be prepared to use a sharp stick or your pump to defend against hostile dogs.

Most main roads on Java include cycle/pedestrian paths. Where there are no bike paths, motorists seem to be more aware of cyclists than in the West. In many Javanese cities, such as Yogyakarta in Central Java, cyclists are the majority and motorists the minority. As usual, Jakarta is the exception; it's not possible to ride around Jakarta. At public places—post offices, markets, schools, big stores—leave your bike at the *titipan sepeda* (bicycle parking area), where the attendant guards the bikes and gives you a claim ticket. The service may be free or cost Rp50-100. At night bring your bike inside your room, or ask the proprietor for the safest storage place.

Since bikes are used so much by the Indonesians themselves, even the smallest villages feature bike shops or someone whose specialty is fixing bikes. The *tukang sepeda* (bicycle repairer) usually sets up shop on a corner. His labor charges are low, mending your puncture while you wait for only Rp500 or so, using only rubber from an old inner tube, a pot of glue, and a homemade hammer.

Health

If you take care with personal hygiene, use caution in what you eat and drink, and get plenty of rest, you'll avoid most health problems while in Indonesia. Most illnesses among travelers are resistance diseases, a result of poor health, eating badly, overindulgence, or overexposure to heat and sun. Upon arrival, first become acclimated to the tropical environment: maintain adequate fluid and salt levels, avoid fatigue, dress light. Jet lag may change your sleeping patterns and eating habits, so schedule early extra rest.

Take a look at the latest World Immunization Chart from the **International Association for Medical Assistance to Travelers** (IAMAT), 417 Centre St., Lewiston, NY 14092, or find out from an official vaccine center which immunizations are currently required for travel to Indonesia. Then double-check with the Indonesian embassy. Tetanus, polio, and yellow-fevervaccines are very effective; others, such as cholera, are not. Typhoid and paratyphoid vaccinations are optional but advisable.

Since no vaccinations or inoculations are at present required except for visitors arriving from infected areas, you won't even be asked for your *Buku Kuning* ("Yellow Booklet"). This is the International Certificate of Vaccination, which records all immunizations and vaccinations. The booklet is available from designated vaccination centers around the world or direct from your doctor. In Indonesia itself, cholera vaccinations are dispensed at Jakarta's Sukarno/Hatta Airport in Cengkareng, though the cheapest place to get immunized in Jakarta is **Dinas Kesehatan**, Jl. Kesehatan 10. Foreigners can get shots at their embassy health unit, set up for use by embassy staff and contract employees, and staffed by foreign service doctors.

For travel health insurance, one of the best outfits is **Travel Guard Internationale** (1-800-826-1300) with a 24-hour Emergency Claims Service.

FOOD AND DRINK

Food- and water-borne infections are perhaps the greatest threats to the traveler in the tropics. Bacterial infections (typhoid, paratyphoid, cholera, salmonella, shigella), infectious hepatitis, and such parasitic infections as guineaworm, bilharzia, bacillary dysentery, amoebic dysentery, worms, and giardiasis can all be transmitted by contaminated food, water, or ice.

It's advisable not to drink local fresh milk or eat ice cream sold by street vendors. Stick to dairy products labeled as pasteurized. **Diamond, Peters,** and **Campina** are quality brand-name ice cream products sold locally. Use powdered whole milk (Dancow brand), cartons of long-life milk, or sweetened condensed milk (Indomilk).

All vegetables and fruit eaten raw should be thoroughly washed, rinsed, or peeled before eating. All meat and fish should be cooked well if you wish to avoid worms. Stick to well-cooked meals served hot. Stay away from rare meats and avoid cold buffets.

WATER AND SALT

Diseases transmitted by water include cholera, typhoid fever, bacillary dysentery, and giardiasis. By Indonesian law, water and ice served in restaurants must be boiled first. Of course, not everyone obeys the law, and unboiled water is often used for washing dishes and cooking certain foods. Avoid ice cubes unless they've been made from boiled water. Hot beverages carry fewer disease-causing organisms than cold beverages. Beer or soda water are about the only non-sweet beverages to drink.

You can consider safe only plastic bottled water (Agua brand is the most widespread) and water you have treated yourself. Though it contains a load of sugar, Fanta is safe for children to drink. Noncarbonated bottled drinks may or may not be safe; use carbonated, bottled, or boiled water for brushing your teeth. The freezing of water does not kill organisms, nor does alcohol in a drink.

Several practical methods make water safe to drink. If boiled briskly for 10 minutes, all the major disease organisms will die. Chemical sterilization, such as water-purification tablets like Halazone, is popular, but watch for side effects. Also, be forewarned that chlorine-based sterilization has proven effective against neither amoeba nor protozoan organisms, including giardiasis. Another chlorine-based method involves adding laundry bleach until a slight chlorine odor is detectable in the water. Let stand 30 minutes before drinking. Adding 5-10 drops of tincture of iodine per liter also works well; let stand for 20 minutes.

When your body sweats you lose salt, so you should add more to your diet. Jet lag and fatigue can be caused by salt deprivation. Loss of body fluids as a result of diarrhea or dysentery also calls for increased salt consumption. Salt tablets are not really necessary, but after heavy physical exercise you might pour a little extra salt on your food. If trekking into remote areas of Indonesia, take along ordinary sea salt. A mixture of salt and water serves as a mild antiseptic.

EXHAUSTION AND HEAT EXPOSURE

Travelers need to adjust to a climate that is extreme by temperate zone standards, possibly producing fatigue and loss of appetite. Acclimating to the enervating heat and humidity of Indonesia could take weeks. First, slow down the pace. Don't overdo it; no one else does. Get plenty of rest. Follow the Indonesian custom of *tidur siang* (napping) sometime between 1200 and 1600, the hottest part of the day. Drink increased amounts of water with fresh lemon and lime juice, and make sure there's salt in your diet. Restrict alcohol and smoking. Avoid rich, fatty foods. Don't eat too much fruit; this can cause stomachaches and diarrhea.

Heatstroke is caused by a breakdown in the body's sweating mechanism. Symptoms are a marked increase in body temperature to over 40 degrees C (105 degrees F) accompanied by reduction in perspiration and sometimes nausea or vomiting. Avoid heatstroke by drinking adequate fluids, taking in enough salt, wearing light clothing, and moderating your intake of alcohol. Though rare, heatstroke is an emergency. The victim should be taken to a cool room, doused with cold water, body fanned and sponged until the temperature drops to at least 39 degrees C (102 degrees F), at which point sponging should stop. Keep the patient at rest.

BALI BELLY

Travelers' diarrhea constitutes 90 percent of travel health problems, affecting about half of the five million visitors to the tropics each year. Sudden changes in climate, food, and water, rather than poor hygiene during food preparation, are generally the causes. If the persists for more than five days, see a doctor. Don't overconsume fruits, especially during December and January. Take in clear fluids such as water, weak tea, juice, clear soup, broth, or soda that has lost its carbonation. The very best liquid is an oral rehydration solution, available in pharmacies everywhere. Gradually add such plain foods as biscuits, boiled rice, bread, and boiled eggs to your diet. Avoid fatty or spicy foods while under treatment, and add dairy products last. Often, after a serious attack, your body is dehydrated and you may experience painful muscular contractions in the stomach. Fruit juice or cola with a teaspoon of salt will counteract this.

Take antibiotics to treat diarrhea, not prevent it. An over-the-counter drug sold in Indonesia that clears up diarrhea is Diatabs. Or one ounce of Pepto-Bismol liquid taken every 30 minutes provides symptomatic relief for most people. Imodium (Arret in Britain) is one of the best non-antibiotic treatments.

MEDICAL CARE AND PHARMACIES

The proprietor of any hotel or *losmen* can usually come up with the name of a reliable and reasonably priced physician or two. If you feel language will be a problem, get the names of English-, German-, or French-speaking doctors from your respective embassy or consulate. Many foreign physicians serve as house doctors in four- and five-star hotels. Or try to find a Chinese doctor in a mid- or fair-sized Indonesian city.

Routine dental care such as cleaning and fillings can be performed in all the main cities. Locate a good *dokter gigi* (dentist) through your embassy or consulate. Complicated root-canal therapy, surgery, or bridge construction and repair is often referred to specialists in Singapore. No certified orthodontists work in Jakarta. Dental floss is hard to find, so bring an ample supply. Jakartan optometrists do satisfactory lenswork, but take an extra pair of glasses or contact lenses, your lens prescription, and contact lens cleaning and storage fluids.

Jakarta has the best medical services. Very possibly the best facility in all of Indonesia is **S.O.S. Medica** (tel. 021-750-6001 for emergencies) in Jakarta. Your first choice for emergencies should be **St. Carolus Hospital**, Jl. Salemba Raya 41, Menteng, tel. 858-0091 or **Pertamina**, Jl. Kyai Maja 43, Kebayoran

Balinese Brahman priest

Baru, tel. 707-211. Particularly good for cardiac cases is **Dr. Cipto Mangunkusumo ICCU,** Jl. Diponegoro 69, Menteng, tel. 334-636. **Sumber Waras,** Jl. Kyai Tapa, Grogol, tel. 596-011 also has a sound reputation, as do **Pondok Indah,** Jl. Metro Dua, Kava UE, tel. 769-7525, and **Setia Mitra,** Jl. Fatmawati 80-82, Cilandak, tel. 769-6000.

You can buy most medicines in Indonesian pharmacies without a prescription. Most international-standard hotels contain pharmacies, and the state-owned pharmaceutical company **Kimia Farma** maintains outlets in midsized towns and cities. The pharmaceutical directory *Iso Indonesia* (Rp9000) provides an explanation of the nature and dosage of available drugs; it's also available in English. If you require a particular medicine over a long period of time—birth control pills, vitamins, blood pressure medication—you'd better bring your own supply. Keep all medicines out of reach of Indonesians; pills are like candy to them.

COMFORT

When relaxing, follow the Indonesian custom of wearing a *sarung,* ideal for this climate. Otherwise wear drip-dry, loose-fitting, light-colored cotton clothes. If your room is clammy and dark, air out your bedding the next morning on a line in the sterilizing sun. When you're too hot, drink water or hot tea. Beards can be quite itchy in the heat, and they scare Indonesian children. At night Indonesians of all ages love to cuddle a skinny, sausage-shaped bolster, the *bantal guling* ("Dutch wife") which looks like a long, soft punching bag. Lying lengthwise on the bed, this pillow absorbs sweat and delightfully fits the contours of arms and legs. If a *bantal guling* isn't available, use a piece of cloth to absorb sweat from delicate areas.

In cheap hotels keep mosquitos at bay by moving your bed under a fan or by using mosquito coils *(obat nyamuk),* which are quite effective, a little nauseating, and available anywhere. Deter the fumigating practices of many hotels by simply telling the person armed with the sprayer *"Tak usah, terimah kasih"* ("Thank you, but it's not necessary"). Electrically powered anti-mosquito devices, known as mosquito mats, are much better and not as toxic; the whole setup costs around Rp12,000. Few travelers use nylon or cotton mosquito nets *(kelambu)* while sleeping, yet you can buy them in both single or family sizes for a song.

Take a *mandi* (shower) as frequently as necessary to stay cool. When staying in a hotel with a *bak mandi* outside the room, don't go into the bath fully clothed. Just wrap a towel around you and take in your soap and shampoo. The happy sound of splashing *mandi* water is heard throughout the day. It's a great boon to travelers in Indonesia that *bak mandi* are often found in airports, train and bus stations, and restaurants the length of the land.

Conduct

Most Indonesians possess split personalities, divided between Western logic and Eastern feeling. Indonesians usually hide such negative feelings as jealousy, envy, sadness, and anger. Prolonged eye contact is avoided, as it may be interpreted as a challenge that could anger another. A Westerner quarreling with an Indonesian is generally assertive and confrontational. But an Indonesian will maintain a calm appearance and ultimately withdraw from a quarrel, usually choosing to deal with the issue later through a third person. Indonesians believe Westerners get angry so quickly because they eat too much meat, take themselves too seriously, and don't know how to laugh at themselves.

BODY LANGUAGE

Such aggressive gestures and postures as crossing your arms over your chest or standing with your hands on your hips while talking, particularly in front of older people, are regarded as insulting. Loud voices are particularly offensive. The feet are considered the lowliest part of the body and, especially on Java, it's offensive to sit with the soles of your feet pointing at people. It's also impolite to use your toes or shoes for pointing, as when indicating something displayed on the ground in the *pasar.* Neither should you point with your forefinger; use your right thumb. If you need to call to someone, extend your right hand and make a motion using the cupped fingers turned downward.

Never use your left hand to touch someone or to give and receive things. If you do inadvertently, say "Ma'af" ("Excuse me"). When giving or receiving something from someone older, or in a high office or elevated status, extend your right arm (but not too far), bring your left arm across the front of your body, then touch your fingers to your right elbow. When passing in front of an elder or high-born person, or person of equal rank whom you don't know, bend your body slightly, particularly if that person is sitting.

INDIVIDUAL VERSUS THE GROUP

There is no place in Indonesian society for the individual. They believe the man or woman who stands alone is unnatural, even absurd. Indonesians are accustomed to sharing their beds with other family members and may feel lonely and frightened when sleeping alone. Someone looking over your shoulder while you're writing is considered normal; why should anyone want to write personal thoughts that no one else may read? Indonesians also want to know your marital status immediately. If you're over 20 years old and say you have no children, Indonesians pity you. To respond, in fact, with an outright "no" is much too blunt. Say instead *"Saya belum beranak"* ("I do not yet have children"). Indonesians commonly use at least four other expressions to denote "no:" *"belum"* ("not yet"), *"tidak terima"* ("I cannot accept" or "you're joking!"), *"tidak senang"* ("not happy"), and *"tidak boleh"* ("not allowed to"). These are softer, more refined, and less provocative ways of saying "no." Anything to avoid unpleasantness and confrontation.

DEALING WITH BUREAUCRATS

Since government offices are so busy, you'll learn to behave aggressively, never letting anyone cut in front of you. Once you reach an official, open with a friendly exchange, then bring up your business. When confronting officials of the Immigration Department, be *extra* respectful, even ingratiating. Play the game. Dress neat and clean. Never get angry, no matter how long and frustrating the wait. If you're trying to move paperwork through an office, or clear something through customs, be courteous but volunteer as little information as possible. Use the telephone whenever you can; it's cheaper than waiting weeks for the mail.

In places unaccustomed to tourists, you'll find the police may harass you. As well as wanting to know who you are and what you're doing in their territory, they'll quickly let you know they run the place, then show off their English and prance their authority in front of the local people. If plunged into a hassle with annoyingly officious cops, customs, or *imigrasi* officials, act stupid, meek, friendly, and innocent. In most cases, they just want you to acknowledge the fact they're real and exercise power over you.

RELIGION

Religion plays a central role in the lives of Indonesians. Don't tell people you're an atheist; people will react with confusion, disbelief, even scorn, believing you're a godless communist. Ask permission to enter or take photos in a mosque. Remove your shoes before entering, and remain silent and respectful as you would in a church or synagogue. Women should dress modestly with long sleeves, trousers, or skirts; men should wear long pants. Menstruating women should not enter. Smoking is prohibited. Don't touch anyone. While the Islamic holy book, the *Koran,* is being read, don't drink or smoke; never put a book or anything else on the holy tome.

Chinese temples and religious monuments are used for religious worship and ceremonies by those practicing Confucianism, Taoism, and Buddhism, and should be granted the same respect as mosques. A sash—usually available at the entrance—should be worn around the waist when entering a Balinese temple. Never touch anybody's head. Most Indonesians regard the head as the seat of the soul and therefore sacred.

DRESS, GROOMING AND HYGIENE

Indonesians are very conservative, so be neat, clean, and fairly careful about what you wear. A *sarung* tied above the breasts is only acceptable on the way to bathe, and

Long after his political disenfranchisement, the Sultan's followers still bring him a daily water offering

wearing shorts, undershirts, and thongs in the streets can be insulting. If you sport a beard you'll be known as *Bapak Jenggot,* "Father Beard." Indonesians will ask how you keep from getting food caught in it, mothers will tell their children you'll eat them up, and others will think you appear angry all the time, like a *raksasa.* Whether bearded or not, children outside of tourist areas—and older people too— will often be afraid of you, though they'll try not to show it.

Indonesians don't normally use toilet paper—many consider it unhygienic—and the plumbing isn't designed to cope with large amounts of it. Most toilets are the floor-level, squat down kind. Covered buckets are sometimes provided in tourist accommdations for the disposal of toilet paper and tampons. It is better to adopt the Indonesian custom of splashing yourself with a dipper after using the toilet. A small cement trough is found next to the squat-down toilet to provide water for the toilet dipper. When finished, throw in a least five full dippers of water to wash waste down. In Indonesia, people don't blow their noses in front of others, but sniffing is okay.

INTERACTIONS

Don't get too annoyed about constantly being asked where you're going. Think up some zany answers, or use the standard ones, like exactly where you're going, if you know, or just *"jalan jalan"* which means roughly "out walking" and covers everything from aimless wandering to purposeful trips to the post office. Or try the Malay response, *"Saya makan angin,"* "I'm eating the wind." This phrase often gets rid of *becak* drivers who won't leave you alone. If people join you on the path or road, make conversation—usually they're not latching onto you forever. Knowing Indonesian allows for a greater range of encounters, as Indonesians are less self-conscious speaking to foreigners in their own tongue. Youngsters still call Western tourists by the Indonesian word for Dutchman, *Belanda*. So when you hear *"Belanda!"* shouted out behind you, turn around and come back with *"Bukan Belanda! Saya orang Selandia Baru!"* ("I'm not Dutch! I'm a New Zealander!") or some such reply. The fixed look of suspicion turns into a smile of appreciation at words in roughly recognizable Indonesian.

If small children offer their services as guides, render payment in ways other than money or candy. Begging creates an endless cycle of dependence, diminishes self-worth, and does more harm than good. Say *"tidak boleh"* ("you may not") to begging children. Offer a look through your binoculars, some pencils, pens, balloons, safety pins, or a small notebook. When in Jakarta or Bali, buy a quantity of the amazing postcards available there, then proffer them as gifts in the Outer Islands.

HASSLES

If a pickpocket probes your jeans or shoulder bag for money, remove the strange fingers, point, and announce to everyone, *"Pencopet!"* In some outlying towns a jeering crowd may follow you around, teasing, taunting, and verbally abusing you. In these cases, try to find a public official, schoolteacher, or police officer with whom you can establish a respectful rapport. Or enter an outlying, untouristed area only with an authority figure to evade encounters with rude, unsavory, or hostile individuals. Often you have surprise on your side and you're gone before a crowd can even gather.

In tourist locales, sellers on foot can be unbelievably pushy. Always be polite at first, expressing your disinterest. If they persist, turn around, face them, and state firmly you're not interested. Keep repeating this in Indonesian and in English, looking them straight in the eye, until they back off. Usually this works quite well, but if it doesn't, say vehemently *"Silahkan pergi!"* ("Please go!").

The ultimate hassle in Indonesia is a bust for selling dope, an offense Indonesians take very seriously. Even your hotel owner or a passerby on the beach can turn you in.

WOMEN TRAVELING ALONE

Women are more likely to be raped in the U.S. or Australia than in Indonesia, but you can expect men and boys here to touch you indecently. Sleazy types tend to hang around train and bus stations, movie theaters, ferry docks, and ports. If obscenely approached, just spit out *"Kau babi!"* ("You pig!"). In this Islamic nation, this invective will get his and the crowd's attention. Hopefully, the humiliation will prevent him from continuing.

When traveling alone, a woman should choose her clothes with care. Except when going to the beach, it's not a good idea to wear short skirts or shorts, braless tank tops, or strapless tops. In particularly strong orthodox Muslim areas, such as Aceh, women shouldn't even wear bathing suits or short shorts to the beach. Don't ask a man to accompany you to the beach as protection; this will be interpreted as an invitation to sex. Don't ever hug an Indonesian man; it will be misinterpreted.

On Bali and in other tourist areas, drivers say such filthy things to women that most soon prefer to avoid taxis altogether. If you want more comfort than a *bemo* provides, hire a car—but eschew all expressions of intimacy with the driver. Never take one driver overnight or for long-term. Don't eat meals with him. Another way a single woman can avoid trouble is to join a group tour. Either way, you will never receive so many marriage proposals in your life.

STAYING WITH PEOPLE

Conversations on buses, trains, and boats can often lead to great places to stay. But be forewarned: staying with a family means absolutely no privacy. Friends and relatives will visit, and anyone in the *kampung* who speaks English will come around to practice. You'll be invited to do things with the family so they can parade you around the village or city street. Small gifts and souvenirs (*ole-ole*) are a common way of showing gratitude and affection to the family you're staying with. If you're invited to dinner, bring a gift of chocolate or a tin of cookies. When attending an event in someone's home, it's customary to leave your shoes outside, then wait to be seated. Don't take photos without permission. Wear clean, decent clothes.

It's not easy for Indonesians to initiate conversations, and they're often relieved when spoken to. They are are very proud of their country and will always ask if you like Indonesia, if you plan to come back. Foreigners can ask Indonesians almost anything and get away with it. Do talk politics, but always in private and never with the army or police. Talk about where they come from, places they've traveled to at home and abroad, or about children (yours or theirs). Don't introduce business into social situations.

TABLE MANNERS

Indonesians always offer to share the meals they're eating when visitors arrive at house, office, or park bench. If invited to dinner, arrive 10 minutes late; it's expected. Once seated, watch your Indonesian host; a guest may not start until the host offers the invitation *"Silakan makan"* ("Please eat") or *"Silakan minum"* ("Please drink"). While at the table, never eat with the left hand. Take a small helping the first time around because your host will be offended if you don't take seconds. It's polite to keep pace with your host. If you empty your plate, it means you want more. If you don't like what's served, it's acceptable to just take a sip or bite. To ask for salt, pepper, soy sauce, or *sambal* is an insult, implying the cook didn't know what spices to add to the dish.

Be careful not to offend your Muslim friends, who are forbidden to eat pork. In their company never ask for or offer dishes prepared with pork or lard. Indonesians are also unaccustomed to eating uncooked food such as salads, cold meats, and dairy products; sometimes Western food can even upset their stomachs. Westerners rarely eat the insides of cattle or sheep, but in Indonesia virtually every part of an animal is consumed. Many traditional families do not talk during meals; conversation starts only after the meal. Cover your mouth with your hand when picking your teeth; only animals show their fangs.

VISITING

Unnanounced visits are traditional. The best time to drop in on people is between 1600 and 1800—after work, food, and siesta, and, in Islamic areas, before evening prayers. It's less polite to visit or call later in the evening, after 2100. It's common for Indonesians to be on your doorstep at 0630 as everyone gets up early. Visits between 1230 and 1530 are considered impolite.

Visitors are never turned away. Allow enough time with your host, as a rushed guest leaves a bad impression. If you're kept waiting for your host to appear, it's a compliment: s/he's changing into nice clothes to receive you. Conversely, s/he'd be offended if you visited only in a *sarung* or T-shirt. The polite way to turn down a visit to someone's house is *"Ya, kapan-kapan, kalau ada waktu"* ("Okay, sometime, if there's time").

It's polite to introduce yourself when meeting strangers. Shake hands when greeting people; men, women, and children will all offer their hands when introduced. Respect is shown by bowing from the waist when passing in front of people, especially older people. Share your cigarettes, and maintain a supply of biscuits for the kids.

Travelers should also be prepared to forego an occasional night's sleep. Make of the night the day. Many forms of entertainment, prayers, and religious festivals run noisily all night long. In some places people stay up the whole night of the full moon simply for the coolness and magic of it. There's plenty of magic in Indonesia.

Java

Introduction

Though Java is the smallest of the Greater Sunda Islands, and comprises only seven percent of the country's land area, it contains 60 percent of Indonesia's population. Here live most of Indonesia's urban population, as well as the majority of its poorest peasantry. Many areas of Java resemble India because of the congestion, the rice paddies, the explosive colors. "I see India everywhere, but I do not recognize it," said the great Bengali poet Tagore when he visited Java in 1927.

The Dutch concentration of resources on Java for several hundred years greatly increased the differences between it and Indonesia's other islands, which the Javanese still consider "Outer Islands." Educationally, it's the most advanced island. Java's universities and technological institutions form the backbone of Indonesia's tertiary education. Java is top-heavy with industry, processing, and modern transport and telecommunication facilities.

With 60 percent of Indonesia's investments concentrated on Java, it's the island of opportunity, the place where young men flock from the rural areas of Indonesia to find jobs. Java also processes raw materials from Indonesia's productive regions: tobacco, foods, beverages, rubber, timber, textiles, machinery. Yet, because of its giant population, Java could never survive if it were left to its own resources; it would be like a head without a body.

THE PEOPLE

With their light brown skin, straight black hair, high cheekbones, and small and slender builds, the Javanese originally belonged to the Oceanic branch of the Mongoloid race. But the Javanese "race" is actually a blending of every race that ever established itself on the island. Most of Java's people belong to four major cultural-lingual ethnic groups: the **Sundanese** of West Java (about 30 million), the **Javanese** of Central and East Java (about 79 million), the **Tenggerese** from the area in East Java around Gunung Bromo (300,000), and the **Madurese** inhabiting Madura Island. Of these, the Javanese are numerically the largest group and the most influential culturally and politically.

HISTORY

Java is the physical center of all the islands, and has always been the metropolitan trading focus for the archipelago. It's the golden mean in both size and location, long the most favored isle for human habitation and thus the most populous and politically powerful. Java's history is long. Compared to the poor archaeological records of the Outer Islands, Java possesses a fantastic amount of documents and monuments. With the wealth generated from huge surpluses obtained from wet-rice cultivation, great precolonial inland empires rose on this island: Majapahit, Singosari, Kediri, Mataram. Ancient Java was a land of peasants and princes, with the peasants laboring and producing for the princes enthroned in their palace cities, providing the massive agricultural wealth to fuel the empire's maritime trade.

The Dutch took possession of the island while Shakespeare was still alive. For a period of 200 years, beginning in about 1723, Java was the key island in the Dutch East Indies empire, paying shareholders in Europe an average dividend of 18 percent per annum. Under Dutch rule Java became known as the garden of the tropics, one of the best-governed tropical islands in the world. It was a wonder of colonial management—a land of railroads, schools, swank resorts, vast well-run estates. You

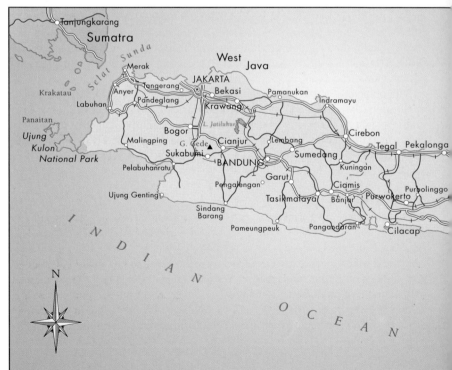

could telephone any point on the island from your hotel, and travel on some of the best-paved roads in Asia. **Batavia,** present-day Jakarta, offered steep white-walled mansions, a maze of canals, overhanging roofs of red tiles, signs all in Dutch—like a street in Rotterdam or The Hague. For 40 years during the 19th century, while the peasants starved, all of Java was turned into a huge work farm, subject to a system of enormously profitable forced deliveries of cash crops. The **Java War** (1835-40) was the last stand of the Javanese aristocracy, Java's equivalent of Bali's *puputan.* The Javanese have said the Dutch had good heads but cold hearts, and claim they lost all their lands because it was precisely the reverse with them.

THE *KRATON*

When the temple city concept arrived from India, the *kraton* developed as its Indonesian counterpart. The fortified palaces of Javanese rulers became the centers of political power and culture. As in India, these fortresses contained all the surrounding region would need in the way of commerce, art, and religion. Cities within cities, they encompassed banks, baths, shops, temples, massage and meditation chambers, schools, workshops, scribe and concubine quarters—everything royalty had a use for.

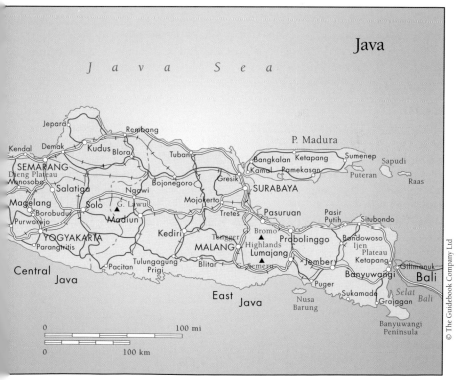

© The Guidebook Company Ltd

Only the *kraton* was open to all the new values and attractions Indian civilization had to offer. The *kraton* adopted and modified first the Hindu caste system, then the philosophical structure of Islam. Only these courts possessed enough wealth for the arts and crafts to flourish. Handcrafted objects were made as ornaments and utensils for the king and court. Though the *kraton* was their origin, crafts eventually spread beyond their walls and into the villages and countryside. Dance also found a home in the *kraton*. The princely courts of Solo and Yogyakarta created their own dance dramas, each style evolving differently. During the colonial period, for the most part a time of peace on Java, artistic expression flowered intensively. The princes, though politically powerless, were still extremely wealthy. The finest wayang puppets, masks, and dance costumes in Indonesia were and are produced in and for the *kraton*.

CUSTOMS

The Javanese claim the level of a people's civilization is measured by the refinement of its system of etiquette. So strongly do they feel this, the Javanese commonly refer to etiquette as *busananing bangsa*, "the garments of a nation." And by this measure, the Javanese pride themselves on being one of the most refined, polite, and cultivated peoples on earth. This cultivation stems from the *priyayi* tradition. *Priyayi* is the gentry class of Java, the old Hindu-Javanese aristocracy who guard and hold such values and ethics as extreme politeness, deference to the aged, soft-spokenness, proper conduct, sophistication, social arts and graces, and artistic skills (dance, drama, music, and verbal eloquence). As a class they consider manual labor undignified—if you can read and write, you must "have clean hands."

BATIK

Java produces the world's finest *batik*. A traditional method of decorating cloth, *batik* is an art of great antiquity. The earliest evidence of *batik*-making dates back to the courts of Central Java. *Batik* centers later developed on the north coast, then spread to other parts of Java. Formerly, *batik* fabrics were used mainly to make sarung, skirts, scarves, and men's headgear; nowadays *batik* is used in housecoats, dresses, blouses, ties, belts, slippers, hats, umbrellas, sport coats, upholstery—anything that can be made of cloth. Even school uniforms in Indonesia feature subdued *batik* patterns.

Most Javanese women cannot afford to wear traditional dress every day, donning instead cheaper Western clothes. During national holidays, however, all women and girls wear the traditional sarung-kebaya outfit, the national woman's dress of Indonesia. A great demand for *batik* has always existed on Java; it isn't just tourists who've guaranteed that *batik* survives and prospers. Still, tourists have undoubtedly accounted for an increase in the making of *halus*, or high-quality, handmade (*batik tulis*) pieces.

Java's principal *batik* centers are Yogyakarta, Solo, Pekalongan, Cirebon, Tasik-malaya, Indramayu, Garut, and Lasem. Each area still produces its own distinctive design and color. Several sizes of *batik* are available. A *kain panjang,* for example, is one meter wide and 2.5 meters long. The sarung is one meter wide and two meters long, sewn into a cylindrical shape and worn as a skirt. sarung are usually worn by men, *kain* by women. A *dodot* is used for high-court ceremonies; its length is four times its width. The *selendang* is a breast and shoulder cloth worn by women.

THE KRIS

At one time all Javanese men, from the age of three, were required to wear this magical, wavy-bladed dagger, and most Javanese are still fond of wearing them. The *kris* is often worn formally by the groom at weddings and by young men to their circumcision ceremonies. Rank is denoted by the method of wearing the *kris,* and it must be worn according to set rules: stuck in the belt in back so that the end of the sheath points to the left, the hilt to the right.

On the best *kris,* hilts incorporate exquisite carvings in ivory or metalwork, decorated with *raksasa* figures (demonic images that drive off evil spirits), little gnome-like men, snakes, or monkeys. The grips of the *kris* of noblemen were often sculpted of gold and set with rubies, diamonds, and sapphires. The ornaments on the blade also provide protection: delicate leaves, *garuda,* or *kala*-figures, and very frequently a *naga* (serpent). *Kris* blades sometimes include up to 31 *lok* (undulations), though more often just seven or nine. An odd number of *lok* ensures good luck. These waves are designed to "saw" flesh for a deeper, ripping stab, and also make the wound difficult to heal.

Some *kris* have a spirit and are capable of sorcery: they can talk, fly, swim, turn into snakes, even father human children. Designs on the blade can ward off demons or render the wearer invulnerable. If pointed at someone or if stabbed into the shadow or footprint of an intended victim, the invisible venom of the *kris* could kill a man. When danger is near, *kris* have been known to rattle in their sheaths.

GAMELAN

Gamelan is the broad name for many varieties of xylophonic orchestras with bronze, wooden, or bamboo keys on wooden or bamboo bases or resting on tubular resonators, balanced on pegs, or suspended. This type of percussion ensemble is found in other forms in Thailand, the Philippines, Madagascar, and Cambodia. *Gamelan* orchestras are the most widespread type of orchestra in the archipelago, especially on Java and Bali. The most sophisticated is the native Javanese *gamelan,* composed of about a dozen musicians and used as accompaniment in *wayang* and dance performances. In its complete modern form, a *gamelan* orchestra could comprise 70-80 instruments, with solo vocalists (*pasinden*) and up to 15 choir (*gerongan*) members.

Native *gamelan* seldom play outside Indonesia because of transportation expenses.

The ethereal sound of the *gamelan* is created when rows of small bronze kettle-shaped discs of varying sizes, with raised nipples, are hit with cudgel-like sticks. These bronze instruments give the *gamelan* its highly distinctive musical range, from thin tinkles to deep booming reverberations. *Gamelan* music can't be compared with the compositions of the West's great polyphonic composers such as Bach, whose music is so mathematically precise. *Gamelan* is much looser, freer, more flighty and unpredictable. Some even feel it is curiously melancholy, even disturbing.

DANCE

After the split of the Mataram Kingdom into the vassal states of Yogyakarta and Solo in 1775, the art of court dancing evolved differently in the *kraton* of each of these cities. As cultural capitals, they've always been artistic rivals: Solo considers Yogyanese dancers too stiff; Yogyakarta believes Solonese dancers are too slack and casual. The differences in the two schools are still recognizable.

In court dancing, the emphasis is on angular graceful poses and smooth subtle gestures. This type of dancing is far removed from Western theories of art and reflects the ultra-refinement of the Javanese courts. Conceived during a time of warring states, classical dancing is executed with all the deliberation of a slow march and the precision of a drill maneuver. Sometimes years of arduous muscular training are required to execute certain gestures—such as arching the hand until the fingers touch the forearm, meant to imitate the opening of flower petals. Dancers are incredibly detached, yet their inaction and long periods of immobility are considered just as important as the action. All these pauses, silences, and motions arrested in space, with lowered eyes and meditative poses, make Javanese dance hypnotic to watch.

The tradition of classical dancing was once considered a sacred legacy by the courts. Dancers selected from lower-class families could serve only in supporting roles in the royal plays. It wasn't until 1918, when the **Krida Beksa Wirama Dance School** was founded in Yogyakarta, that the dance moved outside the walls of the *kraton*. Many village groups have since imitated and diluted the courtly style. Private dance groups perform for anniversaries, wedding receptions, or a *selamatan*. A group can be hired for anywhere between Rp100,000 and Rp600,000; the average cost is Rp250,000. If you hire a troupe to perform, you'll repay the family you're staying with for their kindness, their prestige in the village or *kampung* will rise, and their neighbors will share in the pleasure.

WAYANG

A Javanese word meaning literally "shadow" or "ghost," *wayang* is a theatrical performance of living actors, three-dimensional puppets, or shadow images projected before a backlit screen. The word can also refer to the puppets themselves. In most

Shadow puppet theatre

forms, the dialogue is in Javanese or Sundanese; sometimes Indonesian is used. Most often the chants are in Kawi (Old Javanese), as archaic a language on Java today as Shakespearean English in Great Britain.

All *wayang* drama forms reflect Javanese culture. Characters are judged not by their actions but by their devotion to what is appropriate to their castes, and by their predetermined roles in the drama. Gestures are appreciated more than common sense, style more than content. Courage, loyalty, and refinement always win out in the end, and fate is accepted without question. The *wayang* plays do not just show the direct victory of good over evil. They also display weakness as well as greatness in all the characters and, by implication, in society as a whole.

Besides the abbreviated tourist performances held in Yogyakarta and Solo, *wayang* is staged when some transitional event occurs in a person's life: birthdays, weddings, important religious occasions, or as ritual entertainment during family feasts or *selamatan*. Coming of age (puberty), circumcision, promotion, even the building of a new swimming pool—all could be excuses for a show. While providing entertainment, *wayang* also teaches the meaning, purpose, contradictions, and anomalies of modern life. The policies of the military government are even explained in terms of *wayang* theater, not only by the puppetmasters, but also in newspaper editorials and even in government statements. For example, Krishna, the most widely venerated Hindu deity, has been compared with President Suharto.

Today there are more than 10,000 individual performers of the *wayang kulit* shadow play on Java and Bali. In addition, there are *wayang orang* dance plays and *wayang topeng* masked dancing. The Sundanese prefer *wayang golek,* three-dimensional carved wooden puppets, to the flat leather figures of the *wayang kulit.* In addition to these well-known forms, there are a few rare, vestigial forms such as *wayang beber,* a narrated presentation in which drawings are unrolled, and new forms like Jakarta's *wayang karya,* which features a large puppet stage. On Madura, one troupe of *wayang orang madura* wears masks covering only the top part of their faces, so their mouths are exposed to speak freely. The Chinese of Java have their own form of *wayang golek,* performed only in temples. It's believed *wayang golek* is the last development of all the native *wayang* forms.

The *Dalang*

In the *wayang* forms in which puppets are used, the *dalang* is the puppeteer. The *dalang* is the playwright, producer, principal narrator, conductor, and director of the shadow world. He's an expert in languages and highly skilled in the techniques of ventriloquism. Some *dalang,* or their wives, carve their own puppets, maintaining a cast of up to 200 which are kept in a big wooden box. The *dalang* must be familiar with all levels of speech, modulating his voice and employing up to nine tonal and pitch variations to suit each puppet's temperaments. The *dalang* has a highly developed dramatic sense, and, if he has a good voice, his chants are beautiful and captivating to hear. He must also be intimately versed in history, including complex royal genealogies, music, recitation, and eloquence, and must possess a familiarity with metaphysics, spiritual knowledge, and perfection of the soul. Traveling from village to village and city to city, he has as many fans as a film star.

In ancient times the *dalang* was nothing less than a priest officiating at religious rituals. On Java the *dalang* retains to this day vestiges of his priestly role, particularly in the *ruwatan* performance, a ritual used to ward off evil from a vulnerable child. Once passed down from father to son, the puppeteer's art is now taught only in special schools in Central Java. The working *dalang's* fees depend on his reputation and popularity. It's common for *dalang* of the first rank, such as Nartosado of Yogyakarta, and Amamsoroto, Durmoko, and Supraman of Solo, to demand two million *rupiah* for one night's work. Special appearances can incur additional costs. When a first-class *dalang* performs, only the very best orchestra can be hired; if the *gamelan* is second- or third-rate it will not do the *dalang* justice.

Jakarta

Also known as Ibu Kota, the "Mother City," this sprawling urban center of 10 million people is Indonesia's capital, its brain and nerve center. The world's ideas, technology, and fashions first touch Indonesia here. Jakarta is the nation's literary center and headquarters for its mass media; 21 newspapers are printed here. The city has a film industry, modern theater academy, and prestigious university. Jakarta is where the big contracts are signed, the strings pulled, the rakeoffs diverted. Base for 12,500 companies, 80 percent of all foreign investments come through here, and most of the money stays here.

The chief drama of this city is in its contrasts, a fascinating collision of East and West. Air-conditioned diesels hurtle by peddlers and sleek office towers throw shadows across cardboard hovels. Jakarta contains Indonesia's most expensive buildings and its murkiest slums—great rivers of steel, glass, and granite winding through endless expanses of ramshackle one- and two-storey *kampung*. Here live the most and least educated people of Indonesia. Jakarta is Indonesia's most dynamic, problem-ridden city. Travelers' expenses will run two to three times higher here than anywhere else in Indonesia. Another hard reality is the audacious pickpocketing on Jakarta's buses, and the gangs of youths who relieve travelers of their possessions at knifepoint.

History

Jakarta has the longest continuous history of any modern Indonesian city. The **Tarumanegara inscription**, found near Tanjung Priok, dates from A.D. 500. For centuries merchants met near the mouth of the Ciliwung River, a site destined to be conquered later by empire-mad Dutch, opportunistic English, and Japanese expansionists. When the Portuguese made the first European contact with a Javanese kingdom in 1522, Jakarta was called Sundakelapa. The Hindu *raja's* control of Sundakelapa was broken by Islamic troops on 22 June 1527, a date still celebrated as the city's birthday. The conquering Muslim prince, Fatahillah, then renamed the small Javanese coastal settlement Jayakarta—"City of Victory."

In the early 1600s, Dutch traders established a fortified trading post in Jayakarta. In 1619, they overcame the Bantenese rulers and burned the village to the ground. The Dutch then built a small garrison that withstood twin assaults in 1628 and 1629 by a mighty army of 80,000. Repelling subsequent attacks, the Dutch grew more entrenched. Renaming the site Batavia, for a medieval Germanic tribe, the Dutch built a completely new city of intersecting canals, small gabled houses with tiny windows, and red-tiled roofs—a Little Holland in the tropics. Batavia soon became the trade center for the Dutch East India Co.; from here, Dutch governors sent voyagers out to

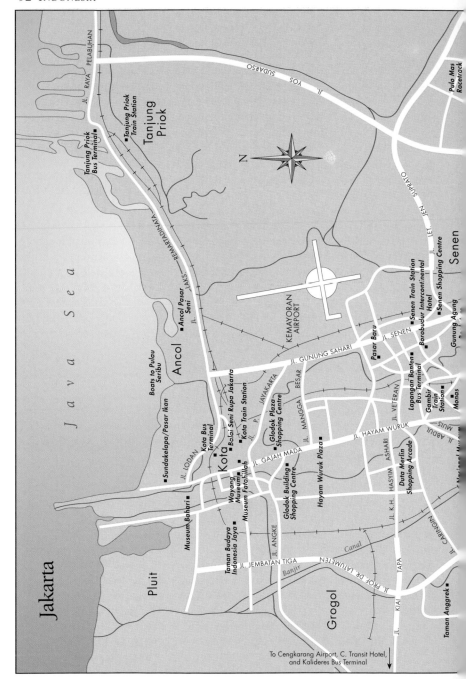

Jakarta

Java Sea

Pluit

Grogol

Ancol

Kota

Senen

Tanjung Priok

Kemayoran Airport

JL. RAYA PELABUHAN

JL. YOS SUDARSO

Pulo Mas Racetrack

Tanjung Priok Bus Terminal

Tanjung Priok Train Station

JL. JAKS. RE.WA.RA.DI.NA.TA

Ancol Pasar Seni

JL. SENI

Boats to Pulau Seribu

Sundakelapa/Pasar Ikan

JL. LODAN

Kota Bus Terminal

Balai Seni Rupa Jakarta

Kota Train Station

JL. JAYAKARTA

Gladak Plaza Shopping Centre

Museum Bahari

Wayang Museum

Museum Fatahillah

JL. GAJAH MADA

Gladak Building Shopping Centre

Taman Budaya Indonesia Jaya

JL. ANGKE

JL. JEMBATAN TIGA

JL. MANGGA BESAR

JL. P. JAYAKARTA

Hayam Wuruk Plaza

JL. HAYAM WURUK

JL. GUNUNG SAHARI

Pasar Baru

JL. SENEN

Senen Train Station

Borobudur Intercontinental Hotel

Senen Shopping Centre

Gunung Agung

JL. LET. JEN. SUPRAPTO

Lapangan Banteng Bus Terminal

Gambir Train Station

Monas

JL. ABDUL MUIS

JL. VETERAN

Duta Merlin Shopping Arcade

JL. K.H. HASYIM ASHARI

JL. KIAI TAPA

JL. CARINGIN

JL. PROF. DR. LATUMETEN

Canal

Banjir

Taman Anggrek

To Cengkarang Airport, C. Transit Hotel, and Kalideres Bus Terminal

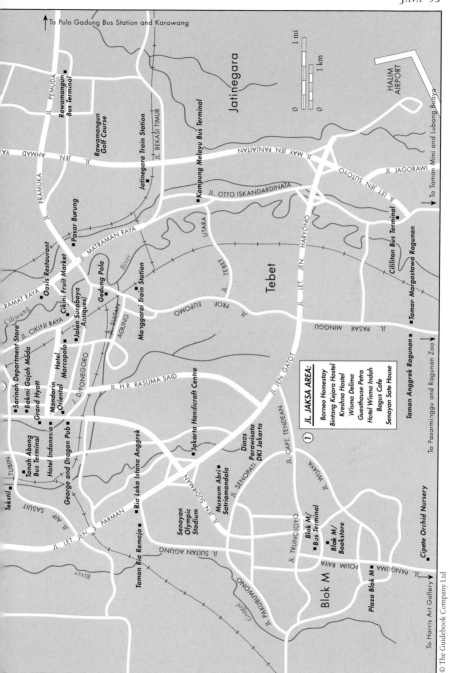

To Pulo Gadung Bus Station and Karawang

Jatinegara

HALIM AIRPORT

1 mi

1 km

To Taman Mini and Lubang Buaya

JL. PEMUDA

Rawamangun Bus Terminal

JL. BEKASI TIMUR

Kampung Melayu Bus Terminal

JL. MAY. JEN. PANJAITAN

JL. JAGORAWI

JL. JEN. AHMAD YANI

PRAMUKA

Rawamangun Golf Course

Jatinegara Train Station

JL. OTTO ISKANDARDINATA

JL. LET. JEN. SUTOYO

Cilliwung

Pasar Burung

JL. MATRAMAN RAYA

UTARA

JL. LET. JEN. HARYONO

Cililitan Bus Terminal

KRAMAT RAYA

Oasis Restaurant

Cikini Fruit Market

River

Gedung Pola

TEBET

Tebet

Taman Margastawa Ragunan

Cilliwung

JL. CIKINI RAYA

Jalan Surabaya Antiques

Manggarai Train Station

JL. PROF. SUPOMO

JL. PASAR MINGGU

To Pasarminggu and Ragunan Zoo

Sarinah Department Store

AGUNG

SULTAN

Bakmi Gajah Mada

Hotel Marcopolo

Mandarin Oriental

JL. DIPONEGORO

JL. H.R. RASUMA SAID

Jakarta Handicraft Centre

JL. JEN. GATOT

Taman Anggrek Ragunan

Grand Hyatt

Hotel Indonesia

JL. CAPT. TENDEAN

① **JL. JAKSA AREA:**
Borneo Homestay
Bintang Kejora Hostel
Kreshna Hostel
Wisma Delima
Guesthouse Petra
Hotel Wisma Indah
Bagus Cafe
Senayan Sate House

Tanah Abang Bus Terminal

George and Dragon Pub

Ria Loka Istana Anggrek

JL. SENOPATI

Dinas Parawisata DKI Jakarta

JL. WIJAYA

Tekstil

TUBIN

JL. AIR SASUT

JL. LET. JEN. S. PARMAN

Museum Abri Satriamandala

JL. JEN. SUDIRMAN

JL. TRUNOJOYO

Cipete Orchid Nursery

RIVER

Taman Ria Remaja

Senayan Olympic Stadium

JL. SULTAN AGUNG

JL. PAKUBUWONO

Ciraol

Blok M/ Bus Terminal

Blok M/ Bookstore

Blok M

Plaza Blok M

POLIM RAYA

JL. PANGLIMA

To Harris Art Gallery

© The Guidebook Company Ltd

open new trading routes. From 1811-1816 Batavia was the base for Sir Stamford Raffles, Java's English administrator while the British occupied the Indies during the Napoleonic Wars. Many of Jakarta's modern (post-1700s) relics and architecture have survived. Thus in Jakarta, more than anywhere else in Indonesia, you can see and feel the effects of the Dutch and English presence.

With the proclamation of Indonesian independence in 1945, the name Jakarta—an abbreviation of its native name, Jayakarta—was adopted. During the Sukarno era, Jakarta was a collection of villages barely held together by the slogans of bombastic nationalism. In the subsequent Suharto years the main avenues were widened and buildings shot up in all directions. The better-known sections of Jakarta are relatively new, though over the last 15 years, the government has begun to revitalize Jakarta's rich collection of historical attractions: colonial fortifications, country estates, cemeteries, mosques, Chinese temples.

SIGHTS

Jakarta lies on a north-south axis. Fronting the city's main drag, **Jl. Thamrin**, are many of the city's largest office buildings, major hotels, theaters, and banks. At Jl. Thamrin's southern end is the new suburb of Kebayoran Baru; at the northern end lies **Lapangan Merdeka** ("Freedom Square") with the towering National Monument. To the north are Kota and **Sunda Kelapa**, sites of the city's Dutch beginnings and oldest remains. Posh **Menteng, Gondangdia,** and **Cikini** (where the diplomats now live) were the most exclusive Dutch residential areas; you still see white villas with tiled roofs and floors and shaded porches. See also the millionaires' row of **Kemang**. Tour the city on Sundays, when the streets have 30-40 percent less traffic.

Kota (Old Batavia)

With its Old World atmosphere, Kota is the oldest part of the city. This relatively small northern area was the waterfront swamp where the Dutch first settled, remaining for 330 years. Surrounded by a moat and thick wall, Old Batavia stretched from Pasar Ikan south to Jl. Jembatan Batu/Jl. Asemba. The Dutch stored their spices in warehouses along the harbor; from majestic buildings surrounding a cobblestone-paved square they administered a vast mercantile empire. The heart of Old Batavia lies where the Jakarta City Museum is today. From Jl. Thamrin, take bus no. 70 (Rp400) or Patas bus no. 16 (Rp600) to Terminal Bis Kota, also called *stanplats*.

Most Kota sights are within walking distance of the *stanplats*. You can visit all the museums in one morning. Near the *stanplats* on Jl. Nelayan Timur see the one remaining 17th-century drawbridge, **Chicken Market Bridge**, which marked the southwest corner of the old Dutch fort. From **Museum Wayang** on Jl. Pintu Besar Utara cross the drawbridge over the Kali Besar to view the only 17th-century building left, the shop owned by PT Satya Niaga. Through the 18th century, ships could sail under the drawbridge and continue up the Ciliwung River.

Glodok

Go wandering in the daytime around Glodok, Jakarta's **Chinatown**, in the immediate area around Jl. Pintu Besar Utara. After the 1770 massacre of Chinese, survivors were forcibly relocated here outside the city walls. Glodok is now a thriving banking, trade, and entertainment center. Hunt for temples along the narrow back streets, lined with Chinese food vendors and shops. Take Jl. Pancoran beside the five-story Glodok Plaza. The Dutch architecture contrasts strikingly with the Chinese buildings with their slanting red-tiled roofs and balconies.

Gedung Syahbandar

This tower-like building overlooking Pasar Ikan in northernmost Kota is a good point to begin your tour. Early in the 17th century, the Javanese erected a military post on this spot to control the mouth of the Ciliwung River and keep an eye on the Dutch who, in 1610, were granted permission to build houses and a *godown* (warehouse). Within months of signing the contract, the unruly Dutch violated it, changing the building material to stone. By 1618, through a series of similarly deceitful moves, the Dutch were firmly entrenced in Jayakarta, their cannons trained on their host's *kraton*. This watchtower, built in 1839 by the Dutch, is one of the few remains of Kasteel Batavia.

Museum Bahari

The Maritime or Naval Museum is located near Sunda Kelapa in the lively Pasar Ikan area (Jl. Pasar Ikan 1). Open Tues.-Thurs. 0900-1400, Friday to 1100, Saturday to 1300, Sunday to 1500, closed Monday (and any other time they feel like it). Museum Bahari consists of two restored Dutch East India Company warehouses. Here the company stored its mountains of coffee, tea, cloth, spices, tin, and copper. One building now contains spice trade memorabilia; the other addresses maritime history. In front of the museum are a wall and sentry box, last remnants of the wall that surrounded Old Batavia in the 17th and 18th centuries. Nearby, explore the multitude of small alleys in the fascinating Pasar Ikan area. Go at dawn when the night's catch is auctioned off.

Sunda Kelapa

One of the most spectacular sights in Jakarta and among the great maritime attractions in all of Java. This 500-year-old harbor area is an easy walk from the Jakarta City Museum. Entrance Rp100. The Ciliwung River—now a clogged and stinking canal—was a vital link to the markets of the outside world for the 15th-century kingdom of **Pajajaran**, located near present-day Bogor. Since then the port has belonged to the Portuguese, Muslims, and Dutch. Though little remains of bustling old Sundakelapa except the name, the harbor is still one of the most important calls for sailing vessels from all over the archipelago. For around Rp3000 boatmen will take you around the waterfront.

Gereja Sion

Also called the "Old Portuguese Church" or "Gereja Portugis," on Jl. Pangeran Jayakarta 1. Emerging from the left side of the Kota train station, walk down Jl. Batu to the bridge; it's on the corner. View the interior (guestbook, donation) Tues.-Sat. 0900-1500. Built in 1693, Gereja Sion is Jakarta's oldest standing house of worship. The Portuguese themselves never built a church in Jakarta, but they imported Portuguese-speaking Indian slaves. Their descendants—freed when they converted to Christianity—eventually became a prominent social class known as Mardjikers or "**Black Portuguese**," though they had only a drop of Portuguese blood. Gereja Sion was restored in 1920, and again in 1978. The interior contains fine 17th-century carved wood pillars, a baroque pulpit, lavish ebony pews, and big copper chandeliers. Many prominent people of Old Batavia are interred in the church graveyard. The most beautiful tomb is that of Governor-General Zwaardecroon; he asked to be buried here so he might "sleep amongst the common folk."

Taman Fatahillah

In front of the Jakarta City Museum is stone-paved Taman Fatahillah, once Batavia's main square. The fountain in the middle—faithfully reconstructed from a 1788 sketch—sits on the foundation of the original. Here the early inhabitants fetched—and later died from—their drinking water. In this square criminals were flogged or beheaded; merry festivals and public markets occupied the site on other days. North of the fountain is a 16th-century Portuguese cannon with the honorific title **Si Jagur** ("Mr. Sturdy"). Because of its phallic shape and clenched fist with thumb protruding between the fingers (a symbol for sexual intercourse on Java), women believed the cannon could cure infertility. Barren women used to offer the cannon flowers, then sit on top of it; the Dutch attempted to end this practice by removing it to a museum. Its Latin inscription, *"Ex me ipsa renata sum"* ("I am reborn from myself") alludes to the fact the cannon was recast from an older weapon. In front of Si Jagur 0600-1400 every day except Sunday is a bustling flea market.

Balai Seni Rupa

This Museum of Fine Arts (tel. 021-271-062) is located on the east side of Taman Fatahillah in a large building with a classical facade. It was built in 1870, and once housed the Department of Justice. Open Tues.-Thurs. 0900-1400, Friday to 1100, Saturday to 1300, Sunday to 1500; entrance fee Rp200, children Rp100. Balai Seni Rupa houses a permanent exhibition of Indonesian paintings from the Raden Saleh era up to contemporary times, including a number of carved tree trunks. A ceramics museum, Museum Keramik, shares the same building. Open daily 0900-1400 except Monday and Friday; tel. 177-424.

Old Batavia Museum

Also known as Museum Kota, or "**Fatahillah.**" Located on the south side of Fatahillah Square right behind Kota station. Entrance Rp200, plus a Rp500 camera charge. Open Tues.-Thurs. 0900-1400, Friday to 1100, Saturday to 1300, Sunday to 1500. Once the City Hall of Batavia (Stadhuis), this magnificent 1710 two-story building is a fine example of Dutch colonial architecture. The whole edifice was converted in 1974 into a museum charting Jakarta's long and dramatic history. The interior is almost devoid of decoration, the floor plan pragmatically designed to serve the needs of bureaucrats and a populace that for 250 years flocked here to obtain marriage licenses, hear sermons, pay taxes, and legalize contracts. Most exhibits are annotated in Indonesian; no numbering system, catalog, or explanations in English. The building contains an amazingly rich collection of massive antique furniture, domestic items, and VOC memorabilia.

Museum Wayang

A puppet museum on Jl. Pintu Besar Utara 27 (tel. 021-279-560). Open Tuesday, Wednesday, Thursday, and Sunday 0900-1400, Friday to 1100, Saturday to 1300. Entrance Rp200. This long, narrow building (1912) and the structure behind it (1939) were built to serve as "the Museum of Old Batavia." In 1975 the collections were moved to the Jakarta City Museum and this building was turned into the Museum Wayang. This two-story building has nine rooms, each containing priceless collections of puppets from all over the world. Go on an off day such as a Tuesday morning, when you'll find the museum almost empty. The museum includes a 1,500-volume library (Dutch, English, and German books) on *wayang*. In back Museum Wayang is a stage surrounded by *wayang beber* scrolls from Solo. At 1000 or 1100 every alternating Sunday *wayang kulit* and *wayang golek* are performed, accompanied by *gamelan*.

National Museum

Also called the Museum Pusat (Central Museum), at Jl. Merdeka Barat 12 on the west side of Medan Merdeka, a 10-minute walk from the Jl. Jaksa area. The building was erected between 1862 and 1868 by the Batavian Society for the Arts and Sciences—the oldest scientific institution in Southeast Asia. Converted into a museum in 1947, it contains the world's richest collection of Indonesiana. Although poorly lit and not dusted since the Dutch left, you could spend a whole day in the prehistory and ethnographic sections, and the Hindu-Javanese antiquities exhibit rivals Leyden Museum in Holland. The museum is open Tues.-Thurs. 0830-1400, Friday to 1100, Saturday to 1300, Sunday to 1500; closed Mondays. Admission Rp200. On intermittent Sundays at 0930 *gamelan* performances are open to the public. Informative guided tours are offered Mon.-Wed. 0930-1030 (free).

MONAS

As you leave the National Museum you'll be facing the National Monument, MONAS, a Russian-built marble obelisk in the center of Merdeka Square between old and new Jakarta in the geographical heart of the city. Started in 1961 to commemorate the struggle for independence, this gigantic phallic needle rises 137 meters and is topped with 35 kg of pure gold leaf symbolizing the flame of freedom. On the sides of the obelisk see the text of the 17 August 1945 Proclamation of Independence and a map of Indonesia. Three meters under the monument is a historical museum, open daily 0800-1700. Entrance Rp500. Dioramas illustrate the archipelago civilization from as far back as prehistoric Java Man; others depict Indonesia's war of independence.

Istiqlal Mosque, Jakarta

Istana Negara

This impressive white-fronted palace, on Jl. Medan Merdeka Utara facing Jl. Veteran, is one of two presidential palaces on the square. First a country house built by a wealthy Dutchman in the late 1700s, it once served as the governor-general's residence. View the front from Jl. Veteran. The lavishly appointed interior boasts Dutch colonial furniture, a neoclassic dining hall, and ceiling decorations resembling Ambonese lace. For a tour, first get permission from the Chief of the Presidential Household, Istana Negara, Jakarta; give it two weeks. Dress or shirt and tie obligatory.

Istana Merdeka

Built by the Dutch nearly 100 years after Istana Negara to replace that aging palace,

this stately edifice was called Koningsplein Paleis. It's been occupied by 15 Dutch governor-generals, three Japanese military commanders, and two presidents of Republik Indonesia. In an emotion-filled ceremony, the Dutch flag was hauled down forever on 27 December 1949. Eyewitnesses state that when the Indonesian bicolor red and white Dwiwarna was raised above the building 100,000 people roared *"Merdeka! Merdeka!"* ("Freedom! Freedom!"), ending three centuries of Dutch colonial rule. The palace was renamed Istana Merdeka, or "Freedom Palace."

Emmanuel Church
At Jl. Merdeka Timur 10 on the east side of the square opposite Gambir train station, this unique classicist Dutch Protestant church was erected between 1834 and 1839. The architect, J.H. Horst, incorporated elements from Greek temples, Renaissance theaters, and the Roman arena in the circular construction. The congregation surrounds the pulpit while the sun bathes the entire interior. Some precious articles in the Emmanuel Church were preserved after several Kota churches were demolished. On Sunday services are delivered in Dutch at 1000, Korean at 1115, and English at 1700.

Istiqlal Mosque
In the northeast corner of Lapangan Merdeka is the massive six-level Istiqlal Mosque. With its minarets and grandiose lines, this is Jakarta's most central and grandest place of Muslim worship. Its size is more impressive than its beauty: the huge white dome can be seen for 15 km and is easily identified from aircraft far out over the Java Sea. On Friday the mosque is crowded with thousands of worshippers; after Ramadan up to 200,000 people crowd in and around it. Reputed to be the largest mosque in Southeast Asia and the second largest in the world, this was one of Sukarno's pet projects. Seventeen years in the making, it was finely crafted from the best materials. English-speaking tours are offered for Rp1000; photos allowed.

Gedung Pancasila
From in front of Hotel Borobudur, follow Lapangan Banteng Selatan and walk down Jl. Taman Pejambon until you reach a "palace" with Ionic columns and pilasters in front of the new Department of Foreign Affairs (Departmen Luar Negeri). Erected in the 1830s, it originally housed Dutch army commanders. After 1918, the big hall served as the meeting place for the Volksraad, the advisory People's Council, which represented minorities in the segregated Dutch colonial system. In this hall—with its typically overdone Dutch interior of dark wood walls, stained-glass ceilings, and marble floors—Sukarno delivered his benchmark speech "The Birth of Pancasila," which laid the constitutional foundation for the modern Indonesian state, and gave the building its name.

Textile Museum

A permanent exhibition of cloths and weavings from all over Indonesia, located in the Tanah Abang area in the southwest section of the city (Jl. Satsuit Tuban 4, tel. 021-593-909). You'll see two giant, stylized *canting* and an Indonesian flag in front of an ornate 19th-century house. Open Tues.-Thurs. 0900-1400, Friday 0900-1100, Saturday 0900-1300, Sunday 0900-1400; entrance fee Rp200. The museum contains 600 pieces representing 327 different styles and processes. If you're planning to spend serious money on fabrics, do some research here first.

NIGHTLIFE

There are also a surprising number of bars, nightclubs, discos, and massage parlors in Jakarta. Most of the city's nightlife revolves around the luxury hotels. **Hyatt's** happy hour runs from 1900 to 2100, with half-price drinks and free snacks; **Hotel Indonesia** offers the same 1800-2000. An active scene has grown up on Jl. Wahid Hasyim near Jalan Jaksa. Prices are high but early-bird discounts are often available before 2200. Some of the best discos, where flashy young Indonesians flock on weekends, include **Faces**, a videotheque that also presents live performances; Rp10,000 entrance fee but free before 1030. Sunday nights are "White Nights," when Caucasians are admitted free. Jakarta's oldest but still most popular disco is the infamous **Tanamur** within walking distance of Jl. Jaksa.

The venerable old **Jaya Pub**, behind the Jaya Building roughly across from the Sarinah Department Store on Jl. Thamrin, is a nice piano bar featuring music and a relaxed atmosphere (usually no cover) where artists, writers, musicians, and filmmakers congregate. The latest addition to the bar scene is the fairly tame but comfortably familiar **Hard Rock Cafe** fronting the Sarinah shopping center.

Ancol Amusement Park

Ancol is a mammoth 551-hectare family recreation park for round-the-clock entertainment. Probably Southeast Asia's largest amusement complex, this shoreline resort lies 10 km from downtown on the bay between Jakarta and Tanjung Priok. If you're already in Kota, you could easily visit Ancol at the same time; from the *stanplats* near Jembatan Dua, get an *oplet* (Rp300) to Ancol. Avoid the park on weekends if you don't like crowds. Prices are high, particularly for some of the Euro-style attractions. In fact, Ancol is all very Western. A concert at Ancol's Pasar Seni, open 0900-2000 daily, is a nice way to spend an evening. Beyond Ancol by the sea is a haunting graveyard, Ereveld ("Field of Honor"), for 2,018 military and civilian victims of the Japanese occupation.

Performing Arts

The tourist office brochure titled *Jakarta Permanent Exhibitions and Regular Performances* includes a useful guide to theater and dance venues; current listings are available in the monthly "Guide to Jakarta." Also watch the English-language newspapers for announcements of performances at the various hotels. The best listing of events is found in the monthly guide, aptly called *What's On.*

Taman Ismail Marzuki (TIM)

The Jakarta Arts Center, Jl. Cikini Raya 73, tel. (021) 322-606, is open daily 0900-2400; low admission. This is Jakarta's Lincoln Center—a large complex of exhibition halls, outdoor cafes, planetarium, and theaters with performances almost every night of the year. Get TIM's

monthly bilingual program from the box office, shops, travel agencies, the Jakarta Visitor's Center, or most big hotels or embassies. Events are also listed in the English-language *Jakarta Post.* Several art galleries in the complex exhibit modern Indonesian art; open Mon.-Sat. 0900 to 1300 and 1700 to 2100.

Gamelan and *Wayang*

Gamelan performances are held at the **Museum Wayang** puppet museum on Jl. Pintu Besar in Kota on alternate Sundays at 1000 for Rp500.

At the **School Of Folk Art** in the Faculty of Fine Arts, National University of Indonesia, see teachers and students playing Cirebon-style *gamelan,* Sundanese traditional dancing, *suling* orchestras, and *wayang* puppet theater. Located at Bakti Budaya, Jl. Bunga 5, Jatinegara near Jl. Matraman Raya. The **Taman Mini Indonesia** cultural park is in Pondok Gede in east Jakarta near Halim Airport. Take a bus from downtown to Rambutan, then a *bemo* to Taman Mini. Dances and cultural performances are held on Sunday 1000-1200 in the pavilions for West Java, Yogyakarta (*wayang kulit*), East Java, and West Sumatra. The park is choked with people but worth visiting for the shows alone.

(above) Javenese gamelan *orchestra, Solo, West Java*

Excellent Javanese *wayang kulit, wayang golek,* and *gamelan* concerts are staged every few Sunday mornings at the **National Museum** from 0930 for only Rp1,000. A must stop for anyone passing through Jakarta on a Sunday. The **Bharata Theatre**, Jl. Kalilio 15 (near Pasar Senen) stages authentic *wayang orang* dramas nightly at 2000 except Monday and Thursday, when there are *ketoprak* performances. This is one of Java's few remaining theaters sponsoring classical drama. Tickets cost Rp3000-4000. Packed with Javanese—abundant local color.

Cultural Centers

The **Ganesha Society** puts on weekly talks and films about Indonesian culture at the **Erasmus Huis**, the Dutch cultural center on Jl. Rasuna Said, tel. (021) 772-325, next to the Dutch Embassy. Get the schedule at the National Museum at Jl. Merdeka Barat. Also check out the **Indonesian-American Cultural Center**, Jl. Pramuka Kav 30, tel. 881-241, which offers Indonesia-related films, lectures, and exhibits. The **Gedung Kesenian**, a whitewashed Romanesque theater near the main post office, presents traditional *wayang orang* performances several times monthly.

Sarinah Department Store

Situated near the Jl. Jaksa area on the corner of Jl. Thamrin and Jl. Wahid Hasyim. Like an Indonesian Macy's, Sarinah has everything from Borneo *perang* and coral

Street vendors, Bandung, West Java

jewelry to *batik* slippers and Batak woodcarvings. A visit to this well-organized department store is sure to satisfy your shopping appetite. Sarinah is a good place for newcomers to acquaint themselves with what's available, though at rather high, fixed prices. Most clerks speak some English. Open daily 0900-1800. Don't miss the Batik Center on the third floor, with its special salesroom for *batik tulis;* reasonably priced handicrafts are found on the fourth floor and a well-stocked bookstore occupies the fifth.

Handicraft Markets

Notable are the 30-40 a/c boutiques of the Jakarta Hilton's **Indonesian Bazaar,** and the 200 kiosks of Ancol's Arts Market, **Pasar Seni,** a delightful outdoor art fair open 24 hours a day. This market is a permanent setting for working artists and craftspeople from all over Indonesia. As at art markets everywhere, you'll find some high-quality items but a lot of junk as well. Good prices. Excellent seafood restaurants abound; stick around for the evening live music concert.

Antiques

Jakarta's densely packed flea market stretches for several blocks along Jl. **Surabaya** in Menteng. These shops offer a bit of everything. Unearth treasures among the fakery and hopeless discards. Many items are of dubious antiquity, having been made the week before in local crafts shops. Arrive in the late afternoon when vendors want to make last sales and go home. To get there, walk or take a bus for Manggarai and get off at Jl. Mohammed Yamin.

Tourist Information

The **Visitor Information Center** (VIC) at Sukarno/Hatta Airport is open daily 0800-2000, closed Sunday. The city's big VIC is in the Jakarta Theatre Building, opposite Sarinah Department Store on Jl. Wahid Hasyim, tel. (021) 315-4094. Open Mon.-Thurs. 0830-1600, Friday to 1700, Saturday until 1300. Specializing in the Jakarta area, staff here hand out free theme-oriented maps, train schedules, and brochures, but you have to ask specifically for what you want.

VICINITY OF JAKARTA

Taman Mini Indonesia

This 120-hectare open-air cultural/amusement park is a window into the cultural and environmental complexity of Indonesia. Traditional-style pavilions exhibit artifacts and crafts of the peoples of each of Indonesia's 27 provinces. It would take a week to see everything. In fact, Indonesians will proudly tell you there's no need to see the rest of Indonesia if you visit this park, which they compare to Disneyland. The complex was formally opened in 1975.

The cultural exhibits and genuine Indonesian architecture are the most valuable aspects of this park. Many structures were dismantled in outlying provinces, then reconstructed here: replicas of houses, temples, mosques, and churches. Every important ethnic group of Indonesia is represented. Near the park entrance, the **Indonesia Museum** is billed as the country's best collection of artifacts and handicrafts—one of the highlights of Taman Mini. A wildlife and natural history museum is featured inside the **Komodo Dragon Museum,** while the six-hectare **bird park** contains 650 bird species native to Indonesia—a great spot to relax. The latest addition is a museum displaying the superb private art collection of the Suharto family.

On Sunday between 1000 and 1400 are outstanding free traditional dance performances, films, and cultural shows at the various pavilions. Get a Taman Mini monthly program in any Garuda office, VIC office, or hotel. Open daily 0800-1700, but most pavilion hours are 0900-1600. They close the gates at around 2000. Entrance fee Rp1000. The park is located 12 km southeast of the city. From Jl. Thamrin in front of the Sarinah Department Store, take bus P16 to Rambutan bus terminal, then bus T01 or T02 to the park.

Lubang Buaya

Means "Crocodile Hole." This massive monument commemorates seven Indonesian officers killed on 30 September 1965 during the alleged communist *coup d'etat,* their bodies ignominiously stuffed down a well. The official name is Pancasila Cakti. Replicas of the six murdered generals and one army officer stand on top of a wall. Ironically, a brother of one of the six senior officers was a high-ranking communist ideologue. The monument is built upon a *pendopo;* take your shoes off as if you were entering a mosque. In front is a parade field where military ceremonies take place. Lubang Buaya is located in a rural setting 16 km southeast of Jakarta in Pondok Gede, three km east of Taman Mini Indonesia. Board a minibus from the highway in front of Taman Mini to the entrance.

Ragunan Zoo

The best and largest zoo in Indonesia, situated in the suburb of Pasar Minggu, about 16 km south of Jakarta's city center. From downtown, take bus 87 or 90 straight to the zoo's entrance. Or take a bus to Pasar Minggu, then get an *oplet* to the front or back entrances. Open daily 0900-1800; entrance fee Rp1000. See a rare species of lesser ape here, misnamed the Klossi gibbon, a sort of pygmy *siamang.* Also baby Komodo dragons, several *anoa,* the *babirusa,* the megapode bird (*maleo*), plus gorgeously plumed birds of paradise. The zoo plays a direct role in conservation—several species of threatened fauna are bred here. Also view the oceanarium and the botanical gardens—one of Indonesia's best—with a wide variety of indigenous plants labeled in Latin.

Pulau Seribu

These tiny tropical islands, the Key West of Java, can best be seen just after takeoff from Jakarta's Airport. Of the seven islands developed as holiday havens, the more accessible are just 10-15 km from Jakarta. Try to visit those islands located as far into the north Java Sea as possible. Coral gardens are found off **Pulau Putri, Pulau Papa Theo, Pulau Genting** (Besar and Kecil), and **Pulau Opak Besar,** all promoted as dive sites.

Superior diving is found on **Burung, Pabelokan, Sibaru Kecil,** and **Sibaru Besar.** with their talcum powder beaches and coconut plantations. On **Pulau Untung Jawa,** site of a Sunday market, are picnic facilities and a campground. Camping is also possible on **Pulau Perak** and **Pulau Khayangan.** Accommodations are cheaper than the international-class hotels of Jakarta; weekday rates are even less, though still not cheap. On weekends and during holiday periods a surcharge of 25 percent is common. Add to this boat fare, local taxes, food costs, and a service tax of 21 percent. Jakartan travel agents should be able to give you details and prices; a three-day, two-night full board package costs around Rp304,500.

The main islands can be reached by boat from **Marina Jaya Ancol** between 0800 and 1000, or from Muara Kamal north of the airport on the way to Tangerang. From Ancol ferries leave around 1030 for touristy Pulau Bidadari; from there you can embark to the outlying islands. Travel among the outlying islands by private or hired boat for about Rp10,000 per hour—you'll feel like a temporary castaway.

West Java

The province's historical name, Sunda, meaning "white," refers to the white ash that covers the land after volcanic eruptions. West Java volcanos are exceedingly active: in 1982 Galunggung erupted, killing 20 people and causing an estimated $25 million in damage, covering villages in the area with mud and thick dust. More recently, a 1993 explosion of Krakatoa killed two American tourists. The capital and cultural center of West Java is the cool mountain city of Bandung, located on a plateau 180 km to the southeast. The main attractions for visitors are the wildlife reserves of Ujung Kulon and Krakatoa, Bogor's world-renowned botanical gardens, and the fine beach resort of Pangandaran.

BANTEN

Banten is renowned for its short-legged bantam hen, *ayam katik,* and its valuable historical remains signifying the advent of Islam in Java. Banten was one of Java's two dominant states in the 17th century. You can view the ruins of the once great Bantenese Islamic kingdom; some portions of a palace have been restored, and a museum houses 200-year-old archaeological objects. To get to Banten, go first to the small

Market day

town of Serang, 95 km west of Jakarta, which serves as the crossroads turnoff to Banten. Once a powerful and wealthy 16th-century center for the pepper trade between the Spice Islands and India, Banten figures largely in West Java history. By 1545 the Portuguese had established a trading station here. The Dutch first set foot on Java at Banten in 1596; their rivals, the British, set up a factory at Banten in 1603 but were expelled in 1683. In 1684 the Dutch vanquished the sultan of Banten's forces and consolidated their power. By the 19th century Banten's deepwater harbor had silted up, becoming a sleepy backwater fishing village.

Towering over the village is the majestic **Mesjid Agung**, built in Hindu-Islamic style by the son of Sultan Hasanuddin in 1559. It contains a small historical museum; closed Sunday afternoon. Northwest of the mosque is **Speelwijck Fortress**, constructed in 1682 and defended until the early 1800s. Climb the single remaining watchtower for a marvelous view. **Klenteng** is a newly renovated 200-year-old Chinese temple with a small museum. Located opposite the fort entrance, it was a gift of the sultan to Banten's large Chinese community.

Surosawan Palace was a heavily fortified compound with archways, main gate, and massive four-meter-high walls. See the ruins of Chinese temples and an old minaret inside the grounds. As a result of Dutch intrigue and manipulative politics, this *kraton* was destroyed by the son of the sultan; the palace was burned down again by Dutch Governor-General Daendels in 1832. Inside the old walls excavations are still taking place; many iron and bronze pieces have been unearthed from workshops where armaments, ammunition, swords, and musical instruments were made.

PULAU DUA BIRD SANCTUARY

Near Banten, off the northwest coast of Java, is the sea-level island of Pulau Dua, within easy reach of Banten's Karanghantu Harbor and one of the world's foremost bird islands. During the breeding season (March-July) its eight hectares are a favorite breeding ground for 40,000-50,000 migratory birds, including species of ice birds. Most visitors base themselves in Serang, Merak, or Cilegon where there are ample accommodations, and make Banten a day-trip. Board a bus from Jakarta's Kalideres station to Serang (Rp2100, two hours). From Serang's Pasar Lama minibus station it's only 10 km and Rp500 by minibus to Banten. Take a short boat ride from Karanghantu Harbor in Banten, or simply walk across the mudflats at low tide.

CARITA BEACH

Stretching down the west coast, from Merak to just south of Labuhan, are some of the most idyllic beaches on Java and a warm sea perfect for swimming, snorkeling, fishing, water-skiing, and sailing. Only three hours by car from Jakarta, Carita is a beautiful, two-km-long, immaculate white-sand shoreline within the protective enclosure of a U-shaped bay. The distant silhouette of Krakatoa can be seen, and the

Carita serves as a convenient base for outings to Krakatoa or Ujung Pandang. Masks, flippers, and snorkels can be rented from the hotels.

For the Carita/Labuhan area, buses leave every hour from Jakarta's Kalideres station for Rp3500 (158 km, three to four hours); look for the sign "Jakarta-Labuhan." Do not take the bus to Merak or Anyer. From the Labuhan bus halt, walk up the road and flag down a colt minivan to the town of Carita; from there colts continue north to Carita Krakatau Beach Hotel (Rp600).

KRAKATOA VOLCANO

In the early misty hours of 27 August 1883, Krakatoa disintegrated in the most violent explosion in recorded history. When the central mountain erupted, it heaved out 20 cubic kilometers of rock, causing the island to collapse and allowing sea water to rush into the fiery crater. Volcanic debris landed on Madagascar on the other side of the Indian Ocean; atmospheric waves circled the globe seven times, and for three years volcanic dust and clouds from the explosion circled the earth, creating sensational multihued sunsets. All remained calm in the middle of the demolished crater until 1927, when a thick plume of steam roared from the seabed, and before long rocks and ash rose far enough to form a small cone. Ominously named Anak Krakatoa ("Son of Krakatoa"), the new mountain has since risen 150 meters above the sea. Renewed seismic activity was detected in 1979. On 15 June 1993, Krakatoa suddenly erupted and engulfed a group of five tourists from England and America, killing two Americans in the firestorm. The Indonesian government now forbids visits closer than three km. However, local boat operators still make the landing against regulations. Proceed with caution.

Labuhan is a fishing village and junction town Rp3500 by a/c bus and 160 km southwest of Jakarta. Two km north of Labuhan on the road to Carita is the PHPA office where you get permits for Ujung Kulon and Krakatoa. You can explore Krakatoa in most cases during a one-day roundtrip. The PHPA staff Labuhan can help with boat rentals, or any villager can lead you to the homes of fishermen who will take you. The least expensive rental is with local fishermen for Rp110,000-120,000, with a four- to five-man crew. Boats from hotels on Carita Beach cost Rp210,000 roundtrip, or Rp420,000 roundtrip on a speedboat. Refunds are never given, even if your boat is forced to turn back, so withhold a portion of the payment until your safe return. The ideal travel season is April-September.

UJUNG KULON NATIONAL PARK

This completely untamed wilderness lies on the far western tip of Java, connected to the rest of the island by a narrow boggy isthmus. Two national parks here total more than 420 square km—one located on the Ujung Kulon peninsula, the other on the main island of Panaitan across a narrow strait.

Opened by the Dutch in 1921 as a refuge for the threatened Javan rhinoceros, the establishment of this last large area of lowland forest on Java has since been credited with saving a number of rare life forms from extinction. Observation towers have been erected at Cigenter, and grazing fields where wildlife can be observed are found at Cijungkulon on Pulau Peucang. On the western tip is a lighthouse, standing near the ruins of an older lighthouse built by the Dutch. Unspoiled beaches with coral formations off the south and west sides of Pulau Peucang and Pulau Panaitan make for spectacular diving, snorkeling, and swimming. No scuba facilities, so bring your own equipment. Best time to visit is April-Aug., when the sea is calmer and the ground not as marshy.

Permits are available from the friendly Forestry Office (PHPA) two km north of Labuhan on the road to Carita. The permit is free, and staff will help with everything, including boat transport and lodging reservations. Pay Rp2000 for a man to go to the market to stock up on provisions. The PHPA office is open Mon.-Thurs. 0700-1400, Friday to 1100, Saturday to 1200. The PHPA camps at Pulau Handeleum and Pulau Peucang offer cooking facilities, water, and cooks, but be sure to bring food and beverages. Guides are available for Rp5000 to show you the other side of Pulau Peucang.

The 90-km passage from Labuhan to Pulau Peucang off Ujung Kulon normally takes 6-10 hours, depending on the weather. Gasoline is not plentiful within the park so make sure there's enough for daily trips from Pulau Peucang to the mainland. Jakartan travel agents offer tours of Ujung Kulon and Krakatoa for Rp265,000-735,000, including all transportation, accommodations in a guesthouse on Pulau Peucang, photo safari with guide, meals, and two nights at relaxing Carita Beach Hotel. Tours are often advertised in the *Jakarta Post*.

Entry is cheaper by land. From Labuhan take a minibus (Rp3000, three hours) to Sumur via Cigeulis; *kapal motor* also depart Labuhan almost every day for Sumur (Rp3500). From Sumur reach Tamanjaya (park headquarters) via motorcycle-taxi (Rp5000 pp). Show your permit at the PHPA office in Tamanjaya, then hire a guide to take you into the peninsula, a six-hour walk to Pos Karangranjang. Buy food for both of you, plus some *kretek* for him. Passage on a local *prahu* from Tamanjaya to Pulau Peucang costs around Rp75,000 one-way.

BOGOR

Located sixty km south of Jakarta (Rp1000 and two hours by bus), Bogor sprawls among hills between the Ciliwung and Cisadane rivers. Its population is 250,000, the majority *pegawai* and their families. Founded over 500 years ago, the city is built around a palace and a huge, verdant botanical garden. Bogor is one of the most important scientific centers in Indonesia, and at least 17 affiliated institutes are scattered all over the city, most of them progeny of the gardens. A town of pretty villas, big trees, and banana, mimosa, and wild almond plants, try to get past the dense traffic to appreciate Bogor's charm.

Istana Bogor

The road from Jakarta runs smack into the lawn of this gleaming white former Dutch governor's mansion, the official residence of the Dutch governor-generals from 1870 to 1942. The palace has not served as a residence since Sukarno's time; the main building is used for official occasions, installations, and ceremonies. Inside the mansion are sumptuously appointed rooms, lavish reception chambers, and a fabulous international collection of fine art. Not normally open to the public, the palace may be visited by prior arrangement through tour agencies like Safairiyah Tours on Jl. Sudirman and Mulia Rahaya Travel in Muria Plaza. You can also arrange tours through most *losmen* and hotels. While admission to the Istana is free, travel agencies charge Rp5000-8000 for their reservation services. If you don't want to go through a tour agency, make a request by letter, including the name of each visitor, the date, and exact time you hope to view the palace. Send to: Head of Protocol, Istana Negara, Jl. Veteran, Jakarta.

Kebon Raya

The Bogor Botanical Gardens, right behind the presidential palace, occupy an incredible 87-hectare estate; this is one of the world's leading botanical institutions as well as an important scientific research center. The gardens have been here for over 170 years; Bogor rose around them. The collection includes 12,695 specimens of native plants from all over the Malay Archipelago and many other tropical regions. During the Forced Cultivation Period early Dutch researchers used these gardens to develop cash crops to provide profits for the mother country. Today, the gardens are still used to collect and maintain living plants, with special emphasis on varieties with profit potential. Kebon Raya is open 0800-1700. Admission is Rp1600, Rp1300 on Sunday and holidays, when it's particularly crowded. To miss the crowds, visit Kebon Raya on a weekday; to avoid the rain, visit in the morning. Guides, some quite knowledgeable and entertaining, are available; negotiate a fee in advance (around Rp6000 per hour).

VICINITY OF BOGOR

Batutulis

Despite the fact Bogor was the capital of the immensely powerful Hindu kingdom of Pajajaran from the 12th to the 16th century, there are few reminders of this period. One of the few remaining physical traces the all-conquering tropical climate has not claimed is Batutulis (meaning "Writing Stone"), an ancient nine-line inscription in Sundanese Sanskrit etched on a conical stone. The inscription attests to the king's supernatural powers, and served to protect the realm from enemies. King Surawisesa decreed in 1533 that the message be written in stone.

The stone is housed in a small building nearly opposite the gate to Sukarno's former home, three km southeast of Bogor's Ramayana Cinema. Open from 0700 until late at night, the *juru kunci* accepts a small donation to let you in, shoeless. The inscription is still sacred to many, and despite the *bemo* whining by outside, the spot still possesses the feel of a place of meditation and devotion. Inside, a ritual of some sort could be going on, people genuflecting on mats, incense burning. One set of footprints, which look like someone stepped onto wet cement, is said to have been imprinted into the stone by the sheer magical strength and power of King Surawisesa. The monarch's knee marks are further evidence of his divinity.

Cipanas

This area of recreational hot springs is a good place to break the journey between Bogor and Bandung. Visit the picturesque market which sells cut flowers, plants, vegetables, and fruit. The hot sulphur baths here (Cipanas means "Hot River") are famous for their remedial powers; the water originates from natural springs on Gunung Guntur. The mountain's top is still bare from an 1889 eruption. Cipanas can be a bit hectic and unpretty at times, a traffic-snarled noisy town surrounding a single peaceful oasis—the president's holiday home. This elegant country house (built in 1750), called **Istana Cipanas**, lies in a park with gardens, triple-canopy jungle, and hot springs. On the grounds is a bungalow where Sukarno composed some of his most famous speeches. On the left after the turnoff to Cibodas Botanical Garden and several km before the town of Cipanas, see the small sign pointing up a dirt track to the right to **Santa Yusup Convent**. This nunnery is a simple and quiet retreat where it's possible to rent rooms if you book in advance. Of the three Buddhist *vihara* in Cipanas, the retreat in the hills is the nicest. Ask for Gereja Buddhist; the entrance is near the Simpang Raya II Restaurant in the town of Pacet. All the *vihara* are under the same *bhikku*, one of Indonesia's leading Buddhist religious leaders. You're given a booklet which explains his philosophy, though it's also okay if you want to practice your own form of meditation here.

Cibodas

The town of Cibodas is the best destination in Puncak for great scenery, mountain treks, botanical gardens, and a good selection of budget guesthouses. The town's big draw is the **Cibodas Botanical Gardens**, a cool, high-elevation extension of the Bogor gardens. Indonesia's first botanic reserve, Cibodas was established in 1862, primarily to protect the region's unusually rich mountain flora. Today the scene of important botanical research, beautiful Cibodas Park covers about 125 hectares and attracts 80,000 visitors a year.

Cibodas is about 10 km beyond Puncak Pass and five km uphill from the town of Cimacan. The turnoff has been improved but you still need to look carefully for the small sign Kebun Raya, or the enormous billboard Cibodas Golf Course. Ask the bus driver to drop you at the turnoff, then wait for a minibus heading up the hill to the gardens. No need for a special charter. Admission Rp1000; open daily 0800-1600, but avoid Sundays unless you love crowds. A rough map is posted at the park entrance.

During the last century the Dutch planted mountain trees collected from Australia, the Canary Islands, South Africa, and many other temperate areas. Alongside the original plantings stand the thick tropical jungle covering the slopes of Gunung Gede. Good paths run through the jungle, some stone-paved; names, both Latin and popular, are displayed on the trees. See 15-meter-high tree ferns (*alsophila*), beds of roses, begonias in full bloom, and an elfin forest where moss-strewn ground and lichen-draped trees impart a fairyland look. Also check out the eucalyptus and lily collections, and a superb view of Gunung Gegerbentang, covered in dense rainforest.

BANDUNG

Roughly 180 km southeast of Jakarta, Bandung is Indonesia's fourth-largest city, with 1.7 million people. Lying in a high valley surrounded by mountains covered in tea plantations, the city is a bustling center of Sundanese culture. It's the site of some 50 universities and colleges, many small academies, and such prestigious institutions as the Nuclear Research Center, the Volcanologists Monitoring Center (VSI), and Indonesia's aircraft industry (IPTN). Indonesia's elite army divison, Siliwangi, is headquartered in Bandung, occupying the former command center of the Netherlands Indies Army. Splendid colonial architecture is another Bandung attraction.

Bandung is also a center for the textile and food processing industries. In the fine arts, musicians, dancers, and artists are lured here from all over Indonesia to study. Once referred to as the "Paris of the East," the Dutch loved Bandung and their long occupation is reflected in the architectural gems as well as the somber middle-class architecture recalling early 20th-century Western European cities—an overabundance of ferro-concrete buildings. Downtown Bandung has unfortunately lost much of its charm and glamour; nowadays it's choked with exhaust fumes and dust. The real charm of Bandung lies in the northern neighborhoods constructed by the Dutch, an historic district of tree-lined boulevards, handsome old houses, and art deco municipal buildings. If you only experience the messy downtown district, you've missed the real highlight of Dutch-era Bandung.

Bandung is a cosmopolitan city with the usual Indonesian mix. The city is split by the railroad tracks: to the north are the richer neighborhoods, to the south the poorer. Because of the numerous universities and colleges housing some of Indonesia's brightest students, this is a youthful city, a haven for academics and intellectuals. Bandung's ITB student leaders pride themselves on being the most radical in all of Indonesia, the catalyst for nationwide student protests and strikes.

Sights

A highly recommended tour starts at the *alun-alun* (visit the tourist office), passes the Merdeka building and continues to Hotel Savoy Homann. Walk up Jl. Braga, then north to the historic Bank of Indonesia, City Hall, and east along Jl. Aceh past Taman Maluku to the impressive Gedung Sate building. Continue north to the ITB campus and Bandung Zoo before returning by bus to city center. Allow a full day. Start your

Love Letters

I love you too much, Connie, he often wrote, to marry you and to bring you here into the life of my own people. You wouldn't be able to live on my earnings, as an Indonesian woman and wife could. Your standard of living is so much higher than ours. And I wouldn't want my wife to live any differently than my own people. I wouldn't want to see my family become an island to itself, far above other Indonesian families. Even though you say that you can make the sacrifice, I cannot accept it. Therefore you're free to live as you please; my love imposes no ties on you. And I say to you, I love you, love you ever so much, will always love you whatever you do, even if you marry someone else, my love for you will never change and I'll always be with you in spirit. I have a duty to fulfil towards my own people here, to vindicate the struggle of my friends who have laid down their lives in the revolution for the liberation of my people. These friends of mine have not died to free my country and then have it bled white by immoral and unscrupulous politicians. Our young people have therefore a duty to work here in our homeland, to open the eyes of the people, to raise their standard of living, until the whole of our people is capable of consciously taking the reins of their destiny in their own hands.

Connie had written back, saying that reading this letter had made her love him all the more and had made her even more determined to be at his side during his struggle.

I love you, wrote Connie, and you know how strong my feelings for you are. You say that if you married me you would feel obliged for my sake to create a separate island, alien to your society. How incredibly little you think of my love for you. Do you imagine that we American women are incapable of loving a man strongly enough to be happy to sacrifice everything for him? What does it matter having to bear the hardships you describe in your letter, having to live in one room, having to share a house with two or three other families and me having to walking tour at the tourist office in Bandung's *alun-alun,* created at the same time (1850) as Gedung Pakuan and the Great Mosque. The **Savoy Homann Hotel** is probably this vigorous period's most superb specimen. The buildings along **Jalan Braga** still retain beautiful stained glass. More glimpses of this era can be seen around Jl. Pasar Baru and Jl. Banceuy. Also check out the **IKIP Building** on Jl. Setiabudi Also known as the Asia-Afrika Building, **Gedung Merdeka** is right in the center of the city

give up the comforts of American life? As if you didn't know there are plenty of Americans who live in badly crowded apartment houses, and, speaking of comforts, I'm sick and tired of hearing about America's prosperity. This expression has been a curse for our people, and I now experience it myself—it has become a curse upon the love that binds us together. Do you really think that we can't live without an elevator, without a pressure-cooker, without a fruit-squeezer, without a washing-machine, without lipsticks, permanent waves and various other products of our giant industries? Don't you know that there are many Americans who long for a life such as in your country, without the complexities of the machine age and all its consequences for human beings? You must realize that I love you, that I want to live by your side, to help you in your struggle to elevate your people. Am I asking too much, my dearest?

And Pranoto had written that he felt deeply how very fortunate he was to be blessed by a love as great as Connie's, but that evidently she hadn't fully understood what he had meant. He found it very hard, in fact, to tell her this—but, to understand the conditions in his country fully, she had to realize that while physical hardships could be overcome by the power of love, there were other things which could not, no matter how great their love.

Here in my country, Pranoto wrote, *there's a plague of mistrust and suspicion of all foreigners, especially the white man, and Americans, Britishers, Dutchmen, Frenchmen—they're all lumped together—all are wicked imperialists and capitalists. And an Indonesian with a Dutch, English, American or French wife is automatically suspect and is distrusted by his own people. particularly if he happens to be opposed to the communists or fanatic nationalists. He is finished then; and far from being any help to him his wife only impedes his efforts to fight on. That's why, no matter how much I love you, and though I know how selfless your love for me is, we must both have the courage to renounce our love to my struggle in my people's cause. I will always be longing for you, Connie, my love!*

~ Mochtar Lubis,Twilight in Jakarta, 1968

on Jl. Asia-Afrika 65 on the corner of Jl. Braga, near the city's *alun-alun*. Built in 1895, it was renovated to its present form by Van Gallenlast and Wolf Shoemaker in 1926. In 1955, President Sukarno invited leaders of 29 developing nonaligned nations to a solidarity conference here. In the building's museum is a fine, well-annotated exhibit commemorating the conference. Open 0800-1300 daily, Friday to 1100, Saturday to 1200.

Premier among Bandung's many colleges and universities is the Bandung Institute of Technology, or ITB, on the north side of the city; take a Dago-bound Honda and get off at Jl. Ganeca. This is the oldest, largest, and one of Indonesia's most prestigious technical universities. ITB was established in 1920 by a group of enterprising Dutch planters, merchants, and industrialists led by the Malabar planter H.A.R. Bosscha. The curriculum, based on the famous Technical High School in Delft, was designed to provide training for native engineers and architects. Yearly, around 30,000 students attend 17 higher educational institutions on campus. ITB has produced many of Indonesia's foremost engineers and political personalities, including Sukarno. Initially criticized for its remoteness from the central area of Bandung, the ITB campus is high, cool, dry, drained, and able to expand. Graceful, soundly built, and functionally brilliant, ITB's original complex is one of the most architecturally important 20th-century buildings in Indonesia.

Ram Fighting

These exciting spectacles are local, low-level competitions which lead to championship matches held annually on the first Sunday after 17 August (Independence Day), when hundreds of rams are brought to the Bandung area to battle for "the cup." The sport is closely tied in with breeders' efforts to upgrade the quality of their rams. Champion rams, which can weigh up to 60 kg and are adorned with names like "Bima" and "Si Kilat" ("Sir Lightning"), are quick to attack and cunning in evasion. A contest usually consists of around 50 ferocious head-on collisions. The Sundanese are orthodox Muslims and forbidden to gamble. Thus

Festival regalia

no money changes hands at these matches; they're staged purely for the pleasure of handlers and breeders. Unfortunately, ram fights are held far less frequently than in the past. Fights are occasionally scheduled at Aki Bohon's house in Cilimus on Jl. Cibuntu, or in the town of Cisuara en route to Lembang. Check with the tourist office or the budget guesthouses near the train station.

Entertainment

Bandung's large student population keeps a half dozen discos filled to capacity on most nights. **Studio East Disco**, Jl. Cipaganti, is the old favorite and considered one of the largest discos in Southeast Asia. **L.A. Disco** on Jl. Asia-Afrika is well located in a musty old shopping complex. Local expats hang out at the **Laga Pub** on Jl. Terusan Pasteur; clean, comfortable, with live music most nights. **O'Hara Tavern** in the Hotel Perdana Wisata is also popular with local Westerners. Another possibility is the **Lingga Pub** in northern Bandung; although quite a distance from downtown Bandung, it's worth the hassle.

The Performing Arts

The Bandung **Music Conservatory** (Konservatori Karawitan), Jl. Buah Batu 212, consists of two parts: ASTI (academic, professional level), and SMKI (for high school students). Ask at the Tourist Information Office, tel. (022) 420-6644, on the *alun-alun* about performances. Take a *bemo* from the Kebun Kelapa bus station or a bus from Perapatan Lima, east of the *alun-alun* on Jl. Asia-Afrika. **ASTI**, the Institute of Fine Arts, often stages performances by its students. Visit any time to see students practice and to ask the lecturers any specific questions. **Gedung Kesenian**, is on Jl. Baranang Siang 1 (Pasar Kosambi area); take a city bus toward Cicaheum. Theater, music, or dances are held every Friday night and sometimes on other nights—*calung* dance-dramas, special film presentations, *wayang orang*, Western theater productions, ballet, drama, *reyog*, even Sundanese country music (*musik keroncang*). Entrance Rp1500.

Shopping and Crafts

Bandung shops are filled with the products of this far-flung archipelago as well as imported goods. West Java accounts for 60 percent of Indonesia's commercial textile production, mostly concentrated in Bandung. For backstreet exploring, cruise Pasar Baru and the streets

Wayang golek *character*

around Jl. ABC (electronics), Jl. Oto Iskandardinata (gold shops), and Kosambi Blok (everything). Pasar Jatayu, a flea market on Jl. Arjuna behind the motorbike parts shop, is a great place to find antiques and secondhand junk. Shops in the *pasar* are normally open until 2100; others are open 0830-1400 and 1700-2030. Also recommended is **Cupu Manik** on Gang Haji Umar (off Jl. Kebon Kawung), only 500 meters from the Sakadarna Losmen, a small *wayang golek* factory. **Pak Ruhiyat**, on Jl. Pangarang (behind no. 22), is a fine *wayang golek* craftsman working out of his home. **Sarinah**, Jl. Braga 10, tel. (022) 52798, sells new *wayang golek* at very good prices (Rp2200-6875).

Ceramics

The government-sponsored **Ceramics Research Institute** (Balai Penelitian Keramik), Jl. Jen. A. Yani 392 near Pasar Cicadas, is concerned with each facet of the operation of turning clay into practical, beautiful objects. The institute turns out everything from small, coarsely finished eggcup-size plant pots and miniature ornamental horses to exquisite copies of classic Chinese vases. On Jl. Sukapura in Kiara Condong, one km from Balai Penelitian Keramik, is a Kasongan-type ceramics center selling lampshades, wall decorations, and the like; farther afield, **Plered** is an active traditional ceramics center southwest of Purwakarta (70 km northeast of Bandung), and the site of an experimental station of the Bandung Ceramics Research Institute.

Tourist Information

The **Bandung Tourist Information Office** is in the northeast corner of the *alun-alun*; open daily 0900-1700. Staffed for the most part by well-informed volunteers who hand out basic city maps and provide sound verbal information on cultural happenings. They also dispense advice on other points of interest on Java and Bali and make hotel and train reservations.

VICINITY OF BADUNG

Malabar Tea Estate

A government-controlled tea plantation at the base of Gunung Malabar in the hills around Pangalengan, south of Bandung. With wide vistas over the valleys below, immaculate buildings, splendid roads, and cultivated fields, this vast estate is an unending delight to the eye. In 1896 K.A.R. Bosscha pioneered its development, and it quickly became famous for its beauty, efficiency, and top-quality tea. Bosscha's name is attached to the Bosscha Observatory, just outside Lembang, north of Bandung. The Bosscha memorial, together with the beautiful house where he once lived, is fastidiously maintained.

Situ Cangkuang

About 17 km north of Garut, this is one of Indonesia's oldest temples and the largest temple in West Java. According to archaeological evidence, this 9th-century *candi* predates Prambanan and Borobudur. In comparison, however, the structure is no larger than a shrine. About 40 percent of the building is original, the remainder carved over the course of a very successful reconstruction completed in 1976. Candi Cangkuang is the only ancient building of its type in West Java.

In 1893, a Dutch archaeologist, Vorderman, noted that Desa Cangkuang contained the ancient tomb of Arif Muhamad and a deformed stone statue. On the basis of that information, an Indonesian archaeologist in 1965 led an expedition that discovered not only the tomb and statue but also the remains of a classical Hindu temple, Candi Cangkuang. Further explorations and excavations have established that this location in the Leles Valley was for several centuries the center of a number of Neolithic, megalithic, Hindu, and Muslim cultures. The more animist aspects of Java-Hinduism still linger today: near the *candi* is a watchman's hut complete with a site for religious ceremonies.

From Leles, 15 km north of Garut, follow the small road to Desa Cangkuang. At the large grass *alun-alun* next to the *mesjid* in the center of town turn left down a good rock road and continue for about three km. Near the village of Cangkuang the hills form a peninsula jutting out into the lake; you'll see the temple among a group of trees. Cross the lake to the island on small boats or on unusual bamboo rafts with seats, or walk around on a small road for two km to reach the temple.

Pangandaran

A favorite beauty spot 88 km southeast of Ciamis and 223 km southeast of Bandung on the south coast near the border of Central Java. This once-small fishing village at the entrance of a small peninsula is almost completely surrounded by the Indian Ocean. The whole peninsula, Cagar Alam Pananjung, is now a wildlife reserve. Hike along the long white-sand beaches, swim in the gentle surf, dive on coral reefs. Pangandaran offers accommodations, restaurants, souvenir shops, a cinema, recreational facilities, and a bank—a good place to unwind. Domestic tourists swamp the place during weekends and holidays, and it's quickly developing a scruffiness typical of many beach resorts. The travelers' cafes serve the standard fare and young guides overcharge for unnecessary tours.

Watch the sun set on the west beach and the moon rise on the east beach. The eastern beach has rough, dangerous surf. Snorkeling is good off Pasir Putih, an excellent coral beach for sunbathing on the west side of the peninsula. Visit the beach south of Pasir Putih and watch turtles and monitor lizards bask in the sun.

Pangandaran Nature Reserve

This 530-hectare *cagar alam* (nature reserve) is south of the village and takes up a whole three-km-square peninsula. Entrance fee Rp1000. The PHPA office stocks maps identifying wildlife habitats and tracing the different paths through the park. Some portions of the reserve are difficult to reach, which helps preserve the animals. Study the map carefully to find a path to take you into the heart, tag along with a walking tour group, or hitch on a jeep. The beach path is a 10-km walk around the entire peninsula at low tide. By motorboat you can travel the same circuit in 1.5 hours for Rp25,000, 15 to a boat. Around Rp4000-5000 per hour for a motorless *prahu*.

Within its relatively confined area, the park seems to have everything: abundant wildlife, caves, teak forests, shady *banyan* trees, grazing fields, scrub areas, mytho-historical remains, seashores, WW II Japanese pillboxes.

Getting There

The typical visitor books a minibus direct from a hotel in Bandung or Yogyakarta to a guesthouse or hotel in Pangandaran. You'll pay premium, but the convenience is often worth the extra cost. Or from Bandung, take a bus to the town of **Banjar** and a second bus down to Pangandaran (six hours total), then a *becak* (Rp1000) to the guesthouse or hotel of your choice.

Central Java

CIREBON

The north-coast town of Cirebon is not on the popular tourist routes. It boasts no golden sandy beaches or trendy restaurants or hotels, but it's a clean, pleasant town, well worth a diversion—especially for its rich variety of arts and crafts and historical attractions. Lying between the sea and the mountains, Cirebon's hot temperatures are often buffered by cool mountain breezes. An ancient precolonial port town near the border of West and Central Java, Cirebon is the meeting point of the Sundanese and Javanese cultures, and the local dialect is a blending of the two. The city's name, in fact, derives from the Javanese word *caruban*, or "mixture." The sultanate here was split into two main houses, Kanoman and Kasepuhan. Both palaces are open to visitors, occasionally hosting court dances and *gamelan* recitals. Also, it must be said the citizens of Cirebon are among the friendliest in all of Java—perhaps due to the scarcity of visitors and the small-town atmosphere. Spend some time chatting with the schoolkids, *becak* drivers, and anyone else who approaches you during your walks.

Telaga Warna, the Dieng Plateau, central Java

Kraton Kasepuhan

The town of Cirebon had long been ruled by Demak Muslims when **Sunan Gunung Jati** founded the sultanate of Cirebon in 1552 and began construction of Kraton Kasepuhan. The palace deteriorated over the centuries until 1928, when it was restored by a Dutch archaeologist. It's located today in the southeast corner of the city, west of the *alun-alun* and next to the graceful tiered-roof mosque Mesjid Kasepuhan. Walk through the split red-brick *candi bentar* into the *kraton*; ornate Chinese carved tigers guard the front gateway. Domestic tourists come in the morning; by afternoon the place is usually deserted as people try to escape the heat. You can take photos inside the museum and in the *kraton* itself. The neatly restored complex comprises 25 hectares. The sultanate has long been stripped of power and the sultan is now a banker. Open every day 0700-1700. Admission Rp1000 plus camera fee; don't pay the so-called "guide fee" for guides fluent only in Bahasa.

Kraton Kanoman

Walk straight through the market, Pasar Kanoman, to this palace built by **Pangeran Cakrabuana** in the 17th century on the edge of what was then the small village of Witana. Woodcarvings on the main door of the hall indicate the opening date (A.D. 1670). Istana Kanoman features a restful courtyard of shady *banyan* trees with children flying kites. The remnants of the old Javanese *priyayi* world lie decaying in overgrown plazas and *pendopo*. In the museum sets of *seni debus* stakes decorate the walls; these were driven into men on Mohammed's birthday each year, a form of mystical self-mutilation in the Prophet's honor. Other exhibits include carvings, weapons, and royal souvenirs from different regencies of Indonesia and abroad. Find the man with the key to the **Gedung Pusaka** (Heirloom Building) inside the *kraton* compound to see the incredible coach of **Kareta Paksi Naga Liman**, the prize attraction of Kanoman. The three creatures depicted on this royal carriage are symbols of earthly and metaphysical powers: the *paksi* or great mythical *garuda* bird represents the realm of the air; the *naga* (snake bird) represents the sea; and the *liman* or *gajah* represents land. All are combined in one Pegasus-like creation called the Paksi Naga Liman. These fused symbols are considered the strongest creatures of their elements. This extravagant carriage, built by Pangeran Losari, was used only during great royal festivals. See also a coach on which the queen sat in the middle of her carved wood "cloud puff."

Taman Sunyaragi

A grotesque three-story red brick and concrete grotto, 4.5 km southwest of town on Jl. Sunyaragi (take minibus BS on Jl. Sisingamanga Raja). Taman Sunyaragi has passed through several transformations since its initial construction as a resthouse for 15th-century royalty. Sunan Gunung Jati used it as a country palace for his Chinese bride,

Ong Tien, who died just three years after arriving on Java. It is, in fact, still referred to locally as "the Pleasure Gardens of the Chinese Princess." At that time the building was adorned with cascading waterfalls and the area was landscaped with small lakes and gardens.

Arts and Crafts

Since the 15th century, Cirebon's well-established Chinese community has influenced the city's unique arts, both in motifs (*megamendung,* or "rock and clouds") and lacquer techniques. Stylized rocks and clouds decorate monochromatic carved door panels, and wooden *wayang* puppets are carved specifically as wall decorations. Much of the wood comes from the *sawo* fruit tree. A Jepara woodcarving (*ukiran jepara*) shop is on Jl. Bahagia 53. Also look up Kardita, a *pelukis becak* (*becak* painter).

The stylistic nuances and bright accents of Cirebon *batik* are found nowhere else on Java. Since the artists' guilds decreed only men could work in *batik,* Cirebon became one of the few places on Java where females did not draw and paint the cloth. Thus the *batik* of this area features bold, masculine designs and large, dramatic portions of free space. *Batik cap* sarung cost Rp12,000-20,000. *Batik kain* in the shops start at Rp20,000. The more expensive *batik tulis* goes for Rp40,000; don't expect lively bargaining as most shops stick to a *harga pesti* (fixed price). Around Pasar Pagi on Jl. Karanggetas are numerous *batik* shops. **Toko Batik Permana,** Jl. Karanggetas 18, and **Toko Batik Saudara,** Jl. Karanggetas 46, are also worth a visit. Finally, check out the **GKBI** (Batik Cooperative) at Jl. Pekarungan 33, which sells a wider selection of Cirebon *batik* than any other outlet. Walk easily to GKBI from Hotel Asia, or take a *becak.* Open Mon.-Fri. 0800-1200, Saturday 0800-1230.

PEKALONGAN

Pronounced "Pek-ALLO-ang." This town has always been a fortress and trade city. The old Dutch Quarter just north of the **Loji Bridge** is comprised of several stately buildings surrounding a grassy park: the old **Resident's Mansion,** imposing **post office, Dutch Reformed Church** (1852), **Kota Madya** (former Dutch city hall), **Societeit Corcle** (Dutch clubhouse), and the remains of a **VOC fort** built in 1753, and later turned into a prison by the Dutch. On 7 October 1945 the Pekalongan residency became the first in Indonesia to free itself from Japanese rule, touching off a violent social revolution which became known in this part of Java as the Tiga Daerah Movement.

Pekalongan *Batik*

Known as Kota Batik ("Batik City"), Pekalongan (pop. 125,000) is an important textile center famed for colorful hand-waxed and stamp-printed *batik* using distinct motifs. This is Indonesia's third leading *batik*-production center after Yogyakarta and

Wax is applied to the fabric during the batik *process*

Solo; Pekalongan even has a **Batik Museum** on Jl. Majapahit, open 0900-1330, closed Sundays. Recognizable by red and blue birds and flowers on white or pink backgrounds, Pekalongan *batik* is some of the most *halus* on the island; you could easily pay Rp250,000 for a fine piece. Prices vary considerably. On average, *batik cap* sarung cost Rp10,000-15,000 while handmade *batik tulis* run Rp25,000-100,000 and up. Start out shopping at **Nirwana** on Jl. Dr. Wahidin and **Kencana** off Jl. Mansyur (Gang Podosugih 1/3). **B.L. Pekalongan**, Jl. K.H. Mansyur 87, tel. (0285) 1358 or 589, is one of the largest *batik* shops; open 0800-1700. **Nulaba Batik** at Jl. Iman Bonjol 47 offers a large selection of designs from all over the northern coast. For lower prices, buy directly from the factories: **PT Rimbung Djaya**, Jl. Jen. Oerip Sumoharjo 20, is opposite *kantor perdangan*, two km from the city; open 0800-1600. **Pandawa Graha**, run by Suryanto Tri, is at Jl. Jawa 24, tel. 1499. For really superb work, visit the Leonardo of *batik*, **Pak Oey Tjoen**, at Jl. Raya 104 in Kedungwuni, nine km from Pekalongan. Unbelievably intricate designs, with eight or nine colors on one piece. Other factories include **Batik Susilo** in the nearby village of Wiradesa and **Umar Hadi Batik** in Buaran village in south Pekalongan. See the *batik* process at these factories any day of the week except Friday.

SEMARANG

The administrative capital of Central Java, Semarang is a busy harbor city; a government, trading, and industrial center; and a major fishing port. The population is 1.2 million, of which 40percent are Chinese. The city is divided into two sections. The mainly residential **Candi** section is up in the cooler hills, where many of the luxury hotels are located; the markets, restaurants, government offices, harbor, and transportation terminals lie in the lower section. The oldest and most picturesque part of town is around **Pasar Johar**; in this area are the taxi, train, and minibus stations and the post and telephone offices.

Semarang is in many ways a more orderly city than Java's other big, important ports, Jakarta and Surabaya. It offers lively nightlife, with many clubs and massage parlors. In fact there's so much business traffic that hotels are often overbooked. Although more a commercial center than a city for tourists, Semarang is a good starting point for many holiday resorts in the mountains to the south. It's the only port open to large ships on this stretch of coast, and cruise ships often call here. From Semarang you can easily visit Ambawara, Kudus, and the temples on Gunung Songo.

Sights

See the remnants of an old **Dutch Fort** on Jl. Imam Bonjol behind Poncol train station; around Tawang station are a number of big dilapidated former **Dutch warehouses**. Distinctive colonial architecture is on display all over the old town north of Pasar Johar; go on foot. The old Dutch section along Jl. Suprapto is wonderfully photogenic. **Gereja Blenduk**, Jl. Jen. Suprapto south of Tawang station, was built in 1753; *blendoek* means "to swell," and refers to the building's unique copper dome roof. **Gereja Bangkon**, Jl. Mataram 908, about the same age as Gereja Blenduk, has been beautifully restored. The amazing **Lawang Sewu** ("One Thousand Doors"), which used to house the Dutch Railway Authority, is easily discernible amongst all the buildings surrounding the Tugu Muda roundabout. Now occupied by the army, it's a hassle to photograph this remarkable structure; you must get permission from the military commander at Bintaldam IV Dina Sejarah, on the other side of the traffic circle.

Museum Jawa Tengah, on Jl. Abdul Rahman one km from Semarang's Ahmad Yani Airport, features fossils, Hindu-Javanese reliefs and statues, and *wayang*. Free entrance. A military museum, **Museum Perjuangan Mandala Bhakti**, lies south of the Tugu Muda Monument. In the center of the city, the candle-shaped **Tugu Muda Monument** commemorates the five-day battle by ragtag Indonesian partisans against elite Japanese soldiers at the end of WW II. Murals on the base show the sufferings of the people under both Dutch and Japanese domination, painted communally by one of the oldest artists' organizations in Indonesia. The modern **Mesjid Baiturahman**, northwest of Simpang Lima, is Central Java's largest and most elegant mosque.

A great cave temple, **Sam Poo Kong Temple** lies on the main road to Kendal about five km west of the city. Take a Daihatsu to Karang Ayu, then another to the temple. One of the largest and most honored Chinese temple complexes in Indonesia, Gedung Batu houses the spirit of a Ming dynasty Chinese admiral, **Cheng Ho**, a legendary Muslim eunuch who landed on Java in 1406 with a fleet of 62 vessels and 27,000 sailors. Twice a month, on Jum'at Kliwon (Friday) and Selasa Kliwon (Tuesday) of the Javanese calendar, multitudes of pilgrims arrive. The main hall, with its tall red columns and beautiful curved roof, is constructed around an inner chamber flanked by two huge dragons. Pilgrims vigorously shake incense and containers of bamboo sticks before these beasts, seeking their fortunes.

SOUTH OF SEMARANG

Ambarawa

In this small mountain town a pivotal clash took place between the Dutch and Republican irregulars in 1949; a huge ugly statue commemorates the famous action. The **Railway Museum** (Museum Kereta Api) exhibits locomotives built from 1891 to 1927 in Germany, Holland, and elsewhere. Free admission; two km from the bus terminal. Visitors also have an opportunity to ride the only cog railway still running on Java by joining a special chartered tour from Ambarawa to the village of Bedono, 17 km uphill. Passengers take their seats in antique coaches, remodeled according to the original designs. A highlight is the 4.5-km section of track southwest of **Jambu** with a notched center rail gripped by a cogwheel. In the middle of the climb the train stops to let passengers hop down and take pictures. The roundtrip journey consumes a day. A group of up to 80 people may sign up for this special tourist attraction, but a week's notice is required. It's also possible to join a group of domestic tourists. Inquire at Exploitasi Jawa Tengah, Kantor PJKA, Jl. Thamrin 3, Semarang, tel. (024) 24500, or at the main PJKA office in Yogyakarta.

Bandungan and the Gedung Songo Group

Bandungan is a popular 981-meter-high hill resort and base for exploring the Gedung Songo temple group, an archaeological park seven km uphill from the town on the slopes of a small valley on the southern side of Gunung Ungaran. First take a minibus to Ambarawa, then from Ambarawa's Pasar Projo take another bus northwest off the main road for about seven km (Rp350, 30 minutes) to Bandungan. The town produces abundant vegetables, fruits, and decorative flowers. The locals hire out horses to explore the surrounding mountain roads.

This is perhaps the most breathtaking temple location on Java. The site was chosen with great care for its magnificent views, encompassing Gunung Ungaran, Lake Rawapening, Gunung Merbabu, and even hazy Gunung Merapi. Although most of the main *candi* in each group were dedicated to Shiva, one shrine was set aside for

Vishnu, a Hindu god rarely worshipped on Java. Don't miss Temple II with its well-preserved *kala-makara* relief on the portal. Entrance fee Rp350; camping Rp550.

KUDUS

Kudus, 54 km northeast of Semarang, originated with the founding of a mosque here in 1546 by **Sunan Kudus**, a Javan *wali* (holy man). Though a staunch Islamic town—censuring looks if you wear shorts—some old Hindu customs prevail: cows may not be slaughtered within the city limits and schoolboys still spend a night at the shrine of Sunan Muria to improve their chances in exams. Kudus is famed as a center for the clove cigarette industry, producing nearly 25percent of Indonesia's annual output. The *kiajis* of Old Town Kudus have a reputation as healers. It's easy getting around town, either walking or by *becak,* which are really cheap here.

Wander the narrow streets of the staunchly Islamic *kauman*; ask directions to the ruins of the Hindu-period **Mesjid Bubar**. One kilometer beyond the *alun-alun* is ancient **Al Manar Mosque**, containing a famous minaret. Built by Sunan Kudus in 1549, this mosque has undergone numerous improvements and modifications. The 20-meter-high, red-brick minaret in front, built around 1685, closely resembles the temple-building style of East Java. Combining both Hindu and Islamic architecture, it actually looks like a Javanese Hindu temple. This *menara* is radically different from minarets in Saudi Arabia or Egypt; it's really just a modified *kulkul* (watchtower) added to fortified temples during Hindu times to warn rice farmers of danger. Now used to announce daily prayers; you can climb the wooden ladder inside for a view of the city.

Clove cigarettes were invented in the 1890s by an entrepreneur who claimed the smoke ameliorated his asthma. Indonesians now smoke over 36,000 tons of cloves a year, outstripping domestic supplies and even importing cloves from Madagascar and Zanzibar. Take free tours of the *kretek* factories of Djarum, Noryorono, Seokun, and Jambu Boh.

Jepara

A small, scruffy, country town 90 km northeast of Semarang on the north coast. Jepara was a main port for the "Second Mataram" of the 17th century, playing an important role in rice export until the harbor silted up. Today Jepara is noteworthy as home to some of the best traditional carvers on Java. Jepara's other name is Kota Ukir, "Carving Town." Except for the hinges, no nails, screws, or metal joinery are used. The wood comes from Blora and Cepu (East Java)—teak mostly, but also mahogany, *kayu meranti,* and *sono.* Coming into town you'll see shops overflowing with tables, chairs, and cabinets piled high inside and out.

Paid by the meter, men come in from the surrounding villages to carve. To see them in action, visit the nearby villages of **Tahunan, Mantingan,** and **Blakanggunung.** Many shops are concentrated along Jl. Pemuda.

YOGYAKARTA

One of the largest villages in the world, Yogyakarta is Java's cultural capital and an important center for higher learning—Java's Kyoto. Its name is often shortened to Yogya—pronounced "JOAG-jah." For centuries a royal city and major trade center, the Yogyakarta *kraton* is the highest-ranking court in Indonesia and "Special Region Yogyakarta" (pop. three million) is responsible directly to Jakarta and not to the provincial head of Central Java. From 1946 to 1950, Yogyakarta was the grassroots capital of Indonesia and the headquarters of the revolutionary forces. Today, with its rich culture, economy hotels, and restaurants, it's a city streamlined for travelers.

Well known as the "main door to traditional Javanese culture," the city draws thousands of talented people from around the world. There are numerous music and dance schools, brilliant choreographers, drama and poetry workshops, folk theater and *wayang* troupes, artists excelling in the plastic arts. It's also one of the best places to shop in Southeast Asia. Yogyakarta is a major *batik*-producing center and, due to increased tourist awareness, this art is developing ever higher standards. The painters and sculptors here are Indonesia's elite, strongly individualistic but increasingly commercialized.

Taman Sari

The ruins of a pleasure park built in feudal splendor between 1758 and 1765 for the sultan and his family. Taman Sari once featured lighted underwater corridors, cool subterranean mosques, meditation platforms in the middle of lily ponds, *gamelan* towers, and galleries for dancing—all in mock Spanish architecture. Princesses bathed in flower-strewn pools, streams flowed above covered passageways, boats drifted in artificial lakes. Tour on foot 0800-1700; Rp500 admission. Students will offer to guide you to secret places.

The *Kraton*

Built in 1757, this is the palace compound of Yogyakarta's sultans—classical Javanese palace-court architecture at its finest. It costs Rp1000 to get into the front portion of the *kraton*, called Pagelaran, and Rp1400 to enter the *Di Dalam*, the inner sanctum. Open Mon.-Thurs. 0830-1400, Friday 0800-1130, Saturday 0830-1300, Sunday 0830-1400. Dress conservatively; men should wear long trousers.

The *kraton* features *batik* and silver workshops, mosques, schools, markets, offices, and two museums, all enclosed by three-meter-thick white walls imitating European fortifications. The interiors are especially reminiscent of prewar Dutch bourgeois mansions. During the war of independence, guerrilla commander Suharto—now the president of the republic—dressed as a barefoot peasant and peddled vegetables at the rear of the *kraton* to confer with the sultan on tactics to use against the Dutch.

Prambanan Temple, near Yogyakarta

The inner court, with male and female steps to the entrance, includes two small museums and a pavilion where you can see classical dance rehearsals each Sunday 1030-1200. On Monday and Wednesday 1030-1200 traditional *gamelan* rehearsals are staged. Both performances are included in the price of admission.

Museums

Musium Biologi, Jl. Sultan Agung 22, displays a collection of plants and stuffed animals from throughout the archipelago; Rp500 entrance fee, open Mon.-Thurs. 0800-1300, Friday until 1100, Saturday and Sunday until 1200.

The **Army Museum** (Dharma Wiratama), Jl. Jen. Sudirman 70, is open Mon.-Thurs. 0800-1300, Saturday and Sunday 0800-1200. This museum records the Indonesian revolution, displaying documents, photos, historical articles, homemade weapons, uniforms, and equipment from the 1945-49 struggle.

Located on Alun-alun Utara, the square north of the *kraton*, is the **Sonobudoyo Museum**, a building constructed in the classical Javanese *kraton* style. Open Tues.-Thurs. 0830-1330, Friday 0800-1115, Saturday 0800-1200, and Sunday 0830-1300; closed holidays. A first-rate collection of Javanese, Madurese, and Balinese arts and crafts, excellent *batik* exhibits, musical instruments (a complete seven-ton iron and copper *pelog gamelan*), palace furnishings, 18-carat gold Buddha, *wayang golek* puppets, woodcarvings, and weapons. Contribute Rp500 as you enter. Finally, about 60 meters from the *kraton's* main gate is the **Kareta Museum**, with old royal coaches and carriages.

Monumen Diponegoro

A reconstruction of Diponegoro's residence, destroyed by the Dutch in 1825, is located four km west of Yogyakarta at Tegalrejo. A 15-minute bicycle ride from town, Rp1000 by *becak,* or take bus no. 1 from Jl. H.O.S. Cokroaminoto. This museum is dedicated to **Prince Diponegoro** (1785-1855), who led partisans during the Java War (1825-30). His *kris* are hung with flowers in glass cases; see also photos of his other sacred possessions and the large commemorative *pendopo*. Visit the hole through which he and his followers escaped to reach Gua Selarong near Parangtritis. After five years of bloody war this nobleman was tricked into negotiations at Magelang, arrested, and exiled to Sulawesi for the remaining 25 years of his life.

Mosques And Churches

Best to visit mosques between sunrise and noon. Dress modestly. Two-hundred-year-old **Mesjid Agung** is on the western side of Alun-alun Lor. This is where the *kraton's* royal *gamelan* are kept during Sekaten week and where the famous *gunungan* procession terminates. **Mesjid Soko Tunggal**, opposite the main gate (Pintu Gerbang) of Taman Sari, was built in the *kraton* pavilion style; stories from the Koran are carved

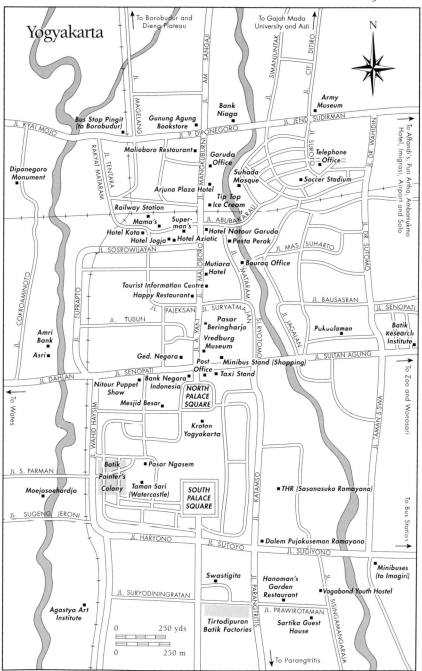

Yogyakarta

To Borobudur and Dieng Plateau

To Gajah Mada University and Asti

N

JL. AM SANGAJI
JL. SIMANJUNTAK
JL. CIT DITIRO

JL. KYAI MOJO

JL. MAGELANG

Bus Stop Pingit (to Borobudur)

Gunung Agung Bookstore

Bank Niaga

Army Museum

JL. JEND SUDIRMAN

JL. P. DIPONEGORO

JL. SURYO

JL. DR. WAHIDIN

Diponegoro Monument

JL. RAKYAT MATARAM
JL. TENTARA

Malioboro Restaurant

Garuda Office

Telephone Office

To Affandi, Puri Artha, Ambarrukmo Hotel, Imigrasi, Airport and Solo

Suhada Mosque

Soccer Stadium

Arjuna Plaza Hotel

JL. MANGKUBUMI

Tip Top Ice Cream

Railway Station

Mama's

Super-man's

Hotel Kota

Hotel Jogja

Hotel Aziatic

JL. ABUBAKARALI

Hotel Natour Garuda

Pesta Perak

JL. MAS SUHARTO

JL. SOSROWIJAYAN

Mutiara Hotel

Bourag Office

JL. DR SUTOMO

JL. SUPRAPTO

Tourist Information Centre

Happy Restaurant

JL. MALIOBORO

JL. PAJEKSAN

JL. SURYATMAJAN

JL. BAUSASRAN

JL. SENOPATI

JL. TUBUN

JL. A YANI

Pasar Beringharjo

JL. SI RYOTOMO

JL. JAGALAN

Pakualaman

Batik Research Institute

Amri Bank

Asri

Ged. Negara

Vredburg Museum

Post Office

Minibus Stand (Shopping)

Taxi Stand

JL. SULTAN AGUNG

To Zoo and Wonosari

JL. DAHLAN

JL. SENOPATI

Bank Negara Indonesia

NORTH PALACE SQUARE

Nitour Puppet Show

Mesjid Besar

JL. WAHID HASYIM

Kraton Yogyakarta

JL. TAMAN'S SWA

JL. S. PARMAN

Batik Painter's Colony

Pasar Ngasem

Moejosoehardjo

Taman Sari (Watercastle)

SOUTH PALACE SQUARE

THR (Sasanasuka Ramayana)

JL. KATAMSO

To Bus Station

JL. SUGENG JERONI

JL. HARYONO

JL. SUTOYO

Dalem Pujokuseman Ramayana

JL. SUGIYONO

Minibuses (to Imigiri)

Swastigita

Hanoman's Garden Restaurant

Vagabond Youth Hostel

JL. PARANGTRITIS

JL. SISINGAMANGARAJA

Agastya Art Institute

JL. SURYODININGRATAN

0   250 yds

0   250 m

Tirtodipuran Batik Factories

JL. PRAWIROTAMAN

Sartika Guest House

To Parangtritis

To Wates

on its pillars. Ethereal Batak hymn-singing vibrates from the **Huria Kristen Batak Protestant Church,** Jl. Nyoman Oka 22, Kota Baru, early Sunday mornings. Attend the Indonesian-style Catholic mass in Yogyakarta's oldest church, **St. Francis Xavier,** Jl. P. Senopati (near the post office); masses are held Saturday at 1730 and Sunday at 0530 and 0700.

Performing Arts

Wayang and dance dramas are performed for both tourists and Javanese. Tourist performances are usually shortened, with just the epic highlights presented. Plays held at **Sasono Hinggil** south of the *alun-alun* are true marathons that start at 2100 and last for nine hours without a break. Tourist performances are not necessarily inferior to the genuine article; often they're better-funded and include more lavish props and costumes than an authentic *kampung* production. You won't be able to understand the words but the magical scenes will fascinate nonetheless. Go to the tourist office, Jl. Malioboro 16, for information on the latest venues and a schedule of performances.

The **Agastya Art Institute,** Gedongkiwo MD III/237, is a training school for *dalang.* Shadow plays are staged here 1500-1700 except Saturday. Entrance Rp3000. *Wayang golek dalang* is also taught; every Saturday 1500-1700 you can see one in action for Rp1750. Also see *wayang kulit* at **Ambar Budaya** in the Yogyakarta Crafts Center, opposite the Ambarrukmo on Jl. Adisucipto, every day 2000-2230; Rp3000. **Habiranda Dalang School,** on the northeast side of the *alun-alun* in the Pracimasono pavilion, puts on free rehearsals each evening 1900-2000 except Sunday and Thursday.

At the **Yogyakarta Kraton** see classical dance rehearsals 1000-1200 on Sunday. Tickets are sold at the door of the palace. *Gamelan* rehearsals Monday and Wednesday 1030-1200; Rp1000. At the **Purawisata** on Jl. Brig. Jen. Katamso, *wayang orang* performances are held nightly with the Ramayana plot; Rp10,000. The biggest venue in town—worth the steep admission fee.

Grhadika Yogyakarta Pariwisata (GYP) is an institution that arranges performances of *wayang orang* at Pendopo Dalem Pujodusuman, Jl. Brig. Jen. Katamso 45, on Monday, Wednesday, and Friday 2000-2200; Rp8500 admission. This is the finest and most authentic Ramayana venue in Yogyakarta; highly recommended for lovers of serious dance.

Ramayana Ballet

These de Mille-like spectacles take place on the enormous stone stage of the Lorojonggrang open-air theater near the Prambanan temple complex on four successive full-moon nights each month from May to August. Cancelled if it rains. This four-episode contemporary *sendratari*-style ballet is based on the traditional *wayang orang* dancing of the classical Javanese theater. The plot is a modernized, dramatized version of the Indian epic poem the *Ramayana*. The Prambanan temple panels are, in effect, reenacted live. The performance lasts 1900-2100. Bring cushions or a sleeping bag to soften stone seats. The tourist info center, major hotels, and almost any travel agency can sell you roundtrip tickets; Rp8000-30,000, depending on the seating. Take note that the *Ramayana* is also perfomed in the covered theater in Prambanan, just opposite the new open-air theater, every Tuesday, Wednesday, and Thursday throughout the year 1930-2200; Rp7000-15,000.

A wayang-kulit puppet

Crafts and Shopping

Spend several days in Yogyakarta before buying so you can discover the right prices at the right places. Be prepared to bargain, with grace. To get acquainted with the full range of crafts offered, visit first the government-sponsored **Yogyakarta Crafts Center**, Jl. Adisucipto across from the Ambarrukmo Hotel. Check out the **Handicrafts by the Handicapped** shop in the Crafts Center. Open daily 0900-1000, this shop sells handicrafts made by disabled people, offers reasonable prices, and provides daily demonstrations.

Also visit **Pasar Beringharjo**, a giant market on Jl. Jen. A Yani, an extension of Jl. Malioboro. Swarming with brazen rats, this one-km maze of market stalls features everything from macrame to mutton to mangos. The people selling textiles and old *batik* here lie like snakes; the unprepared will be robbed blind. Know your stuff. Leather goods and an endless assortment of food, baskets, dry goods, and everyday craft items are sold at reasonable prices in front of and around the market.

Yogyakarta's newest and largest shopping complex is the enormous **Malioboro Plaza** with McDonald's, Matahari Department Store, and Texas Fried Chicken. **Sinar Mas Department Store**, Jl. Malioboro 38, tel. (0274) 4490 or 2613, is a nice store right downtown. **The Art Shop**, opposite the Hotel Garuda, sells high-quality arts and crafts.

Wayang

For the most part, Yogyakarta's *wayang kulit* puppets are made from goat skin, not the traditional buffalo hide; the best cost at least Rp20,000. You'll find *wayang* puppets all over town, but the best place is probably **Pak Ledjar** on Jl. Mataram DN I/370. From Helen's on Jl. Malioboro walk east down the alley to Jl. Mataram, then turn left. Another good place is **Toko Jawa**, Jl. Malioboro opposite the Mutiara Hotel, which also sells musical instruments and Ramayana costumes. *Wayang golek* puppets are made at master **Pak Warno's** on Jl. Bantul, eight km south of Yogyakarta. High-quality *wayang kulit* puppets are created at **Moejosoehardjo's**, Jl. S. Parman Taman Sari 37B, tel. (0274) 2873, west of the Winingo River; he specializes in large *gunungan* screens.

Antiques

Toko Asia, Jl. Malioboro opposite the Hotel Garuda, sells an outstanding collection of old *kris*. Several other small shops are close by. **Madiyono**, Jl. Tirtodipuran 36 (open 0900-2100), has a full range of art antiques. Also worth checking is the group of antique shops in the vicinity of the Ambarrukmo, and the four shops on Jl. Prawirotaman.

Saptohudaya, Jl. Solo km 9 Meguwo, tel. (0274) 62443, sells museum-quality textiles, carvings, Irianese artifacts, and antiques; the best of the best and prices to match. Most *batik* factories also sell antiques. Jalan Taman Garuda is good hunting ground: try **Seni Jaya** (no. 11), and **Pusaka** (no. 22). Probably the most soulful antiques in all Yogyakarta, all at exorbitant prices, are found at **Ardianto**, Jl. Magelang.

Batik

Most of Yogyakarta's hundreds of *batik* outlets open in the mornings, close 1300-1630, then open again at 2100. Look around the galleries before you buy. High-quality *batik* paintings, cheaper than oils, run Rp210,000-525,000 average, but it's worth paying a bit more if it helps improve the art. When shopping, avoid being led into the galleries; it's better to deal directly with the outlets.

You can tour most of the 25 *batik* factories on Jl. Tirtodipuran and Jl. Parangtritis. The majority produce soulless junk. Lots of classy salerooms, but generally they're not the place to buy *tulis* work as most of the pieces are created with the *cap* method. On Jl. Tirtodipuran, see the Chinese-style *batik* at **Plentong**, no. 28; **Batik Srimpi**, no. 22, offers Solo-style work. **Winotosastro**, no. 34, has an excellent selection, including some fine *tulis* pieces and ready-made clothing. **Rara Jonggrang**, no. 6A, displays paintings by at least 15 artists. Another large factory is **Suryakencana**, Jl. Ngadinegaran, with a wide selection in its showroom. **Terang Bulan**, Yogyakarta's *batik* supermarket at Jl. Jen. A. Yani 76, is especially rewarding if you don't know anything about *batik*.

F. **Agus Mudjono**, Mergangsan Kidul, Mg. III/ 102, creates traditional *batik* paintings selling for Rp10,000-350,000. Agus has exhibited his work all over the world. **Tjokrosuharto**, Jl. Panembahan 58, is a large fixed-price shop with a variety of crafts including *batik*. **Siti Astana Bilai-Batik**, Jl. K.H. Dahlan 29, features *batik tulis*; workshop nearby. **Gallery Yogyakarta**, Jl. Gampingan 42 (behind ASRI), is an excellent source for *lurik*, the Javanese homespun. If the color you'd like is not in stock, order it; view the weaving process in the rear.

Ardiyanto Batik, Jl. Taman Garuda, adopts traditional designs for fabric in cotton and silk for dresses, blouses, pillows, and pictures. Limited selection of good-quality *batik* at fixed prices. **Saptohudoyo Gallery**, Jl. Adisucipto near the airport, exhibits works of a variety of artists. **Lod Gallery**, in Taman Sari, sells highly original work by younger artists. The Water Palace area has the best bargains for *batik* paintings—as low as Rp6000—but much of it is amateurish. Also check for possible bargains by top-of-the-line artists at **Amri Gallery**, Jl. Gampingan 67, tel. (0274) 5135, and **Bagong Kussudiardjo**, Jl. Singosaren 9.

Services

Stop at the Tourist Information Center first, at Jl. Malioboro 16, tel. (0274) 66000. From Jl. Pasar Kembang the office is located halfway down Jl. Malioboro toward the main post office; open Mon.-Sat. 0800-1930. An extremely helpful staff, with a town plan, regional maps, and calendar of events. Complete train and bus schedules posted. Beware of strangers who try to pass themselves off as officials from the tourist office.

The **main post office** occupies a historic building on the corner of Jl. Senopati and Jl. Jen. A. Yani. The *pos paket* in a side room will wrap your parcel securely in nylon for only Rp750. The **immigration office** is open Mon.-Thurs. 0730-1330, Friday 0730-1100, Saturday 0900-1230. Located eight km out of town on Jl. Adisucipto on the road to Solo. *Bemo* drivers will let you off right in front.

A WARTEL is attached to the Batik Palace Hotel, offering international telephoning, fax, and telegrams. Fax machines are also found at the better hotels and most guesthouses in Yogyakarta. The Yogyakarta telephone city code is 0274.

Better rates of exchange than Bali or Jakarta. Shop around for the best rate. **Bank Niaga** (Jl. Sudirman) usually provides a good rate; open 0800-1400, Saturday until 1300. Compare the rate with **Bank Bumi Daya**, on Jl. Sudirman beside the Merpati office. **Bank BNI**, adjacent to the main post office, is also worth a try; enter through the foreign exchange door. Other authorized moneychangers located on Jl. Pasar Kembang and Jl. Parangtritis. The moneychanger on Jl. Pasar Kembang near the *wartel* is open daily until 2130.

Yogyakarta on the whole offers good medical treatment; Gajah Mada University is an important center for medical studies. **Bethesda**, Jl. Jen. Sudirman 70, tel. (0274) 2281, is the best local hospital, open 0900-1400, but usually a mob of incompetent interns descends on you. Instead, try a private doctor, 90 percent of whom speak English. Recommended are **Dr. Gandha**, Jl. Pringgokusuman 1, and **Dr. Sukadis**, Jl. Dagen.

VICINITY OF YOGYAKARTA

Kasongan

This potters' village 45 minutes (Rp400) by minibus from Yogyakarta is well known for its animal-shaped, brightly painted children's moneyboxes; Rp1000-4000. Large pots, vases, and bowls for sale. See the potters bisquing pieces in big blazing straw fires. In front of each shop is a display showcase. Customers haggle over prices, which are half what the pieces go for in Yogyakarta's Pasar Ngasem. Can also special-order; allow 10 days. **Bapak Suwarno** in Nidiro village near Kasongan is renowned for his *wayang orang* masks; Rp25,000-50,000.

Kota Gede

Six km southeast of Yogyakarta's city center, Rp6000 for a chartered *andong* or Rp3000 for a *becak* for two. Or take the *bis kota* for Rp250. Kota Gede, founded in 1579, was once the capital of the old Mataram Kingdom and is older than Yogyakarta itself. Silver workshops sprang up to serve the king; nowadays Suharto orders gifts for state guests from here. The town's many busy, clanging silverware shops consume some 50 tons of silver annually. You're free to wander through big workshops full of men and boys using the simplest of handtools, hammering on anvils, filing, polishing, heating, and soldering strips of bright silver.

There are two grades of silver: 92.5 percent sterling, and 80 percent. Display rooms sell a huge variety of pieces, from Rp3000 for a ring set with a semiprecious stone up to several million *rupiah* for a complete silver dinner service for 12. Most of the silver shops inventory the same items, seldom deviating from the sure sellers, but all will make anything to order.

Tom's Silver, Jl. Ngeksigondo 60, tel. (0274) 2818, is the largest and most established workshop, with a large showroom. The workmanship is better, but the prices are also higher. Credit cards accepted, bargain only if you buy wholesale or very expensive items. At **MD Silver** down the street on Jl. Keboan, jewelry sells for less; here you can see *wayang kulit* made from *kerbau* hide. The showroom is open 0800-2000, until 1700 on Sunday; workshop open 0800-1700. Numerous other shops line the streets of Kota Gede, many selling not only silver but tortoiseshell and horn handicrafts, curios, and fake antiques as well.

Imogiri

A cemetery for the royal houses of Yogyakarta and Solo since the early kings of Mataram, Imogiri lies 20 km southeast of Yogyakarta, a 30-minute (Rp450) minibus ride. Climb barefoot up the 345 warm stone steps to the sacred burial ground at the

Prambanan Temple, near Yogyakarta

top. The mighty Sultan Agung was the first Javanese king interred here, his tomb built in the mid-17th century on a small rocky promontory. Since then, nearly every king has found his final resting place on this highly venerated hill. Three major courtyards are laid out at the top of the stairway: to the left are buried the *susuhunan* of Solo, to the right the sultans of Yogyakarta, in the center the Mataram kings. Some graves are over 400 years old.

This is not a place where crowds of tourists come on buses; you have to make an effort to get here, but it's worth it. You may be the only Westerner present; it could be one of the highlights of your visit to Yogyakarta. Hardly anyone speaks English. Pay the entrance fee (Rp800) and sign the visitors book. An important pilgrimage site of ancestor worship, you must wear formal Javanese dress to enter. On the premises men may rent a sarung and women a *kain* and *kebaya* for a modest fee. The Royal Tombs are only open Monday 0900-1300 and Friday 1330-1600; the tomb of Sultan Agung is open around 1430 on Friday, the best day to visit. The graves are closed during Ramadan and no photography is permitted in the graveyards.

Parangtritis

The place to go if you want to take a break from Yogyakarta, Parangtritis is 27 km south on the Indian Ocean. Catch a big bus on the corner of Jl. Kol Sugiyono and Jl. Parangtritis in Yogyakarta all the way to Parangtritis for Rp1000 (includes beach area admission). This is the most popular and accessible of the beaches south of Yogyakarta—a simple seaside resort with wild seas, horse rides on the beach, friendly people, and a handful of foreigners. Take books, *sarung*, and a musical instrument. Accommodations are reasonable, food cheap and plentiful. During the week, life can be simple here and quiet; on holidays and weekends the place swarms with thousands of local tourists.

Visit the excellent freshwater swimming pool and *mandi*. The surrounding area is dramatic, with many jagged cliffs and beaches of meadow-like gray sand dunes and eerie moonscapes stretching for kilometers. Also, walk up the paved road for superb views from the lookout, and do a lunchtime splurge at the stunning Queen of the South Resort.

THE PRAMBANAN PLAIN

It took staggering agricultural productivity to enable pompous feudal monarchs to erect these temples to their own glory. On the rich Prambanan Plain, 17 km northeast of Yogyakarta, are the most extensive Hindu temple ruins in all Indonesia. There's no telling how many more are still under the earth. Lying today among villages and green rice fields with the sharp peak of Gunung Merapi in the background, most of these temple complexes were built from the 8th to 10th centuries. They were abandoned when the Hindu kings moved to eastern Java in the 10th century. Around

1600, all extant temples were toppled by an earthquake. In the 19th century, their blocks were carried off to pave roads and build sugar mills, bridges, railroads. The Dutch started restoration in the late 1930s.

Prambanan Temple Complex

Java's largest temple complex, Rp1000 by minibus from near Solo's Cilingin terminal. Prambanan's central courtyard contains three large structures: a main temple dedicated to Shiva, flanked by one each to Brahma (to the south) and Vishnu (to the north). The complex originally contained 244 minor temples (*candi perwara*), all arranged in four rows. Only several have been restored. The two small *candi* at the side of the main terrace were probably the treasuries where jewels and gold were kept. Admission to the main complex is Rp4000. Open 0600-1800; go early. Vendors line the walkways, plus there's a food and souvenir stall area. See the Ramayana ballet performed here during full moon nights from May to August. Performances nightly in the new, indoor pavilion.

Shiva Temple (Candi Lorojonggrang)

This large central temple was dedicated to Shiva the Destroyer. Built to contain the remains of the Mataram King Balitung, who reigned in the middle of the 9th century and claimed to be a reincarnation of Shiva. Much of the structure had collapsed by the last century and not until 1937 did reconstruction begin. Now a wonder of restoration, this tall, elegant temple is a synthesis of both north and south Indian architectural styles. Almost 50 meters high, for 1,000 years it was the tallest building on Java. Its lavish decorations, statues, and other details all show an outstanding sense of composition. The whole structure is perfectly balanced; while walking around its 20 sides, it never seems to change. See it late in the day when the crowds thin out and the sun turns it gold.

Outlying Temples

Numerous other temple complexes are found along the road between Yogyakarta and Solo. Watch for the small signs posted by the Archaeological Service. Temples **Sambisari, Kalasan,** and **Sari** lie between the airport and Prambanan village. **Lumbung, Bubrah, Sewu,** and **Plaosan** temples all lie more or less north along the same side of the road from the Prambanan complex. To start, follow road signs pointing toward Candi Lumbung. To visit these outlying temples, hire *andong* near Prambanan's minibus terminal for about Rp1000 per hour. It's more enjoyable walking in the cool of the morning on the network of trails. Or take a bicycle. Only Kalasan and Prambanan ask for money (Rp200 each); none but the Shiva temple charge for photography (Rp200).

BOROBUDUR

This colossal, cosmic mountain is one of humanity's most imposing creations—nothing else like it exists. Erected 200 years before Notre Dame and Chartres cathedrals, it predates the Buddhist temple of Angkor Wat in Cambodia by three centuries. Built with more than two million cubic feet of stone, Borobudur is the world's largest *stupa* and the biggest ancient monument in the Southern Hemisphere. See it on a rainy day when water spews from the mouths of its gargoyles. Get an early start in the cool of the morning to avoid the large crowds. Inside the privately managed park you'll find a small archaeological museum, tours on a simulated train, and an audiovisual show on the historical background of Borobudur. Admission Rp4000; Indonesians pay Rp1000.

Although the structure features many characteristics of the Central Javanese style (A.D. 700-950), it has little else in common with other Buddhist temples in Southeast Asia. Persian, Babylonian, and Greek influences are present in Borobudur's art and architecture. Used for veneration, worship, and meditation, this giant monument was an achievement of the Vajrayana sect of the Tantric School of Buddhism, which found acceptance in Indonesia around A.D. 700.

The feudal Sailendra princes—highly advanced technicians—erected it with peasant labor between 778 and 850. No one really knows how this great structure was built, in a time when modern engineering techniques, it is believed, had not yet been

(above) Upper terrace, Borobudur; (opposite) Bas-reliefs, Borobudur

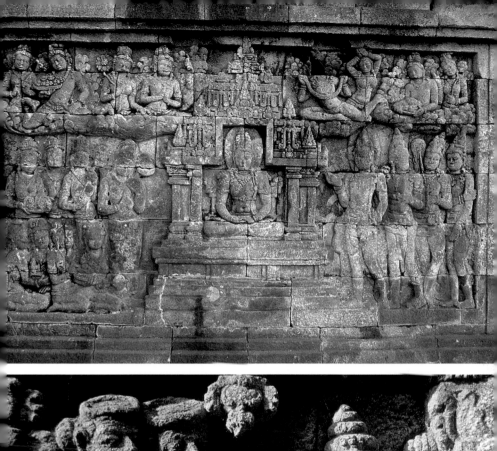

developed. No nation or group of humans could possibly build it today. In 856, the Sailendras were overthrown by Hindus and Borobudur was abandoned soon after its completion. It might have begun collapsing just when the sculptors were applying their finishing touches. The monument was buried under a thousand years of volcanic eruptions and tropical growth until discovered by an English colonel in 1814. In 1855 Borobudur was cleared, but it was only in 1973 that restoration began in earnest. The work was at last completed in 1983 at a cost of some US$25 million. The massive *stupa* is still in an almost continual state of reconstruction.

Turn left upon entering to pay tribute to the gods; those who turn right pay tribute to devils. There are 10 terraces from the base to the main topmost stupa, each representing the individual stages toward perfection. The pilgrim's walk takes you around the temple nine times before reaching the top. The east side's third gallery has the best preserved and most beautiful gateway. Visitors are swallowed up symbolically by the *kala*-monster upon entering, then granted new spiritual life. The walk through the labyrinth of narrow corridors to the summit is over five km.

Reliefs

One of the largest and most complete ensembles of Buddhist reliefs in existence, Borobudur amounts to a virtual textbook of Mahayana Buddhist doctrine in stone. There are 1,500 pictorial relief panels of Buddha's teachings, plus 1,212 purely ornamental panels. Once glistening with bright purple, crimson, green, blue, and yellow paint, over 8,235 square meters of stone surface are carved in high relief, telling scholars much about the material culture of 8th- to 9th-century Java. There are lessons on history, religion, art, morality, literature, clothing styles, family life, architecture, agriculture, shipping, fighting arts, and dancing—the whole Buddhist cosmos. Sculptors trained in the best tradition of Indian classical temple building poured their abundant talents into delicate, intricate detail. To read all the reliefs from the beginning of the story, go through the door on the east side. Because of so many right-angle corners, you're able to see only a few steps ahead. This was designed to force you to take in each phase of the story a frame at a time—like 9th-century TV.

VICINITY OF BOROBUDUR

You can reach other antiquities in the immediate area—Mendut, Pawon, Banon — with local minibuses. The temples belonging to the Borobudur complex—Mendut, Borobudur, and Pawon—fall along a straight east-west axis connecting them to Deer Park in Saranath in India. Pilgrims had to pass each temple to reach Borobudur. You can follow the same pilgrim's route in reverse by making the beautiful walk to **Candi Pawon** (two km), then on to **Mendut** (three km east of Borobudur). Or, if coming from Yogya, take a left to the southwest beyond Muntilan, and the first temple you come to is Mendut, standing quietly alone in the middle of a grassy garden.

Mendut is a genuine 9th-century temple of worship, not a *candi* to the dead. It faces Saranath, where Buddha spoke his first words of deliverance. Originally over 27 meters tall, Mendut was a mound of rubble, home to grazing cows, until it was cleared in 1836. Complete Dutch restoration occurred between 1897 and 1904. The temple dates from A.D. 850, about the same time as Borobudur, and features extensive galleries, terraces, a pyramid-shaped roof, and stupa on top. Erection required very sophisticated knowledge of Buddhist and Shivaistic texts, Indian iconography, symbolism, and monumental architecture. The builders no doubt visited the Indian holy land. Admission Rp100.

Mendut's 30 relief panels are among the finest and largest compositions in Hindu-Javanese art. The stories are drawn from the *Jataka* tales, old Buddhist folk myths involving Buddha's previous incarnations. The stone images in the temple interior are very well preserved, including a 2.5-meter-high Buddha between two bodhisattvas. These colossal statues weren't stolen, simply because of their great weight. Buddha's feet rest upon a stylized lotus blossom; his hand is held in the aspect of a preacher. Architects placed a shaft to one side of the chamber to let in rays from sun and moon to illuminate the Buddha. What was holy to the ancestors of the Javanese is still holy; often there are fresh offerings of flowers and food in the laps of the statues, with incense burning at Buddha's feet. A profound air of tranquility.

SOLO

The cultural linchpin of Java. Sometimes called Surakarta, often spelled Sala, but always pronounced Solo. The population of 500,000 is larger than Yogyakarta's, its sister city. Java's oldest cultural center, considered the island's most Javanese city, Solo is a *priyayi* stronghold. It's the only Javanese city where you see the Javanese written language widely used on buildings and signs. In the hearts of its people, Solo is the traditional capital of the Javanese kingdom—not Yogyakarta. Solo offers everything found in Yogyakarta but the high number of tourists. There are two *kraton*, one even larger and more venerable than Yogya's. Religion is soft and flowing here, unlike the more orthodox form of Islam practiced on the north coast and in West Java. But change is overtaking this ancient capital. Traffic lights are found on all the major intersections; the slick Purwosari shopping center introduced consumer mentality; then, in 1987, the huge new Singosaren Plaza shopping center replaced the venerable old downtown household market Pasar Singosaren.

During the Java War of 1825-30, most of Yogyakarta's *priyayi* families supported Diponegoro, while those in Solo remained loyal to the Dutch. When the Dutch occupied Solo, the *susuhunan* held a reception for them in his *kraton*. This was remembered 116 years later in 1946 when Indonesia became a republic, and the *susuhunan* of Solo was stripped of all authority.

Kraton Hadiningrat

Also called Istana Kasuhunan, or the Susuhunan's Palace, located southeast of the city center. *Susuhunan* means "royal foot placed on the head of vassals paying homage," a title dating from the 1600s. Before 1985, gaudy vulgarity was the dominant theme. The gold vessels, gilded furniture, mirrors, and flamboyant hangings seemed like stage props in the home of a colossal profiteer. Rumors about the *raja's* womanizing and extravagances were rampant and neverending. Living in Jakarta, he neglected upkeep of the palace and failed to propitiate hidden powers.

Finally, in January 1985, catastrophe struck. The main core of the *kraton*, the Dalem Gede—with all its priceless wood architecture and furniture—caught fire. What followed was a comic tragedy. Fire engines which could easily have doused the fire responded quickly but couldn't fit through the main gate. Since the gate was sacred, a powerful symbol of authority, the firefighters refused to smash it down. Consequently, some 60 percent of the palace burned to the ground. The official cause of the fire was a faulty electrical circuit, but it's local belief the prodigal king no longer deserved the protection of the palace spirits, who, as the Javanese say, "went back home." The damaged areas have been rebuilt and the *raja* has moved back to Surakarta and begun to mend his ways. The present *sunan* has six wives, 35 children, and has reigned since the 1940s.

One antique building of great interest that survived the fire is the multistoried minaret **Panggung Songgo Buwono**, seen over the wall in the northeast corner of the courtyard. According to an ancient legend, it was used by the *rajas* of Surakarta as a trysting place with Nyai Loro Kidul, the South Sea goddess. The servants' quarters, the women's quarters, and the priceless library of *lontar* manuscripts also survived the holocaust. Next to the *kraton* is this museum, open 0830-1400, closed Friday. Admission is included with your *kraton* fee. English-speaking guides available. The museum contains a lavish collection of regal pomp, with the carriages being the highlight: superb 18th-century European royal coaches. Also see large, demonic figureheads that once graced splendid royal barges journeying down the Solo River to Gresik in the 18th century. The Art Gallery museum is full of surprises; too bad it's poorly lit.

Mangkunegaran Palace

Mangkunegaran is the 200-year-old palace of the junior line of the royal family. This impressive complex contains a number of carved, gilded teak pavilions amidst a tropical garden, an excellent museum (open Mon.-Sat. 0900-1200, Friday to 1100, Rp1500 admission), a souvenir shop, and one of Java's finest *gamelan* orchestras. The giant *pendopo* reception/dance hall, with its zany painted ceiling of zodiac designs, is one of the finest examples of stately Javanese wood architecture in existence. This smaller court hires its own artisans and dancing masters, and even has its own *gamelan* factory. Various parts and functions of the palace are explained by English-speaking guides. Report to the registration office to pay the entrance fee. Dress conservatively. Open daily 0900-1400, Sunday 0900-1300.

In 1755, when the Mataram dynasty split into rival houses, the reigning *susuhunan's* cousin, Mangkunegoro I, established another small court inside Surakarta's domain. Mangkunegaran II began the palace at the end of the 18th century; it was completed in 1866. After WW II, the royalty business in Indonesia underwent a marked decline. In the early 1970s, to make ends meet, the Mangkunegaran royal family was even forced to establish an adjoining hotel. The young prince of the line died in an auto accident in 1979; the queen "followed her son," literally dying of grief a month later.

After Suharto's ascension to power in the late 1960s, the fortunes of this royal house—to which the first lady Madame Tien Suharto is related—began to improve. With presidential patronage, its financial dealings soon proved extraordinarily successful and members of this "pedigree family" (*keluarga trah*) were suddenly catapulted into key governmental and judicial positions. All this good fortune seemed to confirm accusations of feudalism leveled against Suharto. The palace is presently the official residence of Mangkunegoro VII and his family.

The Javanese orchestra that plays in the southwest corner of the *pendopo* has taken the honorific name Kyai Kanyut Mesem, or "Drifting in Smiles." Originally from Demak and dating back to 1778, it's one of the finest orchestras on Java and older than the palace itself. On Wednesday mornings the *pustaka gamelan* is played, and dance rehearsals begin at 1000 on the *pendopo,* lasting about two hours. Free entrance. Swallows dip and dive amongst the rafters as the *gamelan* plays, seemingly enraptured by the music.

Radyapustaka Museum

Founded in 1890 by the Dutch, the Institute of Javanese Culture is the oldest such organization in Indonesia. The institute's first task was to build a museum, create a library, and publish a monthly magazine. The organization developed rapidly, well known in the world of scholarship, with many foreign cultural historians and Oriental culture experts contributing to its archives over the years. Its present aims include standardizing the Javanese alphabet and offering courses in *Kawi* (Old Javanese), painting, sculpture, *kris*- and *batik*-making, and puppetry.

Located right next to the Sriwedari Amusement Park, the museum contains a fascinating collection of royal paraphernalia, exquisite *kris,* and Javanese crafts. Open daily (except Monday) 0800-1200, Friday until 1100; Rp100. The **City Library** right next door is open 0900-1300, Friday until 1100.

Bird market, Yogyakarta

Shopping and Crafts

Jalan Secoyudan is Solo's shopping street, known for dozens of goldsmith shops. For one of the largest collections of ancient *kris* in Indonesia, visit **Hardjonegoro**, Jl. Kratonan 101. Some of the *kris* are quite famous; expect to pay anywhere from Rp100,000 to five million *rupiah*. To see an *empu*, or *kris* smithy, in action, go to **Pauzan**, Jl. Yosoroto 28/82. A craftsman of *kris* scabbards is **R. Ng. Prodjotjendono**, Jl. Nirbitan RT 16, no. 3.

For the princely sum of Rp2500, select from a vast variety of cassette tapes at dozens of audio shops around town. A bird market, **Pasar Depok**, lies at the northwest end of Jl. Tirtoyoso near Balemkambang Sports Center. Solo's newest addition to the consumer economy is the **Purwosari Plaza**, a good place for Western items. Many boutiques, gold and shoe shops, fabrics, and a big supermarket.

Pasar Triwindu

Off Jl. Diponegoro, just north of Jl. Slamet, an easy walk from Kraton Mangkunegaran. In this flea market you'll find bric-a-brac of every description, often at prices cheaper than in Yogyakarta or Jakarta. Some prize items but a lot of worthless junk as well. Ask to see more refined items often kept under or inside the stalls. Bargain hot and heavy for everything.

Antique Shops

The best include **Eka Hartono**, Jl. Dawung Tengah 11/38; **Toko Parto Art**, Jl. Slamet Riyadi 103; and **Toko Singowidoyo**, Jl. Urip Sumoharjo (heaven for the lapidarist). On display in these dusty shops is a fascinating assortment of relics and curios of the era of Dutch colonialism—delftware, silverware, bronzes.

Other shops along Jl. Slamet Riyadi sell extremely convincing reproductions of 17th- and 18th-century Javanese furniture: herb chests, cabinets, and chairs that look so antique you'd better obtain written verification they're not to avoid problems with customs. Noteworthy also for very fine reproductions is **Mirah Delima**, Jl. Kemasan RT XI.

Wayang

For good-quality *wayang kulit*, expect to pay about Rp15,000 for small ones and Rp20,000 for those larger. Visit the workshop of **Usaha Pelajar**, Jl. Nayu Kidul north of the bus station. The hub of *wayang kulit*-making in the Solo area is **Desa Manyaran**, 35 km southwest; take a bus from Solo's *terminal bis*. Ask for the *kepala desa*, who'll take you around to view the different craftsmen. **Subandono**, Jl. Sawu 8/162, Perumnas Palur, still works in the virtually extinct form of *wayang beber*. In this, the most ancient *wayang* form, the *dalang* unrolls long illustrated scrolls while narrating the pictured tales. His office address is SMKI Konservatori, Jl. Kepathihan, tel. (0271) 2225. He asks Rp10,000-15,000 for a two-meter scroll painted on cloth; 12 scrolls form the complete *Panji* tales.

Toko Bedoyo Serimpi

For theatrical supplies and dancing costumes, visit this small shop at Temenggungan 116 on the corner of Jl. Hayam Wuruk and Jl. Ronggowarsito. A diverse collection of *wayang* accoutrements: gilt slippers for both males and females; all kinds of armlets, headbands, and bangles; different kinds of hats; splendid belts; glittery vests. A classy *batik* shop, Batik Serimpi, lies across the street.

Gamelan Workshop

In **Bekonang** village (10 km from Solo), *gamelan* instruments are made and sold: *kencong* (five in one complete set); *rebab* (two-stringed zithers), Rp40,000; big brass gongs with dragon-stands; whole sets of iron gongs (iron doesn't resonate nearly as well as brass). Browse around the workyard; play the instruments or have them played for you. Another supplier of *gamelan* instruments to the court is **Pak Sarwanto**; his family workshop is at Jl. Ngepung RT 2/RK I in Semanggi, two km southeast of town.

Batik and Textiles

Solo is a *batik*-producing center of long standing. The art form generates both revenue and local pride. Solo-style *batik* designs and the somber classical colors of indigo, brown, and cream are noticeably more traditional than Yogyakarta's. Solo is a better place to buy *batik* than Yogyakarta. Be on the lookout for *Solo malam,* a peculiar local style featuring bright colors against a black backdrop. You can take a *batik*-making course in Solo, usually offered privately in someone's house, or at Warung Baru or Relax Homestay. For traditional *batik* painting, visit **Lawiyan.** Twenty km south of Solo, the well-known weaving village of **Pedan** uses ancient motifs, producing fabric from cotton yarn and silk interwoven with golden and silver thread.

Three major producers of *batik*—Danar Hadi, Batik Semar, and Batik Keris—are based here, well-known brand names that enjoy worldwide sales. These large shops are reliable places to buy; you at least get what you pay for. You pay 10-20 percent more than when shopping in the villages, but at these shops there's a full range of quality—from a Rp5000 shirt to an exquisite Rp222,000 *batik tulis sarung.* You can visit the workshops in back; the shops accept credit cards. Traditional **Batik Semar,** Jl. R.M. Said 132, is best, with friendly and helpful people; watch the *batik* process. The more modern **Batik Keris,** Jl. Yos Sudarso 37, sells fabric and nice *ikat* work.

Centrally located **Danar Hadi Batik Shop,** Jl. Dr. Rajiman 8, is another fixed-price outlet; see the *batik* process here. Open 0800-1600, closed Sunday. Danar Hadi runs another, smaller shop on Jl. Slamet Riyadi, open 0900-1500 and 1700-2100 and on Sundays. There are over 70 other *batik* shops in Solo, many concentrated on Jl. Dr. Rajiman. On Jl. Honggowongso, find several fashion shops where you can buy T-shirts and jeans much cheaper than in Europe or the United States.

Markets and Factories

The largest *batik* and textile market in Indonesia is **Pasar Klewer** ("Hanging Market") on Jl. Secoyudan near the Susuhunan's Palace; open 0800-1600. A mad bustle of stalls offers bright *batik,* Western, and ready-made Indonesian clothes, including stunning *lurik* shirts. Unless you're trained, it's difficult to tell the difference between the extensive variety of mass-produced and fine-quality pieces. The second floor offers better *batik,* but less bargaining. Pasar Klewar doesn't have as much rubbish as Yogyakarta's big Pasar Beringhardjo.

While at Klewer buy some striking *lurik* material, one of the few natural cotton fabrics on Java. With striped, colorful patterns, *lurik* is rough to the touch, like Indian cotton, but it softens with age. Rather than buying poorly sewn ready-made clothes, employ one of Solo's thousands of tailors to sew a dress (Rp3000), shirt (Rp2000), or skirt (Rp2000).

Solo contains at least 300 *batik* factories of various sizes. Most are scattered around the southern part of the city, many others are out along Jl. Adisucipto, and several more are located on Jl. Gremet. The spot to visit is the **Keris Batik Factory** on Jl. Cemani, southwest of the tourist office. Here, in an almost preindustrial atmosphere, 100 men and women produce elaborate *batik*. A great learning experience. This fascinating factory is included with bicycle tours from Warung Baru, or take a *becak* from the tourist office for Rp1000. No direct bus service.

In the factories you can see the *batik* and *ikat*-making processes, but you can't buy material or *sarung* for a *rupiah* less than in the shops. For outstanding, elegant, and expensive *batik tulis*, visit the studio of Ibu Hartini, located behind Pasar Klewer, one of Java's most famous *batik* designers.

Sangiran

This region is known mainly in scientific circles for its extraordinary finds in the fields of paleontology, anthropology, and geology. Since 1891, when a Dutch professor found the skull of Java Man (*Pithecanthropus erectus,* now called *Homo erectus*), this area 15 km north of Solo (on the highway toward Purwodadi via Kalioso) has been the center of intense research. Many prehistoric fossils—human and animal—have been unearthed here. Most of the fossilized remains were buried under layers of fallow earth, laden with lime which helped preserve them. After heavy rains, especially, the fossils turn up in landslides. All the early hominid finds laid the foundations for theories of the earliest human life on Java 250,000 years ago.

The Plestosen Sangiran Museum is a small, unique, and well-organized museum exhibiting extinct elephant tusks; teeth and horns from extinct giant deer, antelope, and other small animals; fossilized mollusks; remnants of stegodon, oxen, rhinoceros, crocodiles, pigs, and apes; and models of *Homo erectus* craniums. Entrance Rp100. Tags identify the items in Latin and Bahasa Indonesia. Although the ape people in the diorama have Indonesian faces, in reality the humans of that time were of a completely different race. Books in the small library may be read on the premises; of special interest is the *Quaternery Geology of the Hominid Bearing Formation in Java.* Visitors can overnight in rooms on the grounds of the old museum up the road; Rp7000. Nice setting.

Candi Sukuh

This Hindu temple on the slopes of Gunung Lawu is just an hour's drive from Solo on the road to Tawangmangu. At Karangpandan, 29 km east of Solo, you'll see a sign at an intersection pointing to Candi Sukuh. The temple was built in the 15th century, late in the Hindu period and just as Islam was penetrating coastal Java. The temple was approached in ancient times by a long flight of steps. The terraced pyramids at Sukuh and nearby Ceto have been compared with the ruins of ancient Mexico and Egypt. Both are dedicated to Bima, the giant warrior god of the *Mahabharata.*

Often referred to as Java's only erotic temple, Sukuh is highly distinctive, with elements not found in other temples in Indonesia. Scholars have conjectured Sukuh was the temple of worship for a family or clan cult, and might have been used for sex education. Tourist agencies won't take you there, considering it too vulgar, and the big tour buses just can't make it up the hill. Offerings are placed on this site by the sultan of Yogyakarta each year, and the temple receives regular visits by Javanese pilgrims.

The shape of Candi Sukuh, with its steps leading to the upper part of the temple, is strikingly similar to the Mayan temples of Yucatan and Guatemala, under contruction at the same time. Walk up three grassy pyramids, passing through three gateways, each atop a flight of stairs, until you come to the main structure, a large stepped pyramid of rough-hewn stone. The temple gate is next to the *kantor,* where you register and flash the tickets you've bought in Nglorok. After, walk down to the bottom of the temple so you can climb up through the gateways. Trails behind the *pondok* lead to the misty heights of Gunung Lawu.

On the stone floor at the top of a steep stone tunnel leading into the complex, large realistic sexual organs are lovingly carved in relief. Devotees still leave flower petals here. Other symbols of love and procreation are found in and around this temple, all executed in an exuberant and unabashed style. Because of the scarcity of available light, bring a tripod or flash to capture the high-quality reliefs. The first representation of a *kris* in Indonesian art is shown in one panel: Bima forging a knife with his bare hands while using his knee as an anvil. *Wayang* clowns are carved in a heavy and gross style compared with the grace and delicacy evident on Central Javanese Hindu temples. Also see carvings of crabs, lizards, tortoises, bats, and nasty underworld creatures. Yoni and phalluses are found in reliefs that depict sexual acts and fetal growth in the womb.

Candi Ceto

Built around the same time as Candi Sukuh, this impressive terraced temple lies 28 km from Karanganyar near the small village of Kadipeso, only a one-hour hike north of Candi Sukuh. At 1,500 meters, Ceto is 600 meters higher and more northerly than Sukuh, one of the most spectacular temple locations on Java. In addition, it's been fantastically restored. Though smaller than Sukuh, the fascinating, lavishly decorated Ceto ruins contain terraces, statues, guardian figures, linga, reliefs, and a wooden *pendopo,* plus stupendous views. Almost no foreign visitors.

Two main narrow terraces make up the complex. At least some portions were built in the 15th century, at the very end of the Majapahit era. Animal themes and figures play an important role, particularly on the higher terraces. As at Sukuh, the Hindu religion was given only nominal obeisance, and it's supposed this temple too was used for fertility rituals.

Candi Ceto, central Java

East Java

A heavily populated area of 30 million people, East Java is packed with bursting cities, towns, and *kampung* along roads running ceaselessly through carefully nurtured rice and canefields. Mountain slopes are home to fruit, coffee, and tea plantations. This rural region was the site of the last powerful Javanese Hindu kingdom, the Majapahit. The island's least touristed province, East Java is more traditional and religious than Central Java; it features few plush tourist amenities, accommodations are relatively more expensive, and it's more difficult and time-consuming to travel here. But for those with the time and transportation, the area's far-flung attractions offer some unusual sidetrips through magnificent countryside. East Java is to Central Java as Mississippi is to Virginia: deep, deep Java, considerably more rural and less touched by the West.

Gua Selamangeleng

Cave hermitages, which ancient Javanese rulers and mystics used as retreats, are a curious feature of East Java not found elsewhere on the island. Sanggrahan village, southeast of Tulungagung, features rare examples of 10th-century bas-reliefs carved on the walls of a cave gouged out of solid rock. Four rooms present scenes of mountains, mysterious clouds, and burials. One of the first known versions of the *Mahabharata* epic was carved here. The story of Arjuna is also carved in an earthy style— voluptuous heavenly nymphs astride clouds descend and attempt to seduce the meditating god. From the intersection on the southeast side of Tulungagung, head south about five km to Sanggrahan. Locals will direct you to a house where you sign a guestbook, then children will take you on a one-km trail through rice fields and across a small river. Signs show the way. This cave lies in a populated area at the foot of the Wajak Mountains; use the great pinnacle of rock as a landmark. **Candi Cunkup,** the foundation of a recently excavated small temple, lies on the northeast side of Sanggrahan. Nice view.

Four km beyond the first cave, **Gua Pasir** also has scenes of Arjuna resisting temptation, though they're not as well executed. These scenes show the love life of the comic dwarves, the *panakawan*. Tragically, Gua Pasir's carvings are now nearly invisible beneath graffiti. The walk out to Gua Pasir through rural East Java is as rich an experience as the cave itself. The area around Boyolinggo village is a black- and white-magic center. In Balairejo, call in on the most renowned magician (*orang sakti*) of them all, Gipowikromo.

Panataran

Ten km north of Blitar and 80 km southwest of Malang is East Java's largest and most imposing complex of ruins. The Panataran temple group took 250 years to build, starting in the 12th century. The structures were most probably the work of the Majapahit. Three gradually rising walled courtyards are laid out on a long field; see dance-play platforms, terraces, shrines, and the same *gapura* gateways found in almost every village in East Java. Temple reliefs show the transition from three-dimensional to two-dimensional representations. The whole complex is very well maintained. Get here early to have the place all to yourself. From Blitar, take a *bemo* or minibus past Jiwut and Ngelok villages to Desa Panataran. The temple complex is down a little road surrounded by rice fields. Open 0600-1700. It's also possible to visit Panataran on a day visit from Malang if you hire a motorcycle from Duta Transport in Malang. The Sri Lestari Hotel in Blitar charges Rp21,000 for a jeep up to the temple, including a stop at Sukarno's Tomb.

One of the most striking structures is the **Naga Temple**, on the second terrace. Once used to store sacred objects, all around it are colossal carvings of protective coiled serpents carried by priests—a sight to make any medieval thief shudder. On the base are reliefs of animal tales. Panataran was constructed more for the commoner than the Brahman. The bathing place southeast of the main temple, built in 1415, shows flying tortoises, the bull and the crocodile fable, winged snakes, and a lion plowing a field. Reliefs also depict Indian Tantric tales, the Eastern equivalent of *Aesop's Fables*. You'll find another bathing place on the road between Ngelok and Panataran. Go through the village toward the complex; around the corner on the left by a river, just before the bridge, is a bathing temple with live spouts. Villagers still use this 16th-century structure for washing clothes and bathing.

MALANG

One of Java's most pleasant and attractive provincial towns. Located in the mountains 90 km south of Surabaya, Malang is a city of well-planned parks, a huge central market, big villas, wide clean streets, abundant trees, and old Dutch architecture. The city was established in the late 18th century as a coffee-growing center and today is known as Kota Pesiar, the resort city. Here it's always spring: Malang is noticeably cooler than other parts of East Java. Seldom does the temperature rise higher than 24 degrees C. With an elevation of 450 meters, it can still get hot during the day, yet the nights are perfect. Although Malang can't compare culturally with a city like Yogyakarta, between the 10th and 15th centuries it was the center of an area of great Hindu kingdoms, and today the surrounding countryside is dotted with well-preserved temples. Buses leave for Malang from Surabaya constantly, Rp1500, 1.5 hours.

The **Djamek Mosque** and the **Protestant Church**, beside one another on Jl. Merdeka Barat, were both founded in the early 1800s. A well-known Chinese temple, **En An Kiong**, is worth visiting. A Balinese temple, **Pura Hindu Bali**, is out of town in Desa Lesanpuro Kedungkandang. The **Malang City Tourist Office** (Baparda) is beside the Balai Kota on Jl. Tugu; open 0700-1400, Friday and Saturday until 1100.

Temples Near Malang

Malang is the best base for visiting East Java's astonishingly rich Hindu ruins. Allow at least a week. Chronologically, the sequence is: Candi Badut, 9th century; Candi Gunung Gangsir, 10th century; Candi Kidal, 13th century; Candi Jago, 13th century; Candi Jawi, 14th century; and Candi Singosari, 14th century. If you want to center yourself outside Malang, try **Pondok Wisata**, in the village Desa Tulis Sayu, near Jago and Kidal. This pleasant religious retreat for Chinese Christians offers room and board for Rp15,000 pp. Rent motorcycles in Malang from Duta Transport on Jl. Majapahit. If you go by *bemo* or minibus, allow more time. Catch a *bemo* from Arjosari bus terminal to Blimbing, a northern suburb of Malang.

Candi Singosari

Ten km north of Malang is the town of Singosari; the local name is Candi Linggo. Dating from the 13th century, this Shiva shrine is the most imposing monument remaining of the murderous Singosari dynasty. It was built to honor King Kartanegara and his priests, killed in a palace revolt. This monarch and his cohorts were the same folks who mortified Kublai Khan's emissaries by cutting off their noses and tattooing "NO!" across their foreheads, an act that precipitated the launching of 1,000 Mongol troop ships against Java in 1293. Candi Singosari's unique feature is its base, serving also as the central *cella* or inner sanctum of the temple. Thus it's called a "cellar-temple" or "tower-temple" by archaeologists. From Arjosari, it's Rp400 by minibus to Singosari village. At the intersection in the northern fringe of town, near where the *bemo* stops, turn west down Jl. Kartenegara next to Bioskop Garuda; the temple is about 600 meters down the road on the right. Ask directions.

Candi Sumberawan

From Candi Singosari, go toward the guardian statues, then turn right down a country road and head northwest for six km until you reach Sumberawan village. Turn right, head up the dirt road about 300 meters, and turn right on a narrow track. You'll probably need a guide, as the narrow trail is unmarked and almost impossible to find. Ask for the gate key if you want to go right up to the stupa, which is about 300 meters further on a trail through rice paddies and across the dam. Spectacular scenery.

Candi Jawi

Candi Jago

Eighteen km east of Malang, Candi Jago is a memorial to the Singosari king Vishnu-vardhana. At Arjosari catch a minibus or *bemo* to Tumpang. About 100 meters before Tumpang's *pasar,* 150 meters down a side road to the left, is Candi Jago. Look for the signpost. Although the temple's roof and body have caved in, it's still one of the most attractive and remarkable temples of the period. Candi Jago dates from the late 13th century, yet has distinct connections with the prehistoric monuments and terraced sanctuaries in Java's mountains.

The monument incorporates Buddhist sculptures, Krishna reliefs, Arjuna's fretful night in his hermitage, earthy scenes from everyday life, and some early and grotesque *panakawan* carvings. See clearly the shift towards two-dimensional figures during this tumultuous dynasty. *Wayang*-like "moving picture" sculptures are placed right next to one another, like figures in stiff parade; the action unfolds counter-clockwise. Temple reliefs are bolder, more vigorous than any earlier style—change was definitely taking place. Jago's gatekeeper will provide a handout about the reliefs with explanations in English. The Sumberwringin watering place is nearby.

Candi Kidal

Kidal village is five km southwest of Tumpang (catch a minibus from Tumpang market). On the far side of the village, you'll see the sign for the temple. This small but lovely sanctuary is an architectural jewel, a nearly perfect example of Singosari temple art. Next to a papaya grove is the richly carved 13th century *candi*—a 12.5-meter-tall burial temple honoring a Singosari king. The recently renovated structure appears quite slender since the base towers up so high, the temple tapering at the top to form a pyramid. To the left of the steps are well-crafted episodes of Garuda carrying the nectar of immortality. Kidal also offers elaborate carvings of medallions and *kala*-heads on the main body, with statues of Garuda guarding the base. There used to be a tunnel beneath the temple leading all the way to Candi Singosari. From Candi Kidal, continue on the road clockwise back to Malang; fabulous scenery.

Mojokerto

Forty-two km southwest of Surabaya. Sukarno attended Dutch primary school here; at that time in the 1920s, it was a very small town. Visit the important **Museum Pur-bakala;** from the south side of the *alun-alun,* head east along Jl. A. Yani to the museum (no. 14), next to *kantor kabupaten.*1 Open 0700-1400, Friday till 1300, Sunday closed. Leave a donation. A magnificent sculptural group of Vishnu carried on the back of Garuda is the centerpiece of a fascinating series of reliefs around the main room. Also known as the Airlangga Statue, one theory holds that the Vishnu figure is a representation of King Airlangga. Taken from the Belahan Bathing Place near Trawas, this piece was probably carved as early as the 11th century. The museum is filled with many other lifelike statues, relics, carved stoned reliefs of daily scenes, and umpteen plaques covered with ancient writing. Afterwards, wander through the original quarter of town with its fine old Dutch houses.

Trowulan

This small agricultural community was once the capital of the mighty Majapahit Empire which, under the ruthless Gajah Mada, controlled most of the archipelago in the 14th century. This ancient capital and major trade center was once completely surrounded by a high brick wall enclosing pools, palaces, playing fields, plazas, and temples. Today, remains lie scattered over a 15-square-km area. Impressively, all the temples were made from brick, with no stonework, granite, or sandstone. All have lost their centerpieces, either to thieves or museums.

Trowulan is 12 km and Rp600 by minibus southwest of Mojokerto, and a 1.5-hour (Rp2000, 60 km) bus ride southwest of Surabaya. Take a bus from Surabaya heading for Mojokerto and Jombang. Ask to get off at the main intersection, which heads to the museum. If coming from Jombang, go to Mojoagung first, then take a minibus to Trowulan. Start your tour from the **Museum Purbakala**. This large, new, well-lit museum is renowned for its remarkable collection of terra-cotta figurines, toys, clay masks, bronze statues, and priestly accoutrements. A superb collection of statues and photographs of ancient sites in East Java is located just behind the museum; don't miss it. The interior collection is a museum of fragments; use your imagination. Open Tues.-Thurs. 0700-1400, Saturday until 1200, Sunday until 1400, Friday until 1100, Monday closed.

You need only good footwear and an adventurous spirit to tour the temples, graves, and gateways. Allow one day. Leave your pack in the souvenir shop at the museum. Follow the museum's tabletop map for directions. Spending 15-20 minutes at each site, looking and resting, it'll take six hours walking or two to three hours by *becak*. When hiring a *becak*, try for the *tur komplet* for Rp8000-10,000, a better deal than visiting a site at a time. **Pendopo Agung** is a restful midpoint between the museum and Candi Bajang Ratu, built by the Indonesian army during a wave of tourist development as an exact reproduction of the 14th-century pavilions traditionally built in front of Majapahit nobles' residences. **Waringan Lawang**, three km from the museum, east of the highway, is a split gateway which once led toward the palace of Gajah Mada. **Bajang Ratu** hardly looks like a temple; it's well maintained and appears quite new even after almost six centuries. Though the best preserved of all the temples, all that's left of the Bajang Ratu compound is a doorway and a bit of the outer walls. Five hundred meters southeast of Bajang Ratu is **Candi Tikus**, once a splendid bathing place with terraces, turrets, and spouts along the walls of the now-dry basin. Two km south of the museum is the cemetery of **Makam Troloyo**, containing possibly the oldest Muslim grave on Java, dating from 1376.

SURABAYA

The melodious name belies the city's true nature—hot, dirty, and noisy, an industrial hub on Java's swampy northeast coast. This is East Java's biggest metropolis as well as its provincial capital. Extending over 300 square km and supporting a population of 3.6 million, Surabaya is the country's second largest city, a modern center for manufacturing, agriculture, and trade, its bustle and din in sharp contrast to the serene agrarian countryside around it. Travelers use Surabaya as a stopover between Bali and Yogyakarta or Jakarta. Surabaya is the main base for the Indonesian navy; for hundreds of years it's been one of Indonesia's most important ports, its facilities second only to Jakarta's. This is also an active center for theater and East Javanese dance forms such as the mesmerizing horse trance dance, *kuda kepang*.

Historical Sights

In the heart of the hotel district is the Buddhist stone statue, **Joko Dolog** ("Fat Boy"), a remnant of the Singosari dynasty. Joko Dolog depicts the great King Kartanegara seated on a pedestal, inscribed 1289. The statue was transferred to this spot from its site near Malang by the Dutch about 300 years ago. Bring flowers and a few *rupiah*. Grahadi, the former residence of the Dutch governors, functions nowadays as the official residence of East Java's governor. Another historic building is the **Hotel Majapahit**; see the old photos in the lobby. Another colorful neighborhood is **Kampung Sasak**. With its winding narrow streets, women in lace shawls, and crumbling old Dutch warehouses, this area offers a good dash of Middle Eastern flavor.

Museums

North of the zoo, at Jl. Taman Mayangkara Mpu 6, is the small ethnographic museum **MPU Tantular**; open daily 0700-0200, Friday to 1100, Saturday to 1230. It houses mesolithic farming tools, Majapahit statuary, Koranic manuscripts, *wayang*, photos of old Surabaya, and a very good paper money collection. Take bus P1 or any C bus on Jl. Pemuda. There's also the inevitable army museum, **Museum Angkatan '45**, containing relics from the war of independence, but it's a long way out on Jl. May. Jen. Sungkono. It might interest Dutch visitors to visit the **Kalibanteng** and **Kembang Kuning** cemeteries, where many of their fellow countrymen have been laid to rest.

Surabaya Zoo

Take a *bemo* or bus (P1 or any C) down Jl. P. Sudirman Kebun Binatang (zoo), just north of the Joyoboyo Bus Station. Open daily 0730-1700; Rp1000 entrance. This is one of the most complete, largest, and oldest zoos in all of Southeast Asia. Unfortunately, the animals are kept in small, dirty cages under terrible conditions. The zoo specializes in exotic birds and nocturnal animals. The Dolphinarium features

Surabaya

J a v a   S e a

N

Tanjung Perak (ferries to Madura)

NILAM TIMUR
NILAM BARAT
TANJUNG PRUIK
PRAPAT KURUNG UTARA
TEL. BAYUR
TANJUNG PERAK BARAT/ TIMUR
KARANG
TEMBOK
BANTENG
BULAK
WONOKUSOMO

To Gresik

GRESIK

KEBALEN TIMUR
KALIMAS BARAT
Ampel Mosque
PEGIRIAN
KERTO PATEN

To Kenjeran Beach

Jembatan Merah Station
RAJAWALI
INDERAPURA
Central Post Office
KAPASAN
Grave of W.R. Supratman

REMBANG
DEMAK
Pelni Office
Governor's Office
Semut Train Station
KAPASARI
KENJERAN
ASEN

DUPAK
Pasar Turi Train Station
P. BESAR W
JAGALAN
KALI NGAGLIK
Kapas Krampang

Grave of Dr. Soetomo
TUJUNGAN
JL. KH. W. AHW
THR and Taman Remaja
Gelora 10 November Stadium
KABANG

KALIBUTUH
Wijaya Shopping Centre
KRANGGAN
AD JAIS
BENGAN
PACAR KEMBANG
KALI KEPITING

Baluran Night Market
PASAR
GENTENG
Tanjungan Shopping Centre
Mayor's Office
WALIKOTA
KEDUNG TARUKAN
KALI WARON

Telephone and Telegraph Office
RAYA ARJUNA
BASUKI
JL. PEMUDA
Bamboo Den
Gubeng Train Station
DHARMAHUSADA

To Tandas

Statue of Joko Dolog
RACHMAT
JL. SUDARSO
RRI (Jl. Pemuda)
Flower Market
Airlangga University

BANYUURIP
KEMBANG KEPUNDONGDORO BALURAN
Hyatt Regency
Antique Shops
JL. KAYOON
Remaja Hotel
DARMA WANGSA
KERTAJAYA

PUTAT
GIRILAYA
BANURIP
WETAN
Pasar Keputran
JL. SUMATRA
Post Office (Jl. Darmo)

DUKUH KUPANG
RA. KARTINI
JL. RAYA DARMO HARJO
Catholic Cathedral (Geraja Katolik)
PUCANOM TIMUR
KALIBOKOR
SELATAN

Taman Tirta Swimming Pool
Musium Ankatan '45
JL. DIPONEGORO
Altea
Hotel Mirama
French Consulate
JAYA SELATAN

JL. MAY. JEN. SUNGKONO
Zoo
Museum MPU Tantular
KENCANA NGAGEL
Restaurant Delby

0   .05 mi

0   .05 km
Joyoboyo Bus Station
NGAGEL REJO KD. BRATANG
Bratang Bus Station
GEDE BARATA JAYA

↙ To Mojokerto
↓ To Malang and Airport Juanda

© The Guidebook Company Ltd

freshwater Mahakam River dolphins from Borneo, sadly cramped in a tiny pool. The hoofed and ruminant enclosures contain the rare Chinese *wapiti,* the *babirusa,* and the *anoa* (dwarf buffalo). Eighteen Komodo dragons devour raw meat in a sandbed enclosure.

Entertainment
On Jl. Kusuma Bangsa, north of Gubeng train station. For purely mindless entertainment, **THR (Surabaya Mall)** is one of the best Taman Hiburan Rakyat parks in Indonesia. Open daily 1800-2400, and not all that crowded. THR features souvenir stands, clothes boutiques, cassette stores, movie theaters, band amphitheater, small train, and Ferris wheels and other carnival rides. Directly to your right inside the entrance are various *warung;* deeper in are ice cream shops, small, fine restaurants, and numerous foodstalls. THR is also a venue for folk performances: *sri mulat* (Javanese comic drama), *ludruk,* and regular performances of *wayang wong* and other open-stage dramas.

Shopping
The city is known, however, for its Chinese and Javanese tailors, who'll cut you a pair of made-to-measure trousers in an hour or so for only Rp15,000. Visit the "Street of a Thousand Tailors," Jl. Embong Malang; *becak* drivers know the location. You'll find **Batik Semar** at Jl. Raya Gubeng 41 at Toko Metro; **Batik Keris** in Toko Sarinah at Jl. Tunjungan 7; and **Rumah Batik Danar Hadi** at Jl. Pemuda 1 near the Simpang Hotel. Besides these big chains, Indonesian fabrics and *batik,* as well as fine jewelry and Javanese artifacts, are displayed at **PT Santi Art Shop,** Jl. Sumatera 52, and **Mirota,** Jl. Sulawesi 24. **Pasar Tunjungan Surya** on Jl. Tunjungan is the place to go for East Javanese handicrafts. The government runs a showroom, **Dinas Perindustrian Jatim,** at Jl. Kedungdoro 86-90; reasonable prices. There are crafts exhibits at least once a month at the **Balai Pemuda** near Mitro Cinema; stalls represent nearly every district of East Java. The **GKBI** *batik* cooperative at Jl. Kranggan 102 is also worth a visit. Some outstanding Indian textile shops lie along Jl. Panggung and Jl. Sasak in the Arab Quarter around Mesjid Ampel.

A whole row of small antique and curio shops lies near the Hyatt on Jl. Basuki Rakhmat and along Jl. Urip Sumoharjo. On Jl. Raya Darmo you'll find **Rokhim** (no. 27) and **Whisnu** (no. 68-74). Good hunting also along Jl. Tunjungan; try **Sarinah** (no. 7) for paintings, silver, and brasswork; and **Kundandas** (no. 97, tel. 43927), for statues, embroidery, and shell handicrafts. The **Bali Art Shop,** Jl. Basuki Rakhmat 143, tel. 45933, opposite the Hyatt, offers a large selection of Chinese porcelain and uncut agate. **Rais Art Shop,** at no. 16 on the same street, near the Hyatt Regency, features other unique antiques.

Tunjungan Plaza, the city's premier shopping center, is Surabaya's Ginza. Walk down the main street, Jl. Tunjungan, an extension of Jl. Basuki Rakhmat, and follow the bright lights. This pretty, colorful area that doesn't shut down until around 2100. An area especially strong on consumer goods such as cameras, sound systems, cassette recorders, and other electronic gadgets.

Markets

A black market behind the zoo sells shoes, jeans, T-shirts, and other cheap goods. **Pasar Keputran**, Surabaya's main night market, livens up around 1900 and is positively chaotic by 2300. The walk to Pasar Keputran is very enjoyable: proceed to the main junction of Jl. Pemuda and Jl. Kayoon and walk one km south. Another big market is **Pasar Pabean**, a dirty, sprawling spot in Chinatown. Worth a visit for the color and clamor and bustle. **Kayoon Flower Market**, along Jl. Kayoon on the banks of Kalimas River, is a park for strollers and lovers. The market sprouted spontaneously after flower hawkers were thrown off public roads in 1960. Here you'll find a variety of tropical shrubs and trees, as well as fresh- and saltwater fish for home aquariums. South of the flower stalls is an active open-air food market. Another flower and bird market is located near Terminal Bratang on Jl. Barat Jaya.

Services

The **East Java Regional Tourist Information Office** (Kantor Penerangan Pariwisata), Jl. Pemuda 118, tel. (031) 472-503, is very helpful; get maps and brochures, and ask for the booklet *Events of East Java.* Inquire after the Madura bull races. The **central post office**, Jl. Kebon Rojo next to Tugu Pahlawan, is open weekdays 0800-1600, Saturday 0800-1230; several telex booths for rent. A more convenient branch is located on Jl. Pemuda, just before the Joko Dolok statue. All packages must be inspected, so leave the contents visible. The **telephone office** (*kantor telpon*) in Tunjungan Plaza offers direct dialing to key cities in Indonesia and the world. *kantor imigrasi*, Jl. Achmad Yani (seven km south of downtown), is open Mon.-Thurs. 0800-1400, Friday 0830-1030, Saturday 0800-1200. The Surabaya telephone city code is 031.

MADURA

An undiscovered gem, this beautiful rugged island is one of the poorest parts of the province. Yet it's blessed with numerous fine white-sand beaches, unpeopled countryside, inexpensive and uncrowded *losmen,* and unique cuisine. Although only 30 minutes from Surabaya by ferry, Madura is almost totally free of tourists. The island is worth more than just a day-trip. Madura is famous for three things: women, salt, and bull races. Some of the best stockbreeders in Indonesia live here. Crowded farmers' festivals, held frequently in special arenas all over the island, attract visitors from around the world. The best day to visit Madura is Sunday, market day.

Madurese craftsmen were inspired by Chinese and European imports, and the island is perhaps best known for its fine beds, screens, chests, and cupboards. Also look for *tempet kue,* three-legged bamboo containers used to store cakes; buy one in the morning *pasar* for Rp1200. Madura *batik* uses rich, bold *mengkudu* red, red-brown, or indigo coloring, incorporating vigorous winged *naga,* sharks, airborne horses with fish tails, and other strange aquatic animal representations. Visit the *batik*-making center, **Tanjung Bumi**, about five km from Bangkalan. In **Telaga Biru**, a ship-building village 15 km west of Ketapang, women draw *batik* designs on cotton cloth loomed at home. Fantastically gnarled, lucky seaweed (black coral) bracelets are also fashioned on Madura. Worn to ward off sickness, these amulets are believed to cure rheumatism.

Madura's capital, Pamekasan, is a slow-moving city, very easygoing, quiet, and undeveloped. The town center is lined with casuarina trees. Bullraces, or *kerapan sapi,* are held in a field about one km from city center. Textiles are quite reasonable here: a 2.5-meter piece of Madurese fabric bought in Pamekasan for Rp15,000 sells for up to Rp100,000 in Jakarta.

Remote Sumenep, 53 km northeast of Pamekasan, is sleepy, rural, almost a village. In the 13th century, Sumenep was an established regency of the Singosari kingdom; the first governor was crowned by King Kartanegara himself. This makes Sumenep one of the oldest *kabupaten* in Indonesia. The *alun-alun* is in the center of town, surrounded by the *kraton,* main mosque, government buildings, and markets.

Mustika Kempang, Jl. Trunojoyo 78, specializes in Madurese-style *batik.* Delftware, old Chinese pottery, furniture, *kris,* and all manner of antique jewelry are on display at the **A. Ba'bud Shop,** Jl. A. Yani, run by an Arab who specializes in *batik.* Eddy, the proprietor of **17 Augustus**, sells old Madurese *batik* and *wayang topeng* masks.

Air Mata

Madura's oldest and most beautiful cemetery sits on a hill near Arasbaya. Its name means "Water of the Eye," or tears. Coming from Ketapang, right after the bridge when you first enter Arasbaya, take a left-hand turn. The minibus driver will drop you off here, or perhaps turn in. About two km down the road is an intersection where you can board another minibus to take you to a little *desa* called Tampegan. If you arrive in Tampegan in the morning, you'll find *dokar* for people going to the market; to Air Mata it's Rp300. Walking is recommended. Within the actual burial compound, you'll be stunned by the vast complex of very old graves. You can easily spend an hour at Air Mata, worth the entrance fee for the tranquility alone. Leave a donation.

Making Conversation

At our first Lebaran party with the University Women's Club Coral was introduced to a youngish, heavy-jawed man in glasses and a lounge suit, whose name she did not catch.

"Are you working at the University?" she asked conventionally.

"Not exactly," he replied.

"But are you connected with it?"

"In a way."

"Do you live in Jogja?"

"Part of the time."

"Have you managed to find a house?" (Houses were rather on our mind at that time.)

"Yes, I have one."

"Do you have to share it?"

"Well, a number of people live there."

The going was distinctly heavy and Coral took the first excuse to leave him. As she reported to me her encounter with this weighty gentleman, a friend sitting beside us gave an exclamation.

"Do you mean the person you were talking to in the passage just now?"

"Yes, who is he?"

"But that's the Sultan!"

Hastily Coral went back, taking me with her, to make her apologies. The Sultan, far from being offended, had been amused. He spoke excellent English and had, he told us, spent two months at a tutoring establishment in Rottingdean, as well as visiting London with an Indonesian students' dance group, which performed at the Queen's Hall in 1936 on behalf of the Chinese Red Cross. He preferred Rottingdean, as it was quieter and he was himself an outdoor type of man.

In this informal manner we first met Kandjeng Sultan Hamengku Buwono Senapati Ing Ngalogo Ngabdulrachman Sajidin Panatagama Kalifah Allah Ingkang Djumeneng Nata Kading IX Ing Ngajogjakarta Hadiningrat, usually called simply Hamengku Buwono IX.

~ Harold Forster, Flowering Lotus, *1958*

MOUNT BROMO

The most popular of all of East Java's travel destinations, this active 2,392-meter-high volcano lies 112 km southeast of Surabaya. The caldera is like a vast, arid amphitheater enclosed by perpendicular walls 350 meters high. This awesome, 2,200-meter-high "sand sea" contains three mountains: Widodaren ("Bride"), Batok ("Cup"), and Bromo ("Fire"), all within one huge crater, the Bromo-Semeru Massif. There are three small crater lakes inside the larger crater, with waterfowl and excellent hiking.

The ideal time to visit is in the dry season (April-Nov.) when you have a better chance of seeing a blood-red sunrise. In the wet, you may as well sleep late and stroll across the sand sea during the warmer part of the day, after the heavy fog has blown away. The temperature on top of Bromo is around 5 C; in July it can drop to zero, so dress warmly. Three times a year the site is overrun by tourists: when an annual festival takes place, over Christmas, and during July and August.

The whole crater, it is said, was dug out by an ogre using half a coconut shell. He performed this Herculean task in a single night, to win the hand of a princess. When the king feared the ogre would succeed, he ordered his servants to pound rice, at which time the cocks started crowing, thinking dawn had come. The ogre couldn't finish the job, and died of grief and exhaustion.

No matter how much you've heard about Mt. Bromo, you won't be prepared for this ethereal, unforgettable spectacle. From Bromo's peak are stunning views of active Gunung Semeru, Java's highest mountain. Although Bromo can still vent steam and ash, smoke profusely, and occasionally boom from the central crater, it has not spewed lava in historical times.

From Surabaya's Purabaya bus terminal ride a bus 2.5-3 hours (Rp2000, 93 km) to the turnoff to Bromo. Unless you're arriving late at night, there's no reason to stop in Probolinggo. Leave Surabaya early so you can make it to Ngadisari, below Bromo, the same day. From the Bromo turnoff to Ngadisari it's Rp2000-2500 by minibus, two hours, leaving every hour or so until 1800. You might have to change buses at Sukapura. The turnoff to Bromo is five km west of Probolinggo on the main highway between Surabaya and Banyuwangi. From Ngadisari to Cemoro Lawang, walk, catch a truck, or take a horse to the rim.

The ascent to the Bromo crater from Cemoro Lawang takes about two hours by foot or 1.5 hours by horseback. For the sunrise, walk down the wall of the big crater so as to arrive on Bromo's narrow rim by daybreak. Take a flashlight. Your motel will wake you up at 0300; you'll hear all the commotion, with horses whinnying outside. Although guides can be arranged in Ngadisari, it's really easy to walk to Bromo without one—just fall in behind the tourists. It costs about Rp5000 to hire a horse. At the top of a rise you'll see a steep 256-step concrete staircase up to the rim. It's possible to walk all the way around the rim, but it's precarious in places and very dusty. You can climb right down inside Bromo's crater, but if you fall into its maw, that's it. After

The smoky granduer of Gunung Bromo

sunrise, you might walk over to the newly constructed Balinese-style temple and then continue around Gunung Batok. A jeep trail heads to the caldera wall, where a paved road zigzags at impossible inclines up to a viewpoint. Superb panoramas. The road splits at the viewpoint, down to the town of Tosari or up to the summit of Gunung Penanjakan.

BALURAN

The entrance to this 250-square-km reserve in the northeast corner of Java is Batangan, just north of Wonorejo, 37 km north of Banyuwangi. The park headquarters at Bekol is 12 km from the main Surabaya-Banyuwangi coastal road. A reserve since Dutch times, a national park only in 1980, Baluran is one of Indonesia's most accessible game parks. Little-known Baluran encompasses a mountainous area which gives way to open forests, scrubland, and white-sand beaches washed by the Bali Straits. Baluran features coastal marshes, open rolling savannah, swampy groves, crab-eating monkeys, and grasslands with huge wild oxen. This is Java's one bit of Africa. There's a campground near the entrance to the park. At the foot of the hill in Bekol, 12 km from the park entrance at Batangan, is a comfortable, modest *pasanggrahan* belonging to the PHPA (Forest Service); capacity 14 people. Rooms cost Rp4000-10,000. No electricity, just lamps and candles. Friendly staff. There's a guard at all times, so your gear is safe. In the early morning you'll be awakened by the strident calls of peafowl and jungle fowl. Plenty of water and cooking facilities, but no meals available. Wear good shoes and bring food, binoculars, and a flashlight.

Baluran is the best place on Java to see a wide variety of wild animals. With its high grasses, flat-topped acacias, dried-out water courses, and herds of animals grazing peacefully, this reserve is strikingly similar to East Africa's famous game parks. Climb up through the mahogany and teakwood forests or tramp across the open grasslands bordering the Madura Strait. You can approach as close as 50 meters to herds of wild buffalos. There are also wild dogs, deer (groups of 30 or more are common), leopards, civet cats, squirrels, fruit bats, macaques, leaf monkeys in the upland forests, and monitor lizards. See wild pigs thunder across savannahs of acacia trees, and a plethora of such birds as green jungle fowl (*ayam hutan*), prancing peacocks (*burung merak*), drongos, and kingfishers. It's not wise to venture out of the jeep or off well-trodden tracks.

THE MERU BETIRI RESERVE

One of the most important reserves on Java. Established in 1972, this 50,000-hectare game park lies on the rugged southeast coast where thickly wooded hills rise steeply to over 1,000 meters. The World Wildlife Fund assisted Indonesia's Forestry Service in drawing up a management plan for the relatively new reserve. To explore, you must be accompanied by a PHPA officer or local guide. A newly built observation tower rises from a cleared savannah. Though best known as the last refuge of the now-extinct Javan tiger, Meru Betiri is also of considerable botanical importance as one of Java's few remaining areas of relatively undisturbed primal montane forest. It's the only known habitat of two of the island's endemic plant species, the *Rafflesia zollingeriana* and *Balanphora fungosa*.

The reserve's two highest peaks, Gunung Betiri and Gunung Tajem, create a sort of rain pocket; this makes the reserve wetter than surrounding areas and accounts for the unbelievably thick jungles. There are even enclaves of true natural rainforests —almost the last on Java—ranging in elevation from sea level to the peak of Betiri.

A comfortable PHPA resthouse, **Taman Rekreasi**, provides food and lodging at Rajegwesi, a small fishing village on a bay within the reserve, about two hours by road from the Sukamade Baru Estate. You can order meals in advance. Another resthouse, closer to the turtle nesting beach, is **Wisma Sukamade** in the Sukamade Baru Estate.

The steep, densely wooded hills of Meru Betiri provided the final stronghold for the indigenous Javan tiger (*harimau macan jawa*), which once inhabited the hilly eastern boundary of the estate. A 1978 study revealed that five or six still survived, but the tigers are now believed extinct. Human interference was the major reason; plantations took over the tigers' traditional valley habitat. Sleek long-bodied panthers (*macan tutul*), pigs, *muncak*, rabbits, squirrels, civets, leopards, black and silverleaf monkeys, and the long-tailed macaque also inhabit the reserve. Sea and shore birds are common. Two species of hornbills (wreathed and the smaller pied hornbill) and egrets and terns are seen most often. Most of the government's conservation efforts are concentrated on the sea-turtle nesting beaches where, in the right season, five species of turtle (green, loggerhead, hawksbill, Pacific ridley, and the leatherback) arrive to lay their leathery, golfball-sized eggs.

Bali

Introduction

This tiny island of nearly three million Bali Hindus, surrounded by a sea of nearly 180 million Muslims, is just a few km from the far eastern tip of Java. When the first Dutch war-yacht pulled into Bali on 22 February 1597, they found a heaven on earth. Bali was really put on the map back in the 1930s when several popular documentaries were made of this paradise-like island. Then the world knew, and Bali has been degenerating into a tourist colony for well-night 60 years now—an Isle of Capri of the Western Pacific. Once known as "Anthropology's Shakespeare," Bali's unbelievably complex and durable social and religious fabric is now finally breaking down under the foreign onslaught.

Big-business tourism has been foisted upon the Balinese by the international consortiums that build hotels and megaresorts—most recently at Tanah Lot—without the consent or consultation of local residents. Most of the money earned by these swank hotels is siphoned back to Java or overseas. Fortunately, the law prohibiting building any structure higher than a palm tree has saved the island, otherwise developers would have taken over completely. Although Bali is only 135 km long by 90 km at its widest, you can still get as lost as you want. There are hundreds of villages that haven't changed in 50 years. You don't need directions; just head for the hills. The best things are still free: orange and gold tropical sunsets, an astoundingly rich culture, the smiles of the children, the sound of the palms, the talcum-powder beaches and coral dive sites. You can still get into temple dances and tourist sites free, and live well for about Rp31,500 a day or less.

Bali is one big sculpture. Every earthen step is manicured and polished, every field and niche carved by hand. The surface of the island is marked by deep ravines, fast-flowing rivers, and, in northern Bali, a west-to-east volcanic chain 1,500-3,000 meters high, an extension of Java's central range. On the plains of southern Bali you see rice fields exquisitely carved out of hills and valleys, sparkling with water or vividly green.

In southern Bali, besides rice, crops of tea, cacao, groundnuts, and tropical fruits flourish. As you head north, the landscape changes from tiers of rice fields to gardens of onions, cabbages, and papayas. Thatched palm huts give way to sturdy cottages made of wood, tile, stone, and volcanic rock. In the higher altitudes you find mountain streams, prehistoric ferns, wildflowers, creepers, orchids, leeches, butterflies, birds, and screaming monkeys. Bali's western tip, Pulaki, is the island's unspoiled, uninhabited wilderness. Legend has it Bali's first inhabitants originated here in a lost, invisible city.

Amandari, Ubud, Bali

HISTORY

Bali is a living museum of the old Indo-Javanese civilization that flourished on East Java over 400 years ago. Prior to 1815 Bali had a greater population density than Java, suggesting its Bali-Hindu civilization was even more successful than Java's. Majapahit refugees were not the first to bring Hinduism to Bali; Indian culture was present in parts of the island as early as the 9th century, and Balinese writing is derived from the Palava script of southern India. Bali today provides scholars with clues about India's past religious history in old sacred texts that have vanished in India itself.

When Gajah Mada of Java's Majapahit Empire conquered Bali in the mid-14th century, East Javanese influences spread from the purely religious and cultural spheres into fine art, dancing, sculpture, and architecture. When that empire fell in the 16th century under pressure from Islamic military and economic invasion, there was a mass migration of Java's Majapahit scholars, dancers, and rulers to Bali. Priests took their sacred books and mythical records, and on Bali they developed unique Bali-Hindu customs and institutions. But Hinduism is only the veneer; the Hindu practices of the new masters were merely superimposed on the deeply rooted aboriginal animism of the Balinese natives, who cling to beliefs dating back to the Bronze Age.

In the early 19th century, Bali's sole export was its highly prized slaves; its imports were gold, rubies, and opium. The island remained obscure for so long because of its lack of spices, precious metals, or aromatic woods, and because of its steep cliffs rising from the sea, deep straits with treacherous tidal currents, and encircling reefs. Surprisingly, the fertile, lava-rich lowlands of Bali were among the last areas occupied by the Dutch and only came under their colonial rule following prolonged resistance.

When a wrecked cargo ship off the south coast was looted by the Balinese at the turn of this century (a traditional practice of island peoples), the Dutch used the incident as a pretext to control the island. One sunny morning in 1906 in Puputan Square, Denpasar, Hindu princes and their families, wearing splendid ceremonial costumes and waving priceless *kris*, charged deliberately into Dutch rifles. This mass suicide (*puputan*), and another two years later in Klungkung, resulted in the annihilation of Bali's most powerful and highest ranking royal families.

The Dutch now held control over the entire island and the glorious Bali-Hindu theater-state, so jealously guarded and preserved for more than a thousand years, came to a bitter end. The *puputan* is commemorated today with a plaque in front of the Bali Museum in Denpasar depicting men, women, and children marching to their deaths.

THE PEOPLE

The Balinese are small, handsome people with round, delicate features, long sweeping eyelashes, and heart-shaped lips. Their cults, customs, and worship of god and nature are animist, their music warm-blooded, their art as extravagant as their nature. Culturally, the Javanese lean more toward refinement and modesty, keeping themselves in check in life and art, while the Balinese prefer the headier, flashier sensations—laughs, terror, spicier and sweeter foods. They're more lavish and baroque in their colors and decorations; they like explosive music and fast, jerky dancing.

Today there's still a distinction between the *wong majapahit,* descendants of 16th-century migrants of East Java's fallen Majapahit Empire, and the Bali Aga, the original inhabitants of the island who retreated into the mountains where they're found to this day, hostile to outsiders. Among the Hinduized Balinese, the three classical Hindu castes are indicated by surnames: the Brahmans with the title Ida Bagus; the Satria with the titles Anak Agung and Cokorda; and the Vaishyas with the title Gusti. Nearly every village has a *puri,* the elaborate residence of a Satria, and a *geria,* the residence of a Brahman. The Bali Aga are Sudra, or casteless, though no Balinese is considered untouchable.

Ninety percent of Bali's population practice Bali-Hinduism. There's also a sprinkling of Muslims in the coastal towns, Buddhists in the mountains, and Christians everywhere. Several thousand Arabs and Indians, many of them hoteliers and textile dealers, live in Denpasar. Some 25,000 Chinese live in the main trading centers of Denpasar, Singaraja, and Amlapura, running the majority of the small retail businesses and restaurants, plus there are around 25,000 resident foreigners.

RELIGION

Outside of India, Bali is the largest Hindu outpost in the world. Put in another way, it's the furthest reaches of the Hindu empire. On Bali Hinduism has developed along lines all its own. In fact, the way in which the Balinese practice their frontier Hinduism is still their greatest art.

Hinduism is at least 3,000 years old and dates from the creation of the *Vedas,* compilations of prayers, hymns, and other religious writings. Hinduism doesn't have a single founder or prophet. There is only one god, though its many different manifestations are named and classified in great detail.

The Balinese call their religion Agama Tirta ("Science of the Holy Water"), an interpretation of religious ideas from China, India, and Java. Agama Tirta is much closer to the earth and more animist than Hinduism proper; the two sects are as different from each other as Ethiopian Christianity from Episcopalian Christianity. If a strict Hindu Brahman from Varanasi ever visited Bali, he'd think them savages. Although the Hindu epics are well known and form the basis of favorite Balinese dances, the deities worshipped in India are here considered too aloof and aristocratic. Often the Balinese don't even know their names. The Balinese have their own trinity of supreme gods, the Shrine of the Three Forces.

The Balinese are scared witless of ghosts, goblins, and the like, which could disguise themselves as black cats, naked women, and crows. Spirits dominate everything the Balinese do, and they are constantly offering fruit and flowers to appease

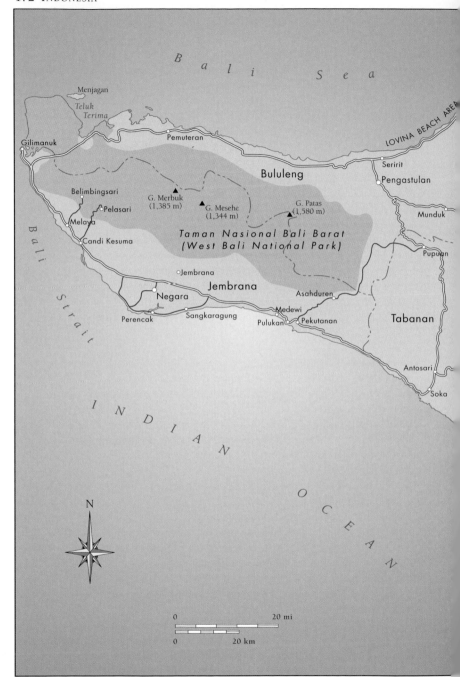

Bali Sea

Menjagan

Teluk Terima

Gilimanuk

Pemuteran

Bululeng

LOVINA BEACH AREA

Seririt

Pengastulan

Belimbingsari

G. Merbuk
(1,385 m)

G. Mesehe
(1,344 m)

G. Patas
(1,580 m)

Munduk

Pelasari

Melaya

Candi Kesuma

*Taman Nasional Bali Barat
(West Bali National Park)*

Pupuan

Bali Strait

Jembrana

Jembrana

Negara

Asahduren

Tabanan

Perencak

Sangkaragung

Medewi

Pulukan

Pekutanan

Antosari

Soka

INDIAN OCEAN

N

0   20 mi

0   20 km

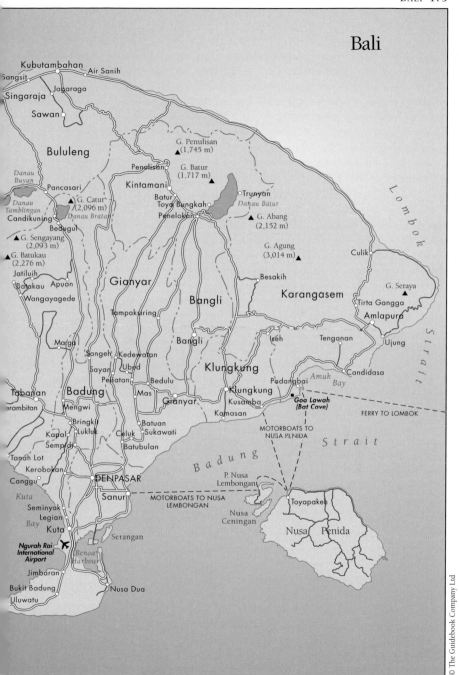

Bali

Kubutambahan
Sangsit   Air Sanih
Singaraja   Jagaraga
     Sawan

Bululeng
              G. Penulisan
              ▲(1,745 m)
        Penulisan   G. Batur
Danau   (1,717 m)▲
Buyan
   Pancasari   Kintamani
Danau   G. Catur   Batur   Trunyan
Tamblingan (2,096 m)   Toya Bungkah   Danau Batur
Candikuning Danau Bratan
        Bedugul   Penelokan
▲ G. Sengayang   ▲ G. Abang
   (2,093 m)   (2,152 m)
▲ G. Batukau
   (2,276 m)   G. Agung
Jatiluih   (3,014 m)▲   Culik
   Batakau   Apuan   Gianyar   Besakih   G. Seraya
Wangayagede   Karangasem   ▲
                                                   Tirta Gangga
         Marga   Bangli   Amlapura
              Tampaksiring   Iseh   Tenganan   Ujung
         Sangeh Kedewatan Bangli
       Sayan   Ubud   Klungkung   Candidasa
Tabanan   Badung Peliatan Bedulu   Padangbai Amuk
Terambitan Mengwi   Mas   Gianyar Klungkung   Bay
         Bringkit   Gianyar Kusamba   Goa Lawah
      Kapal Lukluk Celuk Sukawati Kamasan (Bat Cave)   FERRY TO LOMBOK
      Sempidi   Batuan   MOTORBOATS TO
Tanah Lot   Batubulan   NUSA PENIDA
   Kerobokan   Strait
Canggu   DENPASAR   P. Nusa
Kuta   Sanur   MOTORBOATS TO NUSA   Lembongan
Seminyak   LEMBONGAN   Nusa
Legian   Ceningan   Toyapaken
Bay Kuta   Nusa Penida
Ngurah Rai
International   Serangan
Airport   Benoa
Jimbaran   Harbour
Bukit Badung
Uluwatu   Nusa Dua

Lombok   Strait

Badung

angry deities. If put in our society, a Balinese would show all the classic symptoms of paranoia and neurotic disorders, but on Bali these traits are ritualized and institutionalized. There are sun gods, totemic gods, deer gods, secretaries to the gods, mythical turtles, market deities. Clay figures of the fire god are put over kitchen hearths, bank clerks place pandanus-leaf offering trays on their desks. *Ngedjot* are placed in the courtyards of every house; these offerings consist of little squares of banana leaves holding a few grains of rice, a flower, salt, and a pinch of chili pepper. No one eats until *ngedjot* are placed at the cardinal points in the family courtyard and in front of each house. Though mangy dogs eat the offerings as soon as they touch the ground, their essence has already been consumed by the spirits.

Gods and goddesses, who protect or threaten every act performed by a person during his or her lifetime, inhabit stone thrones and statues or simply hover in the air. Gods are often invited down to visit earth and are gorged with offerings and entertained with music and dance, but eventually they must go back home because they're too expensive to maintain. The Balinese always try to stay on the good side of all the forces. If the spirits are kept happy, the people can relax and even grow lighthearted. Children carry flowers to shrines and learn to dance at an early age to please the gods and the *raja*.

FESTIVALS

There's an unending chain of festivals, over 60 religious holidays a year. The basic tenet of the Balinese religion is the belief the island is owned by the supreme god Sanghyang Widhi, and has been handed down to the people in sacred trust. Thus the Balinese seem to devote most of their waking hours to an endless series of physically and financially exhausting offerings, purifications, temple festivities, processions, dances, and cremations. Festivals are dedicated to woodcarving, the birth of a goddess, and percussion instruments; there are temple festivals, fasting and retreat ceremonies, parades to the sea, celebrations of wealth and learning.

Get a Balinese calendar; besides offering faithful pictorial representations of simple, realistic folk scenes, they show the most propitious days for religious activities. Try to catch one of the full moon ceremonies, a traditional affair that can last for some days. Lots of praying, singing, and dancing—a wonderful opportunity to interact with the people in their own environment on a special occasion. Your hotel owner will tell you what to wear or perhaps even dress you in traditional attire. Incidentally, ceremonies concerning people take place in homes rather than temples. The temples are only used for ceremonies to gods.

Cremation liberates the soul of the dead, allowing it to journey to heaven to rejoin the Hindu cycle of reincarnation. Bodies are buried twice on Bali: once at death, and again after being exhumed and cremated. These funerals are a time of tipsy hilarity, gossip, offerings, and dances, all brightened by continuous *gamelan* music. Because cremations are so expensive, often the dead have to be buried first for as long as it takes the family to raise the necessary money. The deceased is then "re-awakened," the grave opened, and the remains placed on a decorated wood and bamboo tower, a fantastic creation of tinsel, paper, flowers, mirrors, silk, and white cloth. The corpse is then carried in a noisy procession to the cremation grounds. On the way it's spun around on top of men's shoulders to confuse the soul and prevent it from finding its way back to its house where it might make mischief for the living. While tourists trip over themselves taking pictures, the splendid tower, offerings, and coffin are then set ablaze. After the blaze subsides, the eldest son rakes the ashes to make sure all the flesh is burned. To free the soul, the ashes are carried out to sea and scattered.

TEMPLES

At least 20,000 temples grace Bali. If you see *pura* in front of a word, it means temple: *puri*, on the other hand, means palace. All temple complexes and historical sites now charge Rp550 admission, and you must be appropriately dressed. Not all sites require a sash, but all require at least a *sarung*. It's also common to sign a guest book. At some of the more obscure sites beware of guest books in which zeros have been added to all the preceding figures, making it appear donations have been substantial. Menstruating women are barred. Notice the exuberant ornamentation; carvings on temples are like the flowers and the trees. Bring binoculars to observe the extreme detail.

There are temples everywhere—in houses, courtyards, marketplaces, cemeteries, and rice paddies; on beaches, barren rocks offshore, deserted hilltops, and mountain heights; deep inside caves; within the tangled roots of banyan trees. At most intersections and other dangerous places temples are erected to prevent mishaps. Even in the middle of jungle crossroads, incense burns at little shrines. Four sites in particular stand out: **Gunung Kawi, Ulun Dau Batur, Ulun Danu Bratan**, and **Besakih**. The last is the Mother Temple of Bali, the state temple. It lies on the slopes of Gunung Agung, the "Navel of the World," the holiest mountain on Bali, where all the gods and goddesses live.

THE ARTS

There is still no word in the Balinese language for "art" or "artist." A sculptor is a "carver," a painter is known as a "picture maker," a dancer goes by the name of the dance she performs. The Balinese have never allowed artistic knowledge to become centralized in a special intellectual class. Everyone on Bali is an artist. The simplest peasant and most slow-witted worker create something, or are aesthetically conscious as critical spectators. A field laborer will chide a clumsy instrument maker for a job poorly done. Even *dagang,* young girls who run small foodstalls, are skillful practitioners of Bali's classical dances.

A funeral pyre

The purest and oldest example of Balinese art is the ancient mosaic-like *lamak,* which last only a day. Woven by women for Balinese feasts, *lamak* are made from strips of palm leaf, bamboo, and the yellow blades of sugar or coconut palm pinned or folded together to form fancy borders, rosettes, and diminutive tree designs. Hourglass-shaped palm-leaf fertility figures (*cili*) with round breasts and long thin arms—representations of Dewi Sri—appear when rice seeds first sprout.

Carving

The Balinese sculpt with natural media: wood, stone, bone, horn, even deadwood or gnarled tree roots. For the most part, only a souvenir-caliber woodcarving is turned out now, and successful creations are mass produced. There are only about a dozen places in Singakerta, Pengosekan, Kemenuh, and Mas, the main woodcarving centers, that sell high-quality carvings—and they want as much as Rp420,000 for one. You can negotiate a better price for a far superior product by taking note of the artist's name and visiting him in his home workshop. Bring cash. If you want something made to order it'll usually take about two weeks. Bring a photo or picture of what you'd like copied.

If you're looking for quality woodcarvings, go to **Tegallalang, Pujung,** and **Sebatu,** all north of Ubud. This is a great area to meet woodcarvers. Using very simple tools, top-class carvers earn only Rp5000 a day. Prices are cheap, and you'll see items unavailable in the expensive galleries of Mas. The wood used is ebony, jackfruit, teak, tamarind, hibiscus, or frangipani. Statues are usually finished with neutral or black shoe polish.

Stonecarving is related to the craft of woodworking; since soft volcanic rock (*paras*) is used, the technique is much the same. Because Balinese believe constant maintenance of their stone temples is a moral obligation, stone sculpture also serves a religious function. Stonecarving skill is most vividly seen in the distinctive split gates (*candi bentar*), swirling stone friezes, and absurd and menacing mythological statuary. The centers for stonecarving are Kapal and Batubulan; shops selling statues depicting characters from Balinese scriptures line both sides of the road. For something nontraditional, **Wayan Cemul,** just up the lane from Han Snel in Ubud, makes wild and wonderful *paras* sculptures.

Painting

Religious narrative paintings derive from the 14th and 15th centuries when the Hindu population of East Java relocated to Bali. They're characterized by a flat, stiff, formal style, painted according to a very strict traditional formula devoid of emotion. Figures of Hindu gods, demons, and princesses in lime water colors are placed row on row in high state in the realm of the gods. Sometimes up to 15 meters long and four meters wide, these paintings are hung along temple eaves as festive decoration. Modern examples of these cloth paintings are still turned out, especially in Kamasan village (Klungkung Regency). To familiarize yourself with high-quality historical works, visit the collection of paintings at Ubud's **Puri Lukisan Museum.** Many of Bali's finest painters live in and around this village.

The period between the world wars brought heavy changes. Balinese artists stopped painting according to rules and started to recreate their own visual experience. During the years 1933-39, the European artists Walter Spies and Rudolph Bonnet, among others, demonstrated to Balinese artists that painters can be free of set formulas or a single stylistic convention, encouraging them to unfold individually. These Europeans taught them the concept of the third dimension. To understand contemporary Balinese painting, see the **Neka Gallery** in Ubud, the **Neka Museum** north of Campuan, and the superb **Agung Rai Gallery** in Peliatan. Also visit the **Art Center** on Jl. Nusa Indah in Abiankapas, Denpasar, and its permanent exhibition of Balinese painting (open 0800-1700, tel. 0361-222-776), only a 15-minute walk east of Kereneng station. Called the Taman Werdi Budaya, the center also features Balinese and Indonesian maskmakers and woodcarvers. A car park, museum, and small, fixed-price handicraft shops with reasonable prices are also found in the complex.

Learning the rituals at an early age

Shopping

Due to the extravagant sums package tourists pay for Balinese artifacts, prices have become ludicrously high. Clothing, woodcarvings, bone work, and *batik* are usually cheaper in India and other Asian countries, and often of equal or better quality. Although Bali's silversmiths are more inventive, silverwork is just as cheap in **Yogyakarta** (Central Java). The serious shopper needs to obtain the latest edition of *Shopping and Traveling in Exotic Indonesia* (Impact Publications, 9104-N Manassas Dr., Manassas Park, VA 22111 U.S.A., tel. 703-361-7300). On Bali, the asking price in a local market or from a peddler is not necessarily lower than that of an exclusive shop—they both start out at escalated prices.   Balinese silver is 92.5 percent pure and 7.5 percent other metals. When buying jewelry, the price depends on the weight, the design, the stone, or all three. Sellers will often come down 10-20 percent. Gold used in jewelry is three grams of gold to one gram copper. Almost any Balinese town features a gold shop, selling mostly traditional jewelry like earplugs and the large gold rings Balinese men like to wear. Dozens of Europeans sell their own personalized jewelry around Kuta and Legian. Denpasar's **Jl. Sulawesi** has a number of gold shops where you can buy attractive gold articles at a fair, fixed price.

Take advantage of the inexpensive pants, shirts, and blouses available in shops and from beach peddlers—Kuta, Legian, and Sanur are the designer clothes capitals of Asia. In Ubud it costs only Rp5000 and three or four days to secure a perfect fit made to order in a tailor shop, so you shouldn't ever pay a peddler more than that amount plus the cost of material (Rp2000-5000).

The most striking and distinctive cloth native to Bali is *ikat*, known on the island as *endek*, Bali's most visible craft. With its luscious colors, soft diffused look, and striking and primitive patterns, *endek* is worn all over the island for all occasions. The most famous *endek* comes from the village of **Tengenan** in eastern Bali. Also keep a lookout for *kain prada* fabrics woven of silk or cotton and decorated with silver or gold threads or gold leaf. These very colorful kerchiefs are worn by temple girls during festivals. A ceremonial two-meter-long cloth could take from three weeks to a month to weave, depending on the intricacy of the design.

Music

The sound of echoing xylophones, drums, and clashing cymbals is heard all hours of the day and night. Bathers sing in the rivers, rattles clack in the fields, looms tingle with bells, kites vibrate in the wind, little boys walk along lanes imitating the sound of gongs, and flocks of pigeons circle overhead with whistles attached to their feet.

A bronze xylophonic instrument from the gamelan *orchestra*

Some of the finest *gamelan* are made on Bali and cost up to Rp40 million. Every village has its own orchestra, given such names as Sea of Honey or Snapping Crocodiles. All musicians are unpaid amateurs. Anyone may play—a musician might hand over his *gendang* to a spectator during a performance.

Dancing

Balinese dance will probably be the most impressive sight you'll see. With over 1,000 troupes on the island, dance is at the very center of Balinese life. On Java dance is the prerogative of the courts, but on Bali it's most prevalent in the villages. The Balinese consider Javanese dancing boring, while the Javanese think Balinese dancing noisy and vulgar. Dancers on Bali perform for the pleasure of the gods, prestige, and the entertainment of friends and family.

In 1992, Bali's governor decreed that 11 sacred dances may not be performed in hotels. However, a great number of performances are staged especially for tourists; many dance forms have been shortened to please the easily bored foreigner, but just because dances are put on for tourists doesn't mean they're of inferior quality. Try to see dancing in conjunction with a temple festival or other local ritual event. These are free and more spontaneous than tourist performances. On any night of the week you could happen upon any number of different dance-dramas and ballets, honoring a local temple god, dedicating a new temple, exorcizing evil, or celebrating a wedding, tooth filing, or cremation. The stage could be an open dusty courtyard in front of a temple gate or a crossroads beneath the starry sky and towering palms. The dance area will be encircled by hundreds of squatting, sitting, standing people of all ages. The mood is electric.

Watch *gamelan* and dance at **SMKI**, the High School of Performing Arts in Batubulan. There's also **Sekolah Tinggi Seni Indonesia** (STSI) on Jl. Nusa Indah in Denpasar. Or go up to Ubud or out to a village to study dance informally. One way to find a teacher is to first find a style you like by watching performances, then approach the artist directly for lessons. Stay for several weeks; they're glad to have you. Many of Bali's dance teachers are elderly women who know the complete repertoire of the dances. The teacher usually leaves it up to students to decide how much they should pay. A teacher may ask Rp5000 per lesson, but it's highly negotiable. Alternatively, the student may make a substantial donation to the *gamelan* orchestra.

Sports

Bali is a popular scuba and snorkeling destination, famous among divers for its marinelife, superb visibility, and sensational drop-offs. It was on Bali that drift diving became popular, following the development of techniques to accommodate the deep ocean currents surrounding the island. The spectacular **Menjangan Wall** in the northwest part of the island is commensurate with northern Sulawesi's Bunaken.

Baruna Diving, the largest dive operator on Bali (offices in Kuta, Sanur and Nusa Dua) is a good place to start.

The surf breaks for which Bali is famous are at Uluwatu and **Padang**, best when the southeast winds blow onshore during the dry season. During the wet (Jan.-March) surfers nip over to the other side of Bukit Peninsula to Nusa Dua, Sri Lanka, and Sanur where the wind will be offshore. Surfing is the big attraction of the offshore island of Nusa Lembongan; three of Indonesia's most outstanding surf breaks are here.

Cockfighting has been declared illegal by the Muslim Indonesian majority but still takes place on the sly in many villages, usually in the mornings. They may coincide with *upacara* temple ceremonies and festivals, when they are legal. You see only men at the cockfights, though tourist women may attend contests put on for tourists.

Outside **Negara** in western Bali (Jembrana Regency), thrilling regional water buffalo races (*mekepung*) are held on the Sunday before Indonesia's Independence Day (August 14th), and again every other Sunday each September and October. Only the island's handsomest, sleekest bulls—which are not used for plowing or as beasts of burden—are chosen to compete. After extensive training, the huge beasts are dressed up in silk banners with painted horns and big wooden bells. Each team is judged for speed, strength, color, and style. Like Roman charioteers they come thundering down to the finish line, whipping and shouting, mud flying. Jockeys twist the tails of the bulls to gain speed. This festival is staged to please the harvest god. The winning bulls are used for stud and fetch up to twice the market value when sold.

A gamelan and baris *dance performance*

One of the world's top 50 golf courses is on the grounds of the **Bali Handara Ko-saido Country Club** in Pancasari near Lake Bratan. Judged fifth in the world for technical design and service, this 18-hole championship course features tall trees and flowers in riotous colors separating the fairways. Other fine golf courses are at the **Bali Beach Hotel** in Sanur and at Nusa Dua.

Denpasar Regency

Once part of Badung Regency, in 1992 the Denpasar area and Sanur split off and became Bali's ninth *kabupaten*. In addition to the island's capital, Denpasar Regency encompasses Sanur, Benoa Port, and Serangan Island, leaving Bandung more pencil-shaped than ever. Denpasar is the largest and busiest city on the island. An old trading center, its name means "east of the market." It's the headquarters for the government, the media, the island's principal banks, airline offices, and hospitals. Bali's two universities, Udayana and Warmadewa, are also based here. The city's local name is Badung, and you'll hear "Badung" sung out by *bemo* drivers all over Bali. A hot, dusty, cacophonous, former Brahmana-class city, Denpasar has grown fifteen-fold over the past 10 years, and is now home to 367,000 people.

Tanah Lot temple, Bali

DENPASAR SIGHTS

Unless you've got business here, the city has few charms, other than its quiet back alleyways where people are quite friendly. A great place for families to hang out in the evenings is the huge well-kept park in the middle of town, **Puputan Square,** named for the bloody 1906 extermination of the island's ruling class by the Dutch. North of the square is the **Governor's Residence,** built in Javanese *pendopo* style. The largest collection of Baliana in the world is located on the east side of Taman Puputan on Jl. Mayor Wishnu, just south of the tourist office, in **The Bali Museum.** The grand, well-kept complex consists of a series of attractive, grassy courtyards containing all the archetypes of Balinese architecture. The museum's four buildings contain a splendid collection of Balinese art.

Just east of the big *alun-alun* on Jl. Mayor Wishnu, next to the museum, is a Hindu temple, **Pura Jagatnatha,** built in 1953. In the afternoon, people from the surrounding *kampung* come here to pray; the temple's especially busy during the full moon. On a towered throne of white coral sits a bright, gold statue of Ida Batara Sanghyang Widhi in his typical pose. This is the supreme god of Balinese Hinduism. Also visit **Puri Pemecutan** near Tegal bus station on the corner of Jl. Thamrin and Jl. Hasannudin, built in 1907 to replace the original palace of the *raja* destroyed by Dutch artillery. Pemecutan, which shares the complex with Pemecutan Palace Hotel, houses old weapons and a renowned *gamelan mas* which survived from the original *puri.* Don't miss the handsome, four-tiered *kulkul* diagonally opposite the palace with its eight small *raksasa* statues. Chinese porcelain plates decorate the topmost tier.

The Art Center, also called Taman Werdi Budaya, is located on Jl. Nusa Indah in Abiankapas, a Denpasar suburb in the direction of Sanur, a 15-minute walk east of Kereneng station. It houses exhibits of modern painting, woodcarvings, shadow puppets, and giant *barong landung* puppets. This is one of Bali's finest art exhibits. Open Tues.-Sun. 0800-1700 tel. 222-776. One of Denpasar's main attractions is the massive, multistoried, visually fascinating central market, **Pasar Badung** on Jl. Gajah Mada alongside the river. With droves of people and amazing colors, this market is especially strong in plaited ware and inexpensive trinkets. Peep in at **Mega Art Shop,** Jl. Gajah Mada 36 (open 0730-1700, tel. 224-592), for its wide range of Balinese arts—jewelry, leather, puppets, paintings, ceramics, and fine textiles, including reasonably-priced framed weavings from Timor for Rp210,000-262,500 and Sumbu *ikat* for Rp105,000-262,500. Ten percent cash discount. See the incredibly delicate, museum-quality antique gold artifacts from Flores.

SERVICES

The **Denpasar Regency Tourist Office,** Jl. Surapati 7, tel. (0361) 223-399 or 23602, is a five-minute walk from the Bali Museum. Pick up a map of Denpasar and a calendar of events. Open 0700-1400, Friday until 1100, Saturday until 1230. This is the best, friendliest, and most convenient source of information on both the regency and all of Bali. You can temporarily store your backpack here during office hours.

The most modern hospital is **Sanglah**, Jl. Nias, (0361) tel. 227-911, ext. 11. Another hospital, **Wangaya**, is located on Jl. Kartini, tel. 222-141. **Surya Husada Clinic**, Jl. Pulau Serangan 1-3 in Sanglah, tel. 225-249, is the best private hospital. Though it's double the price of public hospitals, the service is better, and the staff better trained and more proficient in English. Open around the clock.

The **central post office** is on Jl. Raya Puputan in Renon, tel. 223-565, which is difficult to get to. Hire an *ojek* from Kereneng station for around Rp2000. Open Mon.-Thurs. 0800-1400, Friday 0800-1100, Saturday 0800-1100. **Bank Ekspor-Impor**, Jl. Udayana 11 (tel. 23981), cashes Thomas Cook traveler's checks and is reliable for wire transfers. A 24-hour moneychanger is at the airport.

SANUR

Sanur is Bali's oldest tourist resort; guesthouses began appearing here as early as the 1940s. Large hotel enclaves, shady lanes, trees, and coral walls give the village a park-like setting. Sanur is smaller, quieter, prettier, safer, and more sheltered than Kuta or Legian. **Museum Le Mayeur**, also called the Ni Polok Museum, was formerly the home of the late Adrien Jean Le Mayeur, the Belgian impressionist painter who moved to Sanur in 1932. The gallery contains 92 paintings captioned in English and Indonesian, local artifacts, and some superb specimens of traditional Balinese carvings. Although Sanur's beach remains white and sandy, in front of La Taverna the shallow and weedy shore has been eaten away by lime removal; Semawang's beach, south of the main Sanur Beach, is nicer. Kite flying is a distinctive event in Sanur. Sponsored by the local *banjar* in the windy, low-lying *sawah* behind the village, competitions take place from July through September. The majority of Sanur's tourist services are found along Jl. Tamblingan.

A kalamakara motif which is hung above the entrance
to a temple for protection against evil spirits

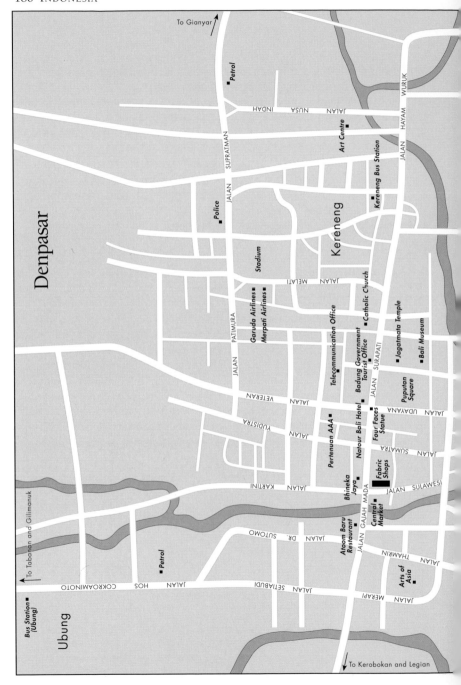

Denpasar

To Gianyar

Petrol

JALAN INDAH
JALAN NUSA
JALAN SUPRATMAN

Art Centre

JALAN HAYAM WURUK

Kereneng Bus Station

Police

JALAN PATIMURA

Kereneng

Stadium

JALAN MELATI

Catholic Church

Garuda Airlines
Merpati Airlines

Jagatmata Temple

Telecommunication Office

Bali Museum

Badung Government
Tourist Office

JALAN SURAPATI

Puputan
Square

JALAN VETERAN

JALAN YUDISTRA

Pertenuan AAA

JALAN UDAYANA

Natour Bali Hotel

Four Faces
Statue

JALAN SUMATRA

Bhineka
Jaya

Fabric
Shops

JALAN KARTINI

JALAN GAJAH MADA

JALAN SULAWESI

Central
Market

Atoom Baru
Restaurant

JALAN DR. SUTOMO

JALAN THAMRIN

To Tabanan and Gilimanuk

Petrol

JALAN SETIABUDI

JALAN MERAPI

Arts of
Asia

JALAN HOS COKROAMINOTO

Bus Station
(Ubung)

Ubung

To Kerobokan and Legian

To Sanur

Petrol

[Television] TVRI

Governor's
Office

Wintosastro

Petrol

Renon

Immigration Office

Post Office

N

500 yds

500 m

0

0

Tiara Dewata
Supermarket Complex

Udayana University

JALAN RAYA PUPUTAN

Perumtel Telephone Office

Police

JALAN DIPONEGORO

To Benoa

Post Office for parcels
(Paket Pos)

Petrol

Hospital

Tegal
Station

Two Brothers
Inn

JALAN TEUKU UMAR

JALAN IMAM BONJOL

To Kuta and Airport

Petrol

Badung Regency

Badung contains the neon-lit tourist swaths of Legian, Kuta, and Nusa Dua. Badung also extends inland to the overtouristed monkey forest of Sangeh and on to the slopes of Gunung Catur (2,096 meters), high in the central mountains. Badung has the island's highest prices and the poshest, most sophisticated hotels. Yet central and northern Badung are regions of fertile rice fields carved exquisitely out of hills and valleys, with small, densely settled villages surrounded by groves of coconut palms. Wealthy southern Bali's temple festivals, ceremonies, and dance performances are lavish and unending.

The drier, sparsely populated club-foot shaped peninsula known as **Bukit** ("The Hill") is attached to the southernmost body of the island by a narrow isthmus. Here, high cliffs fall steeply into the Indian Ocean and surf pounds stretches of isolated coast; this is among the earth's top surfing spots. Although the soil is thin, water scarce, and the climate arid, Bukit is fast becoming an overflow residential area for the mushrooming population of Nusa Dua, Jimbaran, and Tanjung. Between Bukit and southern Bali's fertile plains is the **Ngurah Rai International Airport**, which receives hordes of tourists from all over the world. The bulk of Bali's tourists visit the concentrated international beach enclaves of the south, taking day-trips to sites all over the island.

MENGWI

Sixteen km northwest of Denpasar, Mengwi is Rp600 by minibus from Denpasar's Ubung station. If driving, take the main road to Tabanan through Kapal to the Mengwi turnoff, then proceed north. This quiet town is important as the former seat of a long dynasty of kings; its large temple belongs to the group of Bali state or "national" temples. Since its beginnings in 1634 under Raja I Gusti Agung Anom until its demise in 1891, Mengwi was a separate kingdom that extended its political power as far as Blambangan, East Java. The dynasty was ultimately defeated by the neighboring Balinese kingdoms of Badung and Tabanan.

The elegant **Pura Taman Ayun** is the second largest temple complex on Bali, and one of the island's most beautiful shrines. This trim, impressive garden complex lies only one-half km east of the main highway (turn in at the market), accessible by a long entrance walkway. The original structure dates from around 1740 when ruler Cokorda Munggu built what was to be his state temple on high ground. It's partly surrounded by a wide moat with lotuses, and consists of 50 separate structures. Restored and enlarged in 1937, today Pura Taman Ayun is looked after by descendants of the royal family. It's clean, with toilet facilities, trim gardens, and an orchid nursery. Donation Rp500-2000.

SANGEH

Travel fifteen km beyond Mengwi on the road to Gunung Catur, Rp1000 by *bemo* from Wangaya station in Denpasar to Sangeh's parking lot, filled with Super-Kijangs and Suzuki Katanas and surrounded by a big souvenir shop scene. Here, under towering 30-meter-tall trees, is the holy Monkey Forest, with three clans of sacred, very aggressive monkeys crawling over lichen-covered Bukit Sari ("Nectar of the Mountains") Temple. Built by the royal family of Mengwi in the 17th century, the temple is dedicated to the god Vishnu and was initially used as a place of meditation. Restored in 1973, today it functions primarily as a *subak* temple where offerings to agricultural deities are made. Notice the old statue of Vishnu's mount Garuda, and the relief of a Japanese shooting at an airplane.

LEGIAN

This once dusty, poor seaside village is now just an extension of Kuta, though with a slightly more chic attitude. Legian offers good music, outstanding food, both luxury and budget hotels, sophisticated fashion boutiques, banks, souvenir markets, and *arja, barong, kecak,* and *Ramayana* performances at least every other day. From Denpasar, Legian is Rp600 by *bemo,* or a two-km walk from Kuta Beach on a congested sidewalk beside a busy road running south. It's more pleasant to walk via the beach, though this trek is only safe in the daytime. The shops along Jl. Legian in north Legian feature creative, unusual clothes and cheaper prices than Kuta.

KUTA

Kuta was just a sleepy fishing village on the way in from the airport when it was discovered by seasoned travelers in the late 1960s. Since then, tens of thousands of travelers, surfies, and package tourists have turned Kuta into a gigantic First World yuppie resort. If you accept it for what it is, Kuta can be a fun place to visit. Although rubbishy, cluttered, and increasingly crowded, Kuta offers cut-rate hedonism, nonstop nightlife, fancy restaurants, sophisticated hotels, some of Bali's best shopping, and surprisingly low prices for food and lodging (count on about Rp21,000-25,200 per day). Kuta is still one of the best-value tourist/travelers' hangouts in the world and the liveliest and naughtiest spot on the island.

Kuta's six-km-long crescent-shaped surfing beach, protected by a coral reef at its southern end, and long and wide enough for Frisbee contests and soccer games, is famous for its beautiful tropical sunsets and broad swath of gray sand. Too bad it's so polluted. You can't swim without catching plastic trash in your mouth, hands, and feet. The best waves are the left-handers out on Kuta Reef; the best surfing is from March to July. At low tide, bicycle rides or walks along the firm, moist sand are refreshing. Heading north of Kuta, you can ride for about seven km. At this point either

(following pages) Terraced sawah ricefields

retrace your tracks or turn inland at the thatched roofs of Seminyak's Bali Oberoi and return to Kuta via Jl. Legian.

No less than 15 clubs operate in Kuta, Legian, and Seminyak. Most open late, have no dress code, charge Rp4000-5000 entrance fee, and close at around 0200 (officially, 2400). Kuta's best buys are clothes and sunglasses. The hustling on the beach can be horrific; if you decide to visit Kuta, you better get used to it. Every craft and fakery from every workshop on Bali seems to eventually find its way here. It's all pure junk.

BUKIT PENINSULA

Bukit ("Hill"), a lemon-shaped peninsula at the southernmost extremity of the island, is a dry, rocky land. Oval-shaped and about eight km from north to south, 17 km from east to west, with a maximum elevation of 200 meters, Bukit offers limestone caves, temples perched on the edge of dizzying cliffs, stretches of immaculate isolated beaches, and a dramatic coastline pounded by Bali's most challenging surf. In ancient times, Bukit was considered a dangerous area where great herds of wild *banteng* and water buffalo roamed, driven south by population pressure. Bukit served as hunting grounds for pheasant, wild boar, and deer for the *rajas* of Denpasar and Mengwi; cattle still graze there. So inhospitable is this land that criminals, political enemies, and debtors were once banished here.

Bali's south coast temples all pay homage to the guardian spirits of the sea, but none is more spectacular than **Uluwatu**. This well-maintained complex, one of the *sad-kahyangan* group of the holiest temples of Bali, is the least overwhelmed by tourism and commercialism because of its remote location on the southwestern tip of Bukit. At the end of a beautiful country road, Uluwatu may be reached by public *bemo* from Kuta or Tegal station in Denpasar. From Kuta, it'll cost Rp12,000-15,000 (20 km) to charter a vehicle. From the parking lot, walk 300 meters down a path to the temple; open 0700-1900. Walk up the 71 steps through a strikingly simple limestone entrance to the rectangular outer courtyard. All three courtyards—representing the spiritual, earthly, and demonic realms—are surrounded by hard weathered coral which has enabled the temple to survive for centuries and gives it a brilliant white appearance. Towering over the middle courtyard is an enormous arched *kala* gate flanked by Ganesha guardians, reminiscent of East Javanese temple architecture.

NUSA DUA

The most luxurious hotels on Bali are located in this beach enclave on the east end of Bukit, 27 km south of Denpasar. Named after two raised headlands connected to the east coast by sandspits (Nusa Dua means "Two Islands"), this soulless full-scale, totally self-contained tourist resort has its own parks, roads, golf course, deep-water

Balinese fishermen contribute to the 60,000 tons of fish harvested each year in Indonesia.

wells, sewer system, fire station, police, telephone exchange, banks, emergency clinic, mall, travel and tour agencies, and airline offices. Nusa Dua's beach hotels front a three-km-long beautiful white sand beach with gentle waves and not a rock in sight.

TANJUNG

Three km north of Nusa Dua, the five-km-long peninsula of Tanjung Benoa points toward Benoa Harbor like a long finger. This once sleepy expanse of coconut palms and shallow beach has been transformed into a growing resort area with luxury hotels, dive agents, restaurants, and open-air cafes. Tanjung doesn't have the same feeling of sterile isolation as neighboring Nusa Dua. A nice place for evening strolls is the relatively quiet village of Benoa on the peninsula's tip. For hundreds of years this was an embarkation point for ferries crossing over to Suwungan. More romantic is to walk along the beach southeast of Benoa, past rows of *jakung* pulled up on shore. In Benoa village is a Bugis *kampung* with its small *mesjid*. Don't miss the large, garish Chinese Buddhist *klenteng* picturesquely sited looking out to Benoa Harbor. The annex of this local temple contains bronze icons salvaged from the shipwreck of a Chinese vessel in the 15th century.

Gianyar Peninsula

Gianyar is Bali's richest and oldest cultural region, where much of today's religious life was forged in ancient times. The town of Gianyar is the regency's administrative capital, while Ubud is its cultural capital and most populous town. No part of Gianyar Regency is farther than an hour's ride from Denpasar. Legendary rivers Petanu and Pakrisan course through this region, their sources in the slopes of Gunung Batur. The Pakrisan is particularly rich in historic remains, the river having cut its way through rock cliffs and giant boulders. All along its banks are rock-cut *candi,* monasteries, meditation cells, sacred watering places, shrine compounds, and famous temples.

GIANYAR TOWN

The small, bustling administrative center of Gianyar Regency, 23 km from Denpasar's Terminal Kereneng (Rp700 by *bemo*). It's a *bemo* stop for those heading north to Kintamani or east to Klungkung, and a center for Balinese *ikat* weaving. Its *babi guling* stands and *joged* group are famous all over the island. The poorly staffed tourist office for Gianyar District (Dinas Pariwisata Gianyar) is at Jl. Ngurah Rai 21, opposite the telephone office; it's easier to get info in Ubud.

TIRTA EMPUL

Situated in a valley in the northeast corner of Tampaksiring under a spectacular banyan tree, 37 km northeast of Denpasar at the end of a well-signposted road, the Tirta Empul temple and its 20 small sugar-palm thatched shrines are beautifully decorated and maintained. There's a large square altar dedicated to Batara Indra, and elaborate carvings adorn the lichen-covered walls surrounding the pools. According to tradition, each of the pool's 15 fountains has a specific function: spiritual purification, cleansing from evil, antidote to poison. Tirta Empul's water is looked upon as the holiest on Bali, widely thought to possess magical curative powers.

This is also the area for Bali quilts, hand-painted fabrics quilted by machine, as well as colorful and cleverly designed bedcovers. Two or three km beyond Tampaksiring you'll see quilts flapping in the wind, draped on lines outside at least 12 shops. Prices run Rp75,000-250,000.

GUNUNG KAWI

Two km south of Tampaksiring, on the banks of the upper course of the sacred Pakrisan River, Gunung Kawi ("Mountain of Poetry") lies in the heart of the archaeologically rich Pejeng area, a region where Hinduism first took hold on Bali. This is one of the more impressive historical sites on Bali: a blinding green watery canyon where two rows of ancient blackened tombs have been hewn out of natural rock hillsides as royal memorials.

The whole complex is well-swept and well-maintained and should be visited in the cool mornings or late afternoons when few tourists are about. At the lookout on top of the long, steep stairway, look down upon overwhelming scenery: sunlit waterfalls and palm-studded rice terraces plunging to a deep ravine with a rushing river flowing through it all. The holy water of the river was meant to sanctify the site. Carved into niches on two facing cliffs, the somber and unembellished temples contain no interior chambers, only facades. Built in the late 11th century, the temples are remarkably well-preserved. There are 10 temples in all. Across the gorge is an abandoned hermitage for the keepers of the tombs. All around flows holy water and steep-sided rock walls covered with dripping moss, all of which gives the site an elevated and venerated atmosphere.

Ubud

With its hundreds of art galleries, studios, and souvenir shops, and the flurry and congestion around the two-story market on the main road, Ubud looks like a big commercial scene. But the town and its surrounding collection of villages offers the best value accommodations on Bali, and certainly the best food. In the immediate outskirts, as little as 100 meters from the main road, traditional culture and the demands of the tourist industry coexist to some degree. Ever since the German painter Walter Spies made his home here in the 1930s, Ubud has been a haven for both native and European artists. In an area of 10 square km in and around this village live Bali's most accomplished dancers, musicians, painters, and carvers.

Ubud's main street and lanes are lined with a great variety of shops and kiosks, filled to bursting with woodcarvings, basketry, toy *gamelan* sets, dangling earrings, antiques, clothes, *batik,* bamboo windmills, and paintings. First prices are high— you're expected to bargain. The best time to shop is in the cool evenings. The majority of shops are open from 0900 to 2030 or 2100. **Pasar Ubud** on Jl. Raya in the middle of town houses several hundred shops and stalls. This central market offers low-end clothes in booths upstairs as well as tawdry handicrafts, fans, bags, baskets, and jewelry.

A must is the **Neka Gallery**, established in 1966 in Peliatan. Whereas Puri Lukisan represents only Balinese artists, the Neka Gallery exhibits painters from all over Indonesia, as well as foreign artists who've lived and worked on Bali. The Neka Gallery in eastern Ubud in Padangtegal consists of five different buildings. Paintings cost Rp31,500-21 million; you can get a discount of 10-25 percent. The Neka Museum exhibits and sells some of the highest-quality contemporary paintings found anywhere in Bali. Paintings range from impressionism to abstract expressionism. Open daily 0830-1700.

(above and opposite) There is always time for a game during the festival.

At the south end of Monkey Forest Road is the Monkey Forest, with a beautiful small, cavelike *pura dalem* (temple of the dead) embraced by roots and a holy spring inhabited by a band of irascible gray monkeys. The *pura dalem* on a hill around the corner contains well-executed statues of Rangda devouring children. The temple has been given a facelift—new entrance, information in Balinese and English, and more attractive walkways. It's fairly small and peaceful with no persistent hawkers. Give a donation.

For one-stop service, **CV Three Brothers Wisata** on Monkey Forest Road do everything: car, motorbike, and pushbike rentals; insurance; packing and shipping; postal service, stamps, and parcel delivery; coach tours; shuttle bus tickets; money-changing; cash for credit cards; bus tickets for Java; international and domestic air ticketing; importing/exporting; document clearance; hotel reservations; and laundry. Another full-service agency is **Surya International** on Jl. Raya, tel. (0361) 975-133, fax 975-120; staff will make hotel reservations for you for a fee.

PURI LUKISAN
Meaning "Palace of Paintings," this is Ubud's art museum, situated in a garden with rice paddies and water buffalo out the back windows. Spanning the years between the 1930s and the present, this museum houses one of the island's finest selections of

modern paintings, drawings, and sculptures. The museum was founded in 1954 by Cokorda Gede Sukawati, the *raja* of Ubud and a patron of the arts, and Rudolph Bonnet, a Dutchman who devoted much of his life to studying and preserving the unique quality of Balinese painting.

The museum consists of three big buildings set in beautiful gardens of fountains, statues, and pools befitting a palace. Choose a nice place to sit and relax. Bring a pair of binoculars as the garden is a superb ornithological sanctuary. At present the permanent collection is housed in two buildings; the third is operated by a local painters' cooperative. Here you'll get an overview of all the different stylistic trends in Balinese art. The works in the cooperative are for sale and prices are negotiable; if you see an artist you like, note his name and village and visit his private gallery.

WALKS FROM UBUD

Go to Ubud to get close to the real Bali. All around this sprawling village are scenic rice fields, forested gullies, deep river gorges, lush vegetation, half-overgrown shrines and grottos, beautiful and diversified landscapes, pools, and moss-covered temples carved from rock hillsides. Wake with the sun and set off on foot or bicycle

down any of the village's many lanes. Indispensable companions to bring along are Victor Mason's *Bali Bird-walks*, the Pathfinder trail map *Ubud and Environs*, and bottled water.

CAMPUAN

A crossroads village one km west of Ubud. Walk down a road between huge green embankments, then cross the bridge over a deep river gully. The bridge 25 meters above the river is a vital link between Ubud and the villages of Campuan, Penestanan, Sanggingan and Kedewatan to the west. The walk to and from Ubud has become quite hairraising because of the traffic but staying in a slower-paced village is incentive enough to brave it. Below the Campuan bridge flows the River Oos, which serves as a laundromat and bathing site. Down on the right side two branches of the river meet, a spiritual spot for Hindus. The word *campuan* actually means where two rivers meet, a corruption of *campuran* (as in *nasi campur*). On the spur in between is moss-covered 12th-century Pura Gunung Labuh, an agricultural and fertility temple. Bathe under pure mountain spring water pouring out of a bamboo spout.

PELIATAN

Just 1.5 km southeast of Ubud, Peliatan spreads out along a very busy kilometer-long throughfare from Ubud to the bend in the road at Teges. Peliatan and its neighboring hamlets are known among the Balinese for their internationally famous *legong* troupes and fine *semar pegulingan* orchestra. Because its relative isolation is conducive to studying, Peliatan makes an ideal language lab for learning Bahasa Indonesia or Balinese. Peliatan is a major center for carving and painting. Gifted carvers worth visiting are Nyoman Togog and I Wayan Pasti.

The **Agung Rai Gallery** lies beyond Peliatan but before Negara, one km south of Pande Homestay. One of the finest galleries on Bali, a mammoth art complex of thatch-roofed, traditional-style *bale,* each building houses a different school of Balinese art. At least as much an educational experience as Ubud's Puri Lukisan, these co-op showrooms give you a clear view of the scope and development of modern Balinese painting. See the marble-floored room filled with works costing up to Rp31.5 million. In the private collection in back are the haunting works of noted prewar Dutch, German, and Austrian artists who lived and worked on Bali, exerting a major influence on local painting styles.

YEH PULU

This rarely visited carved cliff face is about one km from Goa Gajah. To get there, start from the Bedulu crossroads. Heading west on the road to Ubud is Goa Gajah; the road east leads to Pura Samuan Tiga; the road south to Gianyar. On this road (Jl. Yeh Pulu) you'll see a sign after one km; take a right, then a left, then a right again. This small road leads almost all the way to Yeh Pulu. Park in front of the small open *bale.* It's a cool 300-meter walk on a well-built walkway to the site. Pay an entrance fee of Rp550, Rp300 for children. The old woman caretaker (*pemangku*) cleans and maintains the reliefs and a statue of Ganesha. For a donation, she'll tell you who's depicted on the reliefs, show you some worn-out carvings on the northern side, and dispense holy water from a clear spring feeding a sacred pool filled with fish. Very calm surroundings, rarely any disturbances.

MAS

An affluent center for the arts 20 km northeast of Denpasar and five km south of Ubud. Historically, the Brahmanic village of Mas ("Gold") is thought to be the place where the wandering high priest Niratha finally settled. Niratha emigrated from East Java in the 15th century and founded temples all over the island. The majority of Bali's Brahmans today claim descent from this venerated Hindu sage. Beautiful **Pura Taman Pule**, on the east side of town behind the soccer field, only 100 meters from the road, is believed to have been built on the original site of Niratha's hermitage (*griya*). A statue of the wandering holy man is near the temple and the *tangi* tree he planted is located behind an altar in the middle courtyard. Regular performances of the *kecak* dance are staged in Mas, and during the three-day Kuningan festival the ancient *wayang wong* drama is staged in Pura Taman Pule's umbrella-studded courtyard.

Bangli Regency

Stretching north to south in central-eastern Bali is the only landlocked regency on the island. Only tiny Klungkung has fewer people than Bangli's population of 180,000, divided into 187 community groups in 73 villages.

With its rugged, overgrown hillocks, wooded ravines, and steeply tiered gardens leading up to immense volcanic craters, the regency encompasses some of the most superb natural scenery on the island. The roads north from Bangli or Tampaksiring climb gradually, the air becomes cooler, and upland crops such as peanuts begin to replace rice. North of Bangli, the road meanders through eerie forests of giant bamboo, finally emerging on one of Bali's most dramatic vistas: the huge 10-km-wide basin of Lake Batur, with the smoldering black cone of Gunung Batur rising behind it.

BANGLI

A friendly, scenic town in the cool, sloping, rich farmlands of central Bali, Bangli is an hour's drive (40 km) northeast of Denpasar. Bangli dates back to A.D. 1204. An offshoot of the early dynasty, the ancient kingdom of Bangli became Bali's most powerful upland court in the second half of the 19th century, largely as a reaction to the Dutch presence in Buleleng. Bangli's prominence, however, never eclipsed the grandeur of the lowland courts, and its influence was not deeply felt in island politics.

Eight royal *puri* were once situated around the main crossroads of town, but now only **Puri Denpasar** is open to the public. Note the sculptures of lions and bodhisattvas inspired by early photographs of Borobudur, and the remarkable painted mural and frieze in the *bale loji* depicting Chinese life in Bangli during the last century.

One of the finest temples of its kind, **Pura Kehen** was founded in the early 11th century by Sri Brahma Kemuti Ketu as a state temple. Each of the three main terraces is connected to the one above by a flight of stairs. The first five terraces make up the outer courtyards (*jabaan*), the sixth and seventh are middle courtyards (*aba tengah*), while the eighth is the sacred inner courtyard (*jeroan*). Steep stairs lead to Pura

Kehen's splendid gateway, the *pamedal agung,* known as "the great exit." *Wayang kulit-*like stone statues on pedestals depicting characters from the *Ramayana* line both sides of the 38 steps leading up the main entrance. The courtyard's walls are inlaid with chipped Chinese porcelain plates, the balustrades of the steps decorated with ornamental carvings. The inner sanctuary features a shrine of 11 tapering *meru* roofs, resting places for the visiting mountain gods.

PENELOKAN

Its name means "Place to Look." This cool, 1,450-meter-high village perches on the rim of a caldera looking out over the sacred, blackened, smoking volcano of Gunung Batur and Lake Batur. Though not a particularly attractive village, views here are magnificent. Penelokan has a high, fresh climate and reasonable *losmen.* There's an admission charge for entering Penelokan, payable at checkpoints as you enter from the south or north. The Penelokan/Kintamani area has one of the worst reputations in Indonesia for horrid, money-hungry, aggressive people. Motorcycle drivers offering to take you down to the lake won't accept anything less than Rp5000. Some *bemo* drivers want Rp8000 for a charter down to the lake. Just laugh and start walking. Someone will come along and offer to take you for the standard fare of Rp1000.

GUNUNG BATUR

After Agung, Batur is the most sacred mountain on Bali. Most often the mountain's only sign of life is an occasional wisp of smoke that drifts across its lava-blackened slopes. The crescent-shaped lake takes up about one-third of the basin's total area. Measuring 13.8 km by 11 km, this is one of the largest and most beautiful calderas in the world. The crater's outer walls, about 30,000 years old, range from 1,267 meters to 2,153 meters above sea level. There are actually two calderas; the floor of one lies 120-300 meters lower than the other. Plan on a full day to explore them both.

You can easily find a guide if you arrive at the trailhead at 0330. They'll come out of the dark and offer to lead you for as little as Rp10,000.

Although you don't really need a guide, the fellow can help you find your way out of the clouds that can envelop the slopes of Gunung Batur without warning. The guides in Toya Bungkah offer three different climbs. The short one, up and back for the sunrise, is Rp25,000-30,000 (four hours). The medium one involves a walk around Batur's three craters, a visit to the bat cave, and a breakfast of eggs boiled by volcanic steam for Rp30,000-40,000 (five hours). The third option is the more interesting tour. Here you get the volcanically boiled eggs with banana and bread, the sunrise, a hike down to the other side of Gunung Batur plus a trip to the "lucky temple" of Toya Mampeh, where lava stopped just meters before the gateway. For this tour they ask Rp60,000-70,000 (all day). All these prices apply to a group (maximum four people) and reflect first offers only.

The easiest approach is from the northwest, beginning at Toya Mampeh. This climb, by way of the volcano's back door, can also begin from the west at Kintamani. Guides here ask Rp25,000 for one to two people plus around Rp5000 for each additional person. If you start on the path from Puri Astina at 0630, you can climb the volcano, rest in the hot springs, and grab a *bemo* back to Kintamani by 1200 or 1300. Though a strenuous ascent, Gunung Batur is the easiest Bali volcano to climb. Make sure you have sturdy shoes; wear long pants and a warm sweater, windbreaker, or sweatshirt. Most tourists are guided to the sandy top of the middle crater. The topmost crater to the north is another hour's climb, along a narrow rim only one meter wide, and the view isn't as fine. At the top is a small shrine to Vishnu. See the sun slowly lighting the whole lake, catch glimpses of Gunung Rinjani on Lombok to the east.

Karangasem Regency

With mighty Gunung Agung dominating the landscape, this regency's scenery is some of the most spectacular on the island. Karangasem is Bali's most traditional region, with rustic villages, hospitable people, and unique festivals. The 861-square-km regency is one of the most untouristed on Bali, removed from the frenzy of development. This is the only area of Bali where a number of archaic dance and musical forms are still regularly practiced and where the High Balinese language is still in common use.

GUNUNG AGUNG

When you fly into Bali, you'll see the shadowy outline of the giant blue-black mountain dominating the landscape. Early in the morning its peak can be seen poking through the clouds from almost any part of Bali. Whether in the bright sunshine or moonlight, a stream of clouds on the crest always trails off in the wind. Between July and October the fit and adventuresome can attempt the ascent of Gunung Agung. It's exhausting, and can be downright dangerous. Don't climb alone, and bring a flashlight, water, warm clothes, an umbrella (a necessity), and trail food. Long pants are also a good idea. Good hiking shoes with nonslip soles are a must for the final steep scramble over loose scree to the summit. Since there are innumerable trails leading skyward, you should have a guide, particularly in the early part of the climb. The cost depends upon how many climbers make up your group and what services, if any, are provided. Fit climbers can complete the whole ascent in a single day. Head back down by 1430 so you can arrive in Sorga, the uppermost hamlet of the slope, by 1730 for the drive back to Selat.

BESAKIH

Bali's oldest, largest, most impressive and austere temple complex is 60 km northeast of Denpasar and one-third the way up the slopes of Gunung Agung. Besakih, actually consisting of three temple compounds, is the "Mother Temple" of Bali and the most important of the island's *sad-kahyangan* religious shrines. It's Bali's supreme holy place, a symbol of religious unity, and the only temple that serves all Balinese. The first record of the temple's existence is from a chronogram dated A.D. 1007, possibly describing the death ritual for Mahendradatta. The great 1917 earthquake destroyed the temple, but it was subsequently restored to its original form. Besakih was again heavily damaged in1963 by a Gunung Agung eruption. The whole complex has since been extensively restored. Get an early start so you arrive about 0800.

Via a series of long stairways, the temple group ascends parallel ridges toward Gunung Agung, the honored birthplace of Bali's deities, tantamount to heaven. Beyond a great unadorned split gate, a broad terrace leads to a *gapura,* which opens onto 50 black, slender, pagoda-like *meru* temples. Long flights of stone steps lead to the main central temple, Pura Penataran Agung. In the third inner court of the central temple is the *sanggar agung,* a beautifully decorated 17th-century triple lotus stone throne representing the divine triad. This is the ritual center of Besakih. Farther up the mountain is another compound, **Pura Gelap,** the "Thunderbolt Temple." Highest, in the pine forests of Agung's southwest slope, is austere **Pura Pengabengan.**

CANDIDASA

Candidasa, meaning "Ten Temples," is named after a shrine in the eastern part of the village. It's a tidy, well-kept, three-km-long European tourist retreat on Bali's southeast coast where the local people are unobtrusive and the hotel folks eager to please. Attracting refugees from the frenetic southern honeypots, Candidasa is the type of place where you think you'll stay two days but end up staying a week. Best in the off-season. Visit nearby Tenganan to shop, and for a fascinating look at the ancient rituals of a traditional society. The sea currents here are unpredictable; swimming is not advisable. If there's no pool where you're staying, you can use a pool in any of the ritzier hotels for around Rp6000. Sunbathing is best on the seawall several meters above. Watch the wind and rain chase fishing craft across the sea. At street level is a statue of the giantess Hariti, surrounded by her many children. Childless couples often come to the temple seeking help from this goddess.

TENGENAN

This is an original pre-Hindu Balinese settlement, long a stronghold of native traditions, located about halfway between Padangbai and Amlapura. At the end of an asphalt country road up a narrow valley, Tenganan is far removed from the Javano-Balinese regions of Bali. Like Trunyan to the northwest, this small village is inhabited by the Bali Aga, aboriginal Balinese who settled the island long before the influx of immigrants from the decaying 16th-century Majapahit Empire. It might appear to be a stage-managed tourist site, but is actually a living, breathing village—the home of farmers, artists, and craftspeople.

The people have completely adapted to the tourist economy; nowadays tables selling palm leaf books are set up at intervals the whole length of the main street. Tenganan is a great place to just hang out; the walled village's quiet pace and somnolent air is all the more accentuated by the complete lack of vehicular traffic, except for the occasional motorcycle. There are no accommodations for tourists; the nearest hotels are in Candidasa.

Except for such visual blights as the row of green power poles down the center of the village's unique pebbled avenues, Tenganan is a living museum in which people live and work frozen in a 17th-century lifestyle, practicing their own architecture, kinship system, religion, dance, and music. Signs of the 20th century are the TV antennas on bamboo poles piercing the thatch rooftops, the motorcycles parked outside the compounds, and the occasional tinny sound of a cassette recorder or radio.

Rectangular in shape (500 meters by 250 meters), Tenganan shares many characteristics with other primitive villages on Nias and Sumba. Broad stone-paved streets, which serve as village commons, rise uphill in tiers so the rain flows down, providing drainage. Each level is connected by steep cobbled ramps. The only entrance to this fortress-like village is through four tall gates placed at each of the cardinal points. The main entrance in the south is called *lawangan kelod*.

Tenganan is the only place in Indonesia where double-*ikat* textiles are made. Rather loosely woven, these so-called "flaming cloths" (*kamben gringsing*) are used only in rites of passage or for ceremonial purposes. Only about six families still know all the double-*ikat* processes (coloring, tying, dyeing), and only about 15 people still weave *gringsing* on small makeshift breastlooms. Within the cloth, reddish or dark brown backgrounds, once dyed in human blood, are used to highlight intricate whitish and yellow designs of *wayang* puppet figures, rosettes, lines, and checks. *gringsing,* and they're generally sold only upon the death of the owner. The really precious *gringsing,* prized by serious textile collectors cost US$3500-5000.

Lontar are palm leaves on which intricate drawings have been etched, usually depicting scenes from Hindu epics. I Wayang Muditadnana makes about one five-page *lontar* book per month, which he sells mostly to tourists for Rp100,000 and up.

AMLAPURA

At one time Amlapura was the seat of one of the richest kingdoms of Bali, tracing its origins back to a 16th century Balinese prime minister known as Batan Jeruk. Lying at the foot of the holy mountain Gunung Agung, Amlapura is today the capital of Karangasem Regency.

Of Amlapura's four palaces, each facing the cardinal points, the most famous is that of the last *raja,* Anak Agung Anglurah Ketut. Puri Kanginan (also known as Puri Agung) is a big complex, surrounded by a thick redbrick wall. Enter the complex through an elaborate three-tiered gate. Inside, an air of slow decay prevails. The fountains have stopped spouting and dragons and serpents sit stonily with wide-open mouths, yet it's a functioning *puri* with connecting walkways over pools and compounds set aside for the royal family.

TIRTAGANGGA

Fifteen km northwest of Amlapura (Rp500 by *bemo*); the turnoff is just one-half km beyond the bridge after leaving Amlapura. One of the prettiest places in all of Bali, Tirtagangga ("Water of the Ganges") is a pool complex built by Raja Anak Agung Anglurah Ketut in 1947 with corvée labor on the site of a sacred spring that emerges from under a banyan tree, the site of a small water temple. This was only one of the old *raja's* weekend retreats; his other water palaces are at Ujung and Jungutan.

With its shallow pools, pleasant cool weather, few mosquitos, great beauty, quiet star-filled nights, and birds chirping over the constant sound of splashing water, Tirtagangga is perfect for relaxation. It's a sublime experience to swim laps in those big flower-strewn pools filled from mountain streams. Pools are drained mornings, but completely fill again by afternoon. It costs Rp700 adults, Rp200 children to use a 45-meter-long pool; you can come and go all day. The water is spine-tingling cold, so wait until noon to plunge in. After 1800 swimming is free of charge, but the water is too cold.

Buleleng Regency

This sprawling, 1,370-square-km regency offers mountain hikes, rustic villages, waterfalls, hot springs, untouched marine and forest reserves, silversmiths, beach resorts, a secluded coastline bordering a placid sea, and distinctive temples. The south end stretches across the foothills of Bali's central volcanos while the north's coastal plain faces the Java Sea. Because of Buleleng's geographic isolation from the densely populated south, it has developed distinct cultural differences in architecture, dance, and art. The regency's capital, Singaraja, has a cosmopolitan air with many ethnic and religious minorities existing in harmony. Tour buses from southern Bali seldom venture over the mountain passes; consequently, there are fewer beggars, touts, and hassles in the tourist enclaves of the region. In the early 1990s, the religious leader of Buleleng, the Pedanda Brahmana of Singaraja's Hindu University, attempted to strengthen the beliefs of the region's Hindus, decreeing that Buleleng's faithful must pay obeisance to God three times daily. Tourists complain about being awakened so early, but it's now custom.

SINGARAJA

Singaraja is a small seaport and the capital of Buleleng District, featuring tree-lined avenues, quiet residential perimeters, a wide market street, rows of bright Chinese shops, and horse-drawn carts amidst frenetic traffic. Singaraja has an entirely different character than Denpasar—more like Java than Bali. Chinese, Indian, Arab, and Buginese traders have called at its port since the 10th century, trading arms, opium, and *kepang* for fresh water, food, livestock, and slaves. Each of these groups has greatly impacted cultural life in the city. In Singaraja you can view sacred *lontar* books at **Gedong Kirtya** at the east end of Jl. Veteran. The 3,000-odd *lontar* in this library record the literature, mythology, magic formulas, medical science, folklore, religion, and history of Bali and Lombok. Many of the *lontar* were looted from the palace in Mataram during the Dutch military expedition to Lombok in 1894.

Festival offerings

A major weaving factory is **Berdikari** at Jl. Dewi Sartika 42, tel. 22217. It special-izes in reproducing ancient, finely detailed Buleleng silk *ikat,* sold for sky-high prices. There are looms in practically every home in the *kampung.* To buy *endek, ikat,* colorfast *sarung,* and gold-threaded *songket,* visit the cottage industry **Poh Bergong,** 10 km south of Singaraja. It's where retailers come to buy at wholesale prices. The **tourist information office,** Jl. Veteran 23, tel. (0362) 25141, is near the Gedong Kirtya; look for the sign from Jl. Veteran.

LOVINA BEACH

Lovina Beach was the first seaside resort to appear in the mid-'70s. Anak Agung Panji Tisna, the ruler of northern Bali, named this stretch of coast after the English word "love" in 1953. To get there, flag down a *bemo* (Rp500) from Singaraja any-where on Jl. Jen. A. Yani. Lovina has since become the generic term for a whole line of small villages and beaches that it has devoured. From east to west, these are: Pe-maron, Tukadmungga, Anturan, Kalibukbuk (or Banyualit), Kaliasem (or Lovina), and Temukus. Kalibukbuk has the most activity, while the fishing villages of Anturan (or Happy Beach) and Temukus are the quietest, with less densely packed restau-rants and accommodations.

Generally, the restaurants, stores, and services are on the south side of the road, ac-commodations on the north. Most are only a short walk from the beach or main road. In Lovina, enjoying beautiful sunsets involves simply walking out on your veranda. You can dive in glass-clear water, find good trekking paths, temples, and hot sulphur pools in the hills, and use centrally located Lovina as a base for day-trips to Tulam-ben, Bali Barat National Park, Pulau Menjangan, the Buddhist monastery, Yeh Sanih, and the lakes and volcanos of the central mountain range. At night fishing fleets head out in their *jukung,* luring fish for netting with kerosene pressure lanterns swaying and glowing yellow along the waterfront. For around Rp5000 you can join them for a two- or three-hour late afternoon trip. The bay is great for swimming: Lovina's warm sea laps lazily at the gray-sand shore during the dry season, quite tame compared to the volatile southern coasts. The wide expanses of sand are great for sunning (espe-cially at Kalibukbuk), and beach masseurs are available for Rp5000.

To spend breakfast with dolphins, buy a ticket the day before from boys on the beach. Average price is Rp10,000 per person and the length of the tour may vary from 2.5 to three hours, depending on the season, the boat, and the captain. Deter-mine in advance how many hours you're going to spend snorkeling versus hours looking for dolphins. When you buy your ticket, give the vendor your room number and someone will wake you with a knock on your door 15 minutes before the predawn departure. It's a 30- to 60-minute trip to dolphin territory. Watch for the different species, particularly the large, slow swimmers that can weigh up to a ton. In any event, you'll get a boat ride, tea, and *pisang goreng* breakfast, and snorkeling on the return trip. Don't let the boatmen go in before the agreed-upon time.

BUDDHIST MONASTERY

Go first to Banjar village, about 18 km west of Singaraja on the highway to Seririt. From the highway where the *bemo* lets you off, walk two km; then, at the intersection just before Banjar Tega's market, turn left up the paved road. Climb another two km to the hilltop monastery. Or take a *honda ojek* (Rp2000) all the way up the steep hill from the Banjar turnoff. Wear long pants or a *sarung* as you must arrive respectfully dressed. *Sarung* rent for Rp500. Entering the *vihara*, sign the guestbook, and give a donation.

This storybook monastery, known as Brahma Vihara Asrama, has a gleaming orange roof, Sukothai-style gold leaf Buddha images, *raksasa* door guardians, stupa with Buddha eyes, and exuberant woodcarvings—a dazzling mix of Balinese Hindu and Buddhist components. Opened in 1970, it's the only Buddhist monastery on Bali. Tibet's Dalai Lama paid a visit in 1982, and Bali's Chinese make regular pilgrimages to this peaceful ashram. Severely damaged in the July 1976 earthquake, it has since been completely restored.

Tabanan Regency

Tabanan is one of Indonesia's richest rice-growing districts, with paddies stretching from the coast to as high as 700 meters on the lower slopes of Gunung Batukaru, the second highest mountain on Bali. Every temple in Tabanan contains a shrine venerating this mountain's spirit, Mahadewa. Tabanan's other major summits are Sangiyang and Pohon.

Three labor-intensive crops of new high-yield rice are grown each year, with soybeans planted in between to rejuvenate the soil. The *subak* of Tabanan average 12-15 tons of rice per hectare, making the inhabitants some of the most productive rice farmers in all Indonesia. Besides rice, there are crops of tea, cacao, groundnuts, and tropical fruits. The regency's higher climes are alpine, with mountain streams, moss, prehistoric tree ferns, wildflowers, creepers, orchids, leeches, butterflies, birds, and screaming monkeys. Lake Bratan in the middle of the regency's central highlands was formed by the volcano Gunung Catur, now inactive. The area is green, opulent, and peaceful, and the people friendly. As you leave Tabanan's southern plains and drive north to Bedugul on Lake Bratan, the landscape changes from tiers of gentle rice fields to gardens of onions, cabbages, and papaya. Thatched palm huts give way to sturdy cottages made of wood, tile, and stone. In the southern villages, the kitchen is separated from the other buildings of the family compound, but in these cold mountain villages, people cook in the same building where they sleep and live.

BEDUGUL AND LAKE BRATAN

A small, friendly lakeside resort in the middle of the central highlands southwest of Gunung Catur, an hour's drive (48 km) from Denpasar on the main road north to Singaraja (30 km away). Bedugul is the name given to a number of villages strung out along the lake's western shore. With its comfortable accommodations, wonderful fresh fruit and vegetables, lakeside views, blankets of fog, and an average temperture of 16-20° C, Bedugul has been a popular weekend retreat since Dutch times. It's a welcome change from Bali's tropical scenery and humidity. Few tourists ever stop here.

Serene Lake Bratan fills the ancient crater of long-inactive volcano Gunung Catur (2,096 meters), which towers over the lake. Over 1,200 meters above sea level, Bedugul is nearly as cool as the Gunung Batur region. Across the lake are some 25-meter-deep caves (Gua Jepeng) dug out by Indonesian slave laborers for the Japanese during the war. The caves are accessible from the rim trail up to Gunung Catur. You can walk there from Taman Rekreasi in about 45 minutes. Don't pass up the beautiful hikes to shrines along the lakeshore and through the steep, jungle-covered hills and pine forests. A lovely *desa* called Kembangmerta, on the other side of the lake from Hotel Bedugul, is two km from the main road or just one km from Ulun Danu Temple. Dotting the whole hillside are holiday homes of rich Balinese.

In front of Hotel Bedugul is the **Taman Rekreasi Bedugul** (Bedugul Leisure Park) complex (admission Rp500, plus parking fee) where you can go parasailing (Rp20,000 for 15 minutes) and rent water-skiing (Rp25,000 for training, tows, and use of jumping ramp) equipment. Motorboats rent for Rp20,000 (30 minutes, capacity four people), covered boats Rp20,500 per tour of the lake (capacity eight people), jetskis Rp20,000 for 15 minutes. Paddleboats (Rp1000) and wooden *prahu* are also available for paddling across to the temple.

A batik depiction of a Javanese gamelan orchestra, Solo Palace Musuem, West Java

Sumatra

Introduction

You'll feel a vast difference between Sumatra and neighboring Java. Sumatra is far wilder, more rugged, more ethnically diverse, and more difficult to get around in. Islam entered some coastal regions of Sumatra more than 300 years before it touched Java. With the exception of northern Sumatrans, the people are generally less educated and poorer than the Javanese, and their culture is not as refined. People are shorter, darker, more wiry—a jungle people. You're apt to find more *kasar* individuals on Sumatra, which—after Java—is sometimes refreshing. Compared to Java, this island has a grand beauty, and the distances and space are enormous.

About the same size and population as California, almost one-third of the island is continuous lowland and saltwater swamp with nipa palms and mangrove trees extending some 1,370 km down the whole east coast. The rivers are shallow and winding; fine white sand beaches, but with rugged surf, are found on the west coast and its offshore islands. An unbroken mountain wall ranging from 1,575 to 3,805 meters marches down the entire western aspect of the island. Called Bukit Barisan ("Parade of Mountains"), this range includes 93 volcanic peaks, 15 of them still active. All major ecosystems are represented in reserves throughout the island, with the exception of lowland rainforests, always the first to come under the chainsaw. The northwest and southwest regions are still quite inaccessible and wild. There's a chain of islands off the west coast—Simeulue, Nias, the Mentawais, and Enggano—with rocky, reef-enclosed coasts. The mangrove forests of Sumatra are the largest and most biologically diverse in the world. In the rainforests trees such as the *ketapang* soar over 60 meters high. The extraordinary *rafflesia* grows up to one meter in diameter—the largest bloom in the world.

Sumatra has a greater variety of wildlife than any other island in Indonesia. The jungle is near at hand and the island's wild creatures have always played a great part in its myth and folklore. Elephants, Sumatran rhinoceros, and large free-ranging populations of Sumatran orangutans are the island's best-known fauna. Orangutans, rhinos, and wild pigs are only found in the north, while the tapir and certain species of monkeys are found only in the south. A cousin to the Javanese tiger, Sumatran tigers occasionally venture into remote villages to take a pig or calf. Other predatory species include the elusive Sumatran clouded leopard, the civet, and a small, striped forest cat called the *macan akar.* One species of orangutan lives on Sumatra, a rare primate found only in the most remote parts of the island. Orangutans may be

Sumatra

Andaman

Sea

THAILAND

South

China

Sea

Subang
Banda Aceh
Tangse
Lhokseumawe
Penang
Meulaboh
Takengon
Langsa
Aceh
Blangkejeren
MALAYSIA
Tapaktuan
Binjai
Medan
Brastagi
Tebingtinggi
Danau
Toba
North
Sumatra
P. Simeulue
Singkil
Prapat
Samosir
KUALA LUMPUR
Rantauprapat
Sibolga
Gunungsitoli
Padangsidempuan
P. Nais
Melaka
Dumai
Telukdalam
Riau
Bengkalis
P. Batu
Pekanbaru
SINGAPORE
Bukittinggi
Tanjungpinang
P. Siberut
Padang
Solok
Rengat
P. Lingga
Muarasiberut
West
Sumatra
P. Sipora
Sungaipenuh
Jambi
P. Singkep
Pagai Utara
Mukomuko
Jambi
Pagai Selatan
South
Sumatra
P. Bangka
Bengkulu
Lubuklinggau
Pangkalpenang
INDIAN
Bengkulu
Lahat
Palembang
Prabumulih
Bintuahan
Lampung
P. Enggano
Kotabumi
Java
Sea
OCEAN
Panjang
Belimbing
P. Krakatau
Serang
JAKARTA
Java

N

Strait of Malacca

KEP. MENTAWAI

KEP. RIAU

0   150 mi

0   150 km

observed in a semiwild state in the Bukit Lawang Rehabilitation Center at Bohorok in northern Sumatra. Another huge reserve, where many of Sumatra's species are found, is the Gunung Leuser National Park of Aceh and North Sumatra. Sumatra is also the home of Indonesia's grandest animal, the Indian elephant.

Bengkulu

Formerly known as Bencoolen, this old coastal town of 70,000 is the capital of Bengkulu Province. A famous 18th- and 19th-century British trading settlement, Bengkulu is rich in history. In 1973 it had only 10 cars, one restaurant, and several small *warung*; the first traffic light was installed in 1979. Today development is accelerating, with paved roads, regular flights, a new port for larger ships, and a dramatic population increase. But Bengkulu is still a small, peaceful town and a pleasure to visit, where long sandy, paradise-like beaches line the coast not far from town. Moderate-priced hotels are generally well run and clean, there are good restaurants, and the local people are friendly and easygoing.

The British, driven from their last stronghold in West Java at Banten, built several fortresses in Bengkulu. After striking a deal with the local *raja* for the exclusive rights to purchase the pepper crop, the first English factory, York, was built in Bengkulu in 1685 about three km north of present Fort Marlborough. Malaria and other diseases soon killed off so many British it was said "two monsoons were the life of a man." Unwilling or unable to pay the natives enough for their pepper, the British had to resort to coercive and repressive measures to maintain production. By March 1719 relations had deteriorated so badly that the Bengkulunese stormed and burned the fort, forcing the British to flee for Batavia and later India. The British did not return until 1724. Sir Stamford Raffles, the founder of Singapore, arrived in Bengkulu in 1818 to revive British fortunes and the failing pepper trade. Over the next several years he freed the slaves and pacified the pepper chiefs, healing the old wounds. But after Raffles was recalled to Britain in 1823, British rule in West Sumatra was doomed.

The tourist office at Jl. Pembangunan 3, Padang Harapan (south of the town center), has little printed info but can help arrange guided jungle excursions to view wildlife or the rafflesia. **Kampung Cina** (Chinatown), with its row of buildings with red-tiled roofs, is the old part of town. **Bengkulu Musium Negeri** is on Jl. Pembangunan, Padang Harapan; open 0800-1400 (except Mondays). Sukarno, Indonesia's first president, who distinguished himself early in his political career by his vocal opposition to colonial rule, was arrested by the Dutch on Java in 1933, brought to Bengkulu, and put under house arrest for nine years. Later, when the Japanese occupied Sumatra, he was captured again. **Sukarno's House** is quite small; it's off Jl.

Sukarno-Hatta, open weekdays 0800-1400, Friday until 1100, Saturday until 1200; closed Monday. Built 1709-1719 by the British East India Co., **Fort Marlborough** is the most formidable fort ever built by the British in the Orient; it is occupied now, as is usually the case with old forts, by the Indonesian army. The whole structure is presently being refinished in cement, which really lessens its historical impact. The well-preserved castle-like parapets around the courtyard contain the original cannon tracks. From its high walls are excellent views of the sleepy harbor, the *pasar,* Kampung Cina, oxcarts, and whirling kites. The back of the fort has been left in its original state; take a walk along the high and windy battlements that overlook the ruins of a rear drawbridge. The old prison with its original bars is now used as a bicycle room for army personnel; inside the compound stand old English gravestones with inscriptions.

Danau Dendam Tak Sudah, a beautiful small lake some eight kilometers southeast of town, is famous for a water orchid *vanda hookeriana)* which grows along its shores—the only place in the world where this species grows wild. The orchid is a protected plant species and may not be picked. When it blooms in June/July and October, the lake is completely surrounded in brilliant pink. The British started to dam the lake during their occupation in the first half of the 19th century, but never finished; its name means "dam not finished." There are no tourist facilities except makeshift *warung* set up in the busy seasons when the orchids bloom. Near the lake are cabanas where visitors may sit and take in the gorgeous view. Two routes lead to the lake. The easiest is by chartered taxi or a public taxi from the village of Dusun Besar. Take the main highway seven kilometers towards Kepahiang, turn left on Jl. Dusun Besar, then walk for 1.5 kilometers. Or take the main highway five kilometers towards Manna and turn left on Jl. Danau and walk for 2.5 kilometers.

Medan

Huge, flat, dusty, sprawling Medan is Sumatra's largest city and Indonesia's third largest, a dominant port and the capital of North Sumatra Province. Though noisy, dirty, crowded, Medan is a necessary departure point for Malaysia or points inland like Prapat and Brastagi. This area used to be a regular battle site in wars between the sultans of Deli and Aceh; *medan* means "level, open field." The city was founded out of a tiny group of *kampung* in a marshy lowland by Sultan Mahmud Perdasa Alam in the 17th century. By 1860 the northeast Deli coastal area had become a highly productive plantation district. All the region's races have converged on Medan. The Javanese originally came to work on the thriving plantations. There are also communities of Sikhs, Acehnese, Riau Islanders, and Arabians, as well as very strong Chinese, Indian, Minangkabau, Melayu, Islamic, and Christian Batak populations.

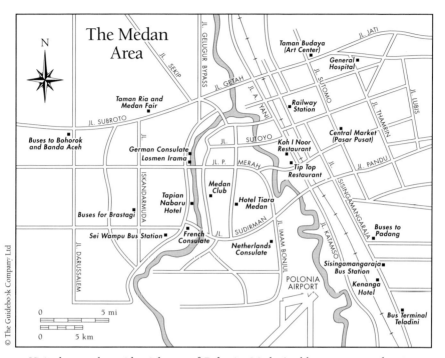

Visit the stately residential area of **Polonia**, Medan's old quarter near the airport with elegant government buildings, parks, and large peaked tile-roof houses built by the colonials. The largest mosque in Sumatra, handsome **Mesjid Raya** (Great Mosque), was built in prewar Moroccan style in 1906. Though seemingly neglected today, this edifice is beautifully and richly decorated, set off by bright stained-glass windows. **Parisada Hindu Dharma Temple** on the corner of Jl. Diponegoro and Jl. Zainul Arifin, is the spiritual hub of Medan's sizable Indian population. The historic palace of the sultan of Deli at Jl. Katamso 66, also called the Maimoon Palace, **Istana Sultan Deli** is an ornate building open all day to the public. For a private visit, apply to the sultan's aide, tel. 22123. Tours can also be arranged. The large villas constructed by Dutch planters are found along wide flowering avenues such as Jl. Jen. Sudirman in the Polonia area, on the west side of Medan across the Deli River, and along Jl. Imam Bonjol and Jl. Balai Kota. **Deli Maatschappij** (now PTP Tobacco Co.) was the first European building, built as a plantation office in 1869. **Museum Bukit Barisan**, Jl. H. Zainal Arifin 8 features mementos from the wartime resistance movement as well as the 1958 Sumatran rebellion; replicas of traditional houses and tribal cultural exhibits are in the back. Open Mon.-Thurs. 0800-1300, Friday 0800-1000, Saturday 0800-1200; free.

For maps and information on Medan and North Sumatra Province, visit the **North Sumatran Tourist Office** (Dinas Pariwisata), Jl. Jen. A. Yani 107, tel. (061) 511-101 or 512-300. Open Mon.-Thurs. 0800-1500, Friday 0800-1200, Saturday 0800-1400. Be sure to change your money in Medan if you're venturing inland, where banks are few and far between and offer lousy rates. **Bank Negara Indonesia**, Jl. Pemuda 12, tel. 22333, gives the best rates.

VICINITY OF MEDAN

Pematang Siantar

Located 128 km southeast of Medan, in one of Sumatra's richest tea- and tobacco-growing districts, Pematang Siantar is North Sumatra's second-largest city and a major transport hub for the whole Simalungan area. A smaller, cooler version of Medan (but just as noisy!), this city is the capital and largest town of the Simalungun Batak tribe, though there are many non-Simalungun people here, including Chinese, Indians, Karo, and Toba Batak. Also the site of Universitas Simalungan, north of town. Pasar Horas, Siantar Plaza, and Pantoan are the town's new, glitzy shopping centers.

Bukit Lawang

In complete contrast to filthy, smelly, noisy Medan, Bukit Lawang is a relaxing village of several hundred people 90 km west of Medan and 15 km west of Bohorok on the edge of 900,000-hectare Gunung Leuser National Park, deep in North Sumatra's backcountry.

Most travelers venture here to view our distant cousins the orangutan in a right environment, but then discover Bukit Lawang is a delightful place to relax as well. People are very friendly and not a few speak quite good English. A high-quality Swedish-made video is shown twice weekly and your questions answered at the **Bohorok River Visitor's Center**. From the village's many *losmen*, it's an easy 20- to 30-minute walk to the free canoe crossing and entrance to the reserve. Obtain three-day permits (Rp3000) at the PHPA office in Bukit Lawang or from the office in Medan (Jl. Sisingmangaraja Km 55). Try to arrive on weekday mornings to avoid hordes of domestic tourists.

At night visit the house where the singers and musicians play; really nice voices. In the nearby village visit the rubber-processing factory; the manager will show you around. Swim in the Bohorok River. You can also rent a rubber inner tube from **Wisma Leuser Guesthouse** or other places (Rp1000) and shoot the rapids downriver for 2.5 hours. It's great fun but can be literally an ass-ripping experience if you have the misfortune to clip a submerged rock at high speed. Wear shoes because of the river's rocky bottom and bring some money in a plastic bag for the bus back.

The Batak

Some scholars believe the word *batak* was originally a derogatory Old Malay term for "robber"; others translate it as "pig-eater." Another theory insists the word originates from Bataha, the name of a Karen village in the Burma/Siam area, the ancient home of the Batak people. The sturdy rice-growing Batak live in fertile mountainous valleys extending up to 200 km north and 300 km south of Lake Toba. The Batak are shorter and heavier than the Minangkabau; they've kept their racial stock pure by living inland, and developed an early reputation for ferocity and cannibalism.

Their society is stubbornly traditional, the majority living in small, independent, self-sufficient, tightly knit villages. But these people also highly value tertiary education, the community sharing the expense of sending the brightest boys in the village to school in Medan or Jakarta. Many Batak are thus well placed in government, academia, and business circles. They're also some of the best chess players in the East; every village has its master. A barefoot peasant stalemated the Dutch World Champion in the Grand Hotel in Medan in 1939, a major event in Batak history.

Racially, the Batak are cousins to such "First Wave" tribes as the Igorots of the Philippines, the Dayaks of Kalimantan, and the Torajans of South Sulawesi. The Batak settled in Sumatra after fleeing Mongol warriors who invaded their highland homes in northern Thailand. Villages were once extremely hostile to one another—you can still find remnants of old bamboo and earth fortifications at Nanggar and Lumban Garaga. Enslavement of war captives and debtors was widespread, and enemies were eaten so they would be utterly obliterated. The Batak tribes retained their own way of life right up to the middle of the 19th century, when Dutch and German missionaries discovered and began to convert them. Their last king, Sisingamangaraja, died in battle against the Dutch in 1907. Samosir Island was the last bastion of the Toba Batak, conquered by tourists in the early 1970s.

Batak headdress, Sumatra

The Final Days of the Rubber Empire

Rubber continued to drop. But at an accelerating pace. The rubber world woke up with a start. No end of letters were written to the editors of the two daily papers in Medan. There were prophecies of a speedy re-establishment; but there were also prophesies of a further drop and total collapse.

The planters were devoured by an unbridled passion for speculation. They had grown used during the fat years to a life of luxury. Everything had grown more expensive—the shops, the hotels. It was easy come, easy go, and the administration had behaved as recklessly as their employees. Lavishly, new appointments had followed one another. Nobody cared. All would be well in the end.

And now suddenly it appeared that nothing would ever be well again. The bonus ran to only a few thousand guilders. And in their need for money to keep up their new standard of existence, they began to buy futures. American shares were especially in demand. There was a feverish activity. Newspapers were opened first at the stock exchange news. The telephone tinkled all day. Expensive conversations ran along the wires to Medan. Stocks and shares rose wildly. Everybody bought, or at least almost everybody. The money that was still over from earlier bonuses was not enough to take back to Holland. No faith was left in rubber. They had to run a risk in order to collect a capital. And now that the gold rush was over, the old desire for Holland revived. So they wanted money all the more, money, money! That was what they had come East for. And sacrificed ten, fifteen, twenty years of their youth.

Rubber continued to drop. One could not stay here for ever. After forty, or forty-five at the most, one was finished by this murderous climate. At that age one was dismissed to make room for new people with young bodies and fresh courage. The company did not bother about one once one had left. That was one's own affair. Estate companies are not charitable institutions. Eight years— five years remained to make one's pile. But what could one earn in these years with prices as they were now? Twenty, thirty thousand guilders at best. That would mean a narrow existence for the rest of one's life. For the miserable little remainder that one had left over for Holland.

Bethlehem Steel was rising, rising. A month, two months were enough to get rich. Then one would have back all the money one had let indifferently slip through one's fingers. And then, of course, one would be careful and save. No more expensive cars. No orgies at the club and in the hotels. No more silk underclothes for one's wife.

Rubber continued to drop. The banks were granting colossal overdrafts. People crowded together. They could not bear the solitude of the home. They had to seek comfort at the club; and there, of course, they drank again and danced, and huddled themselves in each other's arms. They wanted to forget the uncertain future with a wife and child, to forget how they lost their youth. They could not draw back, not yet awhile. They still had credit. Iron necessity had not got them by the throat yet. Besides, they no longer knew how to save. They hardly realized what was luxury and what was not, and their nerves could not bear the grey monotony of work without stimulus. They had poisoned themselves for four years, by their unbridled enjoyment.

Then came the final blw: the collapse of Wall Street. Prices tumbled down. Telephones rang the whole day long. They sold to try to save what was still left to be saved. They lost thousands, and cursed themselves for having gambled. They would have to work now—what else was there left? Work, yes, if the administration would let them.

Rubber continued to drop. It was at production price now. Then it dropped below it. Every pint of latex meant a loss. And every day produced thousands and thousands of pints. Every day, too, saw mass dismissals.

Panic ruled the rubber world.

~ Madelon Lulofs, Rubber, 1933

(following pages) Lake Meninjau, Sumatra

CANNIBALISM

The only human flesh eaters on the island, the Batak were the infamous "head-hunters of Sumatra" in tales of yore. Cannibalism was most prevalent among the Pakpak, although usually only token bits of flesh were eaten for ceremonial occasions, to obtain the attributes, luck, or courage of the victim. Herodotus, the Greek historian, first recorded the practice; Marco Polo in 1292 claimed the Batak ate their parents when they grew too old to work. Marsden, in 1783, wrote the first accurate account of cannibalism; when it was published it shocked the so-called civilized world. Those judged guilty of incest, murder, thievery, or adultery were condemned to be eaten by their fellow villagers, the most degrading of all punishments. In these punitive feasts the victims were not passionately or vengefully killed, but devoured according to fixed ethical rules.

THE ARTS

Older settlements feature a distinctive type of house found nowhere else in Indonesia. Raised on piles soaked for years in mud, these houses are so sturdy they often last 100 years. With not a single nail used, just rope and wooden pegs, the gable ends of these dynamic structures are richly ornamented with mosaics and woodcarvings of serpents, double spirals, lizards, life-giving female breasts, and elongated dark-colored monsters' heads (*singa*) with bulging eyes. The walls are made from heavy planks and the roof rises high, often sloping inward toward the center. The traditional building stays cool indoors even during the hottest part of the day.

Village men make their own music. A *gondang* band consists of cloth-covered metal gongs of different sizes, clarinet-type instruments, and two-stringed lutes made of palm fibers. The Batak are renowned for their powerfully expressive, ethereal hymn singing. Batak women's traditional dancing is ritualistic and slow. The only truly traditional folk dance left is trance dancing, similar to Balinese trance dances —the big difference is that on Bali they're still part of the people's religion. Dance festivals occur on certain dates fixed each year by the priest-doctors. The art of the Batak is an expression of their religious ideas, and is deeply concerned with magic. The Batak are sophisticated in the arts of metalworking, tie-dying, woodcarving, boat-making, and bone, shell, and bark fabrication. All show a mixture of Dongson and Indian influences.

BRASTAGI

A popular resort town in a mountain forest region 70 km from Medan and almost 1,400 meters above sea level. With its cool healthy climate, beautiful scenery, and fine green plantations, this Karo market center is one of the highlights of the journey through Sumatra. At the turn of the century, the Dutch built roads, bungalows, administration buildings, and clinics in Brastagi, and Dutch merchants used to retire here after prosperous careers in Medan. This is still a rich area for European vegetables (including beets, red cabbage, and lima beans), fragrant flowers, and fruits, which are exported to Penang and Singapore. Carrots are so plentiful they're fed to horses. Flies are numerous—make sure your room has a screen. Brastagi makes an excellent base from which to visit live volcanos and Karo villages. **Tugu Perjuangan** is a monument to the Karo people who took part in the '45 revolution against the Dutch. Brastagi has one of the most colorful fruit and vegetable markets in Indonesia on Tuesday and Friday. There are also at least five souvenir shops on the main street, Jl. Veteran.

GUNUNG SIBAYAK
The 2,172-meter summit of this volcano dominates Brastagi's skyline north of town. From Semangat Gunung at the base, it's a 1.5- to two-hour climb to the top. Allow six hours up and back. Start early (by 0700) before it clouds over. Wisma Sibayak and Hotel Ginsata sell maps (Rp500) to Gunung Sibayak. Get a bus to Daulu junction, nine km down the road toward Medan. Buses leave Brastagi for Medan every 15 minutes starting at 0530. From the junction, walk three km to Semangat Gunung, pay the small entrance fee, and give homage to Nini, the mountain's spirit. You don't need a guide as the trail is easy to follow. Be warned that on weekends and school holidays (May-June), a thousand climbers may scamper up Sibayak. After your climb, soak your aching feet and thighs in **Lau Debuk-Debuk** medicinal sulphur springs (Rp500). While in the area see **Sikulikap Waterfall**, only a two-km walk from the hot springs. A new road will someday lead right up to the crater.

Nini Kertah Ernala ("Grandmother of the Gleaming Sulphur") is the mountain's spirit. Be polite to her or suffer the consequences. Locals perform an incense-burning and betelnut-chewing ritual before the climb; the trappings for the ceremony cost around Rp200. On the trail you'll often see cigarette butts stuck on forked sticks—if the cigarette burned evenly and regularly, the climber proceeded; if not, s/he descended and waited for another, more propitious day.

Lake Toba

Lake Toba is the largest lake in Southeast Asia (1,707 square km) and one of the deepest (450 meters) in the world—the Lake Geneva of Southeast Asia. The mythical homeland of the Batak people, it was formed as a result of a mammoth volcanic explosion, believed to be the greatest in the history of the planet. So mighty was this titanic eruption, a veil of incandescent ash wrapped around the earth, plunging it into the darkness of the last ice age about 75,000 years ago. Today surrounded on all sides by pine-covered beaches, steep mountain slopes and cliffs, with Samosir Island sitting right in the middle, Lake Toba is a spellbinding sight. The best-known Batak subgroup, the Toba Batak, live around the lake. One million strong, they are considered the most aggressive, direct, and flamboyant of all Batak groups, and proud of it. The original tribe, the Toba Batak have the purest lineages and speak the most uncorrupted dialect. They can trace their family lines back 10 generations, to a time when any stranger who stared upon them was killed and eaten. This fate probably befell the first missionaries in the area; the last recorded instance of cannibalism took place in 1906. Eighty percent are Christian, but their religion is mixed strongly with ancestor worship. Many isolated Toba Batak tribes living on the lake's west side still haven't had much contact with the outside. Entrance gates of some fortress-like Toba Batak villages are still locked at night against hostile intruders.

Sipisopiso Waterfall lies at the northern end of Lake Toba. From the 120-meter-high lookout point above this beautiful falls is a 360-degree panorama of the waterfall, the precipitous valley below, Tongging, Lake Toba, and mountains—an unforgettable sight. From Brastagi take a *bemo* to Kabanjahe, then ask for the bus to Situnggaling (30 minutes). From there it's a one-hour walk to the falls.

PRAPAT

A busy, congested lakeside resort mostly spoiled by tourism. It has a cool, dry climate, pine-covered beaches, and spectacular views. It's the main town on Lake Toba and the principal embarkation point for ferries to Samosir. Upon entering Prapat, you must pay Rp200 even if you only want to go to Samosir. A tourist office is located near the arched entrance. Drop in at the Batak Cultural Center, Jl. Josep Sinaga 19, to see what's brewing; dances and musical performances are usually staged on Saturday night (Rp1250). Enthusiastic Batak singing and other forms of entertainment are staged on occasion at Hotel Prapat. Saturday is the big market day, when Pasar Tigaraja by the ferry dock swarms with Batak from outlying villages. Woodcarvings, leather goods, curios, and the usual tourist fare are on sale at relatively high prices. Bring sufficient

Lake Toba, north Sumatra

cash, as moneychangers and banks consistently offer poor rates. Butar Sinaga (a.k.a. Mr. Jungle) conducts trekking tours of the area, specializing in orchid treks. Contact him through the Post Restaurant.

Samosir Island

The original home of the Toba Batak, Samosir Island offers a cool, sunny climate, superb hiking and swimming, royal tombs, dramatic Batak architecture, stonecarvings, and very reasonable accommodations and food. Samosir is a more relaxing place to stay than Prapat—quieter, with cleaner water. No a/c, but you don't need it. If you plan to stay a while, bring good books. Watch your gear and close your windows at night, as there is theft from rooms all over Tuk Tuk and Ambarita. No matter what your religion, attend church on Samosir; the ardor with which the people worship and sing in praise of Christ is something to see. The island is technically a peninsula, connected in the west by a narrow isthmus at the foot of Gunung Belirang. The land slopes gently into the waters on the west side while the east edge forms 500-meter-high cliffs.

TOMOK

A traditional village noted for its old stone coffins, Tomok is nine km and 45 minutes across the lake from Prapat. At the intersection of the main and dock roads, climb the steps to the top of a small hill. A huge *hariam* tree houses the spirit of Raja Sidabutar, pre-Christian head of an early tribe. The tree was planted close to his carved tomb 180 years ago on the anniversary of his death. The carved statue of a woman with a coconut shell on her head represents Sidabutar's queen. Mysteriously, the third tomb also bears a woman's face. It is said she was Sidabutar's lover, whom the king said should be killed on the day he died, so they could enter the afterlife together. His orders were followed, and she was allowed her own tomb in the royal cemetery. Her tomb was smeared with her blood; the crimson splotches can still be seen. Nearby are statues and stone chairs.

Inland past dozens of souvenir stands is the Museum of King Soribuntu Sidabutar in a traditional house. Farther inland is another graveyard with stone coffins and old trees. Lining the way are over 200 stands sell artifacts, textiles, clothing, Batak calendars, magic medicine staffs, *pustaha* augury books (Rp10,000), whole carved doors (Rp150,000), two-stringed mandolins, and "antiques" made while you wait. Prices go up when the tourist boats disgorge their cargo, so bargain intensely. Young girls and old grannies weave *ulos* cloths in their booths; better quality blankets cost Rp25,000 (Rp40,000 starting price). The older colorfast ones are Rp350,000-500,000. Better prices for textiles on the other side of the island in Pangururan.

TUK TUK

Tuk Tuk is located on a small peninsula five km and a one-hour stroll from Tomok. Here you'll find the island's best selection of low-priced lodgings and restaurants. Although it's getting touristy, with building everywhere, Tuk Tuk is still quieter and more private than Tomok, and offers frequent ferry connections. You can still find a Batak house for Rp2000 with *mandi*. If you go to bed early, you'll miss some of the best music of your life, especially on Saturday nights—buy a bottle of *arak bangkilo* and join the outdoor groups. Climb up on the grassy plateau between Tuk Tuk and the mountain: sweeping view, perfect meditation venue, weird trees.

HARANGGAOL

This small picturesque village and market town is before Tongging on the northeast edge of Lake Toba. Just before the road from Kabanjahe begins its twists and turns down to the lakeshore, there is a stupendous view above the town and over the lake. A Catholic church and some typical Simalungan-style *ramakh adat* can be seen. On Mondays, one of the largest bulk markets in the area is held here, attended by Karo Batak from the highlands an other Batak tribes from surrounding areas.

Aceh Province

Sumatra's northernmost province and the westernmost province of Indonesia, Aceh seems a nation apart from the rest of the island and the country, and it could indeed support itself very well from its natural-gas revenues alone. Few travelers make it up this far because of Aceh's (mostly unfounded) reputation for religious extremism. If you don't wear shorts or braless jerseys, and you speak some Indonesian, you may find this the friendliest, most civilized province in Indonesia. Its hospitable people, historic architecture and remains, rugged mountains, superlative beaches, and picturesque rural areas will make your trip quite memorable. Two points to keep in mind: beer is largely forbidden to Aceh residents, though foreigners can buy it in hotels and restaurants. And do not carry or smoke marijuana, though locals may offer it to you. The police search likely looking foreigners and throw them behind bars for a few (or many) months if anything is found.

The 5th-century *Liang* annals of China mention a Buddhist state in the Aceh region. In the 7th and 8th centuries Indian traders introduced Hinduism, and by the 9th century Islam made its first inroads into Indonesia at present-day Lhokseumawe. When Marco Polo visited Aceh on his return journey from China in 1292, he wrote an account of the first well-established Islamic sultanate in Southeast Asia. The small sultanates in regions such as Perlak, Bonua, Lingga, and Pidie were all gradually consolidated under one sultanate, with its capital in Great Aceh, where Banda Aceh is today. During the 16th and 17th centuries the capital, Banda Aceh, was a major international trading center that attracted settlements of Indians, Chinese, Arabs, Persians, and Turks. In 1507 began a long line of sultanates which lasted until the final sultan, Tuanku Muhamat Dawot, capitulated to the Dutch in 1903. In the early years of the new republic the Darul Islam movement, based in West Java, attempted to establish a theocratic state in Indonesia. The Acehnese joined the rebellion and it took from 1953 to 1961 for them to reach a compromise with the central government. Although Jakarta has wisely declared Aceh a "Special Autonomous Territory" (Daerah Istimewa) where Islamic law applies, today it is still a very tender area politically.

Yet with all their strict adherence to the precepts of Islam, the Acehnese still give great credence to heretical, almost pantheistic practices. The Islamic judicial system (*hukom*) is the law of the land as long as it does not interfere with *adat*, which remains very strong. Ritual offerings are still employed when planting and harvesting, there is implicit belief in the paranormal such as "invincible" stones, and the interpretation of dreams and omens is widespread. Like so many other places in Indonesia, religion has been adapted to fit local needs. Traditional technology still survives in the interior, but sewing, metalwork, filigree, weapons, and fine unglazed earthenware pottery are all slowly disappearing with the importation of synthetic goods. The lack of tourism hastens their disappearance. Acehnese metalworking is superlative. The finely crafted weaponry, an art developed over decades of holy war, includes shields with Moorish designs and swords with mystic Arabic markings.

Sumatran crocodile

Baturrachman Mosque, Banda Aceh, north Sumatra

BANDA ACEH

Located on the northern tip of Sumatra, this city faces two oceans: the Strait of Malacca and the Indian Ocean. The Sungai Aceh River flows through this busy, noisy, shophouse town, while a big mountain rears up behind it. The center of town is dominated by a massive five-domed mosque. In front is Simpang Lima, the busiest intersection and the city's transport hub. The main city of one of Indonesia's staunchest Islamic regions, Banda Aceh's religious orthodoxy and its harsh treatment of criminals ensures that it is very safe. Everyone prays in Aceh, if only to keep up appearances. Nightlife and entertainment will take all of 10 minutes to experience. Yet the atmosphere is not severe. One's first impression is its neatness and orderliness; it's noticeably more prosperous than other Sumatran cities, and the people seem better dressed, friendlier, and more respectful to outsiders.

In the Middle Ages, this city was a huge multiethnic metropolis with international markets and compounds of Indians, Arabs, Turks, Chinese, Abyssinians, and Persians. At that time Banda Aceh was known as the "Doorway to Mecca," a stopping-off place for pilgrims journeying by ship to the Holy City. Great teachers, poets, and philosophers taught here; schools were everywhere. During the 17th century, under Sultan Iskandar Muda, Aceh reached its height of political power and wealth. Banda Aceh was one of the centers of fierce resistance during the 19th and 20th centuries, when the Acehnese launched a 40-year guerrilla war against the Dutch, whom they fought almost singlehandedly.

Cared for meticulously, **Kherkop,** the Dutch cemetery on Jl. Iskandar Muda, contains an estimated 2,200 graves of Dutch soldiers who died during the Acehnese resistance movement. Nicknamed by the Acehnese "the former Dutch neighborhood," this is one of Aceh's main tourist attractions. Its name means "churchyard" in Dutch. Open 0800-1200 and 1400-1700; visitors should first report to the office. The large three-story museum, **Musium Negeri Aceh,** on Jl. S.A. Mahmudsyah 12, displays local artifacts, weapons, a great range of handicrafts, and ceremonial clothing. Free admission. Open Tues.-Sun. 0830-1800. In the same museum complex is **Rumah Aceh,** a model of an Acehnese aristocrat's home built in 1914 in Semarang. Open Tues.-Sun. 0800-1800. Nearby is the gracious old *pendopo gubernor* where the Dutch governors once lived, now the residence of the governor of Aceh. About 100 meters to the south of the museum on Jl. S.A. Mahmudsyah are **Islamic graves** of Acehnese rulers, including that of Sultan Iskandar Muda. Another group of royal tombs, dating from the 15th and 16th centuries, is on Jl. Kraton.

Mesjid Baturrachman is an unusual mosque with its marble interior is a beehive of religious activity. Built in 1879 by the Dutch, the structure replaced a grand mosque which the Dutch destroyed, together with the sultan's palace and fortress. The elaborate multi-arched facade is a mixture of styles from Arabia, India, and Malaysia. Behind the mosque are two minarets; you can climb one for views over the city. In front is an expanse of gardens and pathways. The *mesjid* may be visited by non-Muslims during non-praying times (0700-1100, 1330-1600). Rules: veiled dress, take off shoes, get the guard's permission (at north gate), no women in menses.

The baths and pleasure gardens of the former sultan's ladies, on the banks of the river on Jl. Teuku Umar near the clock tower. As you come through the front gate of the yard, ask for the key in the building facing you. The story goes that this "Walking Palace" was built for a Malay princess who married one of the sultans of Aceh, enabling her to take an evening walk, not permitted to women at that time. Some also speculate that this stark white structure served as an astronomical observatory, reminiscent of one in Jaipur, India built in the mid-17th century. From the top of Gunongan you can see a small white structure, the sultan's bathing place, on the other side of the road close to the river. It's also locked, so get the key first.

The **Aceh Province Tourist Office** (Kantor Dinas Pariwisata Prop. Aceh), at Jl. Teuku Nyak Arief 92, tel. 22697 or 23692, hands out well-researched brochures and maps. This is one of the best-organized tourist offices in Indonesia.

GUNUNG LEUSER NATIONAL PARK

The largest national park in Southeast Asia and the most important in Indonesia, massive Gunung Leuser National Park (9,000 square km) northwest of Medan remains largely unexplored. Formerly a group of reserves surrounding the well-populated Alas Valley of northern Sumatra, Gunung Leuser became a national park in

1980. The World Wildlife Fund, whose representatives are in Bogor and Kutacane, assist with the park's management. Increasing population pressures in the valley continue to be the biggest management problem, particularly since Gayo, Alas, and Batak immigrants are hardly fazed by the rules and regulations emanating from Jakarta. By tradition, these tribes practice shifting cultivation, which is now illegal.

The park lies for the most part in Aceh Province, though a finger projects into North Sumatra Province almost as far as Brastagi. This wild and beautiful area consists of full and submontane primary rainforest, lowland and swamp forest, and a moss forest above 1,600 meters. Plant species include orchids, dipterocarps, and 50-meter-high hardwood trees. Most of the reserve is rough and mountainous, part of the Bukit Barisan range, with Gunung Leuser the highest point at 3,381 meters. The only lowland areas are the Alas Valley and the lower Kluet River Valley, which slopes down to the west coast of Sumatra at Kandang. Natural salt licks are found in several places; they attract herbivores from elephants to mouse deer, and probably orangutans and some carnivores as well. The park is also a world-class study area for primatologists, with orangutans, gibbons, leaf monkeys, and macaques. Its colorful tropical birds include hornbills, Argus pheasant, and many other species common to Southeast Asia.

There are designated tourist areas near Ketembe Research Station such as **Pulau Latong, Lawe Gurah,** and the **Bohorok** area in the eastern part of the park. Of them, Pulau Latong has better facilities, including three relatively new houses built in a regional traditional style, each with two to three "bedrooms." There's one guesthouse at Lawe Gurah, but it isn't in very good condition. There may or may not be beds in the houses, nor electricity (take candles), nor running water, though river water is drinkable after boiling. The houses do have *mandi*. Eat in Pak Ali's *warung*, a few minute's walk from the Pulau Latong facility, which is the only source of simple cooked food and beverages (including excellent homegrown coffee) or staples. For soft adventurers, **Wisma Cinta Alam** (Rp2000 per person) on the main road a half km south of Ketembe, is nicer, cleaner, and friendlier than the accommodations offered at Pulau Latong and Lawe Gurah.

You can make trips into the forest from the tourist areas. Guides cost about Rp10,000 per day and offer two- or three-day treks. Pak Maringgan and his staff at Wisma Rindu Alam in Kutacane can arrange for guides, take guests to the market for shopping, arrange motorcycle rental, and find inner tubes for river recreation. Lawe Gurah is within a few hours walk of a pleasant hot springs; you can also reach the area from Pulau Latong, though it takes a little longer. One place that has traditionally been good for backpackers is along the **Mamas River.** The Mamas Valley, however, has fallen victim to logging. Reaching the best parts of the Mamas Forest requires crossing the Mamas River, which involves clambering across a wire bridge. Local guides will carry backpacks for less coordinated travelers. In November and December the river is a torrent.

Obtain a park permit (Rp1000) at Wisma Rindu Alam in Kutacane. Since most buses arrive in Kutacane from Medan in the late afternoon when it's too late to try to get a permit, it's better to spend the night in this *wisma* the day you arrive. Pak Maringgan, who runs the *wisma,* is on the staff of the national park and can help you obtain a permit first thing the next morning. Then you can head for the park. Permits are also available directly from the PHPA office in **Tanah Merah**, two km north of Kutacane, open Sun.-Thurs. 0730-1430, Friday 0730-1200, Saturday 0730-1400. Cost is Rp1000 plus three passport photos.

West Sumatra

Densely populated and home to the Minangkabau people, West Sumatra has some of the most exciting scenery you'll ever see: peaks looming over deep canyons and splendid sheltered valleys, villages perched atop deep ravines, great high plateaus with natural air-conditioning, giant mountain lakes, steep rocky coastlines, isolated beaches, terraced rice fields, and unique traditional *kampung*. Two-thirds of West Sumatra is still covered in dense forests and thick jungle, with only about 20 percent under cultivation. Most of the larger Sumatran mammals still inhabit West Sumatra's tropical mountain forests. The giant rafflesia flower is found in the Batang Palupuh reserve north of Bukittinggi and in the forest reserve of Taman Hutan Raya Dr.

Mohammed Hatta, north of Padang. On the offshore Mentawai Islands live such indigenous wildlife as the Mentawai monkey and dwarf gibbons, as well as unusual orchids.

The Minangkabau

Adjacent to Batak territory in West Sumatra is the land of the Minangkabau people, remarkable for their unique matrilineal society. The Minangkabau have a level of political and social equality unique in Southeast Asia. Although sometimes called Orang Padang, they're an interior, not a coastal people. West Sumatra is almost entirely ethnic Minangkabau, who comprise about a quarter of Sumatra's total population and are Indonesia's fourth largest ethnic group. Most Minang are farmers who live in small independent villages. The rest are skilled traders who live in or near the towns. Due to the rich

Rice fields in the vicinity of Lake Minangkabau

soil of the rice fields, their villages are prosperous. They are easygoing, peaceful, self-confident, hardworking, and shrewd commercially—the only ethnic group that can compete successfully with the Chinese in Jakarta. Fervent Muslims, they are one of the best-educated and most vigorous peoples in the whole country; many of the nation's intellectuals, leaders, and authors are Minangkabau.

Padang and Vicinity

The main gateway and largest seaport of the west coast, a center of commerce, the thriving capital of West Sumatra Province, and Sumatra's third largest city. Over 90 percent of Padang's half-million people are ethnically Minangkabau. Padang has one of the heaviest rainfalls in the world (310 centimeter per annum) and can be dreadfully hot, even at 0800 in the morning. Most travelers consider the Minangkabau countryside a better—and cooler—experience than Padang, which has undergone fairly steep inflation recently, so most just do their business, go for a walk along the seawall, see the rusting Dutch ships in the harbor, and move on. Padang's orderliness

Balai Janggo Palace, Sumatra

is unlike Java, and its economy is unusual for Indonesia: it's a city of native, not Chinese, merchants. It's also a strict Muslim town; conservative dress is *very* important. During Ramadan all of Padang's sidewalks are rolled up, its streets empty, its shops shuttered.

See the lovely old homes set back from wide, tree-lined streets in **Padang Baru**, and old Dutch homes along Jl. Sudirman and Jl. Proklamasi. Chinese temples are in **Kampung Cina** (Chinatown). **Adityawarman Museum**, housed in a huge traditional-style *rumah gadang* with two rice barns in front, lies on the corner of Jl. Diponegoro and Jl. Gereja; open 0800-1800, Friday until 1100, closed Monday. Though poorly displayed, inside are antiques and other objects of historical and cultural interest from all parts of Sumatra, plus a special textile room.

The cultural center, **Taman Budaya**, just across from the museum, stages regular music, dancing, and *pencak silat* performances; open 0900-1400. Also check out the happenings at the **Institute of Minangkabau Studies** (SSMR) in Cengke. Padang's university, **Universitas Andalas**, is in Air Tawar. Don't land in jail here. Padang's prison, built in 1819, has appalling conditions even for Indonesia.

The main market, **Pasar Raya**, next to the Balai Kota, has richly decorated *songket* cloth, plus acres of fruit, vegetable hawkers, *dukun,* and blind musicians. The **tourist office** for West Sumatra and Riau is way out on Jl. Khatib Sulaiman, tel. (0751) 28231. In addition to providing pamphlets, several of the staff speak good English, and they can help arrange a *surat jalan* for the Mentawai Islands. Open Mon.-Thurs. 0800-1400, Friday until 1100, Saturday 0800-1400.

BUKITTINGGI

The administrative, cultural, and educational center for the Minangkabau people, Bukittinggi is one of the loveliest, friendliest, most relaxed towns in all Sumatra—a real oasis after bouncing your buttocks raw on the buses getting there. Cool and sunny, nestled in mountains (its name means "High Hill") just south of the equator, this small university town has the country's oldest teachers' college and features many other schools. There are musical taxis, horsecarts, streetsweepers, veiled schoolgirls, regal women walking sedately under parasols, banks of flowers, good restaurants, and a wide selection of reasonable accommodations.

The town is very compact, with many tourist services and bus pickups concentrated along Jl. A. Yani. Providing you're dressed properly, the women are friendly and the men not cheeky. During Ramadan people are more uptight. Most of the businesses are owned by women and run by men. You don't have to bargain so vehemently here, as the Minangkabau usually start with a realistic first price. The area is worth at least a week, and Bukittinggi makes an ideal base.

Bukittinggi

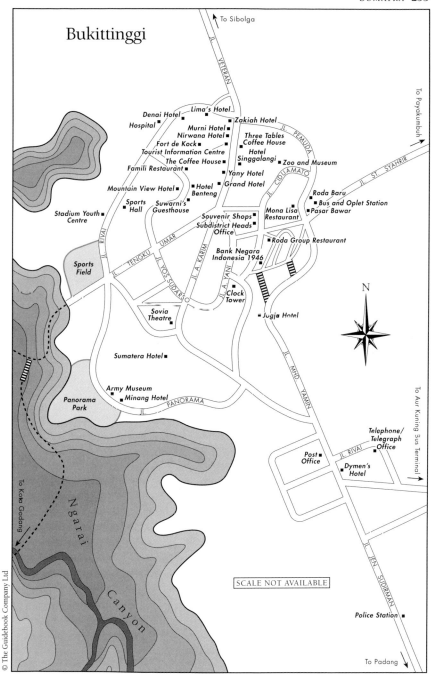

To Sibolga

To Payakumbuh

JL VETERAN

JL PEMUDA

JL ST. SYAHRIR

Lima's Hotel

Denai Hotel ■
Hospital ■ Zakiah Hotel ■
Murni Hotel ■
Nirwana Hotel ■ Three Tables
Fort de Kock ■ Coffee House
Tourist Information Centre ■ Hotel
The Coffee House ■ Singgalangi
Famili Restaurant ■ ■ Zoo and Museum
Yany Hotel ■
Mountain View Hotel ■ ■ Hotel ■ Grand Hotel
Benteng
Sports Suwarni's Roda Baru ■
Hall ■ Guesthouse ■ Bus and Oplet Station
Stadium Youth ■ Souvenir Shops ■ ■ Pasar Bawar
Centre Subdistrict Heads ■ Mona Lisa ■
Office Restaurant

JL CIDUAMATO

JL RIVAI

JL TENGKU UMAR

JL YOS SUDARSO

JL A. KARIM

Sports
Field

■ Roda Group Restaurant

Bank Negara
Indonesia 1946 ■

JL A. YANI

Clock
Tower ■

Sovia
Theatre ■ ■ Jogja Hotel

N

Sumatera Hotel ■

JL MHD YAMIN

Army Museum ■
■ Minang Hotel
JL PANORAMA
Panorama
Park

Telephone/
Telegraph ■
Office

Post ■
Office Dymen's
Hotel ■

JL RIVAI

To Aur Kuning Bus Terminal

To Koto Gadang

Ngarai

Canyon

SCALE NOT AVAILABLE

JL JEN SUDIRMAN

Police Station ■

To Padang

Sights

In the center of town and overlooking the market is a venerable **clock tower** constructed by the Dutch in 1827. The "Big Ben" of Bukittinggi, this clock embodies a Dutch idea and Minangkabau design. Nearby is the **botanical gardens**, where locals may ask to take your picture. The zoo is the highest point in town; just behind the museum, lying within the confines of Taman Bundo Kanduang (Minang for "Kind-hearted Mother") Park. A fantastic place for people-watching; on Sunday the women parade around in their best Minang apparel. It's a must to see the people; the animals are secondary. The zoo (Rp500 entrance) specializes in Sumatran wildlife, and is especially strong on birds. In the center of the park is a beautifully reconstructed traditional-style Minangkabau *rumah adat* (1844) flanked by two rice barns with fine woodcarving. This is the oldest museum (1945) in West Sumatra (entrance Rp200), specializing in local history and culture.

On the southeast edge of town lies **Panorama Park** (Rp100), which looks out over a four-km-long chasm with sheer rocky walls plunging 100-120 meters down to the riverbed below. The sides of the valleys in the Minangkabau Highlands are so steep the buffalo that feed on the grasslands often venture too close to the edge and are killed in the fall. Thus the Dutch nickname for **Ngarai Canyon**: "Buffalo Hole." This canyon, which borders Bukittinggi in the south and west and separates it from the foothills of Gunung Singgalang, is the pride of West Sumatra. Viewed from Panorama Park, it's quite a sight, particularly in the mornings when a veil of mist hangs over the canyon. Don't miss the sunset. Gunung Singgalang (2,877 meters) rises in the background.

Underneath Panorama Park are Japanese tunnels (Gua Jepong) built in WW II. With the help of a guide one can penetrate these bare rock caves for hundreds of meters. From the park, a two-km trail leads down through the layers of faulted volcanic ash, across the river on a small bridge, then up the other side of the canyon to the rim and on to Kota Gadang, a crafts village on the other side of the canyon.

The Dutch built **Fort De Kock** in 1825 during the Padri Wars. Dutch forts like this eventually became towns. Now the site is a small park and scenic viewpoint. Arrive at dusk when giant fruit bats come out, looking like birds without tails. The bats nest in trees in the canyon below Kota Gadang.

Crafts and Shopping

The Bukittinggi area is a center for skilled gold and silver artisans. Both the jewelry itself and the interior of the jewelry shops, done in intricately inlaid wood, are fine examples of Minangkabau expertise. Stones from all over the world are imported and set by craftsmen in their mothers' shops. Also see stones dug from various local mountains, set in brass and hawked in the market, along with colored uncut gems the size of golf balls, and delicate earrings and bracelets hammered out in nearby villages.

Lake Maninjau

A market takes place every day, but Wednesday and Saturday host the biggest, when Bukittinggi is flooded with thousands of Minangkabau who come in from every corner of the highlands. The sprawling market, which literally covers a whole hill, lasts from about 0700 to 1700 and contains everything from antiques and local crafts to produce and spices—a profusion of overpowering smells, colors, and sounds. Get up to it by either climbing the 300-step stairway or use the twisting cart lanes. A sweeping view over the town from the top.

The huge market area is divided into sections: a row of barbers, a row of cigarette-lighter repairmen, rows of crunchy-munchy snacks and sweets stalls, fish market, meat market, countless rows of produce, and perhaps the strangest assemblage of snake oil merchants in all of Indonesia. The market's two levels, Upper Market (Pasar Atas) and Lower Market (Pasar Bawah) are connected by a number of stairways.

Lake Maninjau

Known for its culture, remote location, and beauty, this huge crater lake 38 km west of Bukittinggi is a retreat for famous poets and philosophers. Many visitors consider Maninjau more scenic, cleaner, and friendlier than Lake Toba. The lake is 470 meters above sea level; the 610-meter drop down from the crater's rim is a spectacular drive or walk. The crater holding the lake is one of the largest in the world—a wonder in itself. The lake's deep blue, clear water is always calm. There are facilities for water-skiing,

swimming, fishing, and boating (both motorboats and canoes), but no beaches. Lake Maninjau abounds with fish, which are served up in the many restaurants along its shores.

The ride out to Lake Maninjau on the bus or *oplet* is incredibly scenic. From Bukittinggi's Aur Kuning terminal buses run regularly and take only 1.5 hours (Rp700). The last bus back from Maninjau village leaves at around 1600 (but check!) and tends to be very crowded. On market day, buses return to Bukittinngi as late as 1700. If you miss the bus, and don't want to stay over, you'll have to charter a *bemo.*

Embun Pagi ("Morning Cloud") is a small *desa* and lookout (1,097 meters) 30 km from Bukittinggi, just before the descent down to the lake. Children will approach you selling wonderful straw purses and pandanus palm bags in an infinite variety of shapes, sizes, colors, uses, and prices. Stalls sell refreshments. From Embun Pagi, it's a two-hour walk with 44 sharp switchbacks to the bottom of the crater. Cinnamon plantations slope down to the lake, the green reflecting in the shiny blue water, like the picture of a fantasy world in a child's storybook.

A worthwhile trip is the scenic 16-km road following the north shore of the lake from Maninjau to Muko Muko. This good road continues for 139 km all the way to Padang via Tiku and Pariaman. From Maninjau, first take a bus to Lubukbasang (Rp700), then board waiting buses which take you straight to Padang. The trip around the south shore to Muko Muko is more difficult but even more scenic. Small ferryboats leave from the docks beside Hotel Maninjau to various lakeside *kampung.* Or just rent a canoe from someone and go fishing.

Maninjau Village

A lakeside village at the bottom of the descent from Embun Pagi. Visit the warm springs, 500 meters down the road from the bus stop and a short walk in. Many places rent bikes for Rp4000 per day. There are 11 guesthouses now, and two hotel/restaurants. **Guesthouse Amai Cheap GH,** Jl. H. Udin Rahmani 54, is in an old Dutch house—the most beautiful in Maninjau. Nice rooms with old fashioned beds are Rp4000 s, Rp5000 d. Often full. Quiet **Guesthouse Della Villa** on the Izin Bupati has huge, clean, romantic rooms with high ceilings for Rp4000 s; very friendly people. A popular place for travelers is **Guesthouse Palantha** with about 20 rooms (Rp6000 s); noisy and the food isn't good.

Another good place to stay is **Pillie Guesthouse** (Rp5000) right on the lake, and quiet **Beach Guesthouse** (Rp4000) on the Bayur side of Maninjau village. **Guesthouse Srikandi** has small, hot rooms (Rp4000 s) but the food is the best in Maninjau and reasonably priced (very good breakfast). Another good place to eat is **Goemala Restaurant.** From the porch of one of **Hotel Maninjau's** 30 rooms, you can literally jump into the lake. The hotel restaurant specializes in fresh lake fish. Rent speedboats for sightseeing or water-skiing. On the north side of town is the quieter **Pasir Panjang Permai Hotel,** Rp30,000-60,000 rooms with hot water and breakfast.

LIMAKAUM

Limakaum is five kilometers west of Batusangkar. An old mosque here was constructed wth five stories, symbolizing the five villages of the district. There is also a large, very old *rumah adat* with original mountain *atap* roofing. The "Stabbed Stones" (*Batu Batikam*) and the unexplained "Written Stone" are located in a small park on the north side of the highway near Limakaum. According to existing records, these stones represent a vow of unity between Datuk Perpatih, founder of the Pilang clan, and Datuk Katumanggugan, founder of the Bodi Caniago clan. The set of ancient inscribed stones is near the only hotel in the area, **Mes Kiambang**.

PAGARUYUNG

Form Batusangkar, either walk for an hour and a half or take a *bendi*. Pagaruyung is the former site of the raj's court, heart of the old Minangkabau kingdom. One of the finest man-made objects in Indonesia is the "big house" (*rumak gadang*), called **Istano Pagaruyung**, in the middle of nowhere beyond Pagaruyung. The magnificent building—note the ten-point roof—was erected on the site of another structure which burned down in 1976. There are plans to open a museum inside. Lots of tour buses bring hoardes of day-trippers to the site. Also in the vicinity are rajas' tombs, still maintained as sacred sites.

THE HARAU CANYON

A green fertile valley, 37 km north of Bukittinggi, surrounded by sheer granite canyon walls 100-150 meters high with waterfalls—an astonishing sight. In the Harau Valley is a 315-hectare nature and game reserve, Cagar Alam Harau, with birds, butterflies, monkeys, tigers, steamy rainforests, meadows, waterfalls, a small natural history museum, ranger tours, and an excellent observation point. Pamphlets and map available. The cliffs get steeper as you drive deeper into the park. Only about 20 people a day visit this remote reserve, though on weekends a "study group" as big as 250 could suddenly roll in on three buses. Most Indonesians visit to picnic or to buy exotic orchids at the nursery, which has some very unusual species.

This is an excellent recreation area for mountain climbing and nature hiking. The tigers of the area are protected but the bears are not because of the damage they cause to the fields. Once a week hunters from the surrounding districts gather here to hunt them, assisted by a special breed of hunting dog. These valuable dogs can be seen in Payakumbuh's marketplace, waiting for someone to hire them out to hunt bear. There's no place to stay at the ranger station but you can camp nearby. Bring food. The ranger may be able to arrange for you to stay overnight in one of the nearby hamlets, or in Harau village about three km beyond the ranger station.

The palace of the legendary Raja Adityawarman at Batusangkar

Nias

With its famous megalithic stone altars and furniture, spectacular traditional architecture, and complex religious rites, this fascinating island, 125 km southwest of Sibolga, offers a journey into the past. A magnificent megalithic heroic culture flourished on Nias well into the 20th century; headhunting and human sacrifices were still practiced as late as 1935. In the south part of the island during the 1800s Acehnese slave raiders regularly went on the rampage. Chiefs would carry off captives from neighboring villages and sell them for gold to slave runners. Today this same gold is used for bride-prices at weddings and adorns the headdresses of Niah dancers.

A subdistrict of West Sumatra Province, the island's major city and capital is Gunungsitoli in the north, with the main port Telukdalam in the south. Not far from Telukdalam is the surfing hangout of Jamborai village, which boasts fine beaches and some of the best right-handers in Indonesia. Farther inland are traditional hilltop villages with world-class megalithic sculpture and huge wooden handhewn dwellings on tree-trunk pylons.

STONE JUMPING

Vestiges of the earlier Niah culture also survive in the spectacle of *fahombe* (stone jumping). This frightening sport requires great acrobatic skill, particularly when executed with sword in hand. A solid stone column over two meters high and one-half meter broad stands on the great runway of the village between rows of dwellings. In front of the column is a smaller stone, about one-half meter high. A young man runs from a distance of about 20 meters for the smaller stone, and from it launches himself feet-first high into the air over the column. Much like jumping the high horse in gymnastics, jumpers gyrate around in midair to alight on their feet on rough heavy paving stones facing the column. In olden times stones were covered with sharp spikes and pointed bamboo sticks. *Fahombe* was used to train young loinclothed warriors to clear the walls of enemy villages at night with a torch in one hand and a sword in the other. Stone jumping takes place in all south Niah villages—Bawomataluo, Hilisimaetano, Orahili, Botohili—and costs Rp150,000 for a private showing.

SCULPTURE

There were two phases in the history of Niah classical sculpture—the stonework of the ancient proto-Malayans and the woodcrafts of the 1400s. Though it would be difficult to find a single stonecutter on Nias today, much remains of their megalithic culture, which was of a standard found nowhere else in Southeast Asia. Missionaries who first penetrated the island's interior in the 1930s came across abandoned villages in the mountains with entire inventories of stone sculptures still intact.

These islanders once utilized stone as the most important material of civilization. Stone was used for tools, utensils, pillows, even money. Whole villages are paved with great flat stone tiles; at some sites long stone staircases lead to hilltop settlements. Master masons constructed throne-like chairs twisting with serpents, ornamental tables, bathing places, stelae, and obelisks. Horizontal slabs were erected as memorials to the dead.

Stone slabs carved here are similar in shape to those found everywhere in the early history of the planet, from Stonehenge to Easter Island. Hauled from distant riverbed quarries, Niah carvings were executed in light grayish stone with imagination and superb precision. The villagers themselves are ignorant of where the megaliths originated, who carved them or when. They've also long forgotten the meaning of the magical symbols and rosettes adorning stone pyramids and terraces in front of chiefs' houses and in ceremonial places in south Niah villages, at one time the center of sacrifices.

The old religion is portrayed vividly in Easter Island-like armless statues of ancestral beings distinguished by tall Niah-style headgear, elaborate earrings, sharp features, elongated torsos, large male genitalia, heads with small stuck-on beards, right ears with distended lobes. Note the bold, aggressive stance of the Niah *adu*. At the funerals of chiefs, this wooden image was required so the ghost of the deceased could transfer into it. Statues were also used to propitiate spirits in case of family illness. Well-executed wooden statues start at Rp200,000, but the seller may come down as low as Rp45,000. Smaller ones go for Rp10,000-15,000.

ARCHITECTURE

Southern villages, constructed during the time of internecine warfare, are deceptive fortresses. Bars guarded windows, and trapdoors opened out to roofs. Structures were erected so close together that internal connecting doors made it possible for residents to walk the whole length of the village, sometimes over 300 meters, without ever touching the ground. Many structures featured just a trapdoor in the floor, with no other exits or entrances.

Houses of commoners average four-by-twelve meters; more imposing houses belong to the aristocracy. On these, steeply pitched roofs sometimes soar over eight meters above the height of the walls, with overhanging gables creating a hooded appearance. Rectangular and narrow in shape, these chiefly structures rest on a substructure of stone and massive wooden beams, resisting the tremors that often shake the island. Older houses are made of handhewn polished timbers, ingeniously joined without pegs or nails, with panels and moldings decoratively carved and the roof resting on complicated beamwork.

In remote areas the oldest *adat* houses are still untouched; in the more Westernized villages the people prefer standard Indonesian construction. Nowadays, on more and more *rumah adat,* thatch is replaced with corrugated steel roofs; within a few years old construction techniques will have vanished and the whole silhouette of the typical Niah village will be forever altered. To help preserve what is left, a chief's *adat* house was completely dismantled piece by piece by a Danish professor and shipped back to Europe. In northern Nias, traditional houses are less spectacular, rougher, and more varied.

GETTING THERE

To get to Nias, the quickest is to fly from Medan to Gunungsitoli. SMAC offers several flights weekly (Rp87,000 one-way, Rp92,000 return). The airport is small: only seven-seat Cessna Islanders can land here. SMAC's office is at Jl. Imam Bonjol 59, tel. (061) 515-934 or 516-617, Medan. SMAC also offers a Wednesday flight from Padang. Gunungsitoli's Binaka Airport is 19 km from town; a *bemo* costs Rp3000. If flying out, don't forget to reconfirm your return flight. At the airport, prices for minibus hire to the south start at Rp210,000, but you can bargain down to Rp50,000. The public bus from Gunungsitoli to Telukdalam is Rp6000 (six hours, 120 km). You can also get a boat to Nias, to either Gunungsitoli or Telukdalam, departing Sibolga on the west coast of Sumatra at around 2000 two or three times weekly (Rp7500, 9-12 hours).

Nias man in traditional war costume

LAGUNDI BAY

Twelve km from Telukdalam lie two villages on this horseshoe-shaped bay: Muslim Lagundi and Christian Jamborai, discovered by Australian surfers in the mid-'70s. If you like to swim and sunbathe it's best to stay in Lagundi, as Jamborai on the point is only good for surfing. Lagundi Bay was the main port of South Nias until the Krakatoa eruption of 1883 wiped it out; the port was then moved to Telukdalam. Join the local soccer games on Sunday afternoon. Bring lots of reading material.

The beautiful beach at Jamborai is a 20-minute walk down the shore from Lagundi village toward the west opening of the bay. The surf here can reach over three meters high and travels sometimes 200 meters, with wild sea turtles in the water. Out in the wide bay is a coral reef, then white sand, then another reef over 50 meters wide—an unreal world, like a dream.

BAWOMATALUO

Established in 1878, Bawomataluo (meaning "Sunhill") is the best kept extant traditional village in southern Nias, with superb carvings and high-roofed architecture. It's reached by minibus from Telukdalam (Rp1000, 14 km). Or take the bus to Orahili, then walk a km up the 480 steep stone steps leading to the hilltop village. Bawomataluo is Nias's most accessible, popular, touristy *adat* village. Suharto and Jakarta's police chief have even visited here.

Every two weeks a cruise ship brings 400 people, so it's no surprise prices are quoted in U.S. dollars. The inhabitants will try to flog contemporary wood sculpture and "precious family" *pusaka,* kids pester you for money, villagers offer to pose for photos for a fee. Annoying, but not nearly as bad as Torajaland or Penelokan—this is too important a village, culturally speaking, to pass up. People play chess, sculpt, weave, and slaughter pigs as you walk down the long street laid with big stone slabs. Also visit the other villages of the area. Few roads here; most of the time you have to walk on narrow paths through banana orchards and rice fields.

By far the most fantastic piece of architecture in the whole village, and the finest and largest of its kind in all of Nias, is the imposing chief's palace, called **Omo Sebua**. It's built on wooden pillars nearly one meter thick, with a stepped floor of heavy wooden planks. Visitors sit on the level befitting their rank, the highest level accorded only to the chief. Built by skilled artisans and slaves in 1878, the building encloses a great inner chamber 12 meters long and 10.5 meters wide, with carved decorative motifs on one wall in high relief; on the opposite wall is a wonderful carving in low relief of a two-masted European sailing ship, complete with sailors, cannon, and sea creatures lurking in the depths below. All carvings are in great need of restoration. The spikes of the roof soar 20 meters above the ground, and the building's walls are joined with all the consummate skill of a cabinetmaker. The one eyesore is the ugly sheet-metal roof.

In the village courtyard sits an arrangement of 18-ton stone chairs, where the dead were once left to decay. Also see *menhirs,* obelisks, stone ceremonial benches decorated with simple floral motifs, and a stone disk a foot thick resting on four columns. In all there are 287 stone sculptures, both large and small. Check out the stone slab in front of the chief's house: anchor chain, sharks, whales, young boys swimming, all portrayed in a realistic European style atypical of an ancient megalithic culture. The *kepala desa* explains that these anachronistic carvings date from the islanders' first contact with Europeans, who arrived on their sailing ships with iron chains.

Lampung Province

A wild, forested, district known for its pepper, stunning *tapi* fabrics, and ambitious *transmigrasi* projects. Sumatra's southernmost province has a long coastline with innumerable bays, a rugged mountain interior with game reserves and sea-level swamplands, and some densely populated rural areas that appear to be lifted straight out of Java. It also shares beautiful Lake Ranau with South Sumatra Province. Dormant volcanos of the region range from 2,231-meters-high Gunung Pesagi to 1,645-meters-high Gunung Raya. Pepper, cloves, coffee, and copra are all grown extensively along the rich southern coast, which benefitted enormously from the 1883 Krakatoa catastrophe. Rice, coffee, maize, cassava, and rubber are cultivated inland. Bakauheni, on the southeast tip of Lampung, is the main maritime gateway to Sumatra for overland travelers from Java. Outside of Tanjungkarang and Kalianda there aren't many nice places to stay.

HISTORY

According to folklore, the first people to settle this area came from Batakland. Prior to Islam the Lampungese practiced a syncretic Buddhist-Hindu ancestor cult; *menhirs* and other archaeological remains of this heritage are found on stone inscriptions scattered around the province. To cultivate the valuable pepper spice for sale to European and Asian traders, the sultans of Banten centuries ago sent the first transmigrants to Lampung to carve villages and farms out of the jungle and spread Islam.

From the end of the 16th century until 1808, the sultanate of Benten controlled Lampung (and its pepper) without interfering in local customs. In the 19th century Lampung became a refuge for Banten rebels protesting Dutch rule. In 1855, after defeating the Lampungese hero Raden Intan II, the Dutch monopolized all trade. Today, Raden's grave, built on an earth mound from his Kalianda fortress, is a popular pilgrimage site. In WW II the Japanese drove out the Dutch and established a base in Kalianda to guard the vital Sunda Strait.

THE PEOPLE

The population of the province is divided into two main groups, the native Lampungese and Javanese transmigrants. Traditional native Lampungese villages can be recognized by their well-constructed brown wooden houses raised two meters above ground on pillars, many with a balcony. Often these "balcony houses" feature decorative latticework under the eaves or around the outside edges. The Javanese began settling the area in 1905 when Lampung was chosen as Indonesia's first transmigration site, selected to serve as a receptacle for Java's surplus population and to supply laborers for European plantations. The Javanese soon made up 80 percent of the population. Today, Javanese colonies, with their own traditions, *desa* heads, and social structures, became enclaves in the midst of Lampung, attacking the surrounding rich jungles like swarms of locusts. In 1987, Lampung was Indonesia's second most densely populated province outside Java.

BANDAR LAMPUNG

Formerly called Tanjungkarang, this modern town lies five km north of Telukbetung, a starting point for the journey north. If it's been a while since you've entered one, visit the department store. Catch *oplet* on the main street or use *kijang* or metered sedan taxis (call Taxi 4848 or 333). With the bus and train terminals situated in town, Bandar Lampung has a wider range of places to stay—and is more convenient—than Telukbetung. **Bank Negara Indonesia (BNI)**, Jl. Kartini 51, changes American Express traveler's checks. Visit the ethnographic and archaeological **Museum of Lampung** on Jl. Teuku Umar.

Outside Bandar Lampung are popular beaches, islands, and mountains. Six km southwest of Telukbetung, on the west side of Lampung Bay, is **Nusa Indah Permai Beach**. From Lampasing take the two-hour boat out to Pulau Tegal. Past Lampasing to the southwest are more beaches and coastal scenery. On the east side of this bay are several beaches at **Pasir Putih**, 11 km southeast of Telukbetung. Offshore are the

(above) A Melayu lady from Minangkabau, northwest Sumatra

small islands Dewi, Cendong, and Tengah, reached by *spetbot*. Twenty km southeast of Bandar Lampung are beautiful land-and seascapes at **Tarahan**. A two-hour drive from Bandar Lampung is the 130,000-hectare **Way Kambas Reserve** with an elephant training center. Hire a motorboat at Way Kanan to tour the **Way Wako River**. The **Pugung Archaeological Site** in Pugung Raharjo village (40 km to the northeast) has megaliths and Hindu and prehistoric relics. At **Padangcermin**, 65 km southwest of Bandar Lampung, are nice landscapes and a beach resort.

South Sumatra Province

PALEMBANG

Palembang, with 700,000 people, is Sumatra's second most populous city. For over 1,300 years, the basis of Palembang's economy has been river and ocean commerce. Nearly one-third of total Indonesian government revenue comes from this oil province alone. Much of the city is built on piles over tidal mudflats; the weather could get very sticky and hot. The Musi River divides the city into two sections: the southern half, Ulu, where the majority of the population lives, and the northern half, Ilir, which houses most of the hotels, shops, government offices, and well-to-do residential areas. The **city tourist office**, tel. (0711) 28450, is in the Museum Sultan Machmud Badaruddin II. The **regional tourist office**, tel. 24981, for South Sumatra is located at Jl. Bay Salim 200.

By tradition an ancient Oriental trading center, from the 9th until the 13th century Palembang was one of the world's principal ports. The city was born on pepper, raised on tin, and grew rich on oil. The first tangible signs in the whole archipelago of the arrival of Mahayana Buddhism appeared in Kedukan Bukit near Palembang in the early 600s. The city reached its zenith in the beginning of the 11th century.

The **Mesjid Raya** (Grand Mosque) near the bridge greets you as you come into the city; it was built by Sultan Mahmud Badaruddin in the 18th century. Go for a ride along the road heading upstream beside the Musi River—whole residential areas are built out over the water, featuring some superb examples of traditional architecture. During the rainy season this broad river becomes a lake; the residences built on rafts rise and fall with the water. Palembang's old *benteng* (fort), with its tall whitewashed walls, is on Jl. Benteng just back from the river in the center of the city. It was built in 1780 during the reign of Sultan Ahmad Najamudin II. The *benteng* is now occupied by the army, so permission to enter must be acquired from the fort commander.

Palembang's famous "floating markets" are in the Pasar Ilir 16 area, two km downstream from the bridge. This crowded quarter consists of two km of the scariest, dirtiest markets anywhere, selling anything and everything. Immaculately dressed women shop in the disgusting meat and fish area—the smell is unbearable, there are flies everywhere, sellers wash their cutting boards in the sewer. Just like the *klongs* of Bangkok, boats going to market must travel down these canals. Locals will tell you to be careful walking in this area, which is frequented by "gangsters."

Museum Negeri Sum-Sel is located about five km from downtown, about 300 meters off the road to Jambi and the airport on Jl. Sriwijaya—take a Km 5 *oplet*. See this traditional Palembang house *(rumah bari)*, a solid wooden building made of *kayu tembesu*. The Dutch moved it from the countryside piece by piece in 1931. Megalithic sculpture is displayed as well. Open 0800-1400 Tues.-Thurs., 0800-1100 Friday, 0800-1200 Saturday, 0900-1500 Sunday. Closed Monday.

Klenteng Kwa Sam Yo, between the river and Jl. Sungai Lapangan Hatal, is remarkable for its hundreds of fascinating murals and wall paintings depicting the story of the great Kublai Khan and other Mongolian heroes. Ask to see the vicious-looking self-torture chair, a means for attaining spiritual knowledge through pain and suffering. Another pain-inflicting activity was the immersion of the penitent's hands in boiling oil; ask to see the color photos of the old Chinese whose unscarred hands were so honored.

LAKE RANAU

A giant (40-by-29-km) mountain lake in the southwestern part of the province 330 km from Palembang. Part of the lake lies in Lampung Province. Indonesians go here to enjoy the cool climate, nice scenery, sulphur hot springs, and water sports. This pristine environment—like an untouched Lake Toba—features Gunung Seminung (1,881 meters) soaring up from the southern shore behind the lake. Here, as in much of the Bukit Barisan range, coffee is the most important cash crop; cloves, tobacco, vegetables, and rice are also grown. Culture and language are similar to coastal Lampung to the south.

Bandingagung, the area's largest town, offers several accommodations. All the buses for Ranau Danau terminate here. The town is 12 km west of the main highway; turn in at Simpangsender village. Quieter and more restful is a small resort, **Wisma Putri**, on the lake's eastern shore. Turn in at the sign, eight km south of Simpangsender, or seven km north of Kotabatu. Double rooms cost Rp25,000 but the manager may let you camp outside or sleep on a folding bed in the recreation room. The restaurant serves generous portions at reasonable prices; freshwater fish is the specialty. A 20-minute walk away on the edge of the jungle, with a view over rice paddies, is a waterfall. An elephant training center is in the area.

Kotabatu is the first town on the lake if approaching from the south, and it has a *penginapan*. Kotabatu makes a good base for hiking up Gunung Seminung. Sulphurous hot water can be enjoyed at **Gemuhak Springs**, three km from Kotabatu on the volcano's lower slopes. Just offshore is a small island, **Pulau Mariza**. Beaches are found on the north shore at Bandingagung, Surabaya, and Senangkalang. You can charter boats to tour the lake from Bandingagung and Kotabatu. Boating is best in the morning, as afternoon winds really whip up the waves. Rent a boat and cross the lake to the hot springs.

THE PASEMAH HIGHLANDS

In the Pasemah Highlands between Lahat and Pagaralam are 26 sites with stonecarvings, tombs, and terraced sanctuaries. These remains, which may date as far back as A.D. 100, are said to be the most concentrated collection of monumental symbolic culture in Indonesia. Huge queerly shaped stones are carved into fantastic figures: warriors mounted on elephants, men wrestling a huge snake, animals copulating, frogs, a footprint, waterwheel, even ocean waves. A great number of these extraordinary carvings, menhirs, dolmens, stone cist graves, and terraced sanctuaries were erected at a time when metals were already known in the area. Figures carry swords; wear helmets, rings, and anklets; hold giant bronze kettledrums—artifacts and implements all belonging to the Bronze Age. Many of the figures appear at first to be three-dimensional but are in fact bas-reliefs, the illusion created by the skillful use of the curved surface of the boulders. The modern-day Pasemahans still use some statuary as vow-redemption shrines, calling upon their ancestors to bestow blessings and stave off ill-fortune.

Most sites are found in the subdistricts of Kecamatan Pulau Pinang, Kotaagung, and Pagaralam. The minibus from Bengkulu to Pagaralam takes five hours (175 km, Rp3500). The road via Kepahiang and Tebingtinggi is good. Most sites are easily visited but many are well off the main road. Serious seekers need their own vehicle (Rp60,000-70,000 per day to charter a sedan taxi). It would be difficult to see these sites without a guide unless you speak Bahasa Indonesia; if you don't, consider hiring a guide from your hotel. Allow a full day, between asking directions and arranging transportation, to see the sites just around Pagaralam.

Minangkabau-style rice granary

Nusatenggara

Introduction

Stretching for 1,500 km east from Java, the Lesser Sundas include the six major islands of Bali, Lombok, Sumbawa, Sumba, Flores, and Timor, as well as hundreds of smaller islands and islets. The northern string of islands is a continuation of the volcanic belt that runs through Sumatra and Java as far east as Banda, while Sumba, Savu, Roti, and Timor, forming the "Outer Arc" of the Lesser Sundas, are nonvolcanic.

The population is estimated at close to 10 million, a highly diverse and fragmented cultural conglomeration with hundreds of ethnic and linguistic distinctions. Many of these peoples still exhibit the rudiments of ancient cultures, with beliefs in spirits, ancestor cults, and magic. For the most part, the people are friendly. But you should know you'll cause a great stir when you venture into the interior of the islands, where

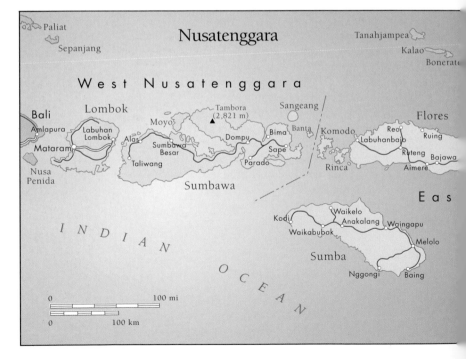

Westerners are a rarity. And in predominantly Muslim territory like East Lombok and Sumbawa, it's important to respect the conservative codes of dress and behavior lest you incur local disfavor, which can extend to fruit and rock throwing.

About 120 million years ago, melting ice caps cleaved Bali and Lombok, creating the 48-km-wide, 600-meter-deep Lombok Strait, the archipelago's deepest. The strait marks the so-called "Wallace Line," named after the great naturalist Sir Alfred Wallace. Sir Alfred observed that all the islands west of Lombok feature tropical vegetation, monkeys, elephants, tigers, wild cattle, and straight-haired Asiatics, while the islands east of Bali are home to thorny arid plants, cockatoos, parrots, giant lizards, marsupials, and frizzy-haired Papuans, typical of Australia. The more advanced placental animals and flora beginning to evolve at that time in Asia proper could not cross the turbulent strait between the two islands. Thus, zoological Model-T Fords such as kangaroos and echidnas were allowed to proliferate on the islands east of Bali because of the absence of predatory mammals.

On the easternmost islands of the chain reside spectacular New Guinea parrots, plus a few Australian species like the cockatoos and honeyeaters who braved the 480-km hop across the Timor Sea. Other than these, Nusatenggara is remarkable for

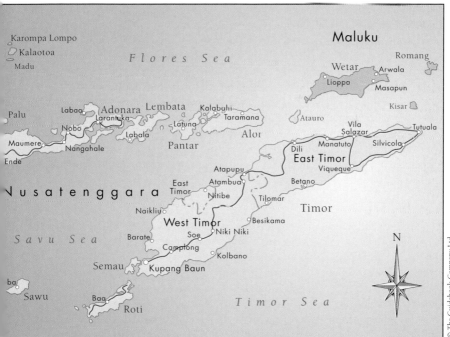

© The Guidebook Company Ltd

the scarcity of its bird species. Whereas Java and Bali have nearly 200 breeding species of Asiatic birds, just across the strait on Lombok there are 68 fewer.

Lombok

This lush, noncommercialized island, fringed by untouched white sand beaches, is currently in the throes of development. Slightly smaller, and drier, than Bali, there's an intact Balinese culture in the western part of the island, with serene temples and palaces. Accommodations in the three main towns—Ampenan, Mataram, and Cakranegara—offer outstandingly good value; the best are owned and run by Balinese.

In the 14th century, Lombok was settled by Hindu-Javanese under the auspices of the powerful Majapahit Empire. Islam was brought to Lombok between 1506 and 1545 by Sunan. In the 17th century, the island was divided into a number of petty princedoms. In return for Balinese support in their struggle against the *raja* of Sumbawa in the early 18th century, the native Sasaks allowed the Balinese to settle in western Lombok. Though the Makassarese were expelled by a joint Balinese/Sasak force in 1677, the Sasaks soon found themselves oppressed by the newcomers from Bali. Over the next several hundred years, they became second-class citizens on their own island. Strained feelings still exist between the Sasaks and the Balinese.

The Dutch colonialists used the conflict between the two groups to their advantage. In the late 19th century, the Sasaks sought assistance from the Dutch, who'd occupied northern Bali in 1882. In 1894, the Dutch mounted an elaborate military expedition to Lombok and demanded a war indemnity of one million guilders from the old raja. The raja accepted but the princes rose up and attacked the main Dutch encampment in Cakranegara. After a bitter month-long campaign of destruction, with the Dutch razing Balinese villages and the Sasaks looting them, the Balinese stronghold at Cakranegara finally fell. Soon after, Lombok formally became a part of the Dutch East Indies.

THE PEOPLE

Lombok's 1.7 million people are a mixture of Islamic Sasak and Hindu Balinese. The poorer Sasaks live in the eastern part of the island, while the Balinese live mainly in the towns and villages of the western central plain. If you want a Bali without the intense culture, religion, and arts, go to Lombok. Here are found Balinese food, customs—even such Balinese festivals as Galungan are celebrated at full throttle. Most of Lombok's Chinese were killed off in the 1965-66 purges; together with Arabs they now comprise only five percent of the population. The aboriginals of Lombok, called the Bodhas, live in the isolated southeast corner—what's left of them.

TRANSPORT

Nusatenggara need no longer be an out-and-back trip from Bali. Bali is still the logical and least expensive jumping-off point; from Padangbai in East Bali there are numerous daily ferries (four to five hours) to Lombok, and regular Merpati flights from Denpasar to Lombok, Sumbawa, Flores, Timor, and Sumba. Merpati flights also depart Darwin in northern Australia for Kupang and Denpasar. Merpati flies from Jakarta to Kupang and from Denpasar to Kupang. Sempati has flights from Denpasar to Mataram, Dili, and Kupang, and from Surabaya to Mataram. Bouraq also flies to Mataram from Denpasar and Surabaya, and from Denpasar to Kupang, Maumere, and Waingapu.

The sleek Pelni ship KM *Kelimutu* sails every two weeks from Banjarmasin to Surabaya, Benoa, Lembar, Bima, Waingapu, Ende, Kupang, Dili, Kalabahi, Maumere, and Makassar, then back to Surabaya. The new KM *Dobonsolo* connects Kupang and Dili to cities along the north coast of Irian Jaya on a two-week circuit. Twice a month, Dili, Larantuka, and Labuhanbajo are connected by the ship KM *Tatamailau* east to points in Maluku and west to Java and Kalimantan. The KM *Awu* links Bima to many ports in Sulawesi and West Kalimantan.

Merpati has fairly reliable flights connecting all the major cities and many smaller towns within this island chain. Flights depart Bali to anywhere in Nusatenggara; flights leaving from Lombok travel only to Sumbawa, Sumba, and Timor. From Sumba, flights are scheduled only to Bima, Denpasar, and Kupang. From Flores, it depends where you are: Labuhanbajo now has an airport, making Komodo a bit more accessible for the jet set; from here there are direct flights to Bima, Denpasar, Ende, Kupang, Mataram, and Ruteng. From Ruteng or Ende, you can fly to almost anywhere. Maumere has flights only to Bali (and on to Java), Kupang, and Bima. From Larantuka you can fly to Kupang and Lewoleba.

Motorized and sailing vessels ply the coasts and travel between islands; in the Solor and Alor archipelagos east of Flores, boats are the principal interisland option. Also, good passenger ferry services link Bali, Lombok, Sumbawa, Komodo, Flores, Sumba, and Timor. These frequent ferries are run by Angkutan Sungei Danau dan Penyeberangan (ASDP), which tends to be even more reliable than Pelni. Frequent non-ASDP ferries also link Larantuka to Adonara and Lembata, and less frequently to Alor.

The larger islands offer buses, canopied trucks with benches, *bemo, dokar,* and minibuses, and you can often hitch a ride (for a fee) with a passing transport truck or motorcycle. With asphalt roads all over Lombok and straight across Sumbawa, it's easy to get around. Move on to Flores and good roads are scarce. There is currently much road work in progress due to earthquake damage, and long stretches are still in fairly poor—yet passable—condition. On Timor, a well-surfaced road goes from Kupang to Dili. And on Sumba a paved road runs between Waingapu to Waikabubak, with good extensions farther on to the east and west.

TOURS

A number of specialized tourist agencies have sprung up in Nusatenggara in the last several years. Of the land/sea tour companies try **Perama Tour and Travel**, with offices in Mataram, Senggigi, Kuta Beach, Bangsal, and the three Gili islands; Bima and Sumbawa Besar on Sumbawa; and Labuhanbajo on Flores. **Island Adventures**, packages similar weeklong trips. **Swastika Tours and Travel**, offers a dozen different options for tours of Lombok and the other major islands in Nusatenggara. In Bima, look for **Parewa Tour and Travel**, tel. (0324) 2525, for special tours to various locales on Sumbawa, Flores, Sumba, and Komodo. Also in Bima is **Grand Komodo Tours and Travel**.

Floressa Tours, tel. (0361) 289-253, in Sanur arranges dive trips to Maumere on Flores for some of the best skin-diving opportunities in Indonesia. **PT Pitoby Travel Service** in Kupang offers tours to Komodo, Kelimutu, and Sumba.

West Lombok

AMPENAN

Formerly Lombok's main seaport but now a crumbling shadow of its former self. Of the three large towns—Ampenan, Mataram, and Cakranegara—Ampenan is the most colorful, with a concentration of inexpensive accommodations and restaurants. The town has a market, shopping area, movie theater, and a few decent restaurants. *Dokar* cost Rp500 to anywhere in town. The west coast beaches are readily accessible from Ampenan.

The **West Nusatenggara Museum** is on Jl. Ponji Tiler Negara, south of Jl. Majapahit. Open Tues.-Thur. 0800-1400, Friday 0800-1100, Saturday and Sunday 0800-1400; closed Monday and holidays. A small collection, with only a few explanations in English. Best are the displays of cloth and *kris*. While in Ampenan, visit the copra factory near Losmen Pabean, toward the harbor. A good antique shop that's been around for years is **Musdah Antique Shop** on Jl. Saleh Sungkar. Several other antique and art shops lie within a couple blocks of the cinema. The **West Nusatenggara Government Tourist Office**, at Jl. Langko 70, tel. (0364) 21866 or 21730, employs a very helpful staff and offers some useful literature, maps, and brochures. Open Mon.-Sat. 0700-1600; closed Sunday and holidays.

NARMADA

Ten km east of Cakranegara, seven km from Sweta by *bemo* (Rp250). From Narmada's *bemo* stop, cross the road and walk down a side street to the entrance (Rp200) of Taman Narmandi (Narmandi Park). In 1801, a raja's summer palace was built here upon an artificial plateau. From a hidden place above the three-tiered

Wet rice planting, Lombok

pools, the old raja used to make his selection of the village lovelies. Built by the king of Karangasem, the large complex encompasses a mixture of Balinese, Islamic, and Sasak architecture. Several *warung* are inside the complex, with plenty more in town. Crowded on weekends. Behind the *bemo* stop, see village handicrafts, clothing, and food in the Narmada market, one of Lombok's largest.

SURANADI AND SESAOT

Suranadi is a small temple and gardens, one of Lombok's oldest, four km north of Narmada and 15 km from Mataram in the hills. See the rebuilt baths of kings carved in the Balinese style with icy clean water bubbling up from natural springs; the pool is said to have been built in exactly the same shape as Lake Segara Anak. At the **Temple of the Holy Eels**, eels swim out of conduits if you drop an egg in the water. Donation requested—Rp500 is enough.

For a little self-indulgence, stay at the formerly colonial **Hotel Suranadi**, tel. (0364) 23686. Reputed to be the finest upland hotel on Lombok, rooms and cottages rent for Rp48,000-96,000; amenities include swimming pool, restaurant, and tennis courts. Service and rooms are not a bad value and the location is fantastic. Perhaps the most unusual thing here is the swimming pool, which consists of sand, round rocks, and ice cold spring water. Meals are rather expensive; up the road is **Wisata** for an alternate Indonesian meal.

Take a *bemo* up the river five km through farming villages to Sesaot, with *bemo* station, market, and forest nearby. The deeper you go, the more proud and *asli* the people become. See people carrying 40-kilo loads of firewood on their heads, trudging in from the rainforest to sell their loads in the market.

LINGSAR

At Lingsar is another sacred eel pool and a large, Balinese temple complex—oldest and holiest on the island—which combines Hindu and Islamic motifs. This worn and faded temple and its pretty courtyard, believed to have been built in 1714, feel more like an Indian *pura* than anything on Bali. The Waktu Telu Muslims and Balinese Hindus worship together here, using different levels of the temple. The Hindu *pura* in the northern part of the complex has four shrines, each dedicated to the gods and god-kings of Bali and Lombok. The Waktu Telu temple, in the southern part of the complex, contains an eel pond dedicated to Vishnu. On all-night festivals during the full moon, sleep in the temple on mats. Lingsar is a highlight of Lombok, an extremely enjoyable experience. Donation Rp500. Buy eggs in the *warung* for the slug-like holy eels. A second, smaller temple is located in the village 200 meters behind.

In the countryside between Suranadi and Lingsar is **Tragtag**, a pure Balinese village on a small hill, as well as many other traditional Balinese villages. Take a *bemo* from close to Cakranegara's *bioskop* direct to Lingsar. You can also take a *bemo* from

Terminal Sweta to Narmada, then board another for Lingsar. From Lingsar's *bemo* stop, it's only a five-minute walk to the temple complex.

THE GILLIS ISLANDS

The three tiny islands of Gili Air, Gili Meno, and Gili Trawangan off Lombok's northwest coast are magnificent. All once depended on the copra trade, but now money comes from tourism. Coconut trees still cover the interior of all three islands, and there is limited cattle grazing and goat herding on Gili Trawangan. The lack of freshwater springs and limited land size has traditionally kept the population small, but water catchment schemes and water transportation from the mainland has changed that. As everything must be brought from Lombok, prices are slightly inflated. While electricity is generated during the evening hours at some establishments, most still use lanterns. Though there are no banks, moneychangers occupy all three islands; a *wartel* office is located on each isle for local and international telephone calls. And while small—you can walk around each isle in a leisurely two or three hours—there is *dokar* transport on all three islands charging Rp500-1000 for a ride along the limited beachfront paths. Many of the accommodations are built up off the ground, have outside *mandi*, thatched roofs, woven bamboo walls, covered verandas, a few chairs and tables, and mosquito nets. Many accommodations rent snorkel masks and fins for Rp3000 per day. At the height of the late summer tourist rush all rooms are rented and some people sleep on the beach. Other small islands off Lombok—particularly south and west of Lembar—now receive travelers looking for more tranquil climes. There are frequent boat connections from Bangsal to and between all three islands.

Sumbawa

Sumbawa (15,600 square km) is made up of rolling uplands, eroded foothills, volcanic ridges, and ancient crater walls. For the most part, the north coast consists of plains and river basins, except for the jagged, towering peak of **Gunung Tambora** on Teluk Saleh. Much of the land is covered with a park-like landscape of large, open tracts of countryside alleviated only by small clusters of trees and shrubs, brown hills, and a mountainous coast with picturesque bays and harbors. Eastern Sumbawa is a rocky, dusty, parched country of stubbly growth and bamboo villages on stilts. The island's rainy season is usually November to April, with little daily variation in temperature.

As big as Lombok and Bali together, Sumbawa has about 800,000 inhabitants. Lying at a transitional point between the Indianized "high" cultures of western Indonesia and the traditional pagan cultures of eastern Indonesia, Sumbawa is a fascinating ethnographic area. Except for a few villages in the Donggo-Mbawa area, there has never been any Christian missionary activity on the island and most islanders are today strict Muslims; there is, however, a powerful undercurrent of animist beliefs and adherence to *adat*.

THE DONGGO AREA

A traditional mountain area west of Teluk Bima, the home of 20,000 swidden farmers called the **Dou Donggo** ("Mountain People"). Speaking an archaic form of Bimanese, they live in patrilineal clans in a dozen villages. Though the Dou Donggo share many cultural traits with Biman lowlanders, they preserve a unique ethnic and religious identity, wear distinctive black clothing, observe their own hierarchical order, and build traditional houses called *uma neuhi*. These rectangular, high-gabled *adat* dwellings, raised on piles and located next to steep cliffs high on mountain ridges, represent probably the original East Sumbawanese house form, once prevalent all over the region.

The darker-skinned Dou Donggo, believed to be descendants of the island's indigenous peoples, practiced until recently an animist religion. They adopted Christianity or Islam only in the last 20 years and practice those faiths with varying degrees of

orthodoxy. This mountain tribe also weaves outstanding cloth on breastlooms. Ask to see the sacred places (*ntsala*), marked by linga, where the gods gather to copulate.

To the Donggo area, about 40 km from Bima, first catch a ferry (Rp2000) from Bima harbor to the port of Bajo, then take the bus from Sila to Donggo. Walk to **Kali** and **Moawa**. Near Donggo, see the stone inscription and the graves of two folk heroes. **Mbawa** is the only village where the black clothing and *uma neuhi* can be seen in everyday use. Alternately take a bus from Bima to Sila; then change buses there. If you get an early start, it's possible to reach Donggo and return to Bima in the same day.

TO KOMODO ISLAND

The ferry to Komodo and Flores leaves from Sape harbor, called simply *pelabuhan*, about four km (Rp1000) by *benhur* from Sape. The regular Sape-Komodo-Labuhanbajo ferry costs Rp9000 pp (bicycles, motorcycles, and cars extra) to Komodo or Labuhanbajo, and an additional Rp4000 from Komodo to Labuhanbajo if breaking your journey in Komodo. The harbor tax is Rp100. On Komodo there's an additional Rp1500 fare (each way) for the transfer *prahu* from the ferry to the national park pier. The ferry leaves from Sape to Komodo (and on to Flores) at 0800 everyday except Friday; allow five hours to Komodo and seven to Labuhanbajo. Reasonably priced private tour boats from Labuhanbajo also run to Komodo and other islands in this crowded strait.

Komodo Island

One of the world's great wildlife regions, this small archipelago nestled between Sumbawa and Flores is home to the Komodo dragon, the sole survivor of carnivorous dinosaurs that thrived in tropical Asia 130 million years ago. The giant monitor lizards—the largest on earth—were only a myth until the turn of this century when a few pearl fishermen were forced to land here one night in a storm. Today, isolated by the strong, unpredictable currents in the straits that separate them, these dry and barren islands draw thousands of travelers from all over the world to view the lizards in their natural habitat. Komodo, as well as the neighboring islands of Padar, Rinca, Motong, and two small areas on Flores south of Labuhanbajo, were made a national park in 1980.

You need a permit (Rp20,000) to visit. The permit, your room charge (Rp5500 a night), and an insurance fee (Rp100) are taken at the front office when you disembark the ferry at Loh Liang. Your visitor permit is good as long as you want to stay, but you must rent a room for every night you remain on the island. From June to August about 15,000 people visit Komodo Island. The rest of the year sees about

Sunset on Sumbawa   *(following pages) Fishing party in Sumbawa*

9,000 people. Most come on cruise ships and sleep on board, but there are 52 beds for rent in several bungalows at the park headquarters.

Loh Liang

Located at the north part of Teluk Slawi, Loh Liang is an area of open grasslands, riverbeds, old *ladang,* savannahs, and a small mangrove swamp on the bay's west end near the coast. It's also the location of the well-kept PHPA camp, two km north of Kampung Komodo. Tourists may only stay in the PHPA camp's visitor accommodations—several large bungalows costing Rp5500 per night. Generator-produced electricity operates until about 2200. There is a cafeteria at the park headquarters which has an extensive menu, though it's somewhat expensive. This is the only place on the island to buy food. To be on the safe side, bring a few emergency food items and bottled water.

Explore **Loh Liang Bay**, a pristine area of white sulphur-crested cockatoos, megapode birds, *wili wili* birds, bellowing Timor deer, and snorting boars crashing through the grass. You can walk from Loh Liang to Kampung Komodo (45-60 minutes) at low tide. Follow only the marked trails to the Poreng Valley. Every time you leave the PHPA camp, a guide must accompany you. When walking, always wear long pants and shoes to protect against snakes and poisonous insects. Other isolated bays in the northern part of the island are **Loh Boko** and **Loh Sorao**, with thick woods, rocky lava cliffs, and unspoiled coral gardens. *Ora* are larger here than on the village side of the island.

Dragon-watching

Best time to see these creatures is May-September. Early in the morning and/or late in the afternoon a PHPA guide takes a group from the Loh Liang camp to the dragon-watching site at **Banunggulung**. One or more guides (Rp2500 each) are required per group. This cost is split among the members of the group. The dry riverbed site is about a 30-minute walk (2.5 km) from Loh Liang. There you can safely view the dragons from above, from the edge of the ravine. Some of the area is protected by a fence. Red clothes and menstruating women are forbidden on this excursion. The whole outing takes about an hour and a half.

Currently, more than 2,000 lizards on the island hunt for their sustenance. Follow the spoor trails left by dragons searching for carrion; these are visible imprints of the Komodo's claws and the scrape of its tail. Have the guide take you to the well-worn dragon trail in **Loh Kalo**. Extending from the bottom of the slope to a burrow complex at a point two-thirds of the way to the top, this 300-meter-long path is devoid of all brush and is used only by the giant lizards.

Never go looking for lizards without a guide. Loh Liang is the safest area, and *ora* here are not abused and killed. In most cases they show no interest in humans and you can often approach quite close to a large feeding dragon without it taking any notice of you. If they do approach, the guides keep them off you with long forked sticks. The younger dragons are the most curious—entering the camp, flicking their tongues at your feet. Often just a slight movement will send them scurrying. Very few lizards will attack humans unprovoked, and most attacks occur in self-defense. Like people, some *ora* are meaner than others, and all should be watched carefully. The infection caused by a bite can be very dangerous.

WATER SPORTS

Komodo is also a marine reserve with fine mangroves and coral reefs rich in diverse marine fauna (such as the *caranx* species) and shellfish. **Teluk Slawi** even has a resi dent population of baleen whales. After you're through viewing dragons, spend the rest of the afternoon snorkeling on the reef. The park office rents fins and asks Rp3000 per day. PHPA can advise you on the best spots, and can arrange boats and canoes. Snorkeling is particularly good off the north coast of the island, teeming with more than 180 species of fish. An outrigger costs Rp5000-10,000 per day. Local fishermen say the sharks are harmless; still, only snorkel in calm water close to the beach. More treacherous than sharks are the four- to five-knot currents in the straits between the islands. Komodo's numerous sheltered coves offer more safety.

Flores

A mostly Christian island becoming more popular with travelers, mountainous Flo res could very well be the highlight of your visit to Nusatenggara. Considered by many one of Indonesia's most beautiful islands, Flores has grandiose volcanoes, high mountain lakes, stretches of savannah, and tropical deciduous forests. Frequently shaken by earthquakes and volcanic eruptions, Flores is riven with deep ravines and rugged valleys, which accounts for the difficulty of travel and the island's distinctive cultures. One spectacular ridge of weathered mountains runs down the middle of the island, with 15 lazily smoking volcanos descending smoothly into the sea on both sides. An unbroken fringe of tangled, buttress-like roots has formed an almost im penetrable barrier along some of the island's coasts. Behind this tidal zone are thick ets inhabited by wild boar. Flores is also well known for its large numbers of domes tic horses.

With its rich stores of sandalwood, textiles, and slaves, the island in the 14th cen tury fell under the economic and political aegis of the Majapahit Empire, which es tablished coastal states. A Portuguese explorer christened the island Cabo de Flores or "Cape of Flowers" in the 16th century. Ironically, Flores has few flowers and was known to Javanese sailors as "Stone Island." In the coastal towns, Florinese began

The Hunter and the Game

There was now little noise. A jungle cock crowed in the distance. Several times a fruit dove, purple-red above and green below, shot with closed wings like a bullet along the clear channel above the stream-bed, soundless except for the sudden whistle of its passage through the air. We waited, hardly daring to move, the camera fully wound, spare magazines of film beside us and a battery of lenses ready in the open camera-case.

After a quarter of an hour, my position on the ground became extremely uncomfortable. Noiselessly, I shifted my weight on to my hands, and uncrossed my leg. Next to me, Charles crouched by his camera, the long black lens of which projected between the palm leaves of the screen. Sabran squatted on the other side of him. Even from where we sat, we could smell only too strongly the stench of the bait fifteen yards in fornt of us. This, however, was encouraging for we were relying on this small to attract the dragons.

We had been sitting in absolute silence for over half an hour when there was a rustling noise immediately behind us. I was irritated; the men must have returned already. Very slowly, so as not to make any noise, I twisted round to tell the boys not to be impatient and to return to the boat. Charles and Sabran remained with their eyes riveted on the bait. I was three-quarters of the way round when I discovered that the noise had not been made by men.

There, facing me, less than four yards away, crouched the dragon.

He was enormous. From the tip of his narrow head to the end of his long keeled tail he measured a full twelve feet. He was so close to us that I could distinguish every beady scale on his hoary black skin, which, seemingly too large for him, hung in long horizontal folds on his flanks and was puckered and wrinkled around his powerful neck. He was standing high on his four legs, his heavy body lifted clear of the ground, his head erect and menacing. The line of his savage mouth curved upwards in a fixed sardonic grin and from between his half-closed jaws an enormous yellow-pink forked tongue slid in and out. There was nothing between us

and him but a few very small seedling trees sprouting from the leaf-covered ground. I nudged Charles, who turned, saw the dragon, and nudged Sabran. The three of us sat staring at the monster. He stared back.

It flashed across my mind that at least he was in no position to use his main offensive weapon, his tail. Further, if he came towards us both Sabran and I were close to trees and I was sure that I would be able to shin up mine very fast if I had to. Charles, sitting in the middle, was not so well placed.

For almost a minute none of us moved or spoke. Then Charles laughed softly.

"You know," he whispered, keeping his eyes fixed warily on the monster, "he has probably been standing there for the last ten minutes watching us just as intently and quietly as we have been watching the bait."

~ David Attenborough, Zoo Quest for a Dragon, 1957

converting to Islam in the 15th and 16th centuries. In 1859, the Dutch took over Flores from the Portuguese and crushed a native rebellion in 1907-08, but it was not until 1936 that they considered the island safe enough for transfer from military to civil control.

The 1,350,000 residents make Flores Nusatenggara's most populous island. Many people describe themselves as *campur* (mixed), naming different island ethnicities— Sikka, Lio—as well as Bugis, Makassarese, and Malay in their paternities. Life in the interior is simple; most Florinese live by fishing, hunting, and simple agriculture revolving around palm and taro cultivation. The indigenous peoples of the deep island areas can still be defensively hostile. Not all Florinese wholeheartedly accept Christianity. Totemism and animism are widespread, and the island is steeped in witchcraft. Megalithic cultures, animist belief systems, and ancestor spirit cults still persist in remote areas.

LABUHANBAJO

This tranquil fishing village, principal port of western Flores, is the favored departure point for Komodo and Sumbawa. It lies nestled into the hillside on a beautiful bay and offers great sunsets over the island-studded sea between Flores and Komodo. Quiet now, it's gearing up for growth—a new pier has recently been built to accommodate larger boats (a Pelni ship now makes a regular stop here); an extension to the airport runway is under construction, which will mean larger airplanes and more group travel; and new hotels, *losmen,* and eateries are appearing in eager anticipation. The airport is on a plateau, about two km from the center of town. The Merpati office is on the way, one half km before the airport. No public transport runs to the airport yet, but some accommodations will shuttle you into town for free. *Bemo* charge about Rp5000 from the airport to town.

Visit the small harbor filled with native and Bugis *prahu.* Stilted Bajo fishermen's houses are built out over the water, with dugout canoes tied underneath. Rent snorkeling equipment in Labuhanbajo from two dive shops. **Varanus Dive Shop** is located 100 meters up from the harbor; it runs dives to various locations including Sebolan, Sebayur, Rinca, and Komodo islands. A two-tank dive with all equipment, transportation, guide, and lunch runs Rp135,000 (two-person minimum). Similar dives are offered by the **Komodo Diving Resort** at the New Bajo Beach Hotel. The best beach around Labuhanbajo is Waecicu, but the snorkeling is second-rate due to reef destruction.

RUTENG

A cool, neat town set amidst the scenic hills of the Manggarai district, with broad streets, photogenic churches, and an airstrip that will put the fear of God in you. Ruteng is reachable by flights from Kupang (Rp121,000) and Denpasar (Rp184,000), with intermediate stops on the Denpasar route at Bima (Rp85,000) and Labuhanbajo (Rp42,000). This village is high (1,100 meters); you might need to don warm clothing by the late afternoon. Embroidered *sarung* are available in the *pasar.* On Jl. Baruk in a traffic roundabout is a newly reconstructed former king's palace. The town itself can be traversed in 20 minutes, so everything you need is within walking distance. *Bemo* around town charge a flat fee of Rp250.

Walk around Ruteng—excellent views of lush paddy fields, hills, mountains, and valleys. This is a large market area; all around Ruteng are the productive mission farms that supply dairy products and meat. Perhaps the best place to see the town, mountains, and surrounding agricultural fields, preferably in the early morning or late afternoon, is at **Golo Curu** is an observation area north of town; take the path that branches left off the road to Reo.

BAJAWA

The grueling ride from Ruteng to Bajawa is spectacular, although there is some grim evidence of slash-and-burn practices. Like Ruteng, this hill town is scenic and refreshingly cool. Don't miss Bajawa's **ancestral poles**; there are a few on Jl. Kartini and a whole group on the edge of town on the road to Ende. Called locally *ngadhu* for men and *bhaga* for women, these totems protect the town and fields against bad spirits (*polo*) and are said to be the resting place of the spirits of clan members. Bajawa makes a good base for excursions into surrounding villages such as Soa, Wago, Langa, and Bena. Gunung Inielika (1,763 meters) may or may not be climbable as it's still considered active, but Gunung Inerie (2,245 meters) can be climbed in three or four hours from the village of Bena.

THE BAJAWA HIGHLANDS

One of the most traditional areas of Flores, and one of great natural beauty, the Bajawa Highlands is home to the Ngada people. Known in early Dutch literature as the Rokka (named after the old name for the region's principal peak, 2,245-meter-high Gunung Inerie), this mixed Malay/Melanesian race, who believe they originated on Java, settled the region during the 17th century. They were conquered by the Dutch in 1907, and Christian missionaries began converting them around 1920. The Ngada occupy the south coast around Gunung Inerie, and inland on the high Bajawa Plateau to Riung in the north. In the highest villages the temperatures can drop to freezing in the rainy season (December to April).

Coconut, *areca, lontar,* palms, tamarind, bamboo, citrus trees, bananas, breadfruit, and mangos grow wild; corn, beans, squash, pumpkins, and other dry-land crops are raised. There is no irrigation system here so only small plots of rice are cultivated in a few riverine areas. The Ngada have domesticated the buffalo and horse, and keep pigs, chickens, and goats. They hunt from horses using bamboo spears and iron-tipped war lances. The Ngada practice ironsmithing and pottery, and dye cloth to make traditional *sarung* with yellow embroidery. This hand-woven cloth often has a black or dark blue background with simple animal designs in patterns. Some designs are tie-dyed.

Ngada villages consist of two rows of up to 50 closely spaced houses facing a central open square. Some of the villages have stone walls, pillars, megaliths, and ritual poles where buffalo sacrifices once took place. Their traditional raised wooden houses consist of living quarters with a high-pitched thatched gable roof (some newer homes now have corrugated metal panels under the thatch) and a low-

Ambulombo Volcano

pitch veranda covered in split bamboo turned concave and convex, alternately, in an overlapping tile pattern. Set about a meter off the ground, the floors are woven bamboo; the walls consist of flat panels of solid teak, some pieces nearly a meter across. In wealthier houses, symbols and figures are carved into these walls. The living quarters are usually about ten square meters in size, with one corner given over to a slightly raised area for the cooking fire. Though small, each dwelling may house up to 20 people. Usually three generations live together in one house, sometimes four generations if the elders live long—and many live to be over one hundred years old.

Roof decorations on the ridges distinguish class for some families. A house-like structure on the ridge indicates the principal upper-class family of a clan. A human figure with knife or spear indicates the principal middle-class family. Lower class and attendant upper- and middle-class family houses are unadorned.

There are many traditional villages surrounding Bajawa where *ngadhu* totems and *rumah adat* can be seen. Always check in with the *kepala desa* before wandering around and taking photos. No longer infrequently visited, villages are cashing in on the increased flow of tourists; some now request that you sign a guest book and leave a Rp1000 (or more) donation.

A clan (not necessarily blood relatives) is made up of at least one upper-class family, one middle-class family, and four lower class families. Children stay in the clan until they marry out (males), start their own clan (if upper class), or are invited by an upper-class couple to form a new clan. This brings great respect upon a family but is very expensive. To start a clan, the couple must erect totems in the village square, one each for the husband and wife, and entertain hundreds of people at a special ceremony. They also must select, invite, and convince at least one middle-class and four lower-class families to join with them in forming the new social unit. Gifts of land or other property are usual compensations for joining. Some villages have only a couple of clans and accompanying totems, while others have over sixty.

BENA

Some say it's the best of the traditional villages in the area. This three-tiered village, 14 km southeast of Bajawa at the foot of the Gunung Inerie volcano, has totem figures and megaliths in the village square surrounded by traditional Ngadanese bamboo dwellings and ritual houses. Overlooking the village is a shrine to the Virgin

Whip fighting, Flores

Mary. Bena burnt in 1961 but was rebuilt in traditional style—there is some corrugated tin under the thatch. Electricity has come to Bena, and it is only a matter of time before it reaches other villages as well. Register at the village entrance; Rp1000 donation. There are *bemo* that run daily to Bena (Rp1000). They have no regular schedule but usually one or two will travel this bumpy road in the morning.

Sometimes trucks also go. Alternately, take one of the frequent *bemo* to Langa and walk the 10 km down the hill and around the base of Gunung Inerie to the village. Perhaps the best is to get a group of four or five together and charter a *bemo* for Rp60,000-80,000 a day.

KELI MUTU

Keli Mutu volcano is one of the more otherworldly sights in all of Indonesia. There are three lakes atop this extinct volcano, two separated by a low ridge and the third several hundred meters distant, all with different colored waters. The colors are in constant flux as the lakes leach minerals from the earth, which dissolve and color the water. Two of the lakes are now different shades of green, one dark and the other milky white; the third is nearly black. From the viewpoint, you can see the complex's highest peak (1,613 meters) and the even higher Keli Bara (1,731 meters) to the south. Rather dangerous trails run along the crater rims, from where the sides drop precipitously into the water. Be careful. Keli Mutu gets quite a few foreign tourists per year, but it's worth it even if there's a crowd. Dry season is April-October.

From Ende or Maumere, take the bus to Moni, from where you start climbing the volcano. It's best to stay the night in Moni and go to the top for sunrise, but it's possible to do Keli Mutu and get back to Ende the same day. On Sunday, busloads of local tourists assault the mountain, most of them directly from Ende. You might get a ride, but they often don't get to the top until around 1100, by which time the mountain has clouded over and there isn't much to see. Or follow Pak Harto's example and go by helicopter; a landing pad was cleared near the top for a visit he made in 1985.

Climb the volcano early in the morning, before clouds roll in. To view the colored lakes by morning light, get up at 0200 and walk the whole 13 km to the top. Start about one km (15-minute walk) out of Moni toward Ende, just past Sao Ria Wisata, where an entrance arch has been set up over the road. The climb will take three to four hours, so carry water, snacks, and a flashlight. About halfway up the mountain, at km six, is the PHPA checkpoint; the entrance fee is Rp400. From the checkpoint it's about six km to the top. You should reach the top around 0600 for sunrise.

Alternatively, a truck to the top (Rp3000 pp one-way) leaves Moni around 0400, getting you there in time for sunrise. The truck leaves the top at 0700 for the return trip to Moni; either pay again to ride down, or walk. From Ende, a *bemo* costs around Rp100,000 roundtrip.

MAUMERE

A port town 148 km east of Ende on the narrow eastern stretch of the island. A pretty place, and easy-going, Maumere is nicely situated on the bay with islands offshore to the north. It's a good base from which to explore this part of the island. In 1992 Maumere met with disaster in the form of a strong earthquake and tsunami. Although the epicenter was out in the bay, the city suffered great destruction. Many buildings were destroyed; some are still in rubble. Cement slabs of others show grim evidence of the damage; buildings stand with large cracks in the walls. Much new construction. Though some large concrete buildings have been erected, smaller bamboo and wood structures are more numerous—they're not only easier, faster, and less costly to build but seem to be more flexible and take violent movement with less damage.

Built like a Spanish town with a main square and market occupying its center, Maumere's principal attraction is its large Catholic church. Inside are paintings of the Twelve Stations of the Cross executed by a local artist with Indonesian characters. The church was badly damaged during the quake of 1992, and there has been no major repair since then. Visit also the old musty cemetery in the rear.

A center of Catholic enterprise, the local mission finances and manages copra and coffee export businesses. The Catholic hospital, St. Elizabeth's (Western-trained staff), in the town of Lela, is the place to go if you get sick on Flores. The old central market was also badly damaged during the earthquake; a new market has been set up on the western edge of town. Buy thick, distinctive Maumere blankets (many times more expensive on Bali); also see Sumatran ivory jewelry carved by local craftsmen. For Maumere-style *ikat* weaving, go to **Harapan Jaya** across from the old market in the city center.

You can change traveler's checks and currency at **Bank Rakyat Indonesia** though the exchange rate is very poor. The bank is open Mon.-Fri. 0800-1200 and Saturday until 1100. The *wartel* is kitty-corner from the bank and is open 24 hours. The **post office** is open Mon.-Thurs. 0800-1400, Friday until 1100, and Saturday until 1230. For photo supplies try Alan Indah or Foto Cantik. Both have rolls of Fuji color slide film, 36 exposures for Rp12,500.

In Waiara, 12 km east of Maumere, are two first-class dive resorts: **Sea World Club**, open since 1975, and **Flores Sao Resort**, one km farther. Both resorts are accessible by *bemo* (Rp500) from Maumere. Daily rates for dives, including all equipment, transportation, and snacks, are Rp110,000-145,000 pp per day; snorkel fins and masks go for Rp7000. Both establishments offer package deals for room and dives up to seven days. Flores Sao Resort also offers diving courses. Get more information from Waiara Cottages—Sea World Club, P.O. Box 3, Maumere, Flores, Indonesia, tel. (0383) 21570, and P.T. Saowisata, Room 6b, Second floor, Hotel Borobudur Intercontinental Offices, Jl. Lapangan Banteng Seletan, Jakarta, 10710, Indonesia, tel. (021) 370-333, ext. 78222 or 78227, or tel. 21555.

LARANTUKA

A picturesque port on the island's far eastern tip, 667 km from Labuhanbajo. Towered over by Gunung Ile Mandiri (1,524 meters), Larantuka hugs the coast. This city has a long-established Eurasian colony and since Portuguese times has been the administrative center for the eastern neck of Flores and the island to the east. Travelers embark for the Solor and Alor archipelagos from Larantuka by crossing the narrow Selat Lewotobi. Larantuka's main street, Jl. Niaga (also called Jl. Yos Sudarso, Jl. Fernandez, and Jl. Diponegoro along different sections), runs along the waterfront. It contains most of the government offices, the town's two churches, and many of the businesses.

For centuries a Portuguese trading center, Larantuka still harbors traces of the Portuguese era in the old stone and stucco houses; in the large-boned, Latin-featured inhabitants in family names such as Monteiros and da Silva; and even in the place-names in town such as *posto* (the town's center). With its prayers, ceremonies, Christmas and Good Friday processions, and Iberian church architecture, the

(following pages) The varied hues of the crater lakes of Keli Mutu volcano

Catholic religious life of Larantuka follows Portuguese traditions. Many of the prayers are recited in broken Portuguese, and during religious processions men carry a bier which symbolically contains the body of Jesus. They wear long white cloaks with high pointed hoods, costumes resembling those donned in Portugal during the Middle Ages. Every Easter, cruise ship passengers and numerous tourists visit Larantuka for its parades.

Old relics from the 1500s and 1600s are still preserved in bamboo chapels as village *pusaka*—vestments, devotional clothes, ivory crucifixes, silver chalices. A statue of a black Virgin Mary, claimed to have been washed ashore in a man's dream, is venerated. An old Portuguese bell hangs outside the **Church of Kapala Maria.** In the corner of the Peca da Penha is the Portuguese font where hundreds of Larantukans where baptized. The 1992 earthquake left its effect in Larantuka, mostly in the destruction of old colonial buildings, but the damage was not nearly as widespread as in Maumere. More destructive is the periodic flooding from waters draining off the steep mountainside at Larantuka's back. In 1979, for example, several villages were swept into the sea and scores of people perished.

Sumba

Outlying, dry, mostly barren Sumba is one of the most fascinating islands of Nusatenggara. Situated south of Flores and midway between Sumbawa and Timor, Sumba is the source of some of the most handsome *ikat* fabrics in Indonesia, and the breeding ground for the country's strongest horses. Here you find an authentic ancient culture with none of the layers of Hinduism, Islam, or Christianity found elsewhere in Indonesia. Lying outside the volcanic belt running through the length of the archipelago, much of interior Sumba consists of extensive plateaus with scattered, irregular hills. The climate is hot and dry, particularly in the east where widespread eucalyptus savannahs and large tracts of flat grasslands and steppe-like landscapes provide good grazing for cattle and support small-scale agriculture. The small unnavigable rivers which supply the island's only irrigation tend to be dry up to eight months of the year.

The 280,000 people of more verdant West Sumba (Sumba Barat) are mainly farmers, while the 150,000 or so East Sumbanese (Sumba Timur) raise horses, cattle, buffalo, and other livestock. Sumbans practice mostly subsistence agriculture: rice, tobacco, and maize are the main crops; coffee and coconuts are secondary. An archaic method of plowing is still used here, in which 20-30 buffalo are driven across flooded fields, trampling them to a muddy consistency. The island's forests yield cinnamon and sandalwood. Greed over the centuries has forced the government to forbid cutting down those few stands of sandalwood that remain; now you need a special license to export the fragrant wood from Indonesia.

IKAT SUMBA

Ikat is a very ancient tie-dye method of decorating rugs, shawls, and blankets. Each completed fabric represents a colossal amount of human labor and only isolated, feudal, agricultural societies like Sumba's still produce these handwoven textiles. Although *ikat* fabrics are also woven on nearby islands such as Flores and Roti, the craft here has reached an unusually high level. Woven from locally grown cotton, the cloths figure prominently in the ceremonial and social life of the island.

Each region has its own distinctive designs and shades. Some heirloom pieces are considered so priceless and magically powerful they cannot be viewed in safety but must be kept in sealed baskets high up among the roofbeams. The really fine blankets, family

Sumba weaving with a skulltree motif

pusaka, you cannot buy. Families already have 1,000 buffalo, so why should they sell a blanket? It's easy to find more cattle, but difficult to make more blankets.

Since *ikat* textiles are now mass-produced for export, a great deal of substandard junk is around. The price is not always indicative of quality; merchants could charge up to Rp150,000 for a worthless piece. Sellers use many, many tricks: if the colors are too faded, the cloth is sometimes painted to make it more vibrant. The fabric could also be starched to make it feel newer. Some traders also boil the fabric in a solution of water, tobacco juice, and *kayu kuning* to give it the look of great age. Caveat emptor..Don't buy immediately; be patient and learn all you can first. On the genuine pieces look for smooth, sharp lines, clean colors (dyes must not run into each other), and intricate, tight designs. Smoothly curving lines is another sign of good work. Bargain relentlessly for each and every piece.

In Waingapu, merchants want as much as Rp400,000 a piece (natural dyes); they can be purchased a little cheaper (Rp100,000 and up) in villages southeast of Waingapu such as Melolo, Rende, Kaliuda, and Pau. The weaving centers of Kawangu and Prailiu are located just outside Waingapu. You won't have to look far; armies of vendors approach you on foot or bicycles, *hinggi* wrapped around their arms, shoulders, and handlebars.

WEST SUMBA

An area of gently sloping hills and savannahs and green forests, agriculturally based West Sumba is known for its giant megalithic stone memorial tablets; traditional villages; conical-shaped, thatch-roofed, high-peaked clan houses; and the *pasola*, a tribal war-game ritual held during Feb.-April. Events in Sumba Barat include *pajura* (traditional boxing), festivals of the Lunar New Year (October and November), Independence Day (17 August), horse races, and the building of *adat* houses and burials (July-Oct.). The isolated Bukambero in the Kodi subdistrict in the extreme west, numbering about 6,000, still practice their ancient ways and are considered a culture apart.

Less dry, cooler, more fertile, hillier, and greener than Sumba Timur, vegetables grow well in Sumba Barat. Many villages are located on a hilltop, a circle of tall houses around the ancestral graves; some villages are still walled and fortified. Houses typically have an open ground floor with chickens and pigs, where the weaving loom might be set up, sheltered from the hot sun. About a meter above is a bamboo floor, the actual living quarters. A veranda is often built on at least one side of the house. Large table-like slabs in the center of each *kampung* serve as a drying rack for roots, rice, buffalo dung, and chalk for *sirih*. Sometimes newly woven baskets are placed here; it's also where children play and old men sun themselves. Pegs-and-pebble gameboards are sometimes carved into the stone.

The *Pasola*

A ritual tribal war which takes place in different villages Feb.-April of each year, beginning several days after the full moon and coinciding with the ritual harvesting of a strange, multihued seaworm. Essentially a jousting match between horsemen carrying long wooden spears and shields, riders are frequently injured and occasionally killed. The government allows the ritual to take place, but spears must now be blunted. Famed as rugged, skilled horsemen, hundreds of Sumbanese combatants charge along circular runways tangent to each other. When their courses intersect they fling spears at each other or try to club opponents from their mounts with the butt end of their spears. Women are the chief observers and supporters of these mock combats, each cheering loudly for her favorites. Big thatch houses, grass-floor shelters, and foodstalls are set up in the spectator area for people streaming in from all over the island. The governor of Sumba and officials from Jakarta might even show up. Before setting out, find out in Waingapu exactly when the *pasola* takes place.

VICINITY OF WAIKABUBAK

Most traditional villages surrounding Waikabubak are accessible by *bemo*, best visited during their colorful weekly open-air markets. Some are as close as one-half km; others, like **Pandedewatu** to the south, are a four-hour walk. Ask villagers along the way for the locations of the big stones, elaborate megaliths, and nice carvings. Different villages bury their dead in different ways, each with unusual carvings and arrangements of stones. The Christian cross is found on more recent graves, alongside such traditional ornaments as buffalo heads (symbolizing power and strength), the horse (a safe trip to heaven), and the dog (faithfulness).

The closest village is **Tarung**, a small hilltop *desa* and ceremonial center (*paraing*) with several tombs one-half km west of Waikabubak. The front of the *adat* houses here are embellished with sets of water buffalo horns, trophies of past sacrifices. If you're waiting for some ritual to take place or just want to relax, swim off the white-sand beach at **Pantai Rua**, 21 km south of town (Rp550, 30 minutes). Or try the natural freshwater pools at **Waikelo Sawah**, 10 km west of the city. *Bemo* will take you to both places.

Eighteen km south of Waikabubak in the district of Wanokaka is the traditional village of **Prai Goli**, believed to contain the oldest megalith—Watu Kajiwa—on Sumba. A few kilometers from Lamboya is **Sodan**, another traditional village, where an important Lunar New Year ceremony occurs in October. The village has a sacred drum, its playing surface covered in human skin from an enemy flayed long ago. The drum is used to call ancestor spirits.

ANAKALANG

Twenty-two km and Rp500 by *bemo* east of Waikabubak on the main road to Waingapu, the focal point of this village is its massive graveyard. Sumbanese believe the present world is just an antechamber to the palace of the next world and that death is the most important event in life. Note the beautifully built thatched, conical homes here, plus a concentration of old burial stones with strong carvings. Every two years a mass marriage ceremony, Purung Takadonga, is held in Anakalang in the early summer.

Check out the nearby village of **Pasunga**, where 50 years ago the last great ruler of the Anakalang Kingdom, Umbu Dongga, was buried in a unique tomb called Resi Moni. Resembling a giant's footstool, the huge 30-ton stone slab (now broken) sat on six short columns. It took two years to carve from a quarry, then thousands of men spent two months dragging the stone to its present site in the village square. The fu-

(following pages) Animist priest on Sumba Island hunting for the year's first 'sea worms'

neral feast lasted a week and 250 water buffalo and scores of horses, pigs, and chickens were slaughtered to honor the departed chief. Another vertical tomb, carved in 1926, features the figures of a man and a woman. Houses in Pasunga stand in two rows like gigantic brown straw hats. The traditional village of **Lai Tarung**, nearby, has numerous old graves.

PRAI BOKUL

In this village an hour's walk north of Anakalang (the path starts opposite the *tempat makam*), the heaviest single megalith on Sumba sits like a fallen meteor. This 70-ton sepulchre, known as **Umbu Sawola**, was erected by one of the richest *rajas* on the island, who hired 2,000 workers to chisel and haul it out of a remote mountain. The slab measures five meters long and four meters wide and rests on short columns. It took three years and three lives to transport it. When the rope broke and killed men it was not considered an accident; the men were but sacrifices to provide the necessary spiritual guardianship for the grave. Ten tons of rice were consumed and 250 buffalo sacrificed in the ritual accompanying the dragging, with priests egging the men on with invocations and chants, all in the belief the stone would ensure the owner's entrance into heaven. The whole project cost Rp105 million to complete, a sum present-day relatives are trying implacably to recoup by charging tourists Rp5000 per photo.

Timor

The easternmost islands of Nusatenggara, the Timor Archipelago—including the Outer Arc islands of Roti, Ndao, and Savu—is the largest of the Lesser Sunda island groups. The population of Timor, the main island (480 km long by 80 km wide), is 1.5 million. Timor was formerly divided between the Dutch in the west and the Portuguese in the east. When Indonesia gained its independence in 1950, the western portion of the island went to the Republic while the east remained with the Portuguese. After a military coup toppled the dictatorship in Portugal in April 1974, the Portuguese sought to rid themselves of all their colonial possessions. In 1975, the Portuguese-controlled half was thus granted complete independence by Lisbon. Fearing that separatism would inspire revolt in parts of Indonesia and that the new government would fall under the influence of communists, the Indonesian military in 1975 invaded and, in 1976, annexed that territory. Now the whole island of Timor, divided into Timor Barat (West Timor) and Timor Timur (or "Tim Tim," East Timor) belongs to Indonesia.

Timor is the fastest-rising island in the world, each year surging three millimeters out of the sea. A central mountain range marches across Timor, from western tip to east. The highest peak at 2,963 meters is Gunung Tata Mai Lau, with several other peaks exceeding 2,000 meters. The island's western half consists of rugged, rocky hills, high plateaus cut by deep valleys, and loose-soiled, grassy terrain. The eastern half is similar but more rugged, with higher peaks, narrower coastal plains, and numerous mountain-slashing rivers. The island's main climatic problem is rain—too little or too much. At the beginning of the wet season the rural people move out to the *ladang* and live in shelters; villages are practically deserted except for old people and children. When the rains really set in, the island becomes impassable anywhere off the main highway. During the dry season (May-Sept.), the Timorese make salt, fell trees, collect beeswax, build houses, relax, feast, and dance. Landscapes during the dry are similar to the parched and brown Australian bush—leaves fall, rivers and wells dry up, drought sets in, the hot winds blow all day long.

Aromatic sandalwood has been Timor's "tree of destiny." By the 16th century Hindu-Javanese traders had discovered it, and by the end of the 19th century nearly all the sandalwood stands had been cut down, leaving behind large areas of open savannah grasslands. Sandalwood first attracted the Portuguese to Timor in the early 1500s. After the traders came the priests. The Dutch captured Melaka in 1641 and, after a prolonged struggle, eventually gained control of Kupang and western Timor. For hundreds of years the Dutch and the Portuguese skirmished over trade interests, but by 1655 the Portuguese had been ousted from all their most important settlements in Indonesia except for East Timor. The heated and longstanding territorial dispute between the Dutch and Portuguese over the sandalwood trade continued until 1904, when the two European powers finally carved up the island. The Portuguese were assigned the eastern half and the small enclave of Ocussi in the west, and the Dutch the remainder. In the 1950s, after the Indonesian revolution, Indonesia took control of the Dutch possessions but refrained from meddling in the Portuguese half. However, on 25 April 1974 military officers overthrew the Salazar dictatorship in Portugal, and the new socialist regime resolutely began dismantling the Portuguese colonial empire, including East Timor.

KUPANG

This 300-year-old trading center is the largest urban area in Nusatenggara and the capital of Nusatenggara Timur. Lying only 483 km from the coast of northeast Australia, Kupang is closer to Darwin than to Jakarta. The vernacular Malay spoken here reflects the wide variety of peoples who settled this area. Christianity is the predominant religion (90 percent), but there is also a small minority of Muslims (descendants of Arab traders), some 3,000 Balinese, a couple dozen Caucasian expats, and the Chinese, who own about 85 percent of the businesses. Kupang has a Catholic university, **Widya Mandira**, and a public university, **Nusa Cendana**. A new tourist office and museum are out beyond the bus station in the new section of town. The museum is a grand place with a small collection, mostly *ikat* (nice samples), some pottery and currency, and ethnographic articles of daily life. Worth a quick look.

In the first half of the 19th century, Kupang was a port of call for English and American whalers. Somerset Maugham's stories of Timor were set here. All the principal government offices are now located north of the city on a plateau called the Walikota. This highland area is cleaner, cooler, breezier and less congested than the city proper. Kupang is a major communications and transport hub for the region, with buses heading out to points in West Timor and Dili, as well as air and sea connections to all over Indonesia.

About 75 meters south of the bridge on the road heading to the harbor is a small road to the right leading to a promontory overlooking Kupang harbor. Some of Kupang's oldest buildings are here. The rather large graveyard has many old Dutch gravestones. Have a Timorese friend take you to one of Kupang's many churches. Masses at the Catholic churches start at 0830 and

(left and above) Megalithic tomb in a Sumbanese village

1030. On Sunday evenings, the streets are full of Bible-toting Timorese going to and from church. Visit the large daily market, lively Pasar Inpres, where you can see all the peoples of eastern Nusatenggara in microcosm: work-hardened rustics from the mountain districts, natives from Roti, Savu, and Flores wearing esplendent woven garments. The variety of *ikat* available on Timor is beyond belief. **Dharma Bakti** runs an *ikat* factory by the cement plant out toward the harbor, surrounded by elaborate murals, where you can watch the actual weaving. **Bank Dagang Negara** offers an outstanding rate for U.S. dollars (one of the best in Nusatenggara), not as good for Australian.

Soe and Vicinity

This big mountain town sprawls across rolling hills 110 km east of Kupang in the Protestant half of West Timor. The fossilized coral all over the landscape looks like lava. Because of its many nearby tourist attractions and cool weather, Soe is the richest area for travelers in West Timor. It's also the capital, as well as the main cultural center, for Timor Tengah Selatan District. At night you'll need a blanket, but all the town's accommodations provide them; in June and July it can drop to 15 degrees centigrade. The Beatrix Tree, 500 meters from Losmen Anda, was planted in 1980 to commemorate the reign of Queen Beatrix of Holland. Every day is market day in Soe, when tribal people come in from outlying villages to sell fresh fruit and vegetables, many wearing the brightly colored traditional garments for which the area is famous.

Horsemen participating in the Posala

Buses run east and west along the main highway to the larger West Timor cities, and north and south along secondary roads (often unpaved) to outlying towns.

Eleven km north of Soe, on the way to Kapan, is **Oehala Waterfall**. Take a *bemo* (Rp300) to the turnoff, then walk the three km down to the parking lot, which is the end of the road. The eight tiered waterfalls are about 100 meters down a ravine. There is no scheduled transportation to the falls, but sometimes *bemo* will make a sidetrip here on their way to Kapan, if there are enough passengers. If you take a *bemo* back to Soe, be sure to be back at the turnoff before dusk, as few *bemo* run after dark. A nice day trip is to take a bus to **Kapan**, 21 km and a Rp750 bus ride north of Soe in the foothills of the Mutis Mountains, a very beautiful and traditional area where orange, apple, and huge grapefruit-like citrus (*jeruk Bali*) are grown. Market day is Thursday, when you see farmers wearing their own textiles (very subdued colors). Northwest of here is a prominent and craggy outcrop called **Nuasusu**, a holy spot of the local king. Walk to Nuasusu along a dirt track, starting a couple of km north of town, past several villages. From Kapan, a road runs northeast to Eban and on to Kefamenanu.

KEFAMENANU

Kefamenanu, often referred to simply as Kefa, is a rest-stop town on the highway about halfway between Kupang and Dili. Kefamenanu is the region's administrative center; it has a post office and *wartel,* but no place to exchange foreign currency. The bus station is about three km from the town center—take a *bemo*. From Kefamenanu, buses to Kupang or Atambua leave around 0630, having circled the town for half an hour before departure. The excellent road to Atambua passes by endless stony pastures and cattle corrals made of sticks or stones. Also along this road are many thatched conical structures, set up on posts and open underneath, in front of the traditional houses.

From Kefamenanu, take a side trip along the north coast to the East Timorese enclave of **Ambeno** (formerly Oeccusi). This is an old port town, with remains of a Portuguese fort and other buildings. The principal town is now **Pante Makassar**; one *losmen*. Life is slow-paced here, with little or no tension from annexation by Indonesia, or the ensuing guerrilla movement that has gripped the rest of East Timor since 1975. On the way pass **Tano**, a traditional village with a great market.

Kalimantan

Introduction

Comprising roughly the southern three quarters of the equatorial island of Borneo, Kalimantan is divided into four provinces that make up about 28 percent of Indonesia's land area, though with only 4.5 percent of its population (seven million). Tourist facilities are relatively developed but visitors are few. Good roads run between Banjarmasin and Samarinda and around Pontianak, but rivers are the main transportation arteries. There are airports in major cities, and airstrips throughout the interior serviced by Pelita, DAS, and missionary aircraft. Half of the territory's land area is under 150 meters in elevation, especially near the coasts. Eighty percent of the territory is jungle; a naturalist recently traveled through the deep interior for 26 days without seeing open sunlight or any sign of cultivation. Upriver travel is often difficult because rivers are too low during the dry season (April-Sept.) and too high in the late wet season (Jan.-March). For these reasons, the best time to visit is in the wet season, either at the very beginning (October and November) or the very end (February to March).

Kalimantan has a wide variety of montane and lowland forests, each an important genetic resource and wildlife habitat. It's estimated that fewer than half the island's endemic species of rainforest plants and animals are known to science. These lowland forests are also rich in wild fruit and nut trees, a significant food source for people, primates, and other animals. With luck, you may see monkeys, gibbons, bearded wild pigs, deer, wild ox, civets, wildcats, flying lemurs, martins, weasels, badgers, otters, porcupines, mongeese, anteaters, squirrels, and bats. Freshwater dolphins thrive in the Mahakam River, playfully following river traffic. The elusive and endangered orangutan lives here and in northern Sumatra. Symbolically, the forest's most important creature is the black hornbill, the Dayak soul carrier.

Borneo was a cultural crossroads in ancient times, a trade center on the route between Java's Majapahit Kingdom, the Philippines, and China. In the 2nd century, the Greco-Roman geographer Ptolemy published an atlas containing an uncannily accurate description of Borneo; Indian traders traveling in merchant fleets no doubt passed on the information. Roman and Marco Polo-vintage Chinese beads have been found here, as well as Hindu-Javanese relics from around A.D. 400. On the Mahakam River, the oldest historic artifacts yet found in Indonesia have been uncovered: three rough plinths dating from the beginning of the 5th century recording in South Indian Palawa script "a gift to a Brahman priest."

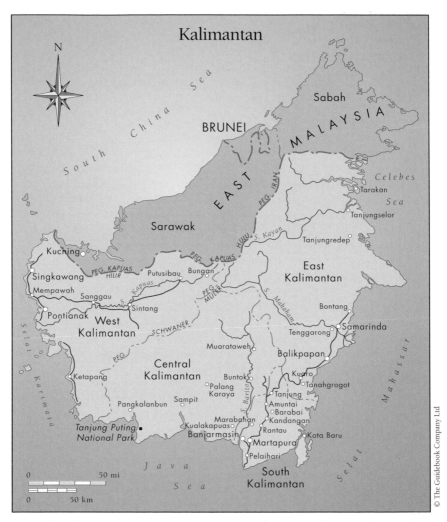

Kalimantan

N

South China Sea

BRUNEI

Sabah

MALAYSIA

Celebes Sea

EAST

Tarakan

Tanjungselor

Sarawak

Kuching

Tanjungredep

Singkawang

PEG. KAPUAS HILIR

Putusibau

Bungan

PEG. KAPUAS

East Kalimantan

Mempawah

Sanggau

Kapuas

PEG. MULER

Bontang

Pontianak

Sintang

West Kalimantan

SCHWANER

S. Mahakam

Samarinda

Tenggarong

Selat Karimata

PEG.

Central Kalimantan

Muarataweh

Balikpapan

Ketapang

Buntok

Palang Karaya

Kuaro

Tanahgrogot

Makassar

Pangkalanbun

Sampit

S. Barito

Tanjung

Amuntai

Barabai

Marabahan

Kandangan

Tanjung Puting National Park

Kualakapuas

Banjarmasin

Rantau

Kota Baru

Martapura

Pelaihari

Java Sea

South Kalimantan

Selat

0   50 mi

0   50 km

© The Guidebook Company Ltd

The first documented European arrival occurred in 1521, when one of Magellan's ships pulled into the harbor of Brunei. Because of the island's inhospitable interior and few natural harbors, the Europeans experienced difficulty in establishing control. Finally, in 1839, the British gained a foothold in the north, establishing the legendary dynasty of the White Rajas who ruled over Sarawak for more than 100 years. During the second half of the 19th century the Dutch concluded treaties with the east coast sultans and assumed autocratic administration of the southern three-quarters, bringing Borneo into the economic orbit of the Dutch East Indies empire. The Japanese occupied the island from 1942 to 1945; ruthless repression resulted in the deaths of as many as 20,000 intellectuals, missionaries, businessmen, and aristocrats. Though both Australia and Britain thought that taking the island was of dubious value, early in 1945 General Douglas MacArthur decided to liberate Borneo and establish an Allied airbase and Pacific port for the British navy. With Indonesian independence, the Javanese gave the territory its new name, Kaliman-tan, meaning "Rivers of Precious Stones"—an apt term to describe the many re-gions of the island known for rich deposits of gold, diamonds, amethysts, agates, sapphires, and emeralds.

THE PEOPLE

Most of Kalimantan's population lives near coastal areas, with Chinese and Malays predominating. Under Indonesia's massive *transmigrasi* program, tens of thousands of Javanese and Balinese families were brought in to settle the island's hinterlands. "Dayak" is a collective name for over 200 different tribes living throughout Borneo's interior. Each *sukuh* (tribe) has a unique tribal name and dialect. Contrary to myth, the Dayak race is light-skinned, resembling the Chinese, with rounded, well-featured faces and slightly slanted eyes. Most of the native Dayak peoples, almost half the terri-tory's population, still live deep inland along the banks of major rivers and tributaries. Recent exposure to modernization is changing traditional life. The Indonesian government is abolishing multi-ple-family longhouses and replacing them with modern, single-family dwellings—a drastic change in village life. Tattooing, mastery of tra-ditional crafts, and the custom of wearing huge bunches of metal earrings to elongate earlobes are all disappearing. Few Dayaks hunt with blowguns and poison darts or spears these days, preferring instead homemade Daniel Boone-style flintlocks. Increasingly, young Dayaks leave their villages to hire on with timber and oil companies or take menial jobs in Kalimantan boomtowns. Chil-dren of wealthy Dayaks study engineer-ing, forestry, and other subjects in In-donesian and European universities.

A Dayak woman dressed for the holidays

Uprising At Sarawak

A letter from Sir James Brooke, the Rajah of Borneo, addressed to a personal friend.

Sarawak was as peaceful as it had ever been, and there was no cause to excite dissatisfaction among the Chinese or raise suspicion in our minds of any hostile designs; yet a conspiracy had been formed which had its ramifications in Singapore and in China. A follower of Tien-te, the rebel chief, had arrived in Sarawak, and some criminals, who had been banished the country, secretly returned from Singapore. I had been unwell for some days, and on the night of the 18th retired early to bed. My servant was sleeping in a room near mine, and Mr. Steel and Nicholets occupied a bungalow close by. Between twelve and one o'clock I was awakend by yells and shots, and seizing my sword and revolver, I opened a window and saw that the house was surrounded. The noise told me it was by Chinese. I opened door by door in the hope of finding means for escape, but in vain. I told Penty that our deaths were at hand, and, as the last hope, went down to the bathing-room, which was under repair. The door was not fastened. I opened it gently, and, seeing a way clear, ran across the lawn to the creek on the right hand of the house, and took the water close under the bows of the boat which had brought the murderers to their bloody work. I carried my sword and pistol across with me. Glad was I to touch ground on the far side, though not above thirty yards. I struggled through the deep mud, and lay down exhausted and panting in the road. Recovering breath, I got to the nearest house, and, launching a canoe, pulled up to the Datoo Bandars kampong. All was in confusion. I was too exhausted to do much, and Hercules himself could not have restored courage or order to such a panic-stricken crowd. Finding all hope of restoring affairs at the Bandars gone, I pulled to the kampongs above, and persuaded the people to secure their women and valuables in prahus, and to cross to the opposite or left bank of the river, so as to prevent the assailants from attacking them by land. My house, Arthur's, and Middleton's were long before this in flames . . . Poor Harry Nicholets was murdered on the grass, trying to reach my house. Crookshank and his wife escaped by their bath-room door. She ran first, and he protected her retreat with a spear in his hand; but, in passing the stable, one of these villains rushed from the opposite side and cut her down. Her husband jobbed his spear into the miscreant's back; but with a twist of his body he wrenched it out, and, seizing the shaft, he struggled to get the spear. Suddenly, however, letting go with his right hand, in which he held a short sword, he cut Crookshank across the fleshy part of the arm. Both staggered; both let go the spear; and Crookshank, weak with loss of blood and believing his wife dead, staggered away and reached me. She, young and beautiful, lay for twelve hours weltering in her blood, conscious and calm in this extremity. One fiend hacked at her head till he cut off the long tresses which protected it; another tore her rings from her fingers; a third—for the sake of our common nature let it be told—gave her water to drink. By this time the remainder of the Europeans had been assured of protection; but when the Bishop asked the leader's permission to carry her to his house, he was told that she should be left to perish. At length the boon was granted, and she was relieved and tended, and is now, praise God, recovering.

Having received intelligence of the withdrawal of the Chinese, Brooke resolved to return to the Sarawak River; but before he could land the Chinese had a second time come down the river in force. Fortunately the steamer *Sir James Brooke*, from Singapore, hove in sight. The Rajah and his party proceeded her to Kuchin, and soon succeeded in driving the invaders out of the town.

The native chiefs having let loose the Dyaks on the Chinese, the latter suffered great slaughter. According to the Straits Times of March 23, at least 1000 Chinese have been killed at the various places; while all the flourishing settlements of the Chinese (except at Kuchin) have been destroyed.

~ Illustrated London News, *2nd May 1857*.

The Penan tribespeople are Borneo's original inhabitants, preceding even the Dayaks. With successive waves of migration over the centuries, the Penan gradually moved inland from the coast to continue their way of life; about 10,000 are left in isolated, scattered pockets in the upper Mahakam and the Apo Kayan.Wizards in jungle craft and masters of the terrain, the Penan live off fruit, wild berries, and game. They hunt with blowpipes, using packs of hunting dogs to track wild pigs. The Penan may live in a village for a few weeks or months, then abandon it to become nomadic hunter-gatherers once again. You might see them in villages bartering their boar-tusk necklaces, panther teeth and skins, bear claws, and orangutan skulls for salt and tobacco. They smoke like locomotives.

DAYAK ARTS AND CRAFTS

Each tribe specializes in its own handicrafts. Most craft products are utilitarian—for agriculture, daily village life, hunting, or fishing. The Dayaks fashion beautiful, high-quality bamboo receptacles of all shapes and sizes. Thin bamboo containers hold firemaking gear, jewelry, tobacco, sewing implements, and yarn; thicker ones store darts for blowguns. Bamboo containers often are completely covered with intricate designs. Men generally do the woodcarving and metallurgy; women do the tattooing, weaving, basketry, beadwork, embroidery, and sewing. Tangled, effusive S-patterns and curlicues are typical Dayak motifs, a mirror of their jungle environment.

The crafts of the Dayak people, Kalimantan

East Kalimantan

It was on the Mahakam River that Hindu culture first arrived in Indonesia, around A.D. 400. Traditional animist culture persists in isolated areas, but many tribes are thoroughly Christianized. Joseph Conrad visited Berau and Tanjungredeb four times, using "that Settlement hidden in the heart of the forest-land, up that sombre stream" as the setting for *Almayer's Folly* and *An Outcast of the Islands,* as well as the second part of *Lord Jim.* Most travelers visit East Kalimantan to explore the lower and middle stretches of the Mahakam River. Another area of interest is the more remote Apo Kayan region near the Sarawak border—a relatively untouched Dayak enclave easily reached with twice-weekly Pelita Air services from Samarinda. This is an area for determined explorers.

Through late 1982 and the first quarter of 1983, the forests of East Kalimantan suffered a grievous loss of 3.5 million hectares. Ranking as one of the worst human-caused ecological catastrophes in history, the "Great Fire" destroyed more than 20 percent of the province's rainforests and eradicated dozens of plant and animal species. Experts attributed the fire to a pattern of unrestrained commercial logging activities.

BALIKPAPAN

The discovery of coastal oil and gas here in the late 1960s quickly transformed traditional village life in the area, making Balikpapan the major economic transport center of East Kalimantan. Stay a couple days to see the combined effects of the oil boom and Indonesian cultural mixing: once-feared Dayaks serve cocktails to expatriates in air-conditioned bars and nightclubs on hills overlooking fishing *kampung.*

The city's central district at the waterfront sprawls up the hills to the northwest. All the main public buildings are on Jl. Jen. A. Yani. Americans, Australians, Europeans, and high-placed Indonesians live on hills overlooking the town. Walk up Pasir Ridge to the Union Oil Complex to see this "other world" of manicured lawns and trees, swimming pools, and modern suburban homes. Below are crowded *kampung* and Pertamina's oil refinery complex—a landscape of gas flares, pipes, tanks, and girders. There's not much else to see. You get the best view of Balikpapan from **Tanki I**, Gunung Dubbs. North of the refinery is a whole neighborhood of houses on stilts connected by wooden walkways over a muddy estuary.

SAMARINDA AND VICINITY

Sixty km upstream from the mouth of the Mahakam River, Samarinda is the capital of East Kalimantan, half the size of Balikpapan. You can see the giant silver-domed Mesjid Raya gleaming in the sun as you approach. A trading town established in

1730, Samarinda is cheaper and more easygoing than Balikpapan. Its location on the northern bank of the Mahakam, with low hills in the background as you come up-river, is lovely. At this point, the Mahakam is up to two km wide at high water and deep enough to accommodate seagoing ships. Logs tied into rafts float everywhere and modern sawmills line the river's banks. All manner of watercraft chug back and forth on the river. Taxi boats depart frequently for upstream destinations, making Samarinda the natural starting point for trips to Dayak villages.

Samarinda boasts one of the largest and most impressive **mosques** in Indonesia. A few Makassar schooners are moored at the south end of the pier. **Mulawarman University** has several campuses scattered around town. Samarinda's red-light district, **Air Biru,** commands an admission fee and is closed Thursday. Lumber mills line both sides of the river; climb the hills northeast of Samarinda to get a look at countryside ravaged by the timber concessions. **Sebarang,** just across the Mahakam, is known for its finely woven *sarung;* buy beautiful pieces for Rp35,000-85,000 and watch the weavers work. Bugis women use a simple loom called the *gedokan; sutera* (silk) thread is used for *sarung samarinda,* woven in many designs and colors and made to last 100 years.

Visit the East Kalimantan tourist office, off Jl. Kesuma Bangsa; not much printed information but an enthusiastic crew. Ask for Dr. Rosihan Anwar. Change money at **Bank Expor Impor Indonesia** or **Bank Negara Indonesia** Mon.-Thurs. 0800-1230, until 1130 on Friday and Saturday. Take plenty of *rupiah* if heading upriver.

TENGGARONG

Capital of the Kutai Regency and site of the former Kutai Kingdom, 39 km up the Mahakam from Samarinda. Though the new road has banished much of the town's charm, the people here are still friendly and there's no officialdom to contend with. Visit the **tourist office,** Jl. Diponegoro 2, for information and advice on traveling in the Mahakam River basin. The Kutai Kingdom has its roots in the old Hindu king-dom of Martapura (Mulawarman), founded upriver at Muara Kaman around A.D. 400. In the 14th century a Muslim kingdom, Kartanegara, was founded downstream nearer the coast at Pamarangan. The two kingdoms waged war until the Muslims won; in 1782 the sultanate moved to a safer spot upstream, the site of present-day Tenggarong. The **Mulawarman Museum Complex,** an imposing white palace, is the town's top attraction. All the gifts Dayak tribes pre-sented to the sultan in recognition of his sovereignty are on display here. China's long contact with the Kutai and Dayak people can be seen in the ceramic collection, which includes Ming china. **Pasar Pagi** is Tenggarong's main market. Dayak crafts are available here, but a better selection is at **Karya Indah Art Shop**: baskets, old stone necklaces, masks, *mandau,* and woodcarvings.

The Mahakam River

This giant muddy river is the highway to the interior. Oceangoing ships travel as far as Samarinda, 60 km upstream from its mouth, to load huge logs floated down to the port. The lower half of the river valley is populated by Muslim Malay groups, including the native Kutai. Dayak tribes which originally moved upriver to avoid Islam have, since WW II, begun to move back into downstream river towns to avail themselves of education, jobs, and opportunity.

Don't expect to see longhouses lining the banks as you chug up the Mahakam; Western-style dwellings are steadily replacing them. Neither will your journey take you through impenetrable tropical forests—much of the jungle is secondary growth or has been clearcut by Weyerhauser. To see Dayak life, head up the river's tributaries, walk inland, or travel far upriver to the Apo Kayan/Krayan regions. You'll see the unusual freshwater dolphin; crocodiles live in swamps and small tributaries of the lower Mahakam but not in the river itself.

The Mahakam up to Long Bagun is navigable year-round. It's best to travel up the smaller tributaries during the rainy season; if they're too shallow, paddle canoes are the only option. Water levels in the upper reaches of the Mahakam can change dramatically in a short time, so don't camp by riverbanks. Plenty of water is available, but you should bring along packaged vittles, as food in the Mahakam region is expensive and unimpressive. Also bring insect repellent, malaria pills, extra batteries,

suntan lotion, toilet paper, flashlight, long pants and shirts, extra film, and water-proof plastic bags to keep everything dry. Supplies are readily available in the lower Mahakam, but prices skyrocket on the middle and upper stretches of the river. Use-ful gifts for your hosts include sugar, *kreteks,* pens, salt, batteries, and liquor.

Samarinda is the usual starting point for trips up the Mahakam. Ordinary river-boats run year-round up to Long Iram, but are limited by a tough series of rapids just beyond Long Bagun. Most travelers who intend to explore the upper Mahakam or trek to West Kalimantan usually take Pelita Air's twice weekly flight to Long Lunuk. Upriver from Long Bagun is a major fork where the Boh River comes in from the east. Longboats and *ketinting* travel up the Boh to the Benahan River. A two-day walk gets you to Mahak Baru in the Apo Kayan. The best maps of the lower Ma-hakam are those from TAD, the big German development program headquartered in Kota Bagun. Tering is the first completely ethnic Dayak village you come to. A church here has an American pastor and a *losmen.* Look for orangutans about 10 km away in the Binulung Daerah area, Kecamatan Muara Kaman; ask the *kepala desa* where they are.

Losmen, homestays, and longhouses are located in almost every village and town along the Mahakam. Standard charge is about Rp5000 per night; this often includes simple meals of rice, vegetables, and river fish. Bring extra food or endure an ex-tremely monotonous diet.

TANJUNG ISUI

Muara Muntai is a good jumping-off point for Tanjung Isui, a beautiful Benuaq Dayak village on the south shore of the giant Danau Jempang, 184 km upstream from Tenggarong. Tanjung Isui is a popular place to view longhouses and traditional Dayak life. See *air tawar* (freshwater dolphins), birds feeding on fish, soft sunsets. There are two longhouses; the one in the center isn't very remarkable. The old long-house is nicer—some handicrafts inside, and lots of *patong* around the courtyard. One *losmen,* but for the same price you can sleep in the old longhouse.

Tanjung Isui is the most popular Dayak village on the tourist trail. You might be able to watch a scheduled dance performance here—touristy, but great for photogra-phers, since authentic rituals and dance are almost impossible to find in these regions.

From Tanjung Isui, reach Mancong and an unimpressive longhouse via a three-hour walk or canoe ride, or a half-hour ride in a car or motorcycle (Rp25,000 return). Four km from Mancong by chartered boat are three villages with better longhouses.

MELAK

This picturesque Muslim riverside town is noted for its nearby orchid forest, **Kersik Luway,** where famous black orchids bloom at the end of the rainy season. Melak has six *losmen;* **Rachmat Abadi,** close to the dock, is the best place to stay. The owner,

Deep in the forests of Kalimantan

Bapak Effendi, can help with trekking details and transport needs. His prices for the latter are high, however, and you're better off with ordinary boats.

The area around Melak is still strongly animist. Stay in villages by asking the *kepala kampung,* and be sure to pay for food and accommodation. There are many easy trails to nearby villages, all commonly used by bicycles and motorbikes. A good gravel road goes to Barong Tongkok (18 km); another road south travels to the orchid reserve at Kersik Luway on the Tanjung Plateau (16 km). The road northwest to Tering Sebarang (cross the Mahakam there) is 43 km; to Long Iram, 51 km. If you get tired of walking, get a lift on a motorbike (Rp4000 from Melak-Barong Tongkok) or truck.

Barong Tongkok

An administrative center in an area of villages, rolling hills, small streams, waterfalls, and gardens—a lovely *kampung* to dwell in for a while. **Wisma Tamu Anggrek,** a small house with a mattress on the floor, is maintained for visitors. **Barong Tongkok Losmen** is acceptable. Ask the local *camat* (headman) about upcoming Kaharigan rituals and nearby handicraft villages. You may stay in the villages; ask the *kepala kampung.* Camping is also a possibility, but ask first. There's usually a swimming hole or *mandi* spot near each village.

There are many hiking possibilities in Kecamatan Barong Tongkok. The terrain is flat or gently rolling; trails pass through groves of bamboo or small trees, gardens and rice fields, areas of overgrown clearings and scattered houses. *Babi hutan* (wild pig) and deer are abundant in the woods west of Barong Tongkok. Walk from Barong Tongkok to Tering on a very pleasant trail in six hours. Blacksmith sites are often found in villages, working a fire pit surrounded by hand-powered bamboo-tube blowers, a trough of water, and simple hand tools.

Long Iram

From Tering, it's an easy 1.5-hour, seven km walk past a lake and over a level terrain of gardens and jungles to Long Iram. It's easy to get here by taxi boat, as well. Long Iram is a friendly town on the equator, the border between upriver and down. You won't see many Dayak here. This is the last place you can count on for finding ice for your beer, *nasi goreng,* large *toko,* or a *kantor pos.* People arriving from downriver won't be impressed, but this is the Big City if you're coming from upriver. The village is about half Muslim, with four mosques. The native Bahau Dayak people are mostly Catholic. Five km east is the village of **Tukul;** there are many lakes around here. Boats of all varieties leave Long Iram often; keep in mind that boats run on *jam karet.* From Long Iram taxi boats head downstream for Samarinda several times weekly (Rp6000-8000). If you're traveling upriver from Long Iram, Data Bilang is six hours, Rp3000, leaving several times weekly.

South Kalimantan

Straddling the equator, this southern province of predominantly flat swampland covers 37,600 square kilometers. Mangrove forests and orchids are abundant and proboscis monkeys live on the Barito River. Modern roads link some cities and villages, but rivers are still the primary transportation network. The Trans-Kalimantan Highway extends from Batakan to Sangkulirang in East Kalimantan. When completed, it will stretch all the way to Tarakan. Banjarmasin, the capital, is famous for its floating houses and markets. The Javanese Majapahit Kingdom took control of this region during the second half of the 14th century; today you can still see Java's influence in men's clothing styles, in some aspects of the region's *wayang kulit* forms, and in Banjarese dance-dramas. Once strictly the domain of the Orang Banjar, South Kalimantan's mangrove-sheltered coastline was unsafe due to piracy until the 1950s.

BANJARMASIN

More than 450 years old, the city is renowned for its floating houses and network of crisscrossing rivers, streams, and canals. Banjarmasin is below sea level, and the water level rises and falls with the tides. Situated on the banks of the Martapura River, 22 km upriver from the sea, Banjarmasin is a convenient base for both Central and East Kalimantan.

The largest city in Kalimantan, Banjarmasin was once populated by pirates; today it's populated by Islamic conservatives, home to over 350,000 people. The Banjarese practice a decidedly more orthodox form of Islam than other Muslim groups on Indonesia's western islands. Thousands make the pilgrimage to Mecca each year; during Ramadan, piercing sirens announce the beginning and end of each day's fast. Modernity is fast approaching, and with it traffic jams, a thriving precious stones market, craft shops, and fine ethnic restaurants.

The city should be seen from the Barito River, which flows red, the color of the spongy peat bogs upriver; take a boat four km to Tamban, where thousands of houses are built on log floats, connected by an intricate system of canals. The well-known Kuin Floating Market lies at the mouth of the Kuin River; hire a canoe at the Kuin Cerucuk Bridge or in central Banjarmasin under the Jl. Yani Bridge for Rp4000-6000 per hour. The market, a gaggle of boats, is visited by shoppers and traders paddling *jukung*, simple dugout canoes. Market day begins soon after sunrise and lasts only until 0900 or so; river traders traverse the waters of Banjarmasin, selling fish, vegetables, fruits, and household necessities door-to-door.

Near the center of the city on Jl. Lambung Mangkurat, across from the Islamic University, is the massive Mesjid Raya Sabilal Muhtadin ("The Road Unto God's Blessings"), built on the site of the old Dutch fort. The main minaret is 45 meters high; the four smaller ones stand up to 21 meters. This modern-art mosque has a copper-colored dome shaped like an alien space vehicle. Visitors with extra time might also visit the Jamin Mosque and the Banjarmasin Museum, situated in a traditional *banjar* house near the Andai River. Visit the South Kalimantan Tourist Office, Dinas Pariwisata Kalimantan Selatan, Jl. Panjaitan 31, tel. (0511) 2982.

VICINITY OF BANJARMASIN

Pulau Kaget is just 12 km south of Banjarmasin by chartered riverboat (Rp40,000 roundtrip). The south end of this tiny Barito River island preserve is an ideal environment for the leaf-eating proboscis monkey, found only on Borneo. These oddly attractive red and silver-gray primates have unusually long, vulnerable noses. You sometimes have to wait two days to see them, and then only with binoculars from your chartered *klotok* 100 meters away.

About one-half hour southeast of Banjarmasin by minibus (Rp1000) from Terminal km 6 on the road from Banjarmasin to Martapura, **Banjarbaru** features numerous modern Indonesian buildings. Banjarbaru is usually cooler and less humid than Ban-

Dayak seer consulting a pig liver

jarmasin. Here you'll see lots of rattan processing, with raw fiber strips expertly peeled, split, twisted, and woven into fine carpets and mats.

Museum Lambung Mangkurat is housed in a building that follows the unique Banjarese architectural style. The present-day collection is paltry, dating only from 1967. The Japanese looted the museum during WW II, and the Dutch got most of what was left. The rest went to the National Museum in Jakarta. The museum covers much of South Kalimantan's history and culture, even Hindu antiquities dating back to the 14th century. The museum's library of coconut shells (Banjar was without paper for centuries) is fascinating; the hollowed-out interiors contain Malay inscriptions. Adjacent is a gallery featuring portraits and landscapes by the Banjar painter Gusti Sholihin, who died on Bali in 1970; his artwork is reminiscent of the French Fauvist tradition.

Cempaka

Extensive diamond-mining takes place along the shores of Riam Kanan, a reservoir near Cempaka, 10 km from Banjarbaru or 43 km from Banjarmasin. Get a public *bemo* to Cempaka from Martapura's bus station or charter one for Rp5000; there are also minibuses from Banjarmasin's Terminal Km 6. Using traditional tools, miners try their luck in the diamond pits. Men dig holes up to 10 meters deep in the sour-smelling clay under a roof of loose thatch. They dig out gravel, sand, and heavy clay soil, handing it up from the pit in small baskets. Young girls carry the heavy load to sluicing areas along canals or the lakeshore, where women wash the raw sludge through sluice boxes, looking for the elusive *galuh* ("the lady")—raw diamonds.

Martapura

Behind the Martapura bus terminal is an enormous market on Tuesday and Friday, crowded with colorfully adorned Banjar women and children, with good prices on almost everything. High-quality diamonds are also sold in Martapura. South Kalimantan province is one of the major diamond-producing areas of Indonesia. Take the minibus from Terminal Km 6 outside Banjarmasin to Martapura (Rp1000, 45 minutes), or travel the short distance north from Banjarbaru or Cempaka.

Near Martapura's bus station and just across the playing field is a diamond-polishing factory—a good place to buy gems. This is a traditional workshop where over 150 people, using 200-year-old methods, work in each shed. Giant wheels, belts, and sluices are used to polish the cut stones—a process requiring two to three days for small gems, 30 days for large ones. Don't buy diamonds unless you know about diamonds. Note that the mines are closed on Friday, and for the 10 days before Idul Fitri. Buy loose stones and have them mounted here, or bargain for gold or silver rings with birthstones or other gems. Near Pasar Martapura are souvenir and gem shops. Martapura also has an impressive mosque.

Central Kalimantan

The province of Central Kalimantan is large (156,610 square km), with vast areas of swampland and lowland terrain in the south. The Muller Mountains border the province in the far north, with the Schwaner Mountains to the west and northwest. Many rivers flow here, draining the highlands. Central Kalimantan receives few visitors, primarily a handful of organized tours that visit the orangutan rehabilitation center at Tanjung Puting. For the visitor willing to travel in local rivercraft and make a few short flights, the rewards are plentiful: undisturbed rainforest, abundant wildlife, and some of the most traditional Dayak villages in all of Kalimantan. Navigable up to 750 km upriver, the **Barito River** is the most expedient and economical way to enter the province. From Banjarmasin you can take the Barito River all the way to Muara Teweh and beyond. Towns here are Islamic, with the ornate domes and spires of mosques nestled away in the trees. Villagers live by fishing, rice growing, and hand-sawing logs into planks. Traditionally, the people of Kalimantan decorate their homes with flowers. Along the Barito River grows the *pasak bumi*, the roots used in Strong Pa medicinal capsules for increasing men's sexual potency. Continuing north, you enter Dayak country and start to notice Christian churches.

PALANGKARAYA

A provincial capital not frequently visited by tourists, Palangkaraya was once intended as the capital of the entire territory. In the 1950s, when President Sukarno visited this town on the Kahayan River (then called Pahandut), he learned it was the mythical birthplace of the Dayak people, where the first human being descended to earth from the upper world. With his usual political astuteness, he ordered that the governor's residence feature eight doors and 17 windows, symbolizing 17 August—the day Indonesia's Proclamation of Independence was signed in 1945. Concrete administrative buildings and asphalt roads suddenly appeared, and a military statue was erected in the center of a great traffic rotary—all totally incongruous and inappropriate in such a remote, undeveloped area. Since Palangkaraya is strategically located on the Kahayan River, the best reason to visit is to make a river journey up to Tewah and Tumbang Mirih.

A surprising find in this small, backwater town is the striking local **Museum Balanga,** complete with classical white fluted pillars. Inside are Chinese ceramics, Kahayan Dayak *kayu besi* guardian figurines, ferocious weaponry, farming and forestry implements, and all types of original Dayak handicrafts. Behind the museum is a small zoo. Take a walk in the gardens; the museum is on five hectares of grounds and another five hectares are reserved as a Taman Budaya ("Cultural Garden"). Be sure to bring all the *rupiah* you'll need before arriving in Central Kalimantan. Except at **Bank Dagang Negara,** Jl. A. Yani 11 in Palangkaraya, you can't change traveler's checks anywhere in the province.

TANJUNG PUTING RESERVE

Established in 1936, this is one of the largest lowland reserves in Kalimantan, with 305,000 hectares. Tanjung Puting consists mostly of a freshwater swamp forest featuring extensive peat bogs, with nipa palm swamps nearer the coast. Dry forest lands are to the north; some *ladang* lie to the east. The reserve covers most of Kotawaringan Sampit, the cape of Tanjung Puting on the south coast of Central Kalimantan between the Seruyan and Kumai rivers. Swamp trekking involves clambering over tree roots and wading—sometimes up to your chest—in the reddish waters. You can also tour the reserve by boat along the Sekonyer River. You must have permission (requires two passport photos) from the PHPA in Kumai to visit the reserve. *A Guidebook to Tanjung Puting National Park*, authored by Dr. Birute M.F. Galdikas, is the best guide available. Get a copy at the park for Rp20,000, or order it from Orangutan Foundation International, 822 Wellesley Ave., Los Angeles, CA 90049, U.S.A., tel. (310) 207-1655.

Camp Leakey specializes in orangutan rehabilitation and research. Since 1971 more than 100 orangutans have been rehabilitated and returned to the wild by the teachers, students, and volunteers of this center. People are friendly and hospitable, but remember this is a working research center—don't overstay your welcome. **Pondok Tanggui** is another rehabilitation center for semi-wild infant orangutans, located 1.5 km upriver from the Rimba Hotel. The orangutans are fed as little as possible to encourage them to go wild again.

The remarkable proboscis monkey is only found on Borneo. Of an estimated total world population of 3,000, some 2,000 live in this park. There are presently 11 groups of proboscis at **Natal Lengkuas Proboscis Research Station.** The guides are first class, the station has good trails and signs, and it's generally more remote and quieter here than at Camp Leakey. Don't be disappointed if you don't see any monkeys; you're almost certain to spot them in great numbers along the river at yhe end of the day. Climb the tower for a great view.

The only official place to stay—and the most convenient—is the **Rimba Hotel**, on the opposite side of the river from the reserve. This wonderful Dayak-style jungle lodge consists of 35 double rooms (Rp52,000 s, Rp117,000 d) raised on wooden stilts above the swamp. Walkways connect the rooms, the beds are comfortable, and the electricity runs 24 hours a day. All rooms come equipped with mosquito nets, shower, fans, and mosquito coils. Backpackers can stay with families at **Tanjung Harapan** for Rp2000 pp, then rent the village boat to Camp Leakey for Rp30,000. This village is only a 20-minute walk from the Rimba Hotel. There's a sister hotel to the Rimba in Pangkalanbun called the **Blue Kecabung.**

Plan on four days to a week for your trip. Pangkalanbun on the Arut River is the area's principal town; get there by flying from Banjarmasin on DAS or Bouraq (Rp75,000). Merpati also offers flights from Jakarta, and there's a daily morning flight from Semarang. It's 12 km by road (taxi Rp10,000) from the Pangkalanbun airport to the forestry headquarters and dock. Hire a *klotok* near the PHPA for the 2.5-hour trip to Pondok Tanggui on the Sekunyer River. From there it's an eight-minute boat ride to the Rimba Hotel. You can also get a public boat to the Rimba for only Rp1000, leaving at 1800 and returning at 1100.

West Kalimantan

West Kalimantan is an immense, rugged, sparsely populated province where travel is slow and expensive. The 1,100-km-long "mother river" of the province, the Kapuas, connects areas near Pontianak with Sanggau, Sintang, Putussibau, and points near the Malaysian border. Life and work here are typical of riverine peoples: catching fish and selling them at market, transporting jungle products from the interior, delivering goods from the city to upriver villages. Pontianak is the point of arrival and departure for the province: hop a ferry across the massive Kapuas to Terminal Siantan on the other side, then take a series of minibuses north to Kartiasa (west of Sambas), south to Supadio, or east to Sintang. The Kapuas River dominates West Kalimantan. Indonesia's longest river, it's also wide and deep—seagoing ships can sail upriver as far as Putussibau.

Vegetation zones include a variety of swamp and lowland forests, jungle areas still pristine with abundant orchids and liana, and montane vegetation at higher elevations. You'll find here numerous snakes, including pythons, as well as such primates as leaf monkeys, the white-handed gibbon, the red-furred *kelasi*, and the *simpai*. Other wild mammals include sun bears, sambar and mouse deer, *muncak*, bearded pigs, porcupines, and fruit bats. Bird species include chattering parrots, rare long-tailed parakeets, pheasant, rhinoceros and helmeted hornbills, and *pitta*. West Kalimantan's population is about 2.2 million; the most densely populated areas are near Singkawang and Pontianak.

PONTIANAK

This overgrown village's name literally means "Vampire Ghosts of Women Dead in Childbirth," and refers to a baleful Indonesian spirit that lures young men into

On the waterways of Pontianak

cemeteries. A bustling, sprawling town on the equator, Pontianak is also known as Kota Khatulistiwa ("Equator City") or the Floating Town. Founded in 1771 by Syarif Abdur, Pontianak is West Kalimantan's center of government, trade, banking, and culture. Just 25 km north of the Kapuas River, Pontianak is a good starting place for trips to interior Dayak villages.

The city has two large girder bridges spanning the river, a massive sports stadium, and numerous canals. Automobile, motorcycle, bicycle, *becak, bemo,* and pedestrian traffic fills the streets day and night.

To get a feel for this bustling city, walk along Jl. Tanjungpura, visit the half dozen **Pinisi schooners** near the fruit market, then continue south along the rickety boardwalk which hugs the banks of the Kapuas. The riverside walk is much more colorful than the drab, congested boulevards. Walk over the **Pontianak Bridge** and continue west along another wooden boardwalk to the old **Sultan's Palace** and adjacent **Sultan's Mosque**. Finally, walk through the **floating village** of Kampung Dalam Bugis—the single most memorable sight in all of Pontianak.

The *kraton* of Sultan Muhammad Hamid, the only remnant of an ancient West Kalimantan kingdom, lies between the two bridges in East Pontianak. The massive 250-year-old **Sultan Jami Mosque**, in all its white-walled splendor, is in Kampung Dalam Bugis, as is **Istana Kadariyah**, the sultan's palace. Take a small boat from the west bank (Rp200).

In the main part of the city, the **Nusa Indah Plaza** is the new shopping area; take a stroll there in the evening. The **Pontianak Theater** nearby is a hive of activity in the evenings. Also south of the river is **Mesjid Mujahidin** on Jl. Jen. A. Yani. **Pontianak harbor**, the center for both foreign and domestic trade, exports such products as rubber and timber. In the evening after it rains, thousands of sparrows swarm along the waterfront. A Chinese temple, **Yayasan Klenteng DW Darma Bakti**, is on Jl. Tanjungpura.

The regional museum, **Museum Negeri Propinsi**, is housed in a splendid building designed by a leading sculptor of Sanggau, Abdulazis Yusnian. Murals depicting scenes from the lives of the Dayak and Malay populations decorate the exterior. Inside is a collection from West Kalimantan's interior and coastal cultures: traditional implements, longhouse replicas, tattooing tools, wood statuary, *ikat* looms, fishtraps, and old ceramics. Open Tues.-Thurs. 0900-1300, Friday to 1100, Saturday 0900-1300. Free admission.

SINGKAWANG

A clean, pleasant, well-built town 145 km northwest of Pontianak, accessible by minibus (Rp2510, three hours) on a picturesque drive from Batu Layang bus terminal. On the way up, stop at Pulau Kijang, a coastal rest stop just before Sungai Duri. Singkawang's climate is cool, much like Bandung. This friendly, very Chinese place has a beautiful lake and pavilion in the center of town; Chinese temples. Unique traditional pottery is made at Saliung, seven km south of Singkawang.

Though less pricey than Pontianak, Singkawang's hotels still aren't cheap. Small *penginapan* offer rooms for Rp5000-8000. Opposite the bus station in the south end of town is Hotel Sahuri. Better values lie in the center of town, two km north of the bus terminal. The town's major attractions are its nearby beaches. Batu Payung is a lovely half-deserted beach where bungalows rent for Rp6000; very popular with the locals. A *losmen* and outdoor restaurants are also available. Hire a sampan from the fishermen. Also visit Gunung Puting, a curiously shaped limestone karst which once served as a Dutch hill resort.

THE INTERIOR

The Kapuas, Indonesia's longest river, is the main highway deep into the interior; along the way you'll see rubber plantations, logging operations, and mostly Javanese settlements until you reach Putussibau. Isolated tribes of Dayak Iban, Sungkung, Bukat, and Kantuk live near the border between West Kalimantan and Malaysia. Trips into the interior by plane or boat usually start in Pontianak. You can travel by boat or plane all the way to the Dayak fishing village of **Putussibau** in Kapuas Hulu ("Upper Kapuas"), nearly 900 km upriver. From here, some travelers boat and hike east across the whole island—extremely expensive, but possible. Beyond Putussibau, the Kapuas is navigable for almost another 300 km. The rest of the adventure involves overland treks, leeches, visits to isolated traditional Dayak villages, and weeks of canoeing and rafting down uncharted rivers.

The journey first reaches the headwaters of the Kapuas, then crosses the mountains to where the Mahakam begins its descent south through East Kalimantan. On the Mahakam, you can reach the coast near Samarinda; or continue on to Tarakan via the Boh and Kayan rivers. A popular option is to fly to Sintang, boat upriver to Putussibau, and fly back to Pontianak—the Borneo experience with minimal hassles.

N

Sulawesi

Celebes

Sea

KEP. SANGIHE

Kalimantan

Santigi

North Sulawesi

Manado Likupang
Bitung
Tondano

Makassar

Toli Toli
Lanu
Biau Kuandang Pimpi Lombagin
Siboa Tomini
Tilamuta
Dumoga Kotamobagu
Marisa Gorontalo Taludaa

Central
Sulawesi

Tinombo

Teluk KEP. TOGIAN

Mapaga Toribulu

Tomini
Malik

Donggala
Parigi Ampana Boalang Luwuk Teku

Selat

Palu Batui Peleng

Pasangkayu

*Lore
Lindu
Reserve* Tojo
Poso *Morowali
Reserve* Kembani Palam

Palam

KEP. SULA

Karosa Gimpu Tentena Bangkulu Taliabu

D. Paso Kolondale KEP. BANGGAI

South
Sulawesi Pendolo *Teluk* Maluku

Mesamba *D. Matana* Sokita *Tolo*

Mamuju Bonebone Malili
Talapang Rantepao Palopo Labota
Mamasa Makale *Teluk* Tolalo *D. Towuti*

Cenrana Polewali Mondeodo Southeast
Sulawesi
Majene Pinrang Enrekang
Siwa *Bone* Wowoni
Pangkajene Kolaka Kendari Monse
Pare Pare Sengkang Baula
Soppeng Benua *Selat Wowoni*
Supangbinangae *Tempe* Watangsoppeng
Baru Watampone Samak Raha Buton
Pangkajene Pising Bone
UJUNG Maros Balangnipa Kabena Muna
PANDANG Malino Sinjai Mawasangka Pasarwajo KEP.
Takalar Tanette TUKANGBESI
Bantaeng Bulukumba
Jeneponto Bira

Benteng Selayar Batuata

Banda Sea

Tanahjampa

Flores Sea Kalaotoa

0   100 mi

0   100 km

© The Guidebook Company Ltd

Sulawesi

Introduction

Four long, narrow peninsulas separated by three great gulfs are joined in the mountainous heart of Sulawesi. The main landmass is 1,300 km long, though in places only 56-200 km wide. Except for some narrow plains, almost all of Sulawesi consists of mountains covered mostly in rainforests and high, uninhabited wasteland. Few areas are more than 40 km from the sea. Lakes are widespread in the interiors. The four distinct peninsulas led to a mammalian evolution in isolation—nearly 40 percent of the birds and a remarkable 90 percent of Sulawesi's 59 species of mammals are endemic. The island's flora consists of sago palms, wine palms, and a palm with a stem that grows corkscrew fashion, shooting out green spouts at each half circle. Ferns here grow in geometric shapes. The best places for observing natural phenomena are in the island's reserves: Morowali, Tanjung Api, and Lore Lindu in Central Sulawesi; Bone-Dumoga, Gunung Dua Saudara, and Panua in North Sulawesi.

On the west coast at Maros, 35 km northeast of Ujung Pandang, a Neolithic settlement and prehistoric remains have been discovered. South Sulawesi ports were an important stop on international spice-trading routes for more than 1,000 years; Buddhist images found at Sampaga on the southwest coast belong to the Indian Amarawati school of art that flourished in the second century. Mysterious megaliths, sarcophagi, and other prehistoric artifacts can be seen in the remote Besoa and Bada valleys of Central Sulawesi, and in North Sulawesi carved stone sarcophagi are scattered over a wide area of Minahasa—remnants of a vanished culture. The peoples of Sulawesi were among the very last to be converted to Islam; the Makassarese came under the sway of emerging Muslim kingdoms on Java's north coast only in 1605. The Portuguese arrived soon after their conquest of Melaka in 1511.

The Dutch gained complete control over the docile Minahasans in the north in the 17th century, but it was a long, bloody struggle to control the independent Muslim tribes of the south. The Japanese occupied the island for 3.5 years starting in 1942; their overriding concern was the maintenance of law and order, the establishment of land defenses, and the efficient extraction of resources needed for the war effort. In March 1957 the commander of the East Indonesia military region based in Ujung Pandang issued the Permesta Charter, demanding greater regional autonomy from the central government and a larger share of national revenues for local development. With the declaration of an autonomous state in North Sulawesi in June of that year, the dissension soon developed into a full-fledged separatist movement.

(clockwise from top left) A necklace of human bone; chewing betelnut; Bugis jewelry; Torajan household

The bombing of Manado and the landing of central government troops on Minahasa in 1958 neutralized the Permesta revolt, though it was not completely suppressed until 1961.

Most of the population is concentrated in the island's southern and northern peninsulas, where relatively flat plains allow for large settlements. The people of the interior are still isolated, retaining their ethnic customs and traditions. The Islamic Makassarese and Buginese, inhabiting the southwestern peninsula, are well known as traders and seafarers. The Torajans, once feared as headhunters, live in the highlands of south-central Sulawesi.

Ujung Pandang

With a population of over 900,000, Ujung Pandang is the sixth-largest city in Indonesia. Formerly known as Makassar, this bustling commercial, shipping, and government center constitutes a major air-sea crossroads between western and eastern Indonesia—the largest and busiest mercantile and communications center in all of eastern Indonesia for over 500 years. It's also the capital of South Sulawesi, with scores of government buildings crowding downtown.

The area surrounding the city was once known as Jumpandang, or Pandan Point, named for its abundant *pandan* (screw pine) trees. A fort was built here by an early sultan of Gowa, to protect the strategic harbor from pirates; today it lies more or less in the center of town. The old fort was subsequently reconstructed by the Portuguese and then the Dutch; the latter renamed it **Fort Rotterdam.** Downtown, a few blocks south of Fort Rotterdam at Jl. Mokthar Lufthi 15A, tel. (0411) 22572, visit **Clara L. Bundt's Orchid Garden and Shells,** a collection of over 200 varieties of seashells (including giant clams), along with her father's 50-year-old orchid nursery. Peak orchid-blooming times are March and September. This is the largest orchid garden in Indonesia open to the public and is definitely worth a visit

Ibu Agung Bahari, Jl. Sulawesi 41, is the most ornate of several Chinese temples found on or near Jl. Sulawesi. This 350-year-old Buddhist temple contains paintings and stone- and woodcarvings—a riot of color. Farther south, on the corner of Jl. Sulawesi and Jl. Bali, is **Long Xian Gong Temple,** built in 1868. The early-18th-century **Tian Hou Gong Temple,** dedicated to a patroness of sailors, is on the corner of Jl. Sulawesi and Jl. Serui.

You'll find the highest concentration of surviving **18th-century architecture** in the oldest part of the city—a European, Chinese, and Christian enclave known as Vlaardingen in Dutch times. The old Dutch **governor's mansion,** now the Indonesian governor's residence, is on Jl. Jen. Sudirman. **Taman Mini Sulsel** on Jl. Dangko is like a miniature version of Taman Mini in Jakarta; the emphasis is on South

Sulawesi architecture, crafts, and culture. Close to the beach with *prahu*; entrance fee Rp1000. Swamps were reclaimed in the city's northeast to provide land for **Hasanuddin University**, established in 1956 and now the largest university in eastern Indonesia.

In a small cemetery on Jl. Diponegoro is **Diponegoro Monument**, a Javanese-style grave and genealogy chart. Indonesians still pay homage at this tomb. Diponegoro, considered Indonesia's first nationalist leader, shrewdly and tenaciously fought the Dutch on Java from 1830 to 1835, until tricked into negotiations and arrested. He

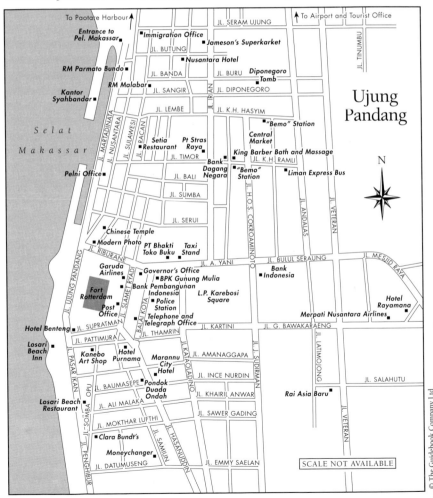

was exiled to Ujung Pandang, where he died in 1855. Lively **Paotare Harbor,** in the northwest end of town, is the city's most amazing sight: rows of handsome, still-active Bugis wooden schooners (*pinisi*) from Banjarmasin, Surabaya, and Kendari. The designs haven't changed since the time of Genghis Khan. Get to Paotare, three km from downtown, by taking bus no. 3 (Rp200) northbound, then walk 200 meters from the last bus stop.

The people at the **tourist office** for South Sulawesi are friendly, offering maps, pamphlets, and excellent information. They also double as a sort of travel agency, arranging for guides, tickets, and car rentals. Open Mon.-Thurs. and Saturday 0700-1400, Friday 0700-1100. Unfortunately, it's inconveniently located four km southeast of the city center on Jl. A. Pangerang Pettarani, tel. (0411) 21142, heading east off the airport road. Take a *bemo* (Rp300) from the central *bemo* station, or a *bis kota* (Rp200) from the Central Market. After office hours, you can find good detailed information at **Mandar Inn Tourist Information,** Jl. Anuang 11, or **Mattappa Tourist Information,** Jl. Pattimura 34.

Shopping

Ujung Pandang is a busy metalcrafts center where exquisite Kendari-style filigree-like silver jewelry is made and sold. The pieces are about 80 percent pure white silver. The Gowanese are known for their brilliant brasswork; brass bells and candleholders from Kuningan look almost Tibetan. The Bugis also produce some of the most attractive pottery in Indonesia. Other regional crafts include unusual baskets and boxes made of orchid fibers from Bone on the east coast of South Sulawesi. Beautiful carved bamboo and wooden artifacts made by the Torajans are easy to find. Street hawkers and shops also sell mounted butterflies—including protected species—from the Bantimurung Waterfall area.

Vicinity of Ujung Pandang

THE MAROS CAVES

The site of some of the oldest art in Indonesia, dating from the Mesolithic period. Handprints and paintings of *babirusa* and deer, believed to be 5,000-10,000 years old, have been found in 55 caves in southern Sulawesi. Small fee to enter. Located in steep limestone cliffs 38 km northeast of Ujung Pandang on the road to Bone, the well-signposted series of caves has been turned into a beautiful archaeological park with shrubbery, forests, clear cool mountain streams, and delightful walkways. Two neolithic cave paintings of pig-deer are reminiscent of those at Lascaux in France. From Ujung Pandang's central station, take a *bemo* 30 km to Maros (Rp500, one hour), then another *bemo* eight km to the entrance of the park.

A Wild Night

A noble tuak *was brought in and served by a slave who had to stand two yards behind me to fill my glass, so long was the pipe. The process had alarmed me in early days, when suddenly a great pipe would be thrust over my shoulder noisily glugging and plopping like an early oil bomb falling until at last a delicate stream of wine, filtered by aromatic leaves stuffed into the mouth of the bamboo, fell into my cup. Every time I myself tried to pour, a long pause in which nothing happened was followed by an uncontrolled torrent of wine and leaves falling as much as a yard beyond the receptacle aimed at.*

I had now discovered the complicated method of obtaining palm wine. It is, in fact, sap taken from the stem of a fruit cluster of the sugar palm which the Torojas call induk. *Every few months the palm, with its huge, dark green mettalic fronds and untidy, black-haired trunk, brings forth a great custer of round, dark fruit. As the fruit approaches maturity a man climbs the palm every third morning for a whole moon and beats the stout stem of the cluster for an hour with a club. At the end of the moon he pierces the stem close to the fruit; if* tuak *flows from the wound the cluster is cut off, and the receptacle after which our friend Timbo was named is hung to catch the dripping from the amputated stump. Between a pint and a quart of wine is collected from the* timbo *at sunset each day, a little always being left at the bottom, or the following day's yield would be unpleasantly sweet. The man who collects the daily pint always cuts a very thin slice from the stump before replacing the timbo.*

The pam is strangley sensitive. The flow of wine will stop if the trunk is struck or if the man who cuts the stump ever washes his hands with soap. A

BANTIMURUNG WATERFALL

Located 41 km northeast of the city in a steep limestone valley with lush tropical vegetation. Cool off at the bottom of 12-meter-high falls, then follow the trail 15 minutes upstream from the first falls to a smaller upper waterfall with fewer people and deep enough for swimming. Also visit the high, one-km-long cave Gua Mimpi (Rp1000 entrance fee), with lights and a walkway. Frequent power cuts, which seem to be deliberate, darken the path, so bring a flashlight. At the end of the cave crawl out to the surface and look down on the valley. Great place to relax. The one place to *thirsty wayfarer may climb any* induk *tree and refresh himself from the* timbo, *though nowadays, unlike the easier former* adat, *he is expected to leave a coin at the edge of the pot.*

As a rule tuak *looks like water you have washed your hands in. When merely collected it is, as the Torajas say, boiling, with the suds working up and down. From twenty to forty hours is the normal age for drinking. It is then what Norman Douglas would call "young, but not altogether innocent."*

The vintage served at Rombalayu's table was the pink Nanggala tuak, *which looks a little like champagne rosé. It was the best I had tasted, and the old chief, abetted by a coy Siindo, declared he would make me drunk on it. Every time I set down my cup a grinning slave poked the pipe over my shoulder and replenished it to the brim. But the liquor is even less intoxicating than post-war beer, and something like two quarts induced no more than a slight preliminary warmth around my heart. (which is, however, all said and done, the best part of intoxication). From the mutterings of the company and the the expectant faces of the girl slaves round the inner doorway I gathered that a more spectacular reaction was looked for. It seemed no more than a fair return for hospitality not to disappoint, so I made a point of swaying slightly on my seat, stammered once or twice and took my cue from Palinggi, who was by now quite tipsy. I was so successful that when I rose to leave the room for a moment a youth sprang forward to support me and remained with me outside lest I shoud collapse in the fresh air.*

~ Harry Wilcox, Six Moons in Sulawesi, 1949

stay is a beautifully landscaped *wisma*; Rp9000, park entrance included. *Warung* serve simple meals near the parking area. To get to Bantimurung, take a *bemo* direct from Ujung Pandang's central *bemo* station to Maros (one hour), then another *bemo* from Maros to Bantimurung (Rp250, 30 minutes). Entrance fee Rp500.

PARE PARE

The second-largest seaport of South Sulawesi, 155 km north of Ujung Pandang, Pare Pare is smaller and slower-paced than Ujung Pandang. A nice, clean city with friendly people, but nothing special except that it's the center of an area known for its delicious rice. Tourists often stop here for refreshment on their way to Mamasa or Rantepao in Tanatoraja. Pare Pare is located near areas that produce large quantities of export commodities, and the town's port is a major embarkation point for cargo and passenger boats to central and northern Sulawesi and over to East Kalimantan.

The harbor is the place to see the Bugis *bago,* with its long bowsprit and triangular mainsail. **Mesjid Raya,** with its white cupola surmounted by a silver spire, is a local landmark. Numerous *toko mas* (gold shops) are located on Jl. Lasinrang. In Cappa Galung village, two km before town, is the **Bangenge Museum of Ethnology,** featuring ceramics, gold ornaments, brassware, traditional implements and clothing dating from the Bacu Kiki kingdom. The curator, Haji Hamzah, is a descendant of its last ruler.

Tanatoraja

The name Toraja was given originally by the Buginese and means "People of the High Country," referring to those who occupy the core of central Sulawesi, from where the four peninsular legs radiate. These ancient peoples are believed to have originated from Cambodia; Toraja legends claim their ancestors arrived in a storm from the northern seas, pulled their splintered boats ashore, and used them as shelters. Today, the principal attractions of Tanatoraja include its houses: shaped like ships, they all face north, the direction of the people's origin. Tanatoraja, or Torajaland, is one of the country's most ruggedly magnificent regions, a high, 3,600-square-km, fertile plateau. These mountains have protected patterns of life and custom which have evolved and changed little over centuries. Makale and Rantepao are the two main towns in the region. In July and August Torajaland is flooded with European tourists toting video cameras. During this time it may be difficult to rent a room in Rantepao or Makale; prices tend to inflate. After the harvest, between September and December, is probably the best time to visit; the people have sufficient funds and free time to spend on such ritual occasions as funerals.

Before the Dutch arrived in 1905, the Torajans were one of the fiercest and most remote people in Indonesia. Headhunters, they displayed the skulls of their enemies in a lodge (*lobo*) in the center of the village. Their skill with blowpipes and spears was uncanny; they could pin small animals and birds at 15 meters, and impale a man at 30 meters. In the late 19th century, Torajaland was known for its coffee, which the Bugis and Makassarese traded for guns and cotton cloth. The Dutch invaded the highlands in 1905, and, after bitter resistence, vanquished and captured the last Torajan warlord, Pong Tiku, at his fortress in Pangala in 1906.

The old religion is called Aluk Todolo ("Worship of the Spirits of Ancestors"). Today it's estimated only 25 percent of the people continue to practice it, while around 65 percent claim allegiance to Christianity and 10 percent to Islam. Aluk Todolo divides the universe and the world of ritual in half: life and death. It's probable that, originally, equal attention was paid to both halves of the ritual world. But because the "life" side emphasized fertility, it was forbidden by Christianity as pagan; ironically, since Christianity has had such a democratizing effect, people can now hold as elaborate a funeral as they wish, and funerals have assumed a much greater importance in Torajan ritual life.

The "Festival of the Dead" is a happy, almost orgiastic occasion. The corpse, embalmed and wrapped in many shrouds and looking like a big striped pillow, is kept company by professional mourners so it won't become lonely during the celebratory feasting. The corpse is carried down from the house and placed inside a granary-shaped structure on a stretcher for transportation to its final resting place, *liang*. These sunken family graves in cliffs came into fashion after thieves from outside Tanatoraja began stealing the gold and jewels interred with the dead. The Batutumonga area is probably the best place to view Torajan burial sites. Open-air tourist museums like Lemo and Londa seem like abandoned ghost-villages.

Getting Around

Torajan guides make trailfinding easier; ask at the hotels. Most speak good English and can organize everything. Guides usually specialize in certain areas and styles of travel. You can rent horses to carry gear for long-distance trips, but it's more pleasant to walk. For an eight-day trip, such as the **Simbuang Loop** passing through or near many traditional Torajan villages, expect to spend about Rp210,000-315,000. Using the map, create your own walks. If you're in a hurry, you can hire minibuses (*kijang*) with drivers for Rp30,000 per day, plus all entrance fees and the lunch/drink costs of the driver and helper. For car, driver, guide, and entrance fees, the rate can go as high as Rp65,000 per day. Signs placed at the start of side roads announce the location of sites. Class one, such as Lemo, Londa, and Kete Kesu, cost Rp1500 pp; class two, like Suaya, Rp1000; and class three destinations like Tampong Allo run Rp500. Admission to remote villages like Batutumonga is free. Cars cost Rp100 extra.

RANTEPAO

Rantepao is a cool, busy, midsized mountain town with potholed roads, a huge market, and wide streets full of honking, bouncing *bemo* and whining motorcycles. A good place to base yourself, especially if walking, since most roads fan out from Rantepao. And despite all the tourists, the city is actually a manageable size, with lots of atmosphere. People are helpful and friendly; except for souvenirs, you're charged the same prices as the locals. It only takes a couple of days to learn your way around. *Becak* cruise up and down Jl. Mappanyuki looking for fares, but you can easily walk almost anywhere.

Funerary effigies carved into cliffside graves by the Toraja

Rantepao's fascinating market, on Jl. Abdul Gani 1.5 km northeast of town, is the region's largest. It offers an enormous variety of produce, merchandise, and handicrafts, and is open every day. See Torajan traditional life firsthand, without ever leaving town. An exotic place to explore—a cornucopia of fruits, vegetables, coffee, *tuak,* poultry, eels, dried fish, bamboo flutes, decorated containers, model houses, hand-forged swords, basketry, and giant conical hats. All is available cheaply—after bargaining, of course. Don't miss the squealing pig market. At Pasar Hewan, in a big open field in Bolu, dozens of tethered *kerbau* are surrounded by their owners and prospective buyers. The spotted buffalo have great ceremonial value and a correspondingly high price—up to Rp7 million. These beasts are rarely found outside Tanatoraja.

Souvenir shops on Jl. Pahlawan offer the best selection of Torajan handicrafts and antiques. Prices are higher than in the market or villages. Look for old woodcarvings, knives, bead necklaces, and *ikat*-dyed cloth. Bargain for engraved and painted boxes, miniature replicas of *tongkanan,* statues made of wood and *kerbau* bone, glass beads.

VICINITY OF RANTEPAO

The walks around Rantepao are gorgeous. A wonderful all-day walk, for example, is from Rantepao to Tikala-Pana-Lokomata-Batutumonga-Lempo-Deri-Bori-Parinding, then back to Rantepao by *bemo.* There are few travelers along the way and you'll enjoy lots of meaningful contact with the villagers. The views from Batutumonga and Lokomata of the *sawah* and Rantepao below are spectacular, especially toward sunset. Set out for more distant villages in the early morning when it's cool; visit villages closer to Rantepao later in the day. Most are quite close to one another and you can easily visit a number of villages in an afternoon. Take lunch with you.

Lemo charges an entrance fee of Rp1500. Rows of *tau-tau* peer down from balconies jutting out from 30 funerary niches carved from the cliffs—one of the largest *tau-tau* groupings in all of Torajaland. The effigies are new, replacing stolen originals. Photographers should arrive early, before the figures are obscured by shadows. See the three traditional houses and two rice barns near the souvenir stalls.

Walk two km south on the road to Makale, then turn east at the sign and continue another two km to reach **Kete Kesu.** At the base of a cliff, 100 meters behind the *tongkonan,* are scattered bones, skulls, and rotted wood coffins with dragon motifs. On the cliff face are *erong* (hanging graves) on wood posts and platforms. Kete Kesu is one of the more commercial, touristy villages in the region. As is **Sullukang,** an old, secluded village about two km past Kete Kesu. This *kampung* has some tall *rante* as well as statues seated in a run-down shack near the village. Look for a sign on the road to Kantor Desa La'bo; the statues are 100 meters beyond.

Nine km from Rantepao is **Pala'tokke.** While human bones crunch underfoot, see two 800-year-old *erong* on the limestone cliff. As at Lemo, these very scenic cliffs are also used for stone graves. Local legend claims the people of Pala'tokke can climb the cliff face like geckos. Entrance fee Rp2000.

Buntao, a village with a *patane* (grave house), is 16 km from Rantepao, Rp500 by *bemo*. Another approach is from Nanggala off the Palopo road; it's a full day's walk via Paniki over a mountainous area. No signs, so keep asking the way. Time your visit for market day. **Tembamba** is a mountain pass village only three km from Buntao—old graves and an awesome panorama.

One km from Rantepao is **Singki Hill**. From the southern edge of town, walk on the road beside the river, cross the bridge, then look on the right for the trail going up the hill—a short but precipitous climb. Good views of Rantepao and surroundings.

Five km from town is **Siguntu'**, a traditional village with views of the valley below. Continue walking past the Singki Hill turnoff to Singki village and beyond, then look for a road to the right up the hill. See the remarkable carving on the nobleman's house, filled with trichromatic symbolic forms. Impressive rice barns; seldom visited. Continue past the Siguntu' turnoff, then turn right on the next road to **Mandoe**, a typical Torajan village six km from Rantepao and just off the Siguntu'-Alang Alang road.

Marante is six km from Rantepao, located on the left just off the road to Palopo. Marante offers a mixture of traditional Torajan dwellings and wooden houses, with some coffins and *tau-tau*. There's a huge step suspension bridge here which daring tourists like to cross. Quite scary.

Nine km farther is **Tandung**, a spectacular area with pine forests, 18-meter-high bamboo, and a gorgeous lake. One-half km off the road to Palopo, 15 km from Rantepao (Rp500 by *bemo*), is **Nanggala**, a traditional Torajan village known for its large *tongkonan* and 14 rice barns with superb carvings—the best around. Entrance fee Rp1500. Packages of beans and ground coffee for sale. Huge fruit bats hang from trees.

Walk north from Rantepao and cross the river, turn left at the intersection, then keep right at the Tikala road intersection to reach **Parinding**. Easy, pleasant, mostly level walking through rice fields. Infrequent vehicles on this route. Parinding is in two parts, both with handsome *tongkonan* and rice barns.

One km beyond Parinding is **Bori**, with one of the best *rante* in the region. Many other villages have *rante*, but here the stones are huge, some towering four meters high. Bori is getting quite touristy—you have to pay to enter now. A small trail near Bori climbs to **Deri**, passing many *tongkonan* on the way.

In **Pangli**, eight km from Rantepao, see the house grave 200 meters above the church; the stone statue features the realistic likeness of a dead man, one Pong Massangka. House graves are built when there are no cliff faces for carving out deep burial pockets; graves are dug into the earth and a small statue or miniature *tongkonan* is built over the top. Each house grave contains members of an entire family, wrapped in shrouds and interred without coffins. Pangli is also the source of a famous *tuak*.

Volcanic lake, northern Sulawesi

About one km north of Pangli, then one km west on a side road, is **Palawa**. This traditional village has numerous *tongkonan* and rice barns, fine examples of Torajan domestic architecture turned into souvenir kiosks. Large numbers of *kerbau* horns are attached to the fronts of some *tongkonan*. Palawa is built on terraces; the highest features seven big houses facing seven big storehouses. Also visit Palawa's Stonehenge-like circle of stones.

Sa'dan To'barana is 13 km from Rantepao. Hyped as the weaving center of Tanatoraja, the cultural significance of the place is greatly exaggerated. Most products, sold at fixed prices, are made to suit the tastes and pocketbooks of package tourists. Women demonstrate traditional weaving at a center near Sa'dan, where you can bargain for old and new cloth. Sa'dan has the best distilleries of the strong palm toddy drink, *tuak sissing biang.*

BATUTUMONGA

A nice place to hang out in the countryside, Batutumonga sits on the slopes of Gunung Sesean, with some of the best trekking in the region and superb views of the valleys below all the way to Rantepao. Batutumonga is the main town in one of the most traditional and remote areas on the island. It's about 23 km by road from Rantepao, but only 11 km by trail via Tikala and Pana. The climb is steep and should be attempted before the afternoon rains turn the trail into slippery mud. *Bemo* also travel to Lempo direct from Rantepao (Rp1500), then you walk one hour to Batutumonga. Or you can take a *bemo* to either Tikala, Bori, or Deri and walk to Batutumonga in a couple of hours.

From Batutumonga walk uphill to the turnoff south to Pana. On this wonderful walk are great panoramas and *rante* stones. From Pana it's 1.5 hours down to Tikala; from there you can take a *bemo* to Rantepao (Rp1500). The complete 670 meter descent from Batutumonga, with beautiful views at almost every turn, takes three to four hours.

PANA TO PANGALA

From Rantepao you can take a *bemo* direct to **Pana** for Rp2000. Near Pana is a very old, hidden set of cliff graves in a wild setting—some of the best *rante* and *liang* in Toraja. After Pana look for a small trail up the bank to the left. If you pass a large school you've gone about 300 meters too far. Coming from Tikala, look for the small trail to the graves on your right, some 300 meters after the school. The *tau-tau* near

A farmer's life

Tikala are rarely visited. It takes a local with a machete to hack a path through the jungle to get to them. You can actually climb up and stand next to them; unusual.

Thirty-five km from Rantepao is **Lokomata**. Take a *bemo* to Tikala (Rp1000), then walk three hours up a steep clay track to Lokomata. Or from Lempo walk 1.5 hours west to Lokomata. A huge, round, three-story-tall boulder beside the road is studded with about 60 boarded-up funereal niches carved into three sides. Many other boulders with graves in this area. Some of the burials are recent, and you might even see a guy chipping away at a boulder. The walk from Batutumonga to Lokomata is level, with nearly continuous panoramas of rice terraces, mountains, and the valley below. Northeast of Lokomata is **Gunung Sesean**, the highest mountain in Tanatoraja. Climb it early in the morning; guide recommended. From Lokomata, walk 45 minutes to the junction to Pana, which you'll reach in a 30-minute walk.

Kijang and trucks drive to **Pangala**, 58 km from Rantepao, a coffee-growing area also known for its dancers. The amazing Wisma Sandro here, owned by a rich man from Jakarta, has rooms for Rp12,000 s or d. Nice and clean, hardly used. Mindblowing to find such extravagance out here in the hills. Food okay but overpriced. Nice walking around here—scenic, friendly people, and the children don't beg. Small trails lead south to Bittuang (36 km, two-day walk) and north to Galumpang (six-day walk). A jeep leaves for Rantepao (Rp4000 per person) from Pangala's market around 1000.

Makale, an administrative center built by the Dutch in 1925, is the district capital. Located 17 km south of Rantepao, Makale's hilltop churches and Torajan-style government buildings overlook an artificial lotus-filled lake. The town is steadily expanding northward along the road to Rantepao, with new hotels appearing each year. Makale's large market is worth a visit to see local produce and the people from surrounding villages. The hospital, **Fatimah**, is at Jl. Pongtiku 103. Some fine walks in the area.

One-half km from Makale is **Tondon**. Walk from the Makale market east on a small road. A row of *tau-tau* in the cliff overlooks cliff graves. Old caskets, bones, and skulls are found in small caves around the cliffs. An easy six-km excursion from Makale is **Suaya**, which has a lovely church. Walk by spectacular, small limestone mountains, then along rice fields. Turn left 250 meters to the village at the base of a limestone hill. In the cliff is a row of 40 amazing *tau-tau* and scattered cliff graves. Suaya is one of the best places to see *tau-tau*.

One km before Suaya is **Tampong Allo**, with seldom-visited hanging graves in a cave. Note the effigy of a mother holding an infant. Because she died in childbirth, she was given a "child" to accompany her in the afterlife. About one km before Tampong Allo is a tree grave. Here only babies nine months or younger are buried in trees, covered in *atap* to protect them from birds and animals.

Eight km from Makale is **Buntukalando**. On the right is a king's *tongkonan*, housing a small museum (Rp300) of royal possessions and Torajan household artifacts. One of the rice barns is unusually large, with 10 supporting pillars instead of the usual six. A *rante* consisting of huge, strangely shaped stones is on the other side of the road.

Sangalla lies six km east of Makale. A palace has been built here on a leveled-off hill with picturesque surroundings. Bear in mind that a Torajan "palace" means "grand bamboo house." Sangala is also the residence of a *tari pageullu* dance troupe, **Group Husik Bambu.**

Twenty km east of Makale, after a fairly level hike, is **Makula**. The old government *pasanggrahan* here has bathtubs inside the rooms, fed by a steaming hot spring. There's also a spring-fed swimming pool outside. You'll find a good natural swimming hole in nearby **Se'seng**. The road then winds for 21 km into the mountains to **Bittuang**, a market town (Monday is the big day). From Bittuang a trail heads north to Pangala (36 km, two days). The 60-km trail to Mamasa in western Toraja can be walked in three days, with gorgeous scenery of valleys, mountains, villages, and rice terraces.

North Sulawesi

A pretty land of vast coconut and clove plantations, high active volcanos, mountain lakes, picturesque villages, hot springs and fumaroles, ancient burial sites, white-sand coral islands, abundant marine life, and outstanding snorkeling and diving. Along this peninsula are six dormant volcanos, each towering 1,800-2,400 meters. The dry season is May to October, rainy season November to April. So near the equator is the Minahasan peninsula that telephone poles cast no shadows at noon.

Heavy, regular rainfall and rich volcanic ash have blessed North Sulawesi with extremely fertile land. The narrow lowlands and valleys of the province have been particularly successful agriculturally, producing rice, vanilla, nutmeg, corn, coconut palms, and cloves. Forest products include rattan, ebony, resins, and gums. Valuable *cingke* (cloves) are grown everywhere in Minahasa, and during harvest their fragrance is everywhere. With an estimated 25 million trees, this is the largest copra production area of Indonesia—18,000 tons exported per month.

North Sulawesi's population of nearly 2.6 million is comprised of an ethnic mix of peoples from mainland Southeast Asia, Indonesia, the Philippines, and the ex-colonial countries of Spain, Portugal, and the Netherlands. A major food and fish processing province, Sulawesi Utara has a higher standard of living and better health care and education systems than most other regions of Indonesia. In fact, this very wealthy province sometimes feels like a separate republic. Its geographic isolation from the rest of Indonesia, and its rebellious history, accentuate this impression.

Most travelers use Manado as a base. Coming from the south, it's possible to travel by bus from Palu (leaving 1700 or 1900) in Central Sulawesi to the North Sulawesi peninsula, then up to Manado via Gorontalo. This approach is still quite challenging (29-30 hours, Rp20,000). For Rp25,000-Rp30,000 you can ride all the way from Palu to Manado. It's easier to fly from Palu to Gorontalo (Rp84,000, three times weekly with Bouraq) and travel the remaining 520 km overland to Manado. Bouraq also schedules flights from Gorontalo to Manado (Rp71,000, four times a week) and Palu to Manado (Rp144,000, three times weekly).

MANADO

The predominantly Christian capital of North Sulawesi Province, this busy city of 420,000 people is built on gentle hills sloping down to a beautiful bay. Two volcanos overlook the city—an inspired setting. Yet for any tourist who is not a water sport enthusiast, Manado holds little of interest; there are few historical sights, no cultural centers or museums of note, and sparse nightlife.

The city has become a collection of the best and the worst in terms of buildings, sanitation, and government services. The most impressive buildings in town, aside from the governor's offices/residence on the hill, are the banks. Surrounding these massive, ugly structures are corrugated tin hovels dominating the entire waterfront boulevard area—very grim even by Jakarta standards. The beach is filthy—human excrement, miscellaneous animal parts, flotsam of all descriptions.

Manado has a large Chinese population. **Ban Hian Kiong** is a small, colorful 19th-century Confucian-Buddhist temple in the center of town (Jl. Panjaitan 7A). The oldest in East Indonesia, this temple is the center of international attention during the Toa Pe Kong festival each February. Climb up to the balcony at the top for a view of the downtown. Near here are several smaller Confucian temples and a **Kuan Yin** temple just before Megawati Bridge. **Kwan Im Tong**, Jl. Sisingamangaraja, is one of the oldest temples in Manado. The city's numerous Christian churches bear such familiar names as Zion, Bethesda, and Advent.

The **Provincial Museum of North Sulawesi**, on Jl. W.R. Supratman, contains cultural artifacts of Minahasa as well as historical remains from Dutch and Portuguese times. Near the waterfront is the large market, **Pasar 45**, a motley sprawl of semi-permanent shops selling just about everything. This is also where all the city's *oplet* seem to converge. **Pasar Bersehati**, near Jumbo Supermarket north of the harbor, is the largest and busiest food market in Manado.

The **North Sulawesi Tourist Office** is now located at Jl. Diponegoro 111, Manado 95112, tel. (0431) 51723 or 51835. Go there for pamphlets and other useful publications; the director is F. H. Warokka. Hours 0700-1400, Friday until 1100, Saturday till 1230. There's also a very helpful tourist information booth at Sam Ratulangi Airport (open 0830-1600) which provides discounts on hotels. **Bank Dagang Negara,**

Jl. Dotulolong Lasut, tel. 63278, has a branch office in Los Angeles which you may use to wire money; the exchange rates are usually the best in town.

AIRMADIDI

In this mountain village, 19 km southeast of Manado, are the best examples of *waruga*, pre-Christian tombs of the ancestral Minahasans. Hewn from single blocks of limestone, *waruga* are shaped like small Chinese temples with enormous roof-shaped covers. Often they're lavishly decorated with intricate animal and anthropomorphic carvings, Portuguese gentlemen in 18th-century attire, or features of important Minahasans. Once common over a large area of Minahasa, as Christianity spread *waruga* were either forgotten or destroyed. Because they contained valuables, many have been plundered. Now they've been collected and assembled in places like Airmadidi.

The name "Airmadidi" means "boiling water"—there are two natural hot springs near the *waruga*, with amazingly clear water. Airmadidi is Rp400 by *oplet* from Manado's Terminal Paal Dua; the *waruga* are just down the road from the Airmadidi *oplet* terminal. A small museum is open 0800-1700. Just before town in Suwaan is **Pongkor**, offering such Minahasan delicacies as baked or fried *ikan mas*; *kolintang* bands play in the restaurant on Saturday nights.

VICINITY OF AIRMADIDI

At **Taman Waruga Sawangan**, 144 ancient *waruga* have been collected within the confines of a tranquil terraced garden. Because they've been so beautifully restored, the *waruga* at Sawangan are more interesting, varied, and detailed than those at Airmadidi. Take an *oplet* from Airmadidi to Sawangan (Rp100, six km). There are other *waruga* sites at **Kema** on the coast south of Bitung, and at **Likupang** on the northern tip of the peninsula.

From Airmadidi, you're within range of some of Indonesia's most beautiful landscapes. It's only a 45-minute *oplet* ride (Rp1000) farther to Bitung or 50 minutes (Rp1000) down to Tondano on Lake Tondano. **Gunung Klabat** is a stiff five- to six-hour climb from the path near the Airmadidi police station. Tackle it during a full-moon night; shiver while waiting for the sunrise at the top. Register with the police before climbing—there may be wild *anoa* on the trail.

TOMOHON

Tomohon is a pretty, windy, sunny town with still-active **Gunung Lokon** (1,580 meters) towering in the background and the sea visible beyond. The smell of sulphur can be very strong. One of the highest villages of the district, the town has a pleasantly cool climate, not unlike a European summer. Known as **Kota Kembang** ("Flower City"), every wooden house seems to be draped with orchid plants, while household gardens burst with enormous zinnias, dahlias, marigolds, and glorious perennial gladiolas. Tomohon is the location of a Christian theology school at nearby **Bukit Inspirasi** ("Hill of Inspiration").

People are very friendly. The town is renowned for its wheelwrights, who supply most of the wheels for the *bendi* of Manado; Tomohon's streets echo with the sound of horses' hooves. A fine market on Tuesday, Thursday, and Saturday features roasted dogs, giant roasted rats, snakes, and bats.

From Manado's Pasar Karombasan, take a public bus or minibus direct to Tomohon (Rp600). Enjoy wonderful views of the city; at night see strings of lights below. Cafes, restaurants, and hot spring spas perch on the side of the road all the way to Tomohon. This pine-forest region offers one of Indonesia's highest concentrations of hot springs. Buy *durian, langsat,* mangos, and other monsoon fruits at **Pineleng**, a village just above Tomohon. The bus continues to climb through the plantations between the volcanos of Lokon and Mahawu.

At **Temboan,** halfway up the mountain to Tomohon, experience real ethnic Minahasan cooking: mice, dog (very peppery hot), wild pig (*babi hutan*), and a gin called *cap tikus,* plus sago wines (*tuak saguer*) of varying potency. The food is heavily spiced, and visitors who don't like hot food should ask for food *"tidak pedas."* Superb views of Manado and the bay. Approaching Tomohon, see the *ikan mas* raised in the ponds on the left.

VICINITY OF TOMOHON

This is a lovely area, comparable to the mountain towns of Java. An oft-expressed greeting in upcountry Minahasa is: *"Pakatua'an wo pakalawiren!"* ("Wishing you long life and health!"). Because of the rich *cingke* cash crops, the people in surrounding villages are comparatively well off. Many horsecarts, so plenty of transportation; Rp500-1000 per ride.

Two km out of Tomohon, on the road to **Tara Tara**, are WW II Japanese ammunition caves. In **Kinilow,** five km before Tomohon, is **Indraloka**, with a large modern swimming pool, natural hot springs, and public baths; hostesses offer rubdowns. Cottages for Rp20,000 s or d.

At **Kakaskasen I,** three km before Tomohon, dances are sometimes held on Saturday night; Rp250 admission. **Kakaskasen II** sits in the shadows of two volcanos, **Gunung Lokon** and **Gunung Mahawu.** Both have crater lakes of considerable beauty, duck-egg blue and smoking, within 1.5 hours walk of the village. Lokon is usually considered the more beautiful of the two, and the casual climb should be no problem for anyone in reasonable condition. Guides for around Rp5000 may be found with the help of the *kepala desa.*

In **Tara Tara,** a traditional mill is located toward the end of the road to the right. Powered by a fast-running stream at the bottom of a small ravine, the immense water wheel drives an intricate maze of belts, pulleys, and wooden gears—the final achievement is the vertical operation of a group of heavy log pounders that pulverize the grain. It's possible to travel along this road to **Tanawangko**, then circle back to Manado.

SONDER

This clove village, 20 km southwest of Tomohon, consists of one main street with three churches (Minahasa, Seventh-day Adventist, Catholic). During the harvest (July-Oct.), one can hardly drive through the streets because of the *cingke* which people have put out to dry on mats—their yards are already overflowing. Even stilted traditional-style wooden homes sport color TV sets, kitchen gadgetry, and expensive furniture. With a per capita income of US$5500, this is one of the richest towns in Asia.

RURUKAN

A colorful 900-meter-high mountain village perched halfway between Tomohon and Tandano, five km up a twisting, rough, mountain road. From the center of the village, take the road to Kumelebuag. Turn right after 400 meters, follow a dirt path for 100 meters, then turn left and go straight along a jungle path to reach some fine hot springs. Backtracking to the village, follow the main road down to Tondano, another six km; this is a beautiful walk with a panoramic view of Lake Tondano.

TONDANO AREA

Tondano is a large market town located in the middle of a fertile rice-growing plateau. Catch a minibus or *oplet* from Tomohon, or from Manado's Terminal Karombasan. Stay at the excellent, clean, and cool **Asri**; Rp18,000 per room includes breakfast, tea, and coffee. Eat at the **Pemandangan** or **Fireball** restaurants on the main road, Jl. Raya Tomohon. From Tondano, continue to other resort towns surrounding **Danau Tondano**, a large, scenic lake beautifully situated between paddies and the Lembean Mountains. This 50-square-km lake, about 30 km southeast of Manado, is the region's largest. Its abundant fish provide a livelihood for the native population. The tiny island in the middle is known as Likri. The waterfall of Tondano is famous.

From Tondano, pay Rp500 to travel around the west or east side of the lake. Eastbound, stop in at **Tandengan** and **Eris**, both with nice views of the lake. Westbound, **Remboken** has a better selection of pottery than Manado; also try the hot springs at the **Taman Wisata**. At **Paso**, bathe in large steaming concrete tanks; ask for *air panas umum* (Rp500). Stay at **Tempat Pemandian Florida**, Rp10,000. From Paso there are lovely views of Lake Tondano across steaming fields of hot springs bubbling amongst the rice.

WATU PINABETENGAN

A megalithic ancestor stone near Kawangkoan, its surface covered in crude, mysterious line drawings and scripts that have never been deciphered. According to Minahasan history, this is the place where their ancestors first divided the land between the people; Watu Pinabetengan means "The Stone of Discussion about the Division." This memorial boulder, two meters high and four meters long, shaped like the top of a *waruga,* has served as a political gathering place for Minahasan elders since time immemorial. There have been at least six major discussions at the stone: the first division of the tribes, a reconciliation of the differences between the tribes, a resolution in the 17th century to drive out the Spanish, a meeting to organize a defense against attackers from Bolaang Mongondow to the south, a 1939 demand for Indonesian independence, and a blessing of the new Indonesian Republic in 1945. Though each of the six Minahasan tribes speaks its own dialect, they are today united as one people; Mina Esa means "Become One" or "United."

From Kawangkoan, take a *bendi* three km (Rp300, 30 minutes) to Desa Pinabetengan. Then walk two km along a road to the site, in a beautiful forest on the slopes of a mountain with a majestic view over Minahasa. Unfortunately, the government has buried the sacred stone in an ugly concrete crypt, like a white-tiled grave. It should have been situated on a lovely grass hillock for everyone to see and enjoy. To make it worse, the concrete roof makes the place even darker, and birds who live under the roof shit on the revered object. A pity, as the site could be an important tourist attraction. Don't visit during the first part of the year: thousands of people converge on the memorial stone during the month of January. Bathe in the hot springs nearby.

Maluku

Introduction

Maluku is divided into three administrative districts: North Maluku, Central Maluku, and Southeast Maluku. The islands are also a transition zone for Asian and Australian flora and fauna, as well as for the human cultures of Melanesia and Southeast Asia. Only about 1.5 million people live here, many of them skilled agriculturalists and seafarers. Animists—Papuan, proto-Malayan, and Negrito—occupy the interiors. Those islands most visited are Ambon, Ternate, Tidore, and the Bandas. The only real urban center in Maluku is Ambon City, or Amboina, on Pulau Ambon.

The total land area of these thousand or so islands is 87,100 square km, about two-thirds the size of Java. The 5,000-meter-deep Maluku Sea adds to their geographical remoteness. The islands vary in size from tiny uninhabited atolls, the tops of submerged volcanos, to Halmahera, Buru, and Ceram, each over 4,000 square km. Lying right in the middle of the great chain of volcanos known as the "Ring of Fire," Maluku is a volatile territory, with 70 eruptions recorded in the last 400 years; earthquakes are not uncommon on Ternate, Ambon, and the Bandas.

Despite unrelenting pressure from timber concessions and human settlements, Maluku still offers the naturalist a striking example of the luxuriance and beauty of tropical animal life. The Aru and Kai islands feature marsupials, including a dwarf species of tree kangaroo only 30 centimeters tall and the tree-living cuscus, a small opposum-like animal.

Yet, in spite of the unbroken chain of islands which seems to link Maluku with the Asian continent, there is a conspicuous absence of land mammals. Wild deer, wild pigs, and the tiny shrew have reached certain parts of Maluku. There are monkeys on Pulau Bacan, and the Sulawesi black baboon and *babirusa* are found as far as the Sula Islands. There are many kinds of honeyeaters, 22 species of parrots, the famous racket-tailed kingfisher, the giant red-crested Malukan cockatoo, and even, on Aru, two species of bird of paradise. On Ceram and the southern islands lives the huge, nearly wingless cassowary.

The vegetation of Maluku is extravagant, with many Australian forms intermingled with the Asiatic. Cloves are found all over Central Maluku; nutmeg is also cultivated. *Kayuputih* (cajeput) oil is derived from the region's eucalyptus trees, while the all-important sago tree provides the main staple in the Malukan diet, as well as bark to make walls for houses and leaves to make roof thatch.

Fishing platform, Maluku

Nutmeg and cloves have brought trade to these islands since at least 300 B.C. They were known by Chinese, Javanese, Indians, and Arabs long before the Portuguese "discovered" Maluku in 1498. In A.D. 846, Ibn Khordadhbih wrote about the "Spice Islands" located some 15 sailing days off Java. Maluku was always treated as a satellite by various Javanese kingdoms; the 13th century Singosari dynasty prospered hugely on the spice trade with Maluku. From the 14th century the spice trade in the islands was dominated by powerful Muslim sultans on Ternate, Tidore, and Djailolo (Halmahera).

For centuries, Europeans could obtain the spices only through Arab traders; European monarchs dreamed of one day controlling the source. The Portuguese navigator Albuquerque captured Goa (India) in 1510 and Melaka (Peninsular Malaysia) in 1511. Soon after, he also located an outstanding map of the smaller islands north of Java, from which the Portuguese were able to trace the origin of nutmeg and mace to the Banda Islands, and cloves to Tidore, Ternate, Halmahera, Bacan, Makian, and Moti. The Portuguese were forced out of Hitu in 1601, and driven entirely out of Tidore and Ambon by 1605.

The Dutch period lasted from around 1605 to 1942. The Dutch tried to create a world monopoly of the valuable nutmeg, cinnamon, and clove trade. In 1607 they gained power by signing a treaty with the sultans of Tidore and Ternate, mandating that the price of cloves was to be fixed, the Dutch would "defend" Ternate against the Spaniards, and the sultan would pay the Dutch for the cost of all battles fought on his behalf. But the Dutch soon imposd a ruthless system of forced cultivation which remained in place for hundreds of years. At the end of the 18th century, world demand for cloves and nutmeg fell drastically. The British and French smuggled out seedlings and succeeded in planting clove and nutmeg trees in their colonies in India and Africa, breaking the back of the monopoly. But it wasn't until 1863, when a liberal constitution was adopted in Holland, that forced cultivation at last ceased and all monopolies were terminated.

After Indonesia declared its independence in 1945, civilians and former military members (KNIL) of the Dutch colonial army created—with Dutch backing—the Republik Maluku Selatan in 1947; the republic broke off ties with Indonesia in 1949. When the Dutch refused the next year to continue backing the new nation, secession was abandoned and some 40,000 sympathetic Malukans were evacuated to the Netherlands. Today a sizable number of Malukans make up the Indonesian population of Holland; many have never seen their homeland.

Maluku is a fascinating ethnographic, linguistic, and anthropological environment. The islands are inhabited by a number of distinct, relatively isolated ethnic groups: the Alfuros, dark skinned frizzy haired proto Malays, the original inhabitants of Maluku; lighter-skinned straight-haired deutero-Malays, who arrived many centuries later; minority groups like Chinese, Arabs, Javanese, and Malukans of European descent who trace their lineage from colonists. One of the major ethnic groups is the Ambonese, living along the coastal areas of the islands of Ambon, Saparua, Nusa Laut, and western Ceram. Roving colonies of "sea gypsies" (*Orang Laut*) moor their boats in the many ports of the archipelago.

Ambon Island

The Uliasser Islands—commercial, communication, administrative and geographic center of Maluku—consist of four mountainous islands southwest of Ceram: from west to east Ambon, Haruku, Saparua, and Nusa Laut. Their total area is 1,295 square km, of which Ambon takes 777 square km. *Embun* means "dew" in Indonesian; this island is almost always enclosed by fog or mist. Predominantly Christian, Ambon is today a sort of "mini-Maluku," offering beautiful tropical landscapes, historic buildings, churches and ruins, picturesque country walks, and fascinating *kampung* with traditions intact. On this island you can photograph some of the most spectacular vistas in the whole archipelago. Officially, the island's main city is called Amboina, although nobody much uses the name anymore—both the island and city are called Ambon. There is tight control on visitors; on arrival you're signed in at the airport's *imigrasi* office, and your hotel must register you with the police.

Ambon has two beautiful bays, Teluk Ambon and Teluk Baguala. The entire island is very mountainous; Gunung Horiel in Leitimor rises to nearly 580 meters; the highest point, Gunung Latua, is nearly 915 meters. Both mountains are volcanic in origin, though dormant. Ambon's rich soil gives rise to nutmeg, clove, cinnamon, betelnut, and palm plantations; a variety of orchids grows wild on shrubs and trees. The main staples are sago, tubers, vegetables, and cassava, which grows wild in swampy areas. Fish provide most of the protein. Cloves and nutmeg are still among the primary cash crops, though not nearly on the scale of the past. Swidden crops such as squash and other gourds, plus spinach, are also cultivated; the Ambonese preference for root crops betrays their Melanesian origins.

Ambon entered quite late into the tumultuous history of the Spice Islands. In 1574, the Portuguese built a fortress on magnificently sheltered Ambon Bay on the site of what is today Ambon City. Ambon became the Portuguese headquarters for the eastern islands, replacing fortresses on Ternate and Tidore. To this day the Uliassers are littered with Portuguese place-names. The Dutch expelled the Portuguese in 1605, and the island remained under Dutch colonial rule from 1605 to 1949, the oldest directly governed Dutch territory in Indonesia. In the first 100 years of Dutch rule, one-third of Ambon's inhabitants were wiped out by diseases or punitive expeditions.

During their 3.5 years of occupation, the Japanese shifted the political balance from the *adat* elite to Ambonese nationalists. Ambon has been flattened by bombs three times since WW II. After independence and before Javanese republican forces could be sent out to replace the Dutch Colonial Army, the pro-Dutch Republik Maluku Selatan (RMS) seceded from Indonesia. This powerful Christian group of soldiers, civilian officials, and members of the traditional elite shared little ethnically, culturally, or spiritually with the Javanese. Resistance was crushed in 1950, although sporadic guerrilla fighting on the neighboring island of Ceram continued into the 1960s and reverberations were felt in Holland even into the 1970s.

AMBON CITY

The administrative capital of Maluku Tengah, Ambon City is a disparate collection of government offices and closely knit *kampung*. Food, accommodations, and transportation in this fair-sized city are as expensive as in Bandung, but the pace is slower. You see few foreigners here except missionaries and occasional Dutch, Australian, or New Zealand tourists. Music is everywhere; all the latest Western tapes pulsate from shopfronts, transistors, and taxi buses, guitars are played on porches and street corners, and everyone owns and exchanges cassettes. Ambon is one of the few places in Indonesia where you see drunks on the street, especially on Sunday afternoons and in the evenings.

This city has had a hard history since the Portuguese first established a fort here 400 years ago. Because of the worldwide popularity of its spices, Ambon has been caught in crossfires and destroyed many times. Before the arrival of Europeans, the land now occupied by the town was called Honipopu, and consisted of four villages. Ambon was for centuries an important way-station for the spice traffic between Ternate and the Banda Islands.

Known all over the Indies as "Beautiful Amboina," prewar Ambon had spacious squares with tall trees, shady cobblestone streets, promenades and gardens, and a charming tree-lined waterfront, with the white houses of the Dutch interspersed among native palm houses. The town was all but demolished by Allied bombs in 1945. A new administrative center, with many government buildings and official residences, was built in the 1970s in the suburb of Karangpanjang—the "Brasilia" of Ambon.

The statue with the upraised sword in the town park is of **Kapitan Pattimura**, who fought against Dutch oppression. The statue is located on the spot where the guerrilla leader was hanged by the Dutch. The memorial to freedom-fighter **Martha Christina Tiahahu**, in the suburb of Karangpanjang, overlooks the whole of Ambon City and Ambon Bay. Tiahahu and her father served in Pattimura's guerrilla forces; she died on a POW ship to Java. Near the statue is the Provincial House of Assembly where elected members meet periodically. In the suburb of Tantui just east of Batumerah, about two km from downtown Ambon, an **Allied Forces Cemetery** was established for the British, Dutch, and Australian servicemen killed in Maluku and Sulawesi during WW II. The Indonesian **Heroes Cemetery** (Makam Pahlawan) is nearby.

Siwalima Museum in Batu Capeo contains historic, craft, and ethnographic objects from all over the province, a surprisingly good collection with many fascinating exhibits: *ikat,* wonderful protective and ancestor statues, woodcarvings, boat models, ceramics. Donation Rp2000. Open 0800-1400; closed Monday and Friday.

The original **Fort Victoria** was built by the Portuguese in 1575 and named Fort Kota Laka. The Dutch overran it in 1605, ending Portuguese control of the Spice Islands. To stamp out Portuguese prestige, the Dutch reduced the fort nearly to its foundations, renamed it Fort Victoria, then expanded and updated the complex over the next 350 years. Now the military occupies the site and only the gate, a few old buildings, and the large bulwarks along the sea remain of the original fort. To enter, obtain permission from the fort commander. Don't take photographs without a permit or your film will be confiscated.

On the road between Poka and the airport is the bloody site where 72 Australian POWs were beheaded during WW II by the Japanese; there's a memorial right off the road, near the water. If taking a taxi in from the airport stop here for a bit. Just before the city is another memorial, marked by a huge statue; see the beautifully kept cemetery with hundreds of graves. A third site is located on the hill by the Siwalima Museum, just a few minutes walk away.

(following pages) Daruba village, Marotai Island

Tempat Masyarakyat Maluku Tenggara is a cottage industry where Tanimbar-style weaving is produced. *Kayuputih* oil is processed and bottled on Ambon, used as a surface balm for itching and may be swallowed for a stomach ache. Most attractively packaged by **Abdulalie** on Jl. Sultan Abdulalie; Rp500-900. The place also sells Minyak Kulit Lawang, which is twice as expensive; this is a hot oil for itching, rheumatism, and the healing of cuts. Also buy pure, green clove oil here for only Rp1000 per bottle.

The **tourist office**, Dinas Pariwisata Dati I Maluku, is on the ground floor of *kantor gubernor* on Jl. Pattimura. Open Mon.-Thurs. 0800-1400, Friday until 1130, Saturday until 1300. The officer for tourism, Mr. Oratmangun, can answer your questions and make it easier for you to visit places that present bureaucratic difficulties.

SIGHTS AROUND THE ISLAND

Soya

There's an air of mysticism about this place. It's said that the last 32 Portuguese families in Maluku were driven to this mountain village in the early 17th century; they held onto their Catholic faith until finally converted to Protestantism. The old church in Soya was built by the Portuguese in 1817. Nearby are huge boulders surrounding a square, once a *baileo*. From the church, turn left and follow a small, twisting footpath, keeping to the right for 15 minutes to the top of Gunung Serimau. If you find the right vantage point, the view from here takes in the long inlet that separates the two peninsulas. On Gunung Serimau there's a foot-high sacred stone chair surrounded by a hedge, believed to be where the first *raja* sat. The trench surrounding the throne area was dug by the Dutch. A WW II concrete pillbox, overlooking Ambon Bay, stands 10 meters away. In a slope in back of the throne is the *tampayang keramat*, a clay water urn which never goes dry. It's visited by locals seeking good fortune, a cure for illness, or a perfect marriage partner. Locals planning to leave the area will take water from the urn to give themselves protection wherever they go. The original urn was stolen in 1980, replaced by the present one.

To reach Soya, take a *bemo* from Ambon. If you want to walk, a red clay path leads southeast of Ambon up to this village (two hours) through a countryside full of steep-sided valleys and rainy hills covered in buffalo grass, palm groves, and Amboina conifers.

Hitulama And Vicinity

Thirty km north of Ambon is the oldest Islamic *kampung* on the island; some believe it was founded by Arab or Javanese traders as early as the 11th century. The Portuguese landed at Hitu in the 16th century; you can still see the ruins of their first trading post. The *kapal motor* for northern Ceram leaves from Hitulama. The section of coastline from Hitu to Liang is very rugged; a fairly good road leads east to **Mamala**, where an unusual traditional event takes place each year at the end of *Ramadan*. Now a form of ritualized warfare, in *sapulidi* (broom-fighting) combatants whip each other with coconut-fiber brooms. A *dukun* treats the open wounds with Mamala oil, which is said to have almost magical curative qualities.

From Mamala, proceed northeast to **Morela**. Though there doesn't even seem to be a trail along parts of this coast, persevere. East of Morela is the old stone fortress of **Kapahala**, captured by the Dutch in 1646. Follow the track into a hilly area past weirdly shaped caves and bizarre rock formations, finally ascending stone stairs to the fortress, protected on three sides by a precipitous drop. Inside are graves of Kapahala's suicidal defenders.

Hila

A village of great tradition 12 km west of Hitulama on a bumpy road, or a Rp1000 (45-km, 1.5 hour) minibus ride from Ambon. The air is heavy with the scent of mace, nutmeg, and cloves, laid out on *tikar* in the streets to dry. The people of Hila venerate several Portuguese helmets, looking upon them as protective mascots and sources of strength. The entire village and its 300 screaming children adopt you. A Christian church here, built in 1772, features a Dutch-inscribed plaque.

The Banda Islands

Nine small volcanic islands 160 km southeast of Ambon on the northeast fringe of the Banda Sea, the Banda Group became world famous in the 17th-19th centuries as the original Spice Islands of the Dutch East Indies. These islands played a gigantic role in Indonesia's early history. To acquire control of the nutmeg trade, in 1619 the ruthless 31-year-old Dutch Governor-General Jan Pieterszoon Coen exterminated Banda's indigenous population—one of the blackest days in Dutch colonial history.

Now comprising the southernmost islands of the Central Maluku District and governed from Ambon, the two main islands are close together and you can get around them easily by *prahu*. There is magnificent scenery, beautiful sandy beaches, puffing volcanos, easygoing accommodations, crumbling Dutch forts and ruined mansions, one of the finest harbors in the archipelago, and peerless coral gardens and reefs.

The Bandas receive a trickle of travelers and odd adventurers. Wealthy tourists, retracing "the footsteps of Magellan," arrive on the luxury cruise ship *Lindblad Explorer*. As yet uncorrupted by tourism, there are few vehicles on the islands; one will meet you at the airport. Theft is practically unknown. Electricity is very sporadic; the generator is turned on at 1800 or 2100 and is always shut off by 0600.

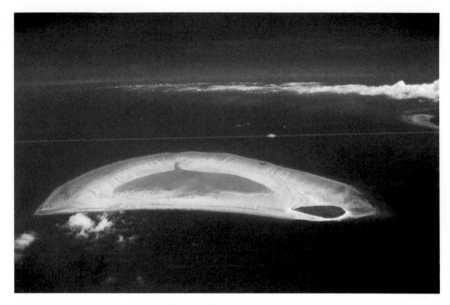

A coral reef off one of the Tanimbar Islands, Maluku

Banda is home to the best-known commercial species of nutmeg, *Myristica fragrans.* The tree, which can grow eight to 12 meters in height, is always in bloom, and the fruit ripens year-round. The islands remain the most important world producer of nutmeg, exporting about 500 tons per year. These islands derive their name from the Javanese word *bandau,* meaning "united"; another interpretation traces the origin to Nusa Banda, "Islands of Wealth."

History

For centuries the Bandanese sold their spices to such traditional regional trading partners as the Bugis, Chinese, and Arabs, receiving in exchange medicine, ceramics, and *batik* and other textiles. The demand for spices as preservatives accelerated in Europe to such an extent that by the 16th century expeditions were dispatched in search of the source. The Portuguese captain Antonio d'Abreu discovered the Bandas in 1511, inaugurating a profitable Bandanese-Portuguese trade which lasted nearly 100 years. Under the auspices of the Dutch East Indies Co., in 1609 Admiral Pieter Verhoeffe brought a war fleet of 13 ships and a thousand men into Bandaneira's harbor to impose an airtight monopoly on all spices leaving the Bandas. After cursory negotiations, the admiral began constructing a massive fort upon the foundations of a former Portuguese fort—a premature and provocative act. Under pretense of further negotiations, the Bandanese lured the unarmed Dutch into an ambush in which the admiral and 45 of his entourage were killed.

Jan Pieterszoon Coen, of whom Dutch historians have said "his name reeks of blood," retaliated and gave no quarter. Invading the Bandas from Batavia with a force of 2,000 men, Coen's mercenaries rampaged through the islands razing villages. Two-thirds of the population was wiped out, the remainder sold into slavery or driven into the hills to die of exposure. Only 1,000 Bandanese survived in the archipelago out of an original population of 15,000.

Coen began setting up a closed horticultural preserve to control the growing and sale of spices. To keep supply down and prices up, nutmeg groves on all but the two main islands were destroyed. Coen carved up the remaining gardens into 68 concessions, or *perken*, which were offered free to Dutch planters called *perkeniers*—mostly rogues and drifters. To work the nutmeg trees on these now unpopulated islands, the holder of each land grant was provided with 1,500 imported slaves. The Dutch East Indies Co. controlled demand and fixed prices, ensuring a guaranteed income for the *perkeniers* and astronomical profits for the company.

During the Napoleonic Wars the English, with great foresight, transplanted prime nutmeg seedlings to their colonies in Sumatra, Penang, Colombo, and Calcutta. The

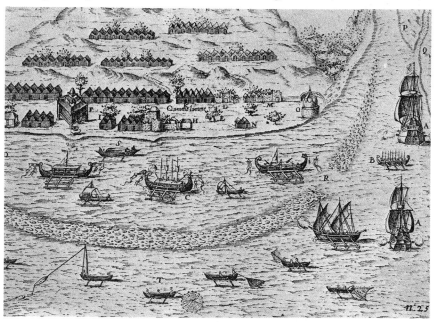

Portuguese ships arrive in the Banda Islands, 16th century

price nutmeg and mace could command on the world market was drastically reduced, and the Bandas became an economic backwater. Rampant graft and larceny finally drove the Dutch East Indies Co. into bankruptcy in the 1790s with a staggering debt of 12 million guilders.

When the new Dutch colonial administration took over the affairs of the shattered company in the early 1800s, it began to institute long overdue reforms. Slavery was abolished in 1862, the plantation workers replaced with imported convicts and gangs of Javanese coolies. The *perkeniers* gained title to their landholdings in the 1870s, but managed their finances so poorly their *perken* were purchased at rock-bottom prices by Chinese and Arab competitors, and by an official government agency created for that purpose. The late 19th and early 20th centuries saw Dutch colonialists sponsoring churches, schools, and public works. In contrast to its stormy beginnings, these tiny islands, under the paternalistic rule of the Dutch, returned to a state of relative peace and prosperity which lasted into the mid-20th century.

By the end of the Japanese occupation, the once beautiful and high-yield nutmeg estates had fallen into sad disrepair. The Dutch at last gave up their Indonesian possessions in 1949, and the Banda Islands lost their importance in the international trade arena forever. During the Sukarno era, the Bandas were associated with the Central Malukan rebellion instigated by the Ambonese, and the nutmeg gardens were nationalized. The whole spice enterprise, rife with corruption, fell into further neglect. The industry has been only partially rehabilitated.

BANDANEIRA

This quiet, peaceful town, today just a few short streets filled with Mediterranean-style homes and shops, was once the Dutch administrative center for the whole region, famous all over the Dutch East Indies for its beauty. Along Jl. Pelabuhan are the grand mansions of the *perkeniers*. Around town are other examples of gracious Dutch colonial architecture, most crumbling into ruin. Two resident cassowaries prance down the middle of the main street—no traffic, so why not? Bandaneira's landlocked harbor, with no visible outlet, was once one of the finest in the Indies. The Merpati flight from Ambon to Banda costs about Rp60,000, departing twice weekly (if enough passengers). There are no banks or fancy restaurants in Banda. Avoid any dealings with the local *imigrasi* office, absolutely the worst in Indonesia.

In the center of town, the **Dutch Reform Church** (1852) overlooks the neglected park surrounding Fort Nassau. The lovely church is a severe structure that replaced an earlier building destroyed in an earthquake. The church has a clock that doesn't work; apparently it clicked its last the very moment of the Japanese invasion 47 years ago. Near the church are a Christian and a Chinese cemetery with lichen-covered inscriptions; the Dutch governor of Banda is buried here. The magnificent **Gov-**

ernor's Palace was once the Dutch *controlleur's* mansion, built in the 1820s with giant granite paving slabs, bright floor tiles, shiny marble, heavily carved beams, huge wooden doors, and shuttered windows. Behind the building, in the garden, is a statue of the Dutch King Willem III. Ask to see the inscription by a 19th-century French prisoner who scratched a lament on the wall. Along Jl. Pelabuhan. Here are the giant *perkeniers*' stone mansions, occupied now by the military or police. One of the grandest of these waterfront buildings is the former **Harmonie Club**, the center of Dutch social life, though today the building is in ruins.

The **Mohammed Hatta Museum** is housed in a building once occupied by the freedom-fighter Dr. Mohammed Hatta. It contains exile memorabilia, as well as the desk and pens he used. The **Rumah Badya** museum, formerly a *perkenier* mansion converted into a mosque, contains artifacts tracing the whole nutmeg culture, plus paintings, big ceramic vases, and old coins.

Fort Belgica is a pentagonal-shaped Dutch fort built in 1611 on the ruins of a 16th-century Portuguese fort, above Bandaneira about 500 meters from the harbor. Although overgrown, the structure is still standing and in fairly good condition considering it was last restored in 1935. Also visit the overgrown, crumbling walls of **Fort Nassau**, below Fort Belgica near the church. Just a gateway, a rusting cannon, and three walls remain of this fort built in 1609 by the Dutch.

Volcanoes

The main harbor of the Bandas is dominated by the **Gunung Api** volcano rising 676 meters out of the sea. Though its main crater is thought to be dormant, the volcano is constantly puffing away and has a treacherous history. On 2 April 1778, a violent eruption was accompanied by an earthquake, hurricane, and tsunami. Fires flared up all over Pulau Neira, destroying 500,000 nutmeg trees and nearly obliterating the town of Bandaneira. In 1820 another eruption occurred. Today you can reach the rim of the crater by first taking a motorboat or canoe from Neira harbor, then climbing up a 500-meter-long footpath; two hours roundtrip. From the top is a splendid view over the town and the whole Banda chain.

Also climb Pulau Neira's 250-meter-high mountain, **Gunung Papenberg**, on a poorly maintained trail, some sections of which have stone steps. The trail begins beyond town and anyone can show you the way. On the side of Gunung Papenberg are the ruined mansions and sheds of the rich Lans family, as well as the dilapidated estates of two other *perkenier* families. Ask the locals about the springs on Gunung Kele, known locally as **Airmata Cilubintang**.

North Maluku

TERNATE

The town of Ternate, now the administrative center for North Maluku, has clung to the side of a smoking volcano since the 1500s. Lying on a flat strip of land on the southeast side of the island, Ternate is a picturesque seaport, the volcano rising majestically above the main street filled with *bemo* and *bendi*. Formerly the capital of the most powerful sultanate east of Ujung Pandang, Ternate today is the second-largest town, after Ambon, in eastern Indonesia and a major shipping center. Though Ambon is more cosmopolitan, Ternate is quieter and more relaxing—except for the earth tremors at night. Ternate's fervent Muslims are in general generous, warm and friendly. Wander down to the harbor at the southern end of town from where you can easily make out the island of Halmahera. South of the harbor area is **Bastion**, where you can catch boats to the neighboring island of Tidore.

The **Sultan's Palace** is above the town on Jl. Babulluh past Benteng Oranye on the road to the airport. Also known as the *kedatan*, the palace has been converted to a museum and is open to the public. The original structure dates from 1234. Take a *bemo* from the Jl. Revolusi station, then walk up the majestic flight of steps to the verandah. Among the royal regalia and heavy atmosphere of decay, you can see by spe-

Man in the middle

Dawn at Halmahera, Maluku

cial request the extraordinary jewelled crown that Drake described in his 1579 visit, though the priceless jewels and ornaments have been replaced by cheap glass stones. There are more forts in and around Ternate than in any other locale of similar size in Indonesia. These crumbling, overgrown ruins once guarded the valuable clove plantations. **Benteng Oranye** is a big fortified trading post right on the edge of town, opposite the *bemo* station. Built by the Durch in 1606-1607, it is now a military complex. The stately fort still has mounted cannon and its VOC seal intact. Informal tours are conducted by the soldiers. From Benteng Oranye it is a pleasant two-km walk north of town to **Benteng Toloko,** just past Desa Dufa on the right. This small, well-maintained Portuguese fort, erected on a hill by d'Albuquerque in 1512, is on the road to the airport. The fort's 16th-century official seal is still quite visible. Take a *bemo* along the road in front of Peng. Yamin to serene, unfinished **Bentang Kayu Merah** (1510) at the south of town.

A fifteen-minute, 11-lm *bemo* ride from town down a lovely road to Kastela is **Bentang Kastela,** erected by the Portuguese in 1522. More than just a fort, Kastela was the center of a town called Ave. The wrecked fortification's gateways still stand, and the remains of the hopistal can be seen in the thick undergrowth. An old Potuguese well nearby is still used by the locals. The ramparts at the circumference of the town are also clearly visible. Fort Kastela, thought at the time to be impregnable, was abandoned only 50 years after it was built. It now protects a papaya patch, and the main road around the island dissects it. From the shore of the village you can see Pulau Maitara between Ternate and Tidore.

TIDORE

The soaring peaks of Tidore and Ternate are only two of ten conical volcanoes which form a line off the west coast of Halmahera. With an area about 78 square km, slightly larger than its sister island, Tidore lies just 1.5 km southwest of Ternate. The southern part of the island is occupied almost entirely by an extinct volcano peak, **Gunung Matubu.** Below the 300-meter level coffee, fruit and tobacco are cultivated. Tidor's northern half consists mostly of hills, with a few level strips along the coast. With its relaxed people and many skilled smiths and craftsmen, Tidore has a completey different feel to it than Ternate. The natives, originally of Alfuro stock, have intermingled considerably with outsiders. Though Islam arrived relatively late—around 1430—the Tidorese are now all Muslim. The only accommodation on the island is in the main town of Soasiu. The best days to visit Tidore are market days, Tuesday and Saturday, when the island's towns are a spectacle of color and transportation is plentiful.

Irian Jaya

Introduction

Irian Jaya is one of the last places on the planet where whole great swaths of earth can still be described as totally wild. There are people here who have resolutely refused to move into any sort of "civilization" as defined by white Europeans. Creatures once thought extinct elsewhere on the globe seem now to flourish here; the Irian mountains, swamps, and jungles are filled with animals and plants unknown and unclassified by Western science. Though tourism has increased markedly since the late 1980s, there are still plenty of places in Irian Jaya that seem to bear no human footprint at all. The territory features wilder landscapes and more impenetrable, treacherous jungle than any other tropical region in the world, including the Amazon Basin.

Most of Irian Jaya is mountainous, with a high central backbone extending for 650 km, dividing Irian into south and north. Some mountains are so high planes must fly between them to avoid turbulence. The highest, Puncak Jaya, is 5,039 meters. Although situated just four degrees below the equator, a number of mountaintops are permanently covered in snow and ice. The climate varies through the highlands. One valley might suffer through a dry season as a second is drenched in the wet, a third receiving rainfall evenly distributed throughout the year. The southern lowlands have a very distinct dry season; in Merauke it sometimes doesn't rain for five straight months.

Because of its phenomenal rainfall—in some places up to 1,000 centimeters per annum—Irian Jaya possesses some of Indonesia's largest rivers. In the south and southwest, they've created mosaic river systems winding through a million square kilometers of mangrove swamps, casuarina groves, and tidal forests. For centuries highland peoples burnt off forests to flush game and prepare the ground for agriculture. This created the great highland grass plains of the Baliem Valley and the Wissel Lakes Country.

The whole territory holds immense fascination for the naturalist. Freshwater and terrestrial vertebrates are nearly all of the Australian type. The coral islands east of the Bird's Head Peninsula in Cendrawasih Bay are famous as feeding grounds for sea turtles and *dugong*, and serve as important nesting sites for seabirds. On land there are cuscus, bandicoots, snakes, tortoises, frilled lizards, and giant monitor lizards. Tree kangaroos with gray-brown coats live in the higher regions. The phalanger has fox-like ears and a long bushy tail. There are 11 crocodile ranches in Irian, each with 300-400 crocodiles; their skins are purchased by such high fashion houses as Gucci and Christian Dior and exported mostly to France.

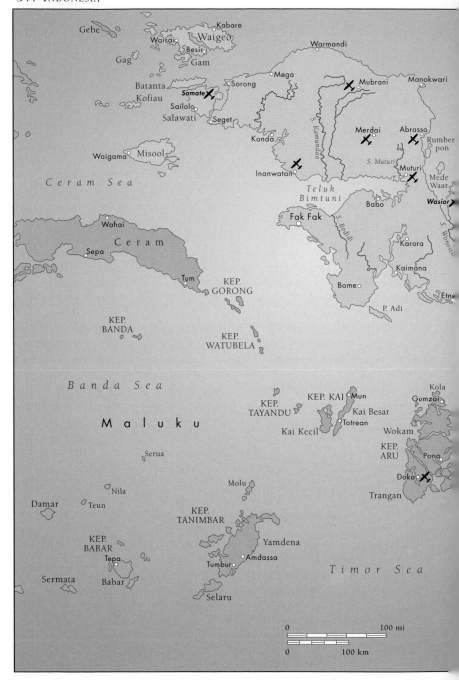

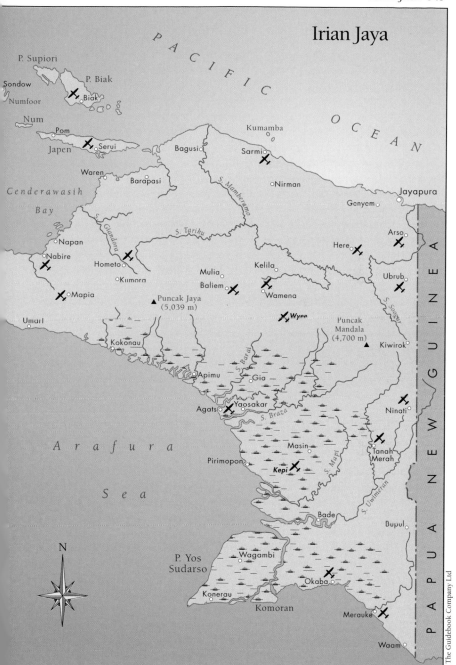

Irian Jaya

Negritos settled New Guinea beginning perhaps 30,000 years ago. During Neolithic times the Melanesians arrived from the east, bringing with them the bow and arrow, the ax blade, pottery, crop plants, the calendar, cowrie shells for money, tattooing, betel-chewing, decorative woodcarving, outrigger canoes and seagoing vessels, the dog and the pig, men's and women's clubhouses, ritualized cannibalism, and warfare. The Malukan spice trade brought Arab, Chinese, and Malay traders were the first to arrive. The Portuguese stumbled upon the island in 1512, the Spanish in 1526, and in 1605 the first Dutch ship, captained by William Janz, reached the mainland, where nine of his crew were eaten by tribesmen.

The Spanish, British, and Germans all tried to establish colonies in the territory, but most ended in disaster. Western New Guinea was officially annexed by the Dutch in 1848. They built their first capital at Manokwari in 1898, then garrisoned men at Fakfak on the west coast and Merauke to the southwest. A settlement at the present site of Jayapura was founded in 1910; this was a political move. The town, located 22 km from the New Guinea border, laid real claim to the western half of the island—keeping it from the Germans, who at the time controlled land east of the border. The highlands of western New Guinea were not penetrated until 1933, when Catholic, Lutheran, and Seventh-day Adventist proselytizers began creeping into the interior. More than a few ended their missions in the stewpot. Well into this century maps of Netherlands New Guinea still included great blank patches in the center marking territory unknown to any white person. By 1938 Hollandia, as Jayapura was then called, had a population of only 800 Indonesians and 400 Dutch.

World War II swirled furiously around this island. By the spring of 1944, General Douglas MacArthur's forces had captured most of the Bismarck archipelago and the Admiralty Islands and neutralized the advance Japanese base at Rabaul. MacArthur then moved westward on the island of New Guinea to prepare for his next campaign, the Philippines.

American forces stormed the beach near Jayapura one April morning in 1944, meeting only token resistance. Over the coming months, Hollandia became a gigantic staging area. Since MacArthur had obliterated most of the coastal towns during the war to uproot the Japanese, as a war reparation gesture he built a new town on the north coast in 1944.

In MacArthur's airy hilltop residence, which overlooked the whole magnificent harbor, he planned the liberation of the Philippines. By October, a huge armada of over 500 ships rendezvoused in Hollandia's harbor. Eyewitnesses reported that the fleet, interconnected by catwalks with thousands of glowing lamps, looked like a great city floating on the water. United States Army camps, where whole divisions once bivouacked, now lie smothered in jungle, and a few rusting landing barges on the beach at Hamadi are the only remnants left. Most of the hulks were long ago turned into spatulas and eggbeaters by Hong Kong merchants.

The Indonesian Republic's claim to the territory was based on the historic half-truth that West New Guinea once lay under the suzerainty of the Malukan sultan of Tidore. The Indonesians also argued that *all* the former Netherlands East Indies were promised to the republic in truce agreements. After years of futile haggling, in the early 1960s Sukarno launched his *konfrontasi* campaign to oust the Dutch. In August 1969, Dutch West New Guinea officially became a part of Indonesia.

THE PEOPLE

Irian Jaya is Indonesia's most sparsely populated province. Only the areas around Manokwari on the east coast of the Vogelkop, the Schouten Islands in Geelvink Bay, the north coast near Jayapura, and several fertile highland valleys feature relatively high population densities. Most regions have fewer than six people per square km or are totally uninhabited. The native Papuans are divided into the Negroids of the high valleys and plateaus whose skins are brown and black, and the coastal and foothills Papuans, a blending of the Melanesian and Negroid races. There's a giddy variety of tribes and over 300 distinct languages, with no one language intelligible to more than 150,000 people. Some languages are spoken by as few as 2,000 people.

Some tribes continue to resist any contact with the outside world. Negritos of the purest blood and a few little-known, extremely isolated pygmy tribes still live in the rough Sudirman Range, raising crops and pigs on land as high as 3,000 meters. Central highlanders still live a largely Stone Age existence. Irianese crafts are less affected by commercialism than in Papau New Guinea. The Asmat of the Casuarina Coast in the south carve striking wooden shields, ancestral and serpent totem poles, dugout canoes, prows, paddles, masks, soul ships, ironwood shields and spears, sago pounders, and grub trays. Traditional colors are red, black, and white.

GETTING THERE

There's no land entry into Irian Jaya. A route popular with travelers is to depart from Cairns in Australia for Port Moresby or Vanimo in Papua New Guinea, where one can apply for an Indonesian tourist visa. From Port Moresby, fly or make your way overland to Vanimo, then hop another flight over to Jayapura. Ujung Pandang is a favorite departure point for Biak and Jayapura. The best months to travel in Irian Jaya are June and July; the weather is drier and it's easier then to find guides.

Jayapura, the provincial capital of Irian Jaya, is not an official tourist gateway into Indonesia, so a 30-day Indonesian visa is required upon arrival from another country. However, foreign tourists may enter the territory via Biak, an island off the northwest coast, and receive the usual automatic 60-day tourist pass. If you intend to enter Jayapura from Papua New Guinea, a visa is fairly easy to obtain from the Indonesian consulate in either Port Moresby or Vanimo. You'll need an onward ticket out of Jayapura and two passport photos; the visa takes two days. From Jayapura to Vanimo, get a

The Dani people of Irian Jaya

Papua New Guinea visa in the consulate in Jayapura or Jakarta. Remember that relations between Indonesia and Papau New Guinea run hot and cold; you can never be sure of the consulate's policy until you actually arrive in either Irian or Papau New Guinea or hear from another traveler who's visited either spot.

When in Irian Jaya itself, you need a *surat jalan* from the police in Biak or Jayapura to visit such places as the Baliem Valley, Agats, Nabire, Oksibil, Merauke, and anywhere near the border with Papau New Guinea. Without proper documentation, travelers may be shoved right back on the plane. You can receive a *surat jalan* quickly and cheaply in Jayapura or Biak. Or obtain a *surat jalan* for Irian Jaya in Jakarta at MABAK, Turun Walikota, Jl. Truno Joyo, Blok M. You must also have your *surat jalan* stamped in the Jayapura police station, even if you've already obtained it in Jakarta. Expect to pay an "administrative fee" of approximately Rp4000. All areas you might visit should be written on the *surat jalan*. Check in with the police within 24 hours of arrival in each town or village. The police in Jayapura can tell you which areas are off-limits.

Jayapura

Known as Hollandia during the reign of the Dutch, this city was the capital of Netherlands New Guinea. At the time it was a small, attractive town in an amphitheater-like setting, with red-tiled roofs sheltering Dutch civil servants. The Dutch put in permanent hardtop roads, expensive dock facilities, and sturdy public buildings. When Irian Jaya fell into the hands of the Indonesian Republic it became Sukarnopurna, then Kota Baru; in the late 1960s it was renamed Jayapura, or "City of Victory," to commemorate its "liberation" from the Dutch.

Located on the northeast coast of Irian Jaya, this thriving, noisy, sweltering provincial capital is wedged into a flat strip of land between steep coastal hills and the sea. The picture-postcard harbor is surrounded by perpetually green hills. Most houses are built on slopes, while the administrative portion occupies the level region beneath. This area contains all the worst features of a modern Indonesian city—dirty streets, polluting traffic, garish blaring cassette shops.

Peopled by an extraordinary mix of gentle Melanesians, immigrant merchants and laborers, and Javanese bureaucrats, in this city Southeast Asia and the Pacific meet. On the streets you'll see tribesmen, vendors with Javanese-style *pikulan,* Minang shopowners, expat oil and timber men, Bugis fishermen, sailors from Makassar, and a trickle of travelers. The town is dead from 1200 to 1600, when most shops and offices close, but in the evenings Japapura's four main streets pulsate with life. Prices are relatively high and it's difficult to bargain. For magnificent views over Jayapura and its harbor, share the charter of a minibus up to **Pemancar Stasiun TVRI**, a steep two-km climb from the highway to the top of a mountain between Jayapura and Hamadi. For nightlife, Jayapura has three discos: the New Scorpio, Tropical, and Chrystals.

Jayapura is still a fairly unpleasant necessity for getting to the Baliem Valley. The police will tell you the *surat jalan* permit office is open 24 hours a day, but don't believe it. Once in, however, it's quite a painless process—you can be in and out within half an hour. Make sure you bring all the relevant juju. The *surat jalan* is now free, but you could always make a donation towards a new office typewriter.

There are three markets in Jayapura. At **Jaya Supermarket** buy cold New Zealand apples and American ice cream. Most craft shops are concentrated in Jayapura's Pasar Ampera, on Jl. Polimak, and at the museum in Abepura. Some of the town's travel agencies and hotels also feature small shops. Irianese *batik* is sold in **Toko Batik Khas Irian** near Disco Chrystals on Jl. Percetakan. The **tourist office** is located in the building to the left of Gedung Gubernor on Jl. Sua Sio, tel. (0967) 21381, open 0730-1500, Friday until 1100, Sunday closed. Take a *bemo* from town (Rp250). Change money at the **Bank Ekspor-Impor**, Jl. Jen. A. Yani. If you have a social visa you need to get your *surat jalan* from Polda police headquarters, Jl. Sam Ratulangi next to GKI Mess (open 0730-1200). This is also where you obtain your permit to visit such points in the interior as Ilaga, Oksibil, Enarotali, and Wamena. Open 0800-2400: you'll need to fill out forms and hand over four passport photos and Rp1000. Get photos at **Happy Photo Studio**, Jl. Jen. A. Yani near Hotel Matoa, or at **Variant Photo Studio** near the Triton.

BIAK

Hot and bright, like glittering sequins, Biak is also known as Kota Karang, "City of Coral." Located just one degree south of the equator on the island of the same name, Biak is a travelers' way station and the easternmost international gateway to Indonesia. An easy, lazy, friendly town, Biak would be all but comatose if it weren't for the screech of jets flying over six or seven times a day. The city serves as a big Indonesian naval base, a supply center for offshore oil rigs in the Sorenarwa Straits and Irian Bay, and a major port for Irian Jaya's tuna industry. Biak also played an important role in General MacArthur's WW II island-hopping campaign through the southwest Pacific.

Today Biak is a typical middle-sized Outer Island town, with restaurants, Chinese supermarkets, and three cinemas. Because of the midday heat, shops open at 0530 or 0600. Biak was well appreciated by the Dutch; even today, everyone seems to speak the language. It's a bird-smuggling center; you can see all manner of exotic birds at Pasar Panir, including "protected" bird-of-paradise skins from Serui. Also for sale are live lorikeets and ravens. Biak woodcarvings are sold at the airport terminal shop and at workshops in the village of **Swapodibo**. On Biak you can buy all the usual Papuan artifacts available on the mainland—stone axes, bows, arrows. They're much cheaper here than in the Baliem Valley.

War Relics

Exploiting the successes of the Hollandia campaign, on 27 May 1944 the Hurricane Task Force of the U.S. Sixth Army landed at Bosnik on Biak Island. The Japanese defense was based on a brilliant use of unfriendly terrain. The Japanese purposely withheld their main forces until U.S. troops had advanced to the rugged limestone hills beyond the beaches. Then, from the cliffs and caves overlooking the advancing Allied columns, the Japanese launched a savage counterattack, succeeding in driving a block between the beachhead and the invading force. After a week of bitter, heavy fighting, the Japanese retreated to a network of enormous interlocking caves known in American military annals as The Sump. During the night the Japanese left their cave positions to launch harassing attacks; by day they fired mortars on the newly captured airdromes. The Americans finally poured aviation gas and TNT down the enemy's long command tunnel, then lit a match: thousands of Japanese soldiers were instantly incinerated.

The cave system, Gua Nippon, is now a tourist attraction. Once a year, Japanese come to pay homage to the 6,000 who died here. To see both Bosnik and The Sump, charter a taxi at the airport for Rp5000 per hour. Or you can reach the caves by walking up a path about 30 minutes from the far side of the airport. More remnants of the war lie all over the beaches and highlands of Biak. Rusted hulls of trucks, jeeps, tanks, and planes remain where they were once abandoned, covered now by flowering creepers. A line of tanks, covered with shells and coral, has been pressed into service as a pier; torpedos have been hollowed out and used as gongs. Bunkers on cliffs face the beaches of the Mokmer Airdrome, and a nearby Quonset hut houses a large family.

AROUND THE ISLAND

Beaches

Biak is primarily agricultural, which has helped preserve the island's virgin beaches and unpolluted waters. From the town of Biak, take a minibus eight km to rocky Yendidori Beach. About 26 km from Biak (Rp600 by minibus) is **Bosnik**, the first Dutch capital of Biak. On the way, don't miss the incredible Telaga Biru ("Blue Lagoon"). Bosnik is a beautiful white-sand beach with palm trees; from here you can see the 17 islands of the Owi Group to the southeast. Near Bosnik is a bird park (*taman burung*) featuring birds from Irian Jaya, including the bird of paradise. Fifteen minutes by taxi past Bosnik the good road ends. Walk one km more and arrive in **Sabah**, a quiet, untouristed fishing village.

In Bosnik you can stay in the **Merau Hotel**, a huge accommodation owned by the Japanese. Down the road is a public beach with a pavilion. This is where the Americans first landed in 1944; see rusted old American landing craft. Children sell shells. If you start from here by roofed boat, it takes only one hour to reach Auki Island, where there are numerous good places to snorkel. Full-day rate is Rp150,000 for up to 15-20 people. Leave at 0800 and return at 1700. There's a nice pool for swimming in the middle of a reef, the coral like undulating mountains of red, green, blue, white, and brown.

Korim Beach

On the north coast, 40 km from Biak, the Bay of Korim is surrounded by rocks and jungle. Ride on a well-paved road through tropical landscapes of Melanesian hill villages, tunnels of butterflies, and tall dead trees with orchids perched on top. Sleep in a house on the beach, or ask the *kepala kampung* for a bed in the very traditional *kampung*. From Biak it's Rp1500 by *bemo* to Korim (one hour); go early, before it rains, when *bemo umum* fill up fast. Near Korim visit the Japanese caves, where human skeletons are displayed. War freaks should seek out John Vandevijver, a half-Dutchman living halfway between Biak and Korim (ask for the *belanda*); he knows a couple of unusual places. Also on the north coast, accessible by dirt track, is the **Biak Nature Reserve**, which protects species of cockatoos and parrots. On **Pulau Sipiori**, two hours away by boat, is another sizable nature reserve.

Warso is a small village northeast of Korim, located at the mouth of a river. From there you can charter a canoe or motorboat to explore upriver. See two waterfalls and exotic birdlife, watch villagers forage from boats or along the banks, visit remote wildlife sanctuaries.

The 150 reefs around Biak offer some of the greatest dropoffs outside the Cayman Islands, some starting only a meter from shore. Together with the big islands of Supiori and Numfoor, there are 43 islands in the Biak-Numfoor District.

The Central Highlands

In the Central Highlands mountain rivers have cut magnificent valleys that are home to hundreds of thousands of people. Because the peaks are higher in the west, the Baliem Valley is more spectacular than its easter counterpart, the Wahgi in Papua New Guinea. The remarkable quiltwork of sweet potato gardens gives the valley an incredibly ordered look. Natives in the area engage in a form of agriculture that is quite different from the slash-and-burn system practiced elsewhere on the island.

Although volcanos are found at the north end of the island there are none in the Central Highlands. Earthquakes are likewise very rare. The Baliem Valley offers an equatorial climate, without seasons, where the steady pressure of the tradewinds makes for rain and sunshine every day. There are no high winds, torrential downpours, or droughts. Because the Baliem climate is so equitable and mild, the natives cannot blame natural disasters on weather-identified supernatural powers, and thus are not a particularly superstititous people.

The pig is all-important in the highlanders' ceremonial and economic life—a crucial part of their social organization, and a major source of protein. The Dani don't eat amphibians or reptiles but catch and consume many insects and almost any sort of mammal, marsupial, or bird, including bats and cormorants. Rats are considered a delicacy, given to young boys who open them with bone needles to remove their entrails. Although the Dani, the area's best known tribe, are not cannibals, the practice has been known to occur among tribes in the southern valleys. In the 1960s an Aso Lokopals raiding party was cut off and wiped out by a group of Hisaro. The twenty dead men were roasted in a big rock fire and ritually eaten. Their bones were placed in the forest on taboo ground, considered extremely dangerous because of its high concentration of angry, vengeful ghosts.

Missionaries were the first outsiders to enter the interior, attempting settlement as early as the 1940s. Many have been and are sensitive, intelligent, and dedicated. Success in conversion has varied from tribe to tribe. In some cases, barely comprehensible Christian doctrines were force-fed to Papuans who already practiced their own proud, integrated spiritual beliefs. Sometimes spectacular shifts to Christianity occurred; other times the missionaries were pretty much ignored. Occasionally, they were eaten.

Since 1977, missionaries have built over 800 schools, 130 hospitals, and 240 first-aid posts, and their private air services are the most extensive on the island. Due to their efforts and those of the Indonesian government, schools all over the central highlands now teach Bahasa Indonesia. The greatest missionary successes came in discouraging war. Only after an area was rendered "safe" by missionaries would government officials and soldiers arrive. Yet the missionaries also brought disease and, to the horror of historians and anthropologists, encouraged the destruction of priceless works of art, fetishes, and handicrafts.

Mummy of a Dani ancestor

*Dani
war dance*

TREKKING

Irian Jaya's highlands are home to very sensitive, fossilized, wholly intact traditional cultures, so visitors must be on their very best behavior. Just because the natives are half-naked, it doesn't mean visitors may bathe naked in the rivers. Though women wear just a G-string girdle, there are involved rules governing how it is worn, according to the woman's age and marital or societal status. Without this scant covering, highland Irianese women feel naked.

If heading into remote areas, take plenty of small bills. Minibuses from Wamena only venture 14 km, as far as Yiwika. Motorcycles are expensive, hard to arrange, and impractical. Your feet will take you to many more places. There are hundreds of kilometers of good hiking trails linking villages throughout the central highlands. Streams not easily forded will have bridges of some sort. Conditions vary widely, depending on terrain and weather. Hiking can be like a Sunday stroll through the park or it can mean clambering over steep slippery rock faces, sliding down muddy paths, and wobbling over dangerous bridges.

If considering a trek into the Baliem Valley it's a good idea to buy most of your provisions in Jayapura. Carry tins and packets of noodles on the plane as hand luggage; don't forget cigarettes and chocolate. Cheap costume jewelry, ballpoint pens, rice, and salt make good gifts. The best present is probably the common safety pin, or *pineti*, which is the Swiss army knife of the Dani culture. They have about 12 different uses for the thing—fishhook, decoration, surgical tool, wood gouger. They seem to like velcro, too. Bring good footwear, a hat, sunglasses, wind- and rainproof gear, a medical kit that includes sterile pads and bandages, light clothing, and a warm sweater and windbreaker for the cool highland nights.

On Pigs

When Arkilaus suggested we buy a pig to cook from the villagers neither of us had any notion to resist him; and presently a half-grown pig was herded in. Arkilaus bargained it down to twenty thousand rupiah, about seven pounds. The owner came with us, to carry the pig over the steep bits, and despite its gentle smile and trusting look I couldn't help thinking of al its roasted meat. The pigman heaved it over his shoulders when we got to the rocky bits of the mountains and released it to trot along beside us when the slope smoothed out. From Iniyei onwards the mountains got worse, running from steep slopes to sheer razorbacks. Even Arkilaus was now flagging behind Yusup and the pigman, who knew the routes, and held the muddy ground well with their splayed toes.

Pigs were at the center of Dani life. The furry grey animal running along beside us was the most important thing they possessed. Some men we saw had lost the top halves of their ears, most likely due to the loss of a favourite pig. In total misery at his desertion a man would hack off his ears with a bamboo knife. Pigs were treated very much like people: sometimes Dani men would whisper into their ears, urging them to be good and get fat. They were often fed on cooked food, and allowed to sleep close to the fire at night. Like children the pigs were considered to have souls, but to be unaware of the religious taboos they should observe; so they were forgiven for rooting in the spirit gardens, or eating food forbidden to the owner's clan. For all that, pigs were killed in huge numbers when necessary, which was only on special occasions.

Nothing could be done without slaughtering pigs. When war was to be waged, pigs were first consulted, then killed and offered to the ancestors to bring good luck. Pigs were the esssential part of the brideprice, and a man couldn't hope to get more than one wife unless he had a lot of them. The great gains, the most senior village elders, could get up to ten wives each if they had enough pigs. Boys couldn't be initiated without eating lots of pork, and first having a live piglet held in front of them to charm the bad spirits out of their chests. When the pigs had been killed the boys could go through mock battles, cold and hunger needed to make them into men. Funerals were also attended by slaughter: the spirit of the dead man was first appeased by being offered plenty of cooked meat, then driven out before he could lay hands on it by men rushing through the compound hurling rocks and shouting. The spirit then had to go and live in one of the Dani ghost-houses: mysterious square huts that only one foreigner had ever been allowed to enter, full of bundles of dried grass bound up to look like humans. If he came sneaking back to the compound to cause trouble he'd be shouted at and told "You go away!"; alternatively he could be called up to help with a war or a ceremony. Spirits were very much taken for granted by the Dani, and their incorporeal presence wasn't at all alarming.

Almost all the marriage, initiation and remembrance of the dead took place at once, in a great pigfeast held by an alliance of villagers every four or five years. The pigs that had been so carefully tended and fattened up were nearly all killed, and there followed three or four weeks of astonishing gluttony, during which some people might eat several whole pigs, being sick in between to fit more in. The more that was eaten the more favourably the ancestors would regard the village and the better would be the anticipated mariages or battles; which was fine for all the Dani, except for the pigs.

~ George Monbiot, Poisoned Arrows, 1988

GUIDES AND PORTERS

Guides and porters are usually easy to find in any village, *losmen,* or airport. Costs can vary widely. It's better to work on a day-by-day basis with village men who ask about Rp2000-3000 per day; a prearranged guide from Wamena will demand Rp60,000 for a five-day trek. Get advice on pay rates from local missionaries, teachers, police, and government officials. Don't expect an Irianese guide or porter to accompany you much more than a day's travel from his village; he might be afraid of old enemies. It's often taboo for them to climb a mountain, believing it will fall down and crush them; it could also be the forbidden home of ancestors.

Never force porters to walk later than they think wise. Mountain Irianese know best where to find good shelter and plentiful firewood. Small boys and young men will fetch water, light fires, cook breakfast, and erect tents; the older men won't. Be prepared to carry your own pack if prices escalate or your porter suddenly decides to return home.

Basket-weaving, Irian Jaya

The Baliem Valley

The Baliem Valley was "discovered" by a wealthy American explorer during a botanical and zoological expedition in 1938. He believed this 1,600-meter-high valley inhabited by a lost civilization. When the clouds cleared, the expedition members beheld a vast, beautifully tended garden of checkerboard squares with neat stone fences, clean-cut networks of canals, and meticulously terraced mountain slopes. The first outsiders to settle here were missionaries landed by floatplane in 1945 near Hetagima on the Baliem River. The Dutch established a settlement at Wamena in 1956, bringing in schoolteachers, new breeds of livestock, modern clothing, and metal tools. Wamena remained under Dutch control for just six short years, until Indonesia wrested West New Guinea from Holland in 1962. The year before, Harvard's Peabody Museum sponsored a major expedition to the Grand Baliem to document the area's stone age culture. This journey is documented in Peter Matthiessen's magnificent *Under the Mountain Wall.* Beyond the Baliem live other peoples, such as the Yali, Mek, and Kim Yal, some uncontacted until the 1960s and 1970s. Villagers here occasionally use human skulls as pillows; the Kim Yal were eating missionaries as recently as 1969.

WAMENA

Wamena is a study in cultural incongruities. Streets are gridded like any small Australian town but flow with very little traffic. In Wamena you'll find Dani tribesmen, Indonesian schoolboys, international aid workers, backpackers, tourists, missionaries, and the police, all strolling beneath cloud-wreathed mountain peaks. There are statues of Dani warriors here, penis gourds pointing proudly upward. Wamena is a Dani handicrafts and marketing center; there are an increasing number of traditional Dani fences and thatched compound entrances erected around town.

Still, it's odd that in a city that's the center of a pig-loving tribal culture the largest and most opulent building is a mosque. Restaurants here are run exclusively by Javanese and Sumatrans. Tribespeople are mustered for the occasional pig feast or as carriers for short walks around the valley, but these activities generate a pittance compared with the economic returns for Indonesians.

Wamena is a small town with row upon row of mission offices, schools, and what seems like hundreds of government offices, all sprawling across the flat Baliem Valley floor. As everything is flown in, prices are some of the highest in Indonesia. You can cut down on your costs if you eat in the markets and stay in the nearby villages. Wamena's market, bustling with farmers selling produce, is the town's premier tourist attraction. This is also the place to view Wamena's extraordinary mixture of cultures and customs—craggy Dani tribesmen, tall stately Minangs, Western-attired Javanese, curly-haired Ambonese. For additional entertainment, the military shows movies every night (Rp2000) and there are regular TV broadcasts. Almost every night the electricity goes out, so be sure to bring a flashlight.

The local market, Pasar Nayak, is an unbelievable hodgepodge of foreign and domestic goods. Stone axes *(kapak)* sell for Rp5000-10,000, the cost depending on size, the type of stone used, and the labor involved. The cheaper variety is sold in the market stalls. Ax blades are mostly common black; green stone is the hardest and considered the finest. At least 20 kiosks in the market sell Dani artificats—bibs, Asmat-style carvings, headdresses, bone and wood carvings, fossils, exchange stones. *Noken,* the cloak-like bark-string bags, come in a variety of sizes and make handy carriers—small ones are Rp3000, large ones Rp7000.

HIKING FROM WAMENA

Walking on the numerous and generally well-maintained dirt footpaths and hard-gravel roads of the Baliem Valley is an invigorating and unforgettable experience. It's difficult to find vehicles—even motorbikes—to charter, and even if you do the cost is high. The climate is ideal for walking, though rains can turn the trails slippery. The people are friendly and welcoming, approaching you on the paths hands extended.

Sinatma is a Protestant mission one hour's walk west of Wamena. From Sinatma walk to the power station dam, then follow Wamena River to two suspension bridges made of vines and rough wood. Continue out to Napua and then over to Walesa.

Pugima is an easy walk from Wamena east across the Baliem River. Walk south on the road beside the airport for about three-fourths of the runway length, then turn left on a path over rocks polished by bare feet, cross the runway—stay alert for planes—and then continue east on the trail to the bridge over the river. The water here is deep and calm enough for swimming. Follow the trail a short distance further to Pugima village, where the chief sells ornately carved arrows at about the same prices as in Wamena.

Woruba makes a nice eight- to 10-hour roundtrip walk to the east of Wamena via Pugima. There's a point here where you can look out over the entire valley. Not a flat walk, the scenery really changes along the way. In Woruba there's a big house with a friendly family from Timor who are happy to put people up for the night, though it's more interesting to stay in nearby *kampung*.

At the end of a two-hour walk north from Wamena is the infamous smoked mummy of Akima. Walk northwest on the compacted gravel road from Wamena, turning left at the intersection, past the jail to Hom Hom. Turn down to the river and cross the bridge. Continue on the dirt road to Akima. A tourist sight, it costs Rp10,000 per group to view the decorated mummy, so if you want to see it take others along with you. The mummy is not for sale; it's the chief's grandfather. These are the Soka people, so don't call them Dani. Akima is also accessible by taxi from Wamena.

An easy five- to six-hour (15 km) walk north from Wamena, **Yiwika** consists of two traditional longhouses, a thatch roof shelter, and a *honnay* surrounded by gardens and women working the fields. *Bemo* run 1100 to 1600 from in front of the Wamena market to Yiwika; a charter for three people costs around Rp10,000 each way. A short walk from Yiwika is the **Lauk Inn**; Rp7000 pp, Rp9000 with breakfast, or Rp12,000 for all meals. Keep a light burning at night to shoo the rats away. Nice restaurant—fresh bread in the mornings.

The Casuarina Coast

The Casuarina Coast is one of the least visited corners of the inhabited world, a desolate, swampy stretch of coast between the Barai and Trikom rivers in southeast Irian Jaya. It was here that Nelson Rockefeller's 23-year-old son Michael disappeared in 1962. An intensely swampy area, all of it borders the coffee-colored waters of the Arafura Sea. At one time the natives' personal adornments, art, woodcarving, music, social organization, and religion were all based on the taking of heads.

The region is named for its huge casuarina trees, an Australasian species with jointed leafless branches. At dusk the sky fills with thousands of flying foxes, swarming down to feed on the ripe casuarina fruit. Here lives the largest of the New Guinea parrots, the *kakatua raja*, or king parrot. Vast mangrove, sago, and bamboo forests crowd the sloping swampland environment, formed of mud sediment over millennia. The natives depend on the surrounding 20,000 square km of forests as a hunting ground.

It is probable that headhunting and cannibalism are still practiced in these swamps, home to some of the most untouched tribes in the world. For centuries the people have prepared human meat like pig meat; the body cut into pieces by the women, then roasted over a fire. Human food has long been known here as "long pig," though it is said human flesh is juicier than the flesh of the swine.

The whole Casuarina Coast is now threatened by ecological disaster. The pristine area of the Asmat and other tribes has been allotted to concessionaires who employ the Irianese to fell trees and float them downriver for collection. There are no reforestation efforts, and overlogging is occurring farther and farther away from the rivers. Even more serious is the erosion caused by uncontrolled logging. Unless timber cutting is stopped, several large rivers could eventually completely submerge the region.

THE ASMAT

Almost the entire Asmat region is covered in water during the rainy season. This is the largest alluvial swamp in the world, a low-lying stoneless territory of bog forests and meandering rivers emptying into the Arafura Sea. Several rivers are wide enough to allow boats to sail up to 50 km upriver; a widely used means of transport is *motor mappi*, the Asmat motorboat. The rivers swarm with shrimp, fish, lobster, crab, freshwater dolphin, sea snakes, and crocodiles. Living along the banks are lizards, known as *cuscus*, that grow longer than the Komodo dragon.

The region's forests contain palms, ironwood, *merak* wood, and mangroves, and are home to crown pigeons, hornbills, and cockatoos. There are grass meadows, and flowers like the Dedrobium orchid.

*Spectacular Irian Jaya
(clockwise from top left) Dani village;
a dramatic outhouse; Baliem Gorge;
waterfall at Biak; mountain algae*

Natives of the region are divided into two main groups: those living along the coasts, and those in the interior. They differ in dialect, way of life, social structure, and ceremonies. The coastal people are further divided into two groups, the Bisman people between the Sinetsy and Nin Rivers, and the Simai people. The 70,000 Asmat, the area's largest tribe, are scattered in 100 villages in a territory of roughly 27,000 square km, an area a little larger than the Netherlands. The tribe was untouched by civilization until recent times. Dutch outposts, missionary settlements, and foreign expeditions finally made inroads on this isolated culture during the 1950s and '60s. Formerly, the families of the entire tribe resided together in houses up to 28 meters long called *yeus*. Today, in such coastal villages as Basiem and Agats, families occupy separate dwellings built on pilings. *Yeus* are still used, but now only by men, as club-houses where bachelors sleep.

The Asmat live on sago, their staple, as well as mussels, snails, and fat insect larvae collected from decaying stumps of sago palms. These last are eaten to the accompaniment of throbbing drums and ritual dances; larval feasts can sometimes last up to two weeks. The Asmat also gather forest products such as rattan, and catch fish and shrimp in large hoop nets. For the most part, these former cannibals and head-hunters live in a constant nightmare of fear, fighting off powerful supernatural enemies by wearing bones of dead relatives around their necks. Constantly carried, fondled, and polished, the bones eventually aquire the patina and sheen of old ivory. In the upper river reaches, tribes wrap their dead in bark and lay them out on scaffolding only a few meters away from the house. The bodies are left there to rot, until only the skeleton is left; then the bones are brought into the house.

The whole estuary region is famous for its carvers. Much of the highly original art of the Asmat is symbolic of warfare, headhunting, and warrior-ancestor veneration. For centuries the Asmat were preoccupied with the necessity of appeasing ancestor spirits, producing a wealth of superbly designed shields, canoes, sculpted figures, and drums. Until the end of WW II, the only tools utilized were shells, animal teeth, tusks, and precious stone axes obtained by trade with mountain people. Today, flattened nails set into wooden handles and iron axes and chisels have replaced the old-style tools; shell and bone are still used for scraping and smoothing finished pieces.

Agats is the starting point for visiting Asmat villages. The missionaries founded a timber mill here and raised wooden walkways all over town; these have since fallen into disrepair and are now quite dangerous in places. It's extremely easy to make arrangements to stay with an Asmat family in town for Rp5000 per night or less. People here welcome you with open arms; they're very affable. Just about anybody will be glad to put you up for a little cash. Only three *warung* in town; all are expensive. Two serve *soto ayam* and nothing else, day after day. The third is run by the same Chinese family who runs the New Asmat Inn and offers more variety—usually dried fish, vegetables, and rice at Rp3000 a meal.

Agats's main attraction is its unique **museum** of primitive woodcarvings and weaponry, run by Father Suwada. Ironwood carvings produced here include hafts for stone axes, one- to two-meter-tall ceremonial shields, sago bowls, copulation figurines, solid wood human heads, arabesque panels, and canoe paddles. There are also knives and necklaces made from the thigh bones and vertebrae of the giant cassowary bird. *Prahu* are painted in bright colors, ornamented with superb carvings. Across from the museum is the **Catholic Mission**, featuring a fantastic library. If you really get bored, at night seek out the dark house in town where you can buy coconut wine for Rp2000 per bottle from a decrepit old man. A lot of backroom card gambling sessions in Agats, but your tablemates never cough up the dough when you win.

GETTING THERE AND AWAY

From Wamena, Merpati flies once weekly to Agats for Rp63,700. Flights are often delayed, postponed, or cancelled. The plane comes to earth on a grass airstrip in Ewer near Agats on the Per River; only small Islanders or Cessnas can safely make the landing. From here you have to catch a boat to Agats (Rp5000, 20 minutes). Sometimes flights leave from Timika, depending on the whims of Merpati, which dispatches the planes from Merauke. You can also rent your very own Merpati Twin Otter in these parts: the tariff is roughly Rp11 million, with an 850-kilogram maximum weight limit.

A *kapal Pelni perintis*, the KM *Nasuna*, sails all the way to Sorong in nine days for an incredibly cheap Rp21,300. Deck class only, though it's possible to rent crew cabin rooms. A worthwhile trip; the ship stops at such remote spots as Bade, Agats, Pomako, Dobo, Elat, Tual, and Kaimana. Food is not included in the fare, but is quite decent—a large plate of rice and vegetables with fish or egg for Rp1000. The usual crowded ship conditions, but not too bad. Members of the crew might let you use their bathroom. From Merauke to Sorong requires 12 days; the ship sits in Sorong for three days, then returns. Another ship runs this route as well, so there's a boat leaving every two weeks. Unless you're packing big money, don't come to Agats planning to visit Asmat villages upriver. Fuel and boat rental prices are high; it costs at least Rp200,000 per day to travel anywhere by boat.

(following pages) A village council, Timor, Nusatenggara

Practical Information

Accommodation

Choose your lodgings carefully. Other travelers are the greatest single source of information on the best places to stay. Second best is tourist offices. In smaller villages, ask the *hansip* (district civilian militia) about homes that put up travelers. The same person who tells you a hotel or *losmen* mentioned in this book no longer exists will also point you to another good one.

Penginapan

A lodging house with very basic facilities—table, chair, bed, thin walls, and a single, low-powered, unadorned light bulb hanging from a cord. *Penginapan* means simply "place to spend the night." You'll find these trader's accommodations all over Indonesia, down little back lanes, often advertised with a sign reading PENG-X followed by the owner's name. The average rate ranges anywhere from Rp5000 to Rp25,000 per night. Most common in small or coastal towns and deep in the interiors of Indonesia's islands.

Losmen

A cheaply run hotel but still quite livable. Bathrooms are usually shared. Room service depends on the particular *losmen*. Here you find interesting people—itinerant merchants, students, *pegawai,* other budget travelers. Architecturally—with their narrow verandas, row of low bamboo chairs, coffee tables, and louvered double windows —*losmen* are descendants of the *pensions* popular at the turn of the century in the Dutch East Indies. Prices range from Rp5000 to Rp25,000. Usually *losmen* are efficiently run by an *ibu* (your hostess, meaning "mother") or a small staff of boys. In Jakarta and other places on Java, a *losmen* could mean a brothel.

Homestays

The phenomenon of homestays, or licensed private homes in tourist villages, is found mainly on Bali and in other areas of the islands popular with travelers. Often named for the family who owns the accommodation (e.g., Homestay Adiyasa), they share many of the characteristics of *losmen* and *penginapan,* but are usually more homey and familiar. You mix more with the family, and simple meals like *nasi goreng* and *mie kuah* are provided.

Wisma

A *wisma* is an Indonesian lodge or small guesthouse with pretensions. Usually it's one story, efficiently run, family owned. *Wisma*-class hotels are actually some of the best accommodations for the money in Indonesia. Costing Rp30,000-50,000, they're comfortable and homey, with first-rate service. *Wisma* often offer flush toilets, and a simple breakfast is included in the price of a room.

Hotels

Hotel associations, with government backing, are cracking down on the heretofore loose use of the term, and now prevent anyone from using the "hotel" appellation without meeting certain standards. My litmus test: if the front desk clerk speaks English, you're probably in a hotel.

The tourist industry has devised two official rating systems to grade the services and facilities of Indonesia's hotels. The *melati* jasmine system is applied to standard hotels, while the *bintang* star system rates the more luxurious places. Five-star (*lima bintang*) hotels cost Rp231,000 to Rp357,000 double occupancy. Most feature all the modern conveniences: a/c, coffee shops, restaurants, swimming pools, tennis courts, shopping complexes. A handful of luxury hotels—like the Amandari and the Four Seasons on Bali—are in a class all their own. They feature fully-equipped, self-enclosed compounds, private staffs, sumptuous surroundings, peerless service, and start at Rp525,000 per night.

For a listing of Indonesia's three-, four-, and five-star deluxe hotels, refer to the "Pacific Hotel Directory" in *Pacific Travel News*, published each June and December, or contact either the Directorate General of Tourism (Jl. Kramat Raya 81, Jakarta) or any Indonesian Tourist Office.

There are also small, efficient, clean, well-managed business hotels all over Indonesia. These offer very good value.

WEST JAVA

JAKARTA

Budget
Wisma Delima, on Jl. Jaksa 5 (tel. 021 337-026) The best known of the budget hotels, Wisma Delima hasn't changed much in 10 years—bad lighting, slimy *mandi*, stuffy, noisy, cramped dormitory beds for Rp6000. Rooms upstairs are nicer. All right for a few days. The receptionist, Ricky, is a nice guy. Be aware you'll have to come home at midnight (1300 on Saturday), when the gate is locked.

Family Homestay, Jl. Kebon Sirih Barat Dalam 1, tel. 335-917. A spacious family home with about six extra rooms upstairs for guests. Clean and friendly—Vilhelm speaks Dutch and English.

Hotel Tator, Jl. Jaksa 37, tel. 392-3941. With fan rooms from Rp14,000-24,000 and a/c rooms from Rp35,000, this accommodations is very well run by a Torajan woman: good security, exceptionally clean, nice dining area, good restaurant with Indian/Indonesian/Western food, laundry service with ironing, and other nice little touches like use of the phone in the office. Good value.

Wisma Ise, Jl. Wahid Hasyim 168, third floor, tel. 333-463. Reached by walking from Jl. Jaksa along Jl. Wahid Hasyim, then crossing Jl. Thamrin and walking on the right side. Only a five-minute walk east from Sarinah Department Store.

Wisma Ise offers 20 newly remodeled rooms for Rp12,000-24,000—a nice, quiet, spotless place with magnificent large patio and good breakfasts. Call from the airport to reserve a room. The family will wake you for your 0500 flight and even drive you to the airport.

Moderate
Sabang Metropolitan, Jl. Agus Salim 11, tel. 344-0303. Running only Rp115,500-178,500, the Sabang is a better deal than the international-class hotels. Clean, efficient, central, fully outfitted rooms with pool, restaurants, newsstand, business center, and funny rules (no people of opposite sex in rooms, no smelly fruits). Always ask for the discount.

Cipta Hotel, Jl. K.H. Wahid Hasyim 53, tel. 390-4701, fax 326531 with a/c rooms Rp154,000-175,000 near Jl. Jaksa. Clean and modern Ask for the 30 percent discount; the place is hungry for business.

Marcopolo, Jl. Teuku Cik Ditiro 17-19, tel. 230-1777. Patronized for the most part by small businesspeople from all over Asia, this is one of the cheapest places for an ice-cold draft beer and great dinner buffet in an a/c, fairly sophisticated environment. Offering very reasonable rates (Rp94,500-126,000 including tax and service), the Marcopolo is just right for cleaning up and resting after some hard traveling.

Luxury
The Mandarin Oriental Jakarta, Jl. M.H. Thamrin, tel. 314-1307, fax 324-669. Certainly the most elegant of Jakarta's top hotels—the top choice of international businesspeople for its business center, well-appointed rooms, and attentive service.

Hotel Borobudur Intercontinental, Jl. Lapangan Banteng Selatan, tel. 380-5555, fax 384-2150. The largest hotel in Indonesia (1,172 rooms), HBI also has tennis and squash courts, a large pool, and an outdoor cafe where an opulent buffet brunch is served every Sunday. Rates: Rp945,000-2.5 million. In its restaurant read newspapers in every language.

Jakarta Hilton, Jl. Jend. Gatot Subroto, tel. 570-3600. Surrounded by gardens, the Hilton shares a 32-acre site with several authentic Batak tribal houses, a Balinese temple, and even a jogging path; this whole complex is a luxurious enclave (Rp420,000-630,000) well insulated from the downtown bustle, with swimming pool, health club, tennis courts, bowling alley, shopping arcade, nursery, and an American restaurant.

Grand Hyatt, Jl. M.H. Thamarin Kav. 28-30, tel. 390-1234, fax 310-7300. A luxurious 455-room hotel in the heart of the business district with a huge pool and several high-class restaurants—another favorite among those who can afford it (Rp630,000-1 million). The downstairs shopping complex has several bookstores, inexpensive cafes, and a great *nasi padang* restaurant in the basement..

BOGOR

Budget
Puri Bali Losmen, tel. (0251) 317-498, at Jl. Paledang 30.An excellent choice is this small, cozy, clean, spacious, and centrally located *losmen*, only 400 meters from the entrance to Kebon Raya; Rp15,000-25,000. The 80-year-old Balinese proprietor, I Made Taman, former head of Indonesia's national parks, is a delightfully knowledgeable, helpful, garrulous man who speaks good English, German, and Dutch and plays the guitar and violin. He and his two sons make gracious and lively hosts.

Firman Pensione, at Jl. Paledang 28, tel. 323-246. Next door to Puri Bali, this friendly, family-run hotel has rooms for Rp10,000-30,000 and dorms for just Rp4000. Firman has evolved into the primary backpackers lodge because of its low prices and friendly managers.

Moderate
Abu's Pensione, Jl. Mayor Oking 15, tel. (0251) 322-893. Because of its superb location just behind the railway station, Abu's is the best mid-priced place with clean dorm beds for Rp6300, rooms overlooking the river for Rp16,800 with outside bath or Rp21,000 with inside bath, and Rp63,000-94,000 for deluxe rooms. Abu's pro-

vides great meals on a garden patio next to the local ravine. Also offers a number of tourist and travel services.

Rikin's, Jl. Cibural Indah, tel. 314-070. This family-run guesthouse offers lodging for Rp30,000 with all meals included. Rikin speaks Dutch and a little English. For moderate costs, he will drive you around to remote rubber plantations, tapioca factories, and *desa*. Recommended.

Luxury

Mirah Sartika Hotel, tel. (0251) 312-343, fax 315-188. A venerable, Dutch-era hotel with a central location down a small alley and spotless a/c rooms for Rp63,000-126,000.

Wisma Permata, Jl. Raya Pajajaran 35, tel. 318-007, fax 311-082. Another *tempoe doeloe* relic which charges Rp70,000-95,000, with hot water, huge rooms and bathrooms, big beds, breakfast, and adjacent steakhouse restaurant.

BANDUNG

Budget

Yossie Homestay, Jl. Kebon Jati 53, tel. (022) 420-5453, fax 420-9758. Owned by Josep and his American wife, this is the newest and cleanest choice. Rooms in immaculate condition cost Rp9000-12,000; dorm beds just Rp4000. Yosep also runs tours to nearby volcanoes, hot springs, and silk weaving villages, and sends direct minibuses to Pangandaran. Live folk music in the evenings.

Sakadarna International Travelers Homestay, Jl. Kebon Jati 34, tel. 420-2811. Clean; dorm Rp4000 and rooms from Rp10,000-12,000. Includes a restaurant. The friendly owners offer tours of the surrounding area (Lembang, Tangkuban, Ciater, Dago), can arrange direct minibuses to Pangandaran, and dispense free brochures with maps and useful information.

Hotel Surabaya, tel. 436-791, near the train station. An old Dutch art-deco hotel with economy rooms Rp10,000-18,000, standards Rp12,000-20,000, and elaborately furnished (period beds, antiques) rooms in the rear from Rp45,000. An old world experience.

Moderate

Hotel Melati, near the train station. Probably the best of the moderate hotels, clean and reasonably priced at Rp37,000-45,000.

Trio Hotel, tel. 615-055. Though situated near the redlight district, it's a spotless place with rooms for Rp70,000-105,000. Actually a great location: lively at all hours plus dozens of nearby *warung*, *durian* stalls, nightclubs, and excellent Chinese restaurants.

Luxury

Hotel Perdana Wisata, tel. (022) 438-238, fax 432-818. Plentiful, pleasant, with all the modern conveniences, this brand new deluxe hotel is managed by the Holiday Inn group. Strange location on a busy street, but rooms are superb at Rp147,000-210,000. Pool and Japanese restaurant.

Savoy Homann Hotel, Jl. Asia-Afrika, tel. 432-244, fax 436-187. A venerable art deco classic with large rooms (Rp210,000-357,000) off a lovely inner garden. Though the hotel is a recognized architectural masterpiece and retains a distinct bygone charm, the place seems disorganized and rooms need upgrading. The Garuda/Merpati office is right across the street.

Grand Preanger Hotel, JL. Asia-Afrika 81, tel. 431-631, fax 430-034. Bandung's best five-star hotel, superbly managed, with a renovated art deco wing and 150 rooms in the new tower, plus pool and nightclub with rockin' Filipino bands. Rooms cost Rp315,000-462,000, or try the Garuda Suite for Rp4.2 million. One of the best hotels on Java.

CENTRAL JAVA

CIREBON

Budget

Hotel Asia, Jl. Kalibaru Selatan 15, tel. (0231) 202-183. A Chinese-run hotel and the best-value *losmen*-style accommodation in Cirebon. Situated in an old Dutch home, the whole building is itself an antique. Quite centrally located down a quiet street facing a canal. Rates range from Rp12,000 to 20,000. *Nasi gudeg* vendors come around the courtyard in the mornings. A masseuse works the premises (Rp2500). The English-speaking manager can answer any specific questions and offers a useful information package with local transportation tips.

Moderate

Cirebon Plaza Hotel, Jl. Kartini 54, tel. (0231) 2061 or 2062. A clean, modern hotel on the road from Bandung; Rp30,000 s or d for a/c rooms with *mandi*; coffee shop and restaurant.

Grand Hotel, Jl. Siliwangi 98, tel. 208-623. This old colonial hotel offers a multitude of large rooms in every price range: Rp35,000-60,000 for a/c rooms in a central location. Has all the amenities, plus great service and style.

Luxury

Bentani Hotel, Jl. Siliwangi 69, tel. (0231) 203-246, fax 207-527. Pool, three restaurants, and decent a/c rooms for Rp105,000-160,000.

Park Cirebon, Jl. Siliwangi 107, tel. 205-411, fax 205-407. Features a deluxe lobby, pool, and 91 rooms priced at Rp126,000-210,000. A favorite of expats working the Pertamina oil refineries to the west of Cirebon. This hotel also operates the **Sangkan Hurip Park Resort** in the mountain town of Kuningan just outside Cirebon.

SEMERANG

Budget

Hotel Singapore, Jl. Imam Bonjol 12, tel. (024) 543-757. A clean and quiet hotel with friendly managers. Rooms cost Rp9000-12,000, probably the best cheapie in Semarang.

Hotel Oewa-Asia, Jl. Imam Bonjol. In the noisy center of the city, rooms in the back are quieter and run Rp8000 with wall fan and two beds. In the front building rooms run Rp15,000 with *mandi*, toilet, but plenty of noise. The ice water is a nice touch.

Hotel Jaya, at Jl. M.T. Haryono 87, tel. 23604; Rp10,000. A big, breezy hotel with large, fairly clean rooms with inside *mandi*. Secure; gate closes at night. Isolated location but one of the better cheap hotels in town.

Moderate

Blambangan Hotel, Jl. Permuda 23, tel. (024) 21649. The best deal are their higher-priced rooms (Rp15,000-25,000); also dorm beds from Rp6000. Popular and often filled with Indonesian tourists. Well-run.

Surya, Jl. Bonjol 28, tel. 540-355, fax 544-250. A good midpriced hotel with economy rooms from Rp22,000 and a/c rooms Rp25,000-30,000. Rates include tax, service, and breakfast.

Luxury

The **Telomoyo**, Jl. Gajah Mada 138, tel. 20926 or 25436. Central, with 67 a/c rooms and large open courtyard. Nice lobby with a homey feel. Popular with Dutch package tourists and Japanese business travelers. Higher-priced rooms are a better value; European food is served in the restaurant.

Hotel Santika, Jl. A. Yani 189, tel. 314-491. This hotel offers Rp26,000-31,500 rooms with a/c; telephone, in-house video, restaurant. This flashy hotel is located opposite Es Teler, one of the best *bakso* restaurants on Java.

Siranda Hotel, Jl. Diponegoro 1, Candi Baru. tel. (024) 313-272. Air-conditioned rooms start at Rp60,000 for the first floor, and descend in price as you ascend in height. There's no elevator, so you'll get a lot of exercise. Built in 1974 for Indonesia's first PATA conference, today the Siranda is a little frayed at the edges, but still a good value. Offers beautiful views at night.

The **Patra Jasa**, Jl. Sisingamangaraja, tel. 314-441, fax 314-448. Sits lordly above the city with beautiful rooms complete with a/c, refrigerator, and TV for Rp210,000-525,000. Restaurant, coffee shop, bowling alley, tennis courts, swimming pool, billiards, travel bureau, drugstore, bank. The best tourist hotel in Semarang.

YOGYAKARTA

Budget

Beta Losmen, Gang I, Pasar Kembang area. Inside one of its own *kampung*, this is one of the largest; clean, friendly, secure; usually full in July and August.

Gandhi Losmen, Gang II, Pasar Kembang area. Charging only Rp5000-8000 for rooms with fans (no breakfast), this is one of the cheapest and best accommodations around. The family is very friendly and helpful, and there's free tea as well as laundry service—a secure place with a beautiful garden.

Moderate

Hotel Kota, Jl. Pasar Kembang. Beautiful, spacious rooms for Rp12,000-20,000. Nicely laid out, secure, clean, showers in some rooms, leafy gardens, tea. Drawbacks: the front rooms are noisy, it's run like a boarding school, Rp20,000 pp deposit required. No guests admitted between 2330 and 0530.

Asia-Africa Hotel, Jl. Pasar Kembang 9, tel. (0274) 66219, fax 4489. Rents economy rooms for Rp13,000-30,000 with attached bathrooms and a/c rooms with private patio for Rp28,000-45,000. Nice, cool central courtyard.

Peti Mas Guesthouse, Jl. Sosrokusuman, tel. (0274) 61938, fax 71175. By far the best of a half-dozen choices on Jl. Sosrokusuman is this clean, quiet, and nicely decorated guesthouse with attractive pool and garden restaurant. Fan rooms cost Rp20,000-45,000, a/c rooms Rp46,000-82,000.

Sartika Homestay, Jl. Prawirotaman 44 A, tel. (0274) 72669. Receives rave reviews from travelers, the best accommodation in the neighborhood. Afi, the friendly English-speaking manager, is always ready to answer questions and provide any services for a pleasant stay. Room rates are Rp15,000-20,000 including breakfast, tasty snacks, and drinks.

Luxury

The Puri Artha, Jl. Cendrawasih 9 (just off Jl. Solo near Pasar Baru). One of the better small hotels in town. Well-run, attractive, with a good restaurant and swimming pool, costs about Rp63,000-105,000. *Gamelan* in the evening, and each Thursday and Sunday the staff will take you to play tennis. Book well in advance as the Puri Artha often fills up with package tourists.

The Ambarrukmo Palace, Jl. Solo, tel. 66488, fax 63283. Another fine example of Javanese *kraton* architecture, about seven km down Jl. Solo toward Prambanan. Hamengku Buwono VII built it in the 1890s. Rates are Rp180,000 for the cheapest single room, Rp750,000 for the presidential suite. The shops in the arcade charge ridiculous prices. There's also a small post office and bank.

Natour Garuda Hotel, Jl. Malioboro 72, tel. 66353, fax 63074. A high-priced colonial-style hotel in the center of town; Rp250,000-750,000 including tax, service, dinner, and Ramayana performance. Built in 1911, then rebuilt in 1938. The rooms have been completely restored and modernized, with a new seven-story annex added in the rear.

SOLO

Budget

Losmen Solo Homestay, on narrow lane to the north of Jl. Ahmad Dahlan. With its spacious courtyard, friendly help, and acceptable rooms (sometimes noisy) for Rp5000-8000, this is one of the most popular traveler's places to stay. Located in the Jl. Ahmad Dahlan neighborhood of old Dutch buildings, narrow alleyways, trendy cafes, and a dozen more decent *losmen* in the Rp5000-10,000 price range.

Keprabon Hotel, at Jl. Dahlan 12, tel. (0271) 32811. A real rarity—an old Dutch hotel with art deco touches in the period windows and furniture. Simple but clean rooms face a quiet inner courtyard.

Westerners, on Kemlayan Kidul 11, tel. (0271) 33106. Except for the screeching birds in the morning and the almost compulsive sweeping, let nothing untoward be said about this delightful family-style accommodation; Rp5500-7000 for small but adequate rooms, plus two VIP rooms for Rp8500-9500. There's a kitchen (with utensils), telephone, laundry area, bicycles for rent, breakfast, and a good notice board. Relax in open-air sitting areas with flowering plants—an island of peace in the center of the city, where, as the name implies, only Westerners can stay. Well known to *becak* drivers.

Relax Homestay, Jl. Empu Sedah 28 (off Jl. Gatot Subroto).This popular homestay is an excellent nearby alternative. Six fabulous, spacious rooms in the main building for Rp7000-10,000 and 10 smaller cubicles for Rp6000. Well-run, nice garden, and very quiet even though it's in the heart of Solo.

Moderate
Hotel Dana, Jl. Slamet Riyadi 286, tel. 33891, fax 43880. One of the best deals in the Rp15,000-24,000 price range. Spacious doubles come with fan, *mandi,* and veranda; nice courtyard, quiet for downtown (just across from the tourist office).

Putri Ayu Hotel, Jl. Slamet Riyadi 293, tel. and fax 46155. Commodious, quiet, extremely clean rooms. Though about 2.5 km out of town on the road to Yogyakarta, a *bis kota* passes by right out front (Rp150)—or take a *becak* for Rp500.

Luxury
Kusuma Sahid Prince, Jl. Sugiyopranoto 22, tel. (0271) 46356, fax 44788. Once considered the top hotel in town. On estates formerly owned by members of the royal family, this aging 50-room relic charges from Rp180,000 up to Rp2.1 million for a luxurious suite. If you feel heatstroke coming on, pay Rp3500 to plunge into the Olympic-size pool.

Hotel Sahid Sala, Jl. Gajah Mada 82, tel. 45889, fax 44133. Top choice in town; plush rooms cost Rp105,000-210,000. A major 1994 addition now provides the cleanest and most modern rooms in Solo. Swim at the Kusuma, but stay at the Sahid.

EAST JAVA

SURABAYA

Budget
Bamboo Denn, Jl. Ketabang Kali 6A, tel. (031) 40333. This well-known accommodation is a 20-minute walk from Gubeng railway station. Pay Rp5000-9000 for tiny hot rooms, or Rp4000 for a bed in the okay dorm. You'll be asked to talk before a class of mostly Chinese students; these conversational English classes subsidize the low cost of the rooms. Perhaps a convenient place to stay for those overnighting in Surabaya on their way to Yogyakarta, Jakarta, or Bali. Dismal, but definitely cheap. Public transport, travel agent, and public telephone nearby.

Hotel Santosa, Jl. Embong Kenongo 40, tel. 43306. Rents rooms for Rp10,000-15,000. The front row of rooms, facing a small garden, is best —tolerably clean, and not a bad deal for a major city. Communal *mandi*.

Bina Dirga Angkasa, Jl. Embong Kenongo 52, tel. 42687. This family-run hotel charges Rp12,000 for the cheapest rooms; it's very secure and has a travel agent in front.

Moderate
Remaja Hotel, Jl. Embong Kenongo 12, tel. 41359, fax 510-009. In the Rp55,000-65,000 range plus 21 percent tax and service—a small, efficient businessperson's hotel, with a/c and mice.

Olympic Hotel, Jl. Urip Sumoharjo 65, tel. 43216. If you want to be right in the middle of it, this is the place—Rp12,000-26,000. Located on a busy extension of Jl. P. Sudirman, this old hotel couldn't be more central. *Bemo* stop just 50 meters south, Nitour and Garuda offices are close by, and you can eat at nearby Wiena Restaurant.

Hotel Kalimantan, Jl. Pegirian 202-A, Kampung Sasak. The best deal in Kampung Sasak is on the other side of the Kalimas canal: charges Rp9000 non a/c, Rp13,000 a/c. It's secure and has a garden, travel agency, and restaurant in front which gives room service. This hotel is within walking distance of Jembatan Merah, the historic Mesjid Sunan Ampel; the Kalimas wharf area is only two km away.

Luxury

Majapahit, Jl. Tunjungan 65, tel. (031) 69501. In the middle of the business/entertainment district, this fully equipped hotel charges Rp69,000-140,000 for a/c rooms with balcony, refrigerator, bar, and restaurant. It was here in 1945 that the Dutch flag was ripped down and the Indonesian flag raised in its place, an incident which helped precipitate the Battle of Surabaya.

Mirama Hotel, Jl. Raya Darmo 68-72, tel. 69501, offers a/c rooms with TV and refrigerator, restaurant, and bar. **Garden Hotel,** centrally located at Jl. Pemuda 21, tel. 47000, has a/c, a swimming pool, a good Chinese restaurant, and a bar—one of the best values in this price range.

Hyatt Regency, Jl. Basuki Rakhmat 124-128, tel. 511-234, fax 521-508. With its beautiful decor and service, this elegant four-star property is one of Indonesia's best high-class hotels: Rp420,000-630,000. Features video movies, health club, business center, and nightclub.

Garden Palace Hotel, Jl. Yos Sudarso 11, tel. 479251. The city's newest international-class hotel. Spacious a/c rooms with video, bar, TV, pub, ballroom, 24-hour coffee shop and restaurant.

BALI

DENPASAR

Budget

Wisma Taruna Inn, Jl. Gadung 31, tel. (0361) 226-913. Lying on a quiet back street, two km from the city center (Rp200 by *bemo* or a 20-minute walk). From downtown Denpasar, walk up Jl. Hayam Wuruk and turn left at the Arya Hotel, approximately 100 meters down on the right. Rates Rp5000 s, Rp10,000 d (without breakfast); in the off season even lower. Rent motorcycles and bicycles here. Other amenities include laundry service, beverages, and food. Friendly houseboys. This hostel is only a 10-minute walk from the Kereneng bus terminal, which provides transport to all of eastern Bali.

Bali International Hostel, Jl. Mertasari 19, Banjar Suwung Kangin, Sidakarya, Denpasar Selatan, tel./fax 63912. A big, new hostel (opened in 1993), well-suited for young people and student groups. Be sure to book ahead as the hostel could be occupied by a group. Rates: Rp10,000 for fan cooled rooms, Rp15,000 pp for a/c. Each room holds two to four beds. Restaurant. Very clean and safe; lockers provided. Get a taxi as it's a bit out of town—the area is bounded by Sanur, Denpasar, Kuta and the airport. Just two km from beach. Tours and sporting activities can be arranged.

Two Brothers Inn, Jl. Imam Bonjol. On the main road to Kuta Beach, this *losmen* is only a five-minute walk from the Tegal *bemo* terminal and a 10-minute fast walk from downtown. Go down the lane (Gang VII/5) to the right of Banjar Tegal Gede. One of the cheapest *losmen* in Denpasar (Rp10,000 to 15,000 d without *mandi*), the Two Brothers is clean and safe, with electricity, sitting toilets, showers, fragrant flowers, free tea and coffee. Caters exclusively to travelers. It's also quiet, except for the dog chorus at night. Excellent value; please don't try to bargain. Try local meals in nearby *warung* and a small restaurant 200 meters away; ask proprietor Ibu Anom for the best eateries. From Two Brothers you can easily walk or take a *bemo* into town (Rp350), or just stroll down the lane in your swim gear with your towel over your shoulder and thumb a *bemo* (Rp800) to Kuta Beach.

Hotel Adi Yasa, Jl. Nakula 23 (tel. 22679). Central and cheap, they ask only Rp8500 s, Rp15,000 d with bathroom and breakfast. The 22 rooms, which may be hot and muggy and needing refurbishing, all face a pleasant, central garden. Request a fan. When getting off the long-distance bus at around 0500, this is a convenient transit place to stay as it's only 1.5 km from Ubung station.

Moderate

Sari Inn, Jl. Mayjen Sutoyo, tel. 222-437. Has 15 large, comfortable rooms with *mandi,* fan, and tea—very reasonable at Rp15,500 s, Rp20,000 d. An inexpensive *rumah makan* is 200 meters away. Call the inn from the airport and the owner will pick you up for Rp10,000.

Losmen Elim, Puri Oka, Jl. Kaliasem 3, tel. 224-631. This 17-room accommodations charges Rp15,000 s, Rp25,000 d; Rp50,000 for a/c front rooms. Breakfast extra, no hot water, all the hot tea you can drink.

Hotel Puri Alit, Jl. Sutomo 26 (P.O. Box 102, Denpasar), tel. 228-831, fax 288-766. In the heart of Denpasar, the Puri Alit has 22 rooms. With fan Rp16,000 s, Rp20,000 d; with a/c Rp30,000 s, Rp35,000 d. Private bath, tub, shower. For reservations, call the head office at Jl. Hang Tuah 41, Sanur, tel. 288-560, fax 288-766.

Luxury

Pemecutan Palace Hotel, Jl. Thamrin 2 (P.O. Box 489), tel. 423-491. Recently renovated, with 45 rather ordinary rooms ranging from Rp30,000 s to Rp45,000 d, most with a/c and phones; no hot water. The restaurant serves Chinese, Indonesian, and Western food. Amenities include laundry and a car rental service. Quiet, despite its central location. housed in a rebuilt palace—the royal occupants were annihilated in the 1906 *puputan.* Today, you may observe the day-by-day activities and rituals that still take place in the extensive courtyards of the *puri.* The singing birds add a nice touch. Ask to see the old *meriam* (cannon), an 1840 gift to the raja by the Dutch.

Cottages Tohpati Bali, Jl. Bypass Ngurah Rai 15, tel. 235-407, fax 232-404. Located northeast of Denpasar in the suburb of Tohpati, choose this hotel if you want more spacious surroundings, away from the city's hustle and bustle. Luxury facilities—cottages surrounded by tropical trees and flowers, pool and sunken bar, piano bar, restaurants, shops, fitness center, putting green, tennis courts, and a contracted beach in Sanur with "every water sport available."

Natour Bali Hotel, on Jl. Veteran 3 (P.O. Box 3, Denpasar), tel. 225-681. Centrally located, just a short walk from Jl. Gajah Mada and the Bali Museum, this venerable three-star, 73-room hotel is the closest thing to first-class accommodations in Denpasar. Built by a Dutch shipping company in 1927, this was Bali's first tourist hotel, and though it's becoming rather frayed, it still retains vestiges of its charming past with a palm-shaded lobby, antique black fans, art-deco lamps, dark wood finishings, and shady walkways. Here stayed the early Western anthropologists and writers. Rates: Rp92,400 for rooms with a/c, ceiling fans, private bathrooms, hot water, TV, video, and a sound system. Suites are Rp150,150. Other amenities include gift shop, bar, and the Puri Agung Restaurant.

KUTA

Budget

Yulia Beach Inn, on Jl. Pantai Kuta 43, tel. 751-862, fax 751-055. Only two minutes from the beach. The 48 rooms start at Rp20,000 s, Rp25,000 d for fans and shared bath and rise to Rp45,000 s, Rp50,000 d for bungalows with fridge, a/c, private bath, and hot water. Also available are safety deposit boxes; postal and laundry service; car, motorbike, bicycle, and minibus hire; and daily tours starting at about Rp15,000 pp.

Rita's House, tel. 751-760, in an alley between Poppies Lane I and Poppies Lane II. Though close to the beach, rooms cost only Rp15,000 s, Rp20,000 d. Quiet and away from the intense hustle. If heading for the beach, turn right into the lane just before the Tree House Restaurant. Rita's sets up tours, has parking spaces, and can recommend *batik,* music, and painting teachers.

Pension Dua Dara, Segara Batu Bolong Lane, just off Poppies Lane II. Each room (Rp8,000 s and Rp10,000 d for a small, Rp12,000 d for a large) has bath, fan, and terrace. Very clean and tidy. An incredible deal if you don't mind such inconveniences as no bathroom mirrors or towel racks. Safety deposit boxes, free breakfast including coffee, toast, and jaffle, plus tea all day. The drinks are cheaper than in restaurants. Phone available. Caters mostly to young Australian surfers.

Lusa Inn, Gang Bena Sari. With spacious yard/garden, good security, and big rooms for only Rp15,000 s, Rp20,000 d, this is one of the quietest, prettiest *losmen* on Kuta. The little lane of Gang Bena Sari is halfway down from Kuta to Legian on the left-hand side, running between

Jl. Legian and the ocean. The lane has relatively sparse traffic, a great traveler's eatery (El Dorado), about five quiet *losmen*/homestays, and a *warung*.

Komala Indah II, Gang Bena Sari. Also noteworthy. Here you can live in a Balinese compound in a bungalow with shower, bath, sink, fan, mosquito nets, good beds, tile floors, and private garden. Rooms with Asian toilets run Rp8,000 s, Rp12,000 d; newer rooms with Western flush toilets are Rp12,000 s, Rp15,000 d. The place is clean, safe, quiet, private, and only a five-minute walk to either Jl. Legian or the beach. Free tea, jaffle breakfast. Nice boys run it.

Moderate
Poppies Cottages, P.O. Box 378, Denpasar, tel. (0361) 751-059, fax 752-364. Offers luxury, charm, privacy, and security in the heart of Kuta for Rp120,000 s, Rp135,000 d in 20 delightful Bali-style bungalows. Poppies is peacefully enclosed in its own complex on Poppies Lane, a maze of stone paths meandering through lush gardens and lily ponds. Each unit has a/c, ceiling fans, fridges, hot water, baby cots; some have kitchens. Efficiently managed, Poppies provides complete room service, babysitters, pool, free airport transfers, even parking. Book early—steady and loyal clientele.

Pendawa Inn, tel. 52387, South Kuta. Located down a lane lies across from the Hotel Kartika Plaza. Beautiful, well-kept garden, clean rooms with showers and Western toilets, friendly people. Tranquil and a bit away from the rush, this is a little oasis in the midst of bustling Kuta. It's about a five-minute walk to the beach, near a good and inexpensive restaurant, the Puspa Ayu. Rates: Rp14,700-29,400 s, Rp33,600 d (three classes). Discounts for stays of a week or more. Jimmys with a/c can be hired for about Rp42,000 per day.

Asana Santhi Willy Inn, Jl. Tengal Wangi 18, tel. 751-281. A good deal in the middle of Kuta, Willy's has 26 rooms (Rp63,000-94,500) featuring antique furniture, tasteful art, verandas, and private open-air garden bathrooms under big mango trees—cheap, quaint, cool, quiet, beautiful, and full of character. Small pool, IDD telephones. Go down the lane before Lita Beach Club and turn right.

Sandi Phala Beach Resort, Jl. Kartika Plaza, tel. 753-042, fax 753-333. This beachfront hotel has spacious, well-designed two-story bungalows (Rp73,500 s, Rp84,000 d). From the private terrace is a great view of the pool, the beach, the sea, and the sunset. High season surcharge is Rp21,000; tax and service 15.5 percent extra. Sunken bar. Great sandwiches and cocktails in the beachside Warung Sunset Restaurant. Rent *jukung* or jet-skis out front for Rp50,000.

Luxury
Natour Kuta Beach Hotel, Jl. Pantai Kuta, P.O. Box 393, Denpasar, tel. (0361) 751-361. Has 32 quiet bungalows with lush gardens overlooks the beach. The oldest (1936) of Kuta's hotels, it was built in the native style in 1930s. Units are priced at Rp150-235,000, suites run Rp346,300. There's a Garuda agent in the hotel.

Kartika Plaza Beach Hotel, P.O. Box 84, Denpasar, tel. 751-067, fax 752-475. This spectacular five-star resort hotel has 304 elegant rooms and suites, plus 81 Balinese-style bungalows set in a huge 12-hectare garden. Clearly in the splurge category, it boasts an Olympic-size pool and an impressive full-size and well-equipped fitness center, including three clay tennis courts with instructors, massage rooms, weight room, and two jacuzzis. Rooms in the four-story wings, which wrap around the giant pool and gardens, cost Rp210,000 for garden view or Rp231,000 for ocean view. Standard bungalows (Rp220,500 s, Rp241,500 d) are cozy with their own pool.

Kuta Beach Club, Jl. Bakung Sari, P.O. Box 226, Kuta, tel. 751-261, fax 71-896. Dead center to all the action, 200 meters from the beach but peacefully set back 300 meters from the street. Its 120 plushly furnished bungalows cost Rp94,500 s, Rp115,500 d. Pool, sun decks, tennis, mini-tennis.

Pertamina Cottages, Jl. Pantai Kuta, P.O. Box 121, Denpasar, tel. 751-161. In a class by itself, sprawling over 10 hectares, this handsome hotel has 255 modern, two-room, four-square, red-brick, beautifully appointed cottages from Rp189,000 to around Rp1.7 million per day. Though comparable accommodations can be found for less, the isolation is splendid with closed-circuit TV, fresh flowers daily, shopping arcade, open-air stage, two restaurants, bars, convention facilities, tennis courts, pool, badminton, and three-hole golf course. A minibus conveys meals and guests through the grounds. A favorite with package tourists and Indonesian businessmen. Only a five-minute drive from the airport, the southernmost hotel in Kuta.

UBUD

Budget
Rona's Accommodations and Book Exchange, Jl. Tebesaya 23, tel. 96229, fax 619-5120. The ideal place to acclimate. Rona's is hardly ever empty, but when it is call for a free pickup in the Ubud area. The rooms, though basic, are excellent—comfortable, cleaned daily, and cheap (Rp10,000 s, Rp12,000 d). Price includes mosquito net, fan, towels, soap, toilet paper, wardrobe, private bath. Rona's also has Rp20,000 bungalows with showers (no hot water) and deluxe rooms for Rp30,000 with double bed, wardrobe, shower, flush toilet, and sink. The Indonesian food served in the restaurant is high quality and cheap, with a large and varied two-course breakfast and free tea or coffee all day. Luggage storage, security box, and use of multilingual library are free. Also available: laundry service, moneychanger, dance and shuttle bus tickets, tour service.

Arja Inn, Jl. Kajeng 9, you have your own *mandi,* mosquito net, and comfy bed. Lovely family, very private—all for only Rp15,000 d. Friendly **Artini I** asks Rp7000-8000 s, Rp12,000-15,000 d for rooms with their own *mandi,* sizable veranda, magnificent garden, and award-winning breakfast. Quiet. Artini Restaurant is opposite. **Frog Pond Inn** gets consistently wonderful reviews. The owner is friendly and the rooms have billowy beds, clean white sheets, private *mandi* and toilet, and bottled water; surrounded by a tropical garden.

Gandra Accommodations, Jl. Karna 88, Ubud Kelod. Beautiful gardens, clean rooms, great breakfast of fresh fruit and jaffles, free storage service, helpful family, nice garden. Dip into some of the old novels. One of the best accommodations for the price in Indonesia (Rp8000-10,000 s, Rp10,000-13,000 d), yet only five minutes from Ubud's center. Walk down Monkey Forest Road 100 meters and turn left at the sign. A small shop sells blankets, clothes, and film at reasonable prices.

Warsi's House, Monkey Forest Road. Rooms have fans, two double beds, Western toilet, shower with ventilator, inside tub with hot water, towels, and good security. Upstairs rooms (Rp35,000) overlook the family compound, beautiful gardens, and possibly the best view of the Monkey Forest. The room rate includes a large breakfast of banana pancakes, fresh fruit salad, tea or coffee; toast and eggs also available. Warsi is a sharp businessperson and also owns a boutique. She likes to dress her guests up in traditional attire and take them to temple festivals.

Moderate
Pringgajuwita Water Garden Cottages, Jl. Bisma Ubud 80571, tel. and fax 975-734. A classy place with 25 rooms in two different classes: standard Rp78,000 s, Rp84,000 d and deluxe Rp105,000 s, Rp115,500 d (plus 15.5 percent tax and service). You get the service, decor, and comfort of any of Ubud's six international-standard hotels at half the price. All rooms have hot water, private verandas, fans, Balinese-style furniture, and woodwork finishing. The generous, high-quality breakfast (0700-1000) comes with wholegrain bread and homemade jam. The bungalows for Rp115,500 are the best deal, with luxuriant gardens, jungle-enveloped swimming pool, restaurant on leafy pavilion, plus lots of conveniences. Only about an eight-minute walk from Ubud's center, yet very quiet with only the sound of birds in the mornings. Ideal for groups. Well-run by a charming and conscientious manager.

Dewi Sri Bungalows, Jl. Hanoman in Padangtegal, P.O. Box 23, Ubud 80571, tel. 975-300. A haven in the rice fields with three different classes of self-contained bungalows: standard Rp63,000, second story Rp84,000, or suite Rp105,000; American or continental breakfast included. The duplexes are really nice, with a private bedroom upstairs, relaxing open-air living area below, and walled open-air bath. Hot water, pool, attentive staff, coffee shop. A ten-minute walk from Jl. Raya, its main draw is the antique exterior and interior.

Ibu Masih Bungalows, Monkey Forest Road, tel. 975-062. Room with bed, fan, private bathroom, shower and breakfast for Rp20,000-50,000. Also check out the new place with the same proprietor, Masih Accommodations, about 20 meters beyond the football pitch off Monkey Forest Road. Prices for the six bungalows range from Rp15,000 s to Rp25,000 d; enormous upstairs rooms have pyramidal ceilings and magnificent bathrooms and verandas. Ibu Masih is a marvelous lady who'll teach you dancing, talk to you about art, and make a royal tour of her guests each morning. Masih's personable homestay is just a 10-minute walk from Ubud's "downtown."

Oka Kartini, Jl. Raya, Padangtegal, tel. 975-193, fax 975-759. Located 150 meters before the post office as you're entering Ubud from Peliatan. Out of the busy center of Ubud with all its traffic and sellers, Oka's restful, Balinese-style bungalows with intricately carved reliefs and palm thatch, surrounded by pool and gardens, are in the Rp63,000-84,000 range with hot showers; other rooms go for as little as Rp21,000. Oka worked for six years as a guide in the Puri Lukisan and is well informed about painting. She'll store your luggage while you travel around, find you a dance teacher, and hand out free treats. Public transport is close at hand, or ask for airport transfer by private car (Rp42,000 for two).

BANGLI

Budget
Artha Sastra Inn, Jl. Merdeka 5, tel. (0366) 91179. This original raja's palace has seen better days, but the potted plants and palace court architecture give it a unique feel. Sleep in the bed of the last king of Bangli and participate in the ritual life of a *triwangsa* family. Funky, decaying rooms outside with *kamar mandi* are Rp6000 s, Rp9000 d. Slightly less run-down are the five larger rooms in the interior of the *puri* with inside *mandi,* costing

Rp10,000 s, Rp15,000 d. These are adapted from traditional Balinese *bale* and feature ancient carved doors and antique furniture. Rate includes breakfast of banana or pineapple pancakes. Inexpensive menu, but the food is not that great. Ideally located in the center of Bangli near the bus station. Coming into town from Denpasar, the palace complex is on the right.

CANDIDASA

Budget
Dutha Seaside Cottages. A nice, family place on the north end of the village—run like a large commune. Dutha has its own beachfront, with good swimming. Rooms cost Rp8000 s to Rp20,000. Tariff includes breakfast, or just go in the kitchen and make your own tea or coffee. Frequent parties and Balinese feasts. A real traveler's place, clean and quiet.

Kelapa Mas. Very popular and almost always full, rooms range in price from Rp10,000 to Rp30,000. Simply and minimally maintained, with a lovely seaside location in a banana and coconut grove. Cottages facing the sea are the best.

Homestay Ida. An uncrowded, six-room accommodations in the eastern part of town just before the lagoon. Ida's charges Rp30,000-40,000 for traditional bungalows in a coconut grove. No hot water.

Nani Beach Inn, near the Ramayana. Quiet and friendly, bungalows with *mandi* for Rp15,000 d. which includes a good breakfast. Very close to the beach.

Moderate
Anom Beach Bungalows. To get away from the crowds, head 10 minutes west of Candidasa to Sengkidu. This hotel asks Rp25,000 for one of eight bungalows with fan, shower, and breakfast. Excellent restaurant on the premises. Snorkeling equipment for rent.

Candidasa Beach Bungalows II. tel. 751-205. A big, centrally located two-story hotel with an open-air bar and a pool. Despite the packed-in feeling, rooms are spacious, and breakfast—especially the banana pancakes—is excellent. All rooms have fans, a/c, hot water, Western-style bath, fridge, and TV. Cost: Rp58,800 s, Rp69,300-84,000 d.

Luxury

Nirwana Cottages, Sengkidu, tel. 236-136, fax 235-543. Ten traditional one-story cottages go for Rp73,500-Rp105,000. Close to the water, Nirwana is clean, private, and low-key. Superb location, nice rooms, and wholesome homecooked food.

Watergarden, tel. and fax 235-540. Twelve luxurious Balinese-style cottages. All bungalows (Rp126,000 s, Rp136,500 d) have a/c, ceiling fans, and large wooden-decked verandas. Amenities include pool with waterfall, room service, restaurant, IDD, laundry and ironing, safety deposit, library, flight reconfirmation, mountain bikes, and tour and transport services. An elegant place.

Puri Bagus Villa. A relaxing, clean, and comfortable hotel tucked away amid the palms in Sumuh fishing village past the lagoon: 50 well-designed, spacious bungalows for Rp126,000 s, Rp136,500 d. Nine units (Rp31,500 surcharge) and two suites (Rp367,500) face the ocean. Terrace verandas, but beware of slippery tiles after it rains. Good 24-hour security, an unobtrusive, friendly staff. Pool, restaurant. Coral reef out front. Reservations: Jl. Bypass I Gusti Ngurah Rai 300 B, P.O. Box 419, Denpasar 80001, tel. 751-223, fax 752-779, or direct to the hotel at 235-238 or 235-291, fax 235-666.

Candi Beach Cottages. On the white sands of Mendire Beach in Sengkidu, this high-class accommodations charges Rp126,000-189,000 for luxurious rooms. Amenities include two bars, two restaurants, water sports, pool, tennis courts, a fitness room, spa, occasional *barong* dances, tour service, and free shuttle into town.

TIRTAGANGGA

Budget

Dhangin Taman Inn. Set in a nice courtyard and garden, this is the first *losmen* you come to as you're entering the watergardens. Its 13 basic rooms vary in price from Rp10,000 to Rp15,000 s, depending on size, view, and baths.

Tirta Ayu Homestay. Offers four bungalows right inside the water palace. Cost is Rp20,000 d, including pool admission and breakfast; laundry service is extra. New two-story bungalows on the homestay grounds are priced higher. A good deal.

Hotel Taman Sari. Outside the palace complex, offering 25 rustic rooms (Rp7000 s, Rp8000 d) with bathrooms, showers, and a view of the sea. The two front rooms are quietest. Electricity is only on 1700 to 0700, and there are far too many ants and mosquitos, but the price is right.

Rijasu. Next door to the Taman Sari is this simple but immaculate homestay with complimentary breakfast and tea. Same price as the Taman Sari but the rooms are cleaner and nicer, with 24-hour electricity. Laundry, but no telephone. Excellent food just next door.

Moderate

Kusuma Jaya Inn. East of the water palace, up 99 steep steps, are 18 hillside bungalows which rent for Rp15,000 s, Rp20,000 d for the basic unit or Rp40,000 for a larger unit with huge beds, fan, and big open-air bathrooms. Rates can be bargained down. Superb views (especially at sunrise and sunset) taking in the glittering sea and Gunung Agung. Service is excellent, food well-prepared and reasonable.

LOVINA BEACH

Budget

Parma Beach Hotel, tel. 23955. This old but well-kept hotel has nice rooms looking out on gardens that meet a black-sand beach. Rates: Rp15,000-25,000 in the low season; Rp18,000 s, Rp30,000 d in the high season for four classes of rooms. No additional charges. Reasonably priced kitchen. Friendly staff.

Astina's, P.O. Box 42, Singaraja 81151. Though rooms are a bit dark, rates are only Rp7000 s, Rp8000 d with outside *mandi*, or pay Rp11,000 s,

Rp12,000 d for larger Bali-style bungalows with inside *mandi*, sink, shower, carved furniture, fan, and breakfast; cheaper in the off season. Nice gardens. Their quiet location, north of Ayodya's, is away from everything but a short walk to anything. Good value.

Happy Beach Inn. Reasonably priced at Rp8000 s, Rp10,000 d for rooms with fans; cheaper rooms are Rp5000. The two bamboo rooms in the back of Happy's are the best, only Rp10,000. The food is inexpensive and great—try the fish wrapped in banana leaves, black rice pudding with ginger, or the dinners, when staff cooks a big suckling pig and serves *nasi campur* with calamari (Rp2000).

Chono's, Kalibukbuk, tel. 23569. On the main road, only a five-minute walk from the beach. Clean, spacious rooms with good beds and large baths. Rates: Rp15,000-20,000 for rooms with a fan, shower, and private toilet; simple breakfast included. Transport, car rental, sightseeing and snorkeling tours, and laundry and baggage storage service. On its second story, Chono's has a nice restaurant that hosts buffets and dances regularly.

Krisna Beach Inn, on Jl. Seririt 13 km west of Singaraja in Temukus. Best of the several accommodations in Temukus, with eight clean rooms (Rp10,000 s, Rp18,000 d) in a U-shaped compound facing the ocean. Krisna's has an open-air restaurant pavilion (open 0700-2200) serving fresh seafood. Special features include laundry service, swimming out front on a nice private beach, and a splendid coral reef just offshore.

Moderate
Nirwana Cottages, tel. (0362) 22288, fax 21090. Lovina's largest and oldest accommodations on the beach 500 meters from the main road. The brick, bamboo, and thatch structures feature flush toilets, showers, and enclosed outdoor patios. Five classes of rooms range from Rp10,000 to Rp50,000. Good restaurants are within walking distance.

Angsoka Cottages, tel. 22841, fax 23023. Only two minutes from the beach. Cozy rice-barn units for Rp15,000 (outside *mandi*) and detached bun-galows with a/c, inside *mandi*, hot water, and a nice veranda for Rp60,000. Amenities include restaurant and bar, helpful staff, laundry service, IDD telephones, pleasant gardens. Located in the heart of Kalibukbuk, with moneychangers, restaurants, art shops, and ticket agents close at hand. Angsoka has an attractive pool with a sunken bar surrounded by bamboo and *angsoka* flowers. Spiffy and relaxing. Book at the front desk for shuttle service, marine excursions, or dolphin watching. Luxury accommodations at a budget price.

Baruna Beach Cottages, P.O. Box 149, Lovina Beach, Pemaron, tel. (0362) 23745 or 23746, fax 22252. Sheer comfort and relaxation. Rooms or bungalows (the latter feature Western toilets) run from Rp35,700 to Rp109,200. Make reservations at least two weeks in advance. Heading west out of Singaraja, the first village you reach is Pemaron. Set amidst landscaped gardens, the Baruna can't be beat, a totally self-contained resort right on the beach, offering a poolside bar, boutique, cultural shows, sauna and massage services, sailing, windsurfing (Rp12,000 per hour), snorkeling and dolphin trips (Rp3000 and up), and motorbike and bicycle rentals (Rp10,000 per day). American, Indonesian, or continental breakfasts cost Rp8500-19,000, lunch or dinner Rp8500-Rp22,000.

Celuk Agung, Anturan, P.O. Box 191, Singaraja 81101, tel. (0362) 23039, fax 23379. Most of the sixteen comfortable bungalows have private baths, showers, hot water, satellite TV, and fridges. Prices range from Rp42,000 s, Rp52,500 d for standard (no a/c) to Rp105,000 s, and Rp115,500 for the suites. Most of the hotel's grounds are devoted to gardens. Facilities include a bar, a reasonably priced restaurant, pool, tennis and badminton courts, laundry, safe-deposit boxes, and transport service. Nice views of rice fields and the sea. Quiet, good value.

Banyualit Beach Inn, P.O. Box 116, Singaraja 81101, tel. 41789, fax 23563. Gets high marks for its traditional bungalows with clean and tidy rooms, *mandi* with plants, Western toilets, bedside phones. Room rates are Rp15,000-45,000 in three classes. Some units have verandas nearly touching the water, and it's only a 10-minute walk to the main road. Nice surroundings, quiet, fine restaurant, good security, and an accommodating staff. Staff can organize tours; transport; snorkeling, scuba, fishing and sailing outings; and dolphin-watching trips. Credit cards accepted.

Luxury
Aditya Bungalows, P.O. Box 134, Singaraja 81101, tel. 22059. Charges Rp90,000 for deluxe rooms with a/c, hot water, private terrace, TV, fridge, and sea view; Rp70,000 for rooms with a/c and a garden view; Rp50,000 for rooms with hot water and a fan; and Rp40,000 for rooms with a fan and *mandi*. Friendly managers. Aditya's also runs a very efficient and handy travel service.

Bali Lovina Beach Cottages, tel./fax 22385. Between Arjuna and Permata, this 30-room hotel is pure luxury living: immaculate cottages with bath, shower, and hot water are Rp94,500 s, Rp105,000 d for superior rooms; Rp84,000 s, Rp94,500 d for standard rooms; Rp63,000 s, Rp73,500 d for rooms with fan. Credit cards accepted. Restaurant, beautiful pool, poolside bar, beach access, very few beach hawkers. Water sports offered include sailing, snorkeling, fishing, canoeing, windsurfing, and dolphin-watching tours.

Palma Beach Hotel, Jl. Raya Puputan 17X, tel. 225-226 or 225-231, fax 61659. Lovina's swankest, largest, and most expensive hotel—a quiet, luxury marine resort that caters to package tourists. Nineteen standard rooms go for Rp126,000 d; superior class rooms are more spacious, with open-air bathrooms, fridge, TV, and garden for Rp157,500 d. Live karaoke weekly, a coffee shop and restaurant, tennis court, large pool facing the beach, and open-air fitness center. Make reservations at the Denpasar office, Jl. Raya Puputan 17 X, tel. 25256, fax 25231. Watch for Palma's business cards offering a 20 percent discount.

BEDUGUL

Budget
Hadi Raharjo Hotel and Restaurant, tel. (0362) 23467. Three km south of Candikuning in Bedugul village at the junction of the road to the lake, this basic, 10-room hotel charges Rp15,000 for 15 rooms with private *mandi,* cold water, breakfast included. Good value.

Mini-Bali between Candikuning and Bedugul. Appropriately named for its six tiny Rp15,000 rooms, small beds, and the truly mini portions served in its restaurant. One room (Rp20,000) has a private *mandi*. Spartan yet clean.

Moderate
Hotel Bedugul, tel. 29593. On the lake's southern shore, this immense property seems to have absorbed all the adjacent, less expensive hotels. This is why they are able to get away with charging Rp73,000-94,500 for rather decrepit motel-style lakeside rooms. Also, 36 bungalows face the lake (Rp63,000-Rp105,000) with private *mandi* and hot water plus breakfast. All prices subject to 15.5 percent tax and service. Patronized by rich Chinese, Jakartans, and Japanese who seem to be the only ones able to afford the waterside restaurant (lunch buffet Rp9325) where the quality of the expensive Chinese-Indonesian food is not that high. A wide range of water sports is offered. A scene for people who like people.

SUMATRA

MEDAN

Budget
Krishen's Yoghurt House (formerly Jacky's Traveler's Centre), Jl. Kediri 96. Still popular with travelers. Dorm beds are Rp3500, rooms Rp7500 d. The restaurant's walls are plastered with insider's travel info, photos, and notes proclaiming what a wonderful man Jacky is. This copious collage of information ranges from the basic to the most obscure, from the markets of Medan to the rainforests of Aceh. There's even a signed photograph of Joe Cummings on the wall. The restaurant serves decent fruit juice, homemade yogurt, and tasty Indian food. Jacky is undoubtedly helpful and he speaks impeccable English. He maintains a book exchange so you can top up on reading material here, in any language.

Tapian Nabaru, Jl. Hang Tuah 6, tel. (061) 512-155. Houaws in an old Dutch home by a river and tree-filled park, it's only a 10-minute walk from Kampung Keling (the "Ginza strip" of Medan), and five minutes by *mesin becak* from the airport. Not the cleanest or friendliest of places but it's cheap and quiet. Big or small rooms cost Rp5500 per person; dorms Rp2500. Breakfast (Rp1000) consists of bread, jam, egg, and coffee or tea, or eat in Kampung Keling.

Sarah's Guesthouse, Jl. Pertama 10 (behind Astra Toyota on Jl. Sisingamangaraja). Has Rp6000-7500 rooms, or Rp10,000 with *mandi*. Dark and spartan, but quiet, clean, and safe. Buy bus, ferry, and airline tickets here—transport is available to the airport.

Losmen Irama, in a little alley off Jl. Palang Merah 1125. Centrally located, only 50 meters from the intersection of Jl. Imam Bonjol and quite close to Danau Toba International Hotel. Though its rooms could be small, hot, and stuffy, it's cleaner than many. Some rooms have been upgraded with bunkbeds, so you now have to pay for three, even if you're only two. Rooms with *mandi* cost Rp7500, dorm beds Rp2500.

Wisma Yuli, Jl. S. M. Raja Pagaruyung 79B, tel. 323104. Clean rooms with fans for Rp7500 s (including breakfast). The street is off Jl. Sisingamangaraja, opposite Mesjid Raya.

Moderate
Hotel Sumatra, Jl. Sisingamangaraja 21, tel. (061) 24973. Sweatboxes for Rp25,000 s (Rp35,000 d with fan and *mandi*).

Kenanga Hotel, Jl. Sisingamangaraja 82 (near Mesjid Raya), tel. 712-426. Clean and central, with nice rooms from Rp5000 to 30,000. Tourist information desk, moneychanger, small bar. Good value. The restaurant serves either a continental, American, or Indonesian breakfast for under Rp4000.

Luxury
Hotel Dharma Deli, Jl. Balai Kota 2, tel. (061) 327-011, is an old colonial-style hotel, the former Dutch Hotel de Boer. The hotel's famous gardens

have now been turned into private suites (Rp350,000 and up). The cheapest rooms cost Rp100,000, with an extra bed. Amenities include hot water, a/c, a great lobby, bar, and shops. Right across the street is the historic old post office. Take note that at any of Medan's expensive class of hotels, if you book through a travel agent or make an appeal at the reception desk itself, you can often receive a 10 percent discount.

Tiara Medan, Jl. Cut Mutiah Medan 20152, tel. 516-000, is Medan's leading hotel, with full facilities and outstanding service. Its elegant, lavishly appointed rooms are expensive. Try booking at Natrabu Travel to the left of the hotel; Morris will sell you a voucher for Rp90,000 d. The Tiara features two international restaurants, bars, a coffee shop, taxi service, pool, and health club. Ideal for businesspeople as the commerical district is nearby.

Danau Toba International Hotel, Jl. Imam Bonjol 17, Box 490, tel. 327-000, is a large, well-established, high-priced hotel with bar, restaurant, pool, and bowling alley. This modern hotel has a/c rooms (Rp90,000-150,000) with high balcony views looking out over the city, swimming pool, and tennis court. Avoid the hotel's restaurants: the food is either fiendishly expensive or demonically dreadful.

Polonia Hotel, Jl. Jen. Sudirman 14-18, Box 303, tel. 325-300. Asks Rp90,000 per room or Rp150,000 for a suite. The Polonia is centrally located with very good service and in-room video, swimming pool, health center, and reputable Chinese restaurant.

SAMOSIR ISLAND (LAKE TOBA)

Moderate
Carolina's in Tuk Tuk, tel. 41520. This hotel offers 30 rooms and Batak-style bungalows on the slope of a small hill overlooking the lake. Truly luxurious motel-style units are Rp45,000; cheap and simple rooms are Rp7500 with outside *mandi* or Rp12,500 for one inside. The food is reasonable and imaginative—great breakfasts with freshly baked bread. Carolina's has its own pier and a private swimming cove.

BRASTAGI

Budget

Losmen Merpati, Jl. Trimurti 4. Set off the street and very quiet. One of the cheapest (RP4000 s, Rp7500 d) places in town. It's clean an has good rooms with shower and *mandi,* also a restaurant with good food.

Moderate

Bukit Kubu Hotel, Jl. Sempurna 2, tel. 20832. You'll feel like Dutch colonialist at this gracious hotel. Rp90,000 for a suite (no breakfast), Rp 25,000 for the cheapest room. Built in 1939, this is one of Indonesia's most faithfully preserved Indies-style hotels, with complete and original Dutch furnishings, restaurant, and a fire at night in the lounge. Nice bar where you can drink Bujit Kubu Slings with real *marquisha* juice. The vast and immaculate lawn surrounding the hotel is a golf course.

BUKITTINGGI

Budget

Pelita Express, Jl. A. Yani 17, tel. (0752) 22883. This lodging offers both a palce to sleep and a tour and travel service. The manager St. Armen, charges Rp4000 for a basic room and Rp 10,000 fr a room with a private bathroom.

Gangga Hotel, Jl. A. Yani 99. A big eambling building with very affordable Rp9000 rooms with *mandi.* The hotel is centrally located with nice sitting areas and a ticketing and taxi service.

Hotel Benteng, off the bottom of Jl. Tengku Umar, tel. (0752) 22596 or 21115. Highly recommended with reliably clean economical rooms (Rp10,000) with shared *mandi* and views. Higher-priced rooms offer hot water and balconies. The Bentang has a spacious lobby with bar; the restaurant serves expensive European, Chinese and Indonesian food. Good security. Staff also organizes tours of the area aimed at the highlights of the Minang culture.

Moderate

Wisma Sitawa, on Jl. R. Rival. A reasonable guesthouse about five minutes from downtown, and near the public swimming pool. Clean, quiet, with a family atmosphere. Courtyard garden; free tea, coffee, and toast for breakfast.

Minang Hotel, Jl. Panorama 20, tel. (0752) 21120. The Minang is set ina beautiful garden overlooking Ngarai Canyon; Rp35,000 plus tax for the cheapest, smallest rooms, or Rp45,000-53,000 for rooms with bathtub and hot water. Only a kilometer from the *terminal bis,* this well-run guesthouse may be full so make reservations.

PADANG

Budget

Hotel Tiga Tiga, Jl. Pemuda 31, tel. (0751) 22633. Offers economy rooms for Rp6000 s, Rp10,000 d; standard with fan for Rp15,000 s, Rp20,000 d; and VIP a/c rooms for Rp18,000 s, Rp25,000 d. Cozy and friendl. A *penjaga* waits outside if you arrive early in the morning on the bus.

Moderate

Hotel Hang Tuah, Jl. Permuda 1. tel. 26556. Lots of extras at this hotel. Rooms Rp11,000-23,000, all with *mandi.* Economy rooms have two fans, higher priced rooms a/c an TV. Nearly opposite the bus terminal, the hotel offers clean, spacious, well-lit rooms. Friendly and helpful staff. The restaurant downstairs serves continental breakfast, included in the room price.

Luxury

Pangran's Beach Hotel, Jl. Ir H. Juanda 7, tel. 22584, 22512, 22085, or 27411. This is Padang's top hotel, a "marble palace" with rooms and suites for Rp79,875-221,875. Rates don't include the 15 percent tax and service. Offers views, a/c. telephone, TV, a restaurant specializing in steaks, bar, 24-hour room service, laundry, and taxi. Accepts credit cards.

PALEMBANG

Luxury

Hotel Swarna Dwips, Jl. Tasik 2, P.O. Box 198, tel. 313-322, telex 27203, fax 28999. This is Palembang's best hotel, recently renovated and one of the nicest in Sumatra. The colonial-era old building has large rooms for Rp20,000 but is rather run down and stuffy. The cheerier newer building ofers modern motel-like rooms overlooking a neighborhood od red-tile roofs and quiet streets. Everything—telephone, light, bells, a/c—seems to work. Taxi and *becak* service out front. Rooms range Rp50,00-113,500.

SULAWESI

UJUNG PANDANG

Budget

Hotel Nusantara, Jl. Sarappo 103, tel. (0411) 3163, near Jl. Sulawesi. An Islamic traders' hotel close to the harbor, with Floresian staff, color TV, and drinks in the lobby. Relax on the second- and third-floor balconies and look out over the busy market street below. The rooms (Rp5000 s, Rp7000 d) are tiny but usually clean; windows don't close—lots of mosquitos for company; rats in the hallways. An automatic alarm system will have you up for predawn prayers at the mosque next door. Popular with travelers.

Dolly's Homestay, Jl. Gunung Lompobatang 121, tel. 318-936. A more agreeable budget accommodation than Hotel Nusantara, right in the middle of town, a 1.5-km Rp1000 *becak* ride from the main harbor. Rooms, including a good breakfast, are Rp5000 s, Rp7000 d. The proprietor, Mr. Rein, speaks fluent Dutch and English. He keeps a book of traveler's testimonials that is a very good source of information about Sulawesi, Kalimantan, and other islands. Clean.

Mandar Inn, Jl. Anuang 11, Box 245, tel. 82349. One of the best places to stay for independent travelers. It has a very helpful staff, and offers information leaflets in five languages as well as a film of the tourist resorts of South Sulawesi. Very clean and located in a quiet neighborhood, about one km from the beach. Food is available in the hotel at the same prices as the local *warung*.

Moderate

Hotel Wisata, Jl. Hasanuddin 36-38, tel. (0411) 24344 or 22186. Much less expensive than the big

hotels but it's clean and well-located. Shared bathroom, good breakfast, good service (porter). Avoid the least expensive rooms in the older part of the hotel in back—they're stultifyingly hot and lack ventilation. Ask for the newer and quite nice rooms in the front. Eat in the hotel restaurant (Rp2000), or try one of several good restaurants nearby.

Hotel Purnama, Jl. Pattimura 3, tel. 3830. Though centrally located just to the south of Fort Rotterdam, it's expensive for the drab rooms offered (Rp11,000-17,000 with breakfast).

Ramayana Satrya Hotel, Jl. Gunung Bawakaraeng, tel. 22165 or 24153. Take a *bemo* from downtown for Rp200 or alight from the *bemo* passing in front of the hotel from the airport. Rooms start at Rp14,000 s or d but because of the immense number of mosquitos an a/c room is recommended. Can be pretty dingy and mildewy. Many of the hotel policies—such as a 10 percent "tax" added to the already rip-off breakfast—seem designed to wheedle as much money out of people as possible. Staff is exceedingly lazy and the food is terrible. A male who tries to stay here with an Indonesian woman will be thrown out. Still, the Ramayana is undeniably handy for early morning bus departures to Tator—they leave from right across the street, and the hotel is just down the street from the Merpati office.

Hotel Widhana, Jl. Botolempangan 53, tel. 22499. Rates are Rp30,000-55,000 for large, quiet, clean and comfortable a/c doubles. It's located in the center of town close to prime tourist attractions and shopping areas.

Pondok Delta, Jl. Hasanuddin 25, tel. 22553. A family hotel charging Rp35,000-45,000 (breakfast included) for good a/c rooms. Great food, cheap laundry rates, refrigerator in front—the kind of place you leave your key in the door. U.S. aid workers stay here months at a time, and it's a great place for kids.

Luxury

Marannu City Hotel, Jl. Sultan Hasanuddin 3-5, tel. (0411) 21470 or 21806. The city's top hotel, near the post office, Garuda office, and shopping area. Room charge is Rp110,000 (plus 21 percent tax and service) for big, well-lit rooms with fridge, TV, video, and all the amenities, including coffee shop, bar, billiard room, large swimming pool, and occasional buffets. Worth the price. Avoid the restaurant—Rp21,000 for overpriced, ordinary meals.

Makassar Golden Hotel, Jl. Pasar Ikan 52, tel. 22208, fax 71290. Terrific—the best view of any large city hotel. This three-star hotel features commodious rooms, super magazine kiosk, disco, pool. Don't miss the sunset. Standard rooms Rp115,000 s; Toraja-style cottages at Rp155,400 s, Rp172,200 d right on the sea. Add to all prices tax and service charges. The restaurant is the pits and the food takes forever to arrive.

Pondok Suada Indah, Jl. Sultan Hasanuddin 14, tel. 7179. For something cheaper and more authentic, check out this old Dutch-style right across from the Marannu. With 14 enormous and slightly overpriced rooms at Rp35,000 s, Rp40,000 d (plus 10 percent tax), it feels like a guesthouse with a colonial air.

Hotel Victoria Panghegar, Jl. Jen. Sudirman 24, tel. 21292 or 21228, fax 21292. A large, modern and expensive luxury hotel with outstanding service—the city's most "Westernized" international-standard hotel.

MANADO

Budget
Penginapan Jakarta Jaya Jl. Hasanuddin. Very popular with travelers, almost always full, except when they periodically decide not to receive foreigners. Reach this *penginapan* by *oplet* traveling to Tuminting (Rp200). It's near the Megawati Bridge.

Flamboyan, across the street from Penginapan Jakarta Jaya. The most likely place to accept your presence—especially if you have some foreign coins to give the owner. Quite basic (Rp4000 per person) but adequate rooms. Very good eats downstairs, and a balcony over the rather noisy street.

Hotel Kawanua, Jl. Sudirman 40, tel. (0431) 63842. Opposite the hospital in Kampung Kodok. The nice lobby does not accurately represent the poor condition of the rooms (Rp24,000, not bargainable).

Nusantara Diving Center, Molas. A diving/snorkeling club outside of the city. Negotiate for a quiet a/c bungalow with hot water, tub and shower, and enclosed patio for around Rp15,000 per day.

Moderate
Guesthouse Maria, Jl. Sam Ratulangi. Good value for Rp25,000-30,000. Very clean, with good food, and easy to locate. From this guesthouse, catch any *oplet* along Jl. Sam Ratulangi into town. Returning, catch one to either Sario or Waneo.

Hotel Minahasa, Jl. Sam Ratulangi 199, tel. (0431) 62559. In an old Dutch mansion, it rents fan rooms for Rp30,000 and a/c rooms for Rp38,000. Sheets and towels are changed every day, incredible meals, plus tea, snacks, and *zirzak*. Excellent people, good service.

Hotel Jeprinda, Jl. Sam Ratulangi 37, tel. 4049. Conveniently located opposite a travel agent, near downtown and the main post office. No restaurant. At Rp20,000 s for rooms with fan, Rp25,000 for a/c, this is not a bad deal, but not as good as the Minahasa.

Wisma Charlotte, Jl. Yos Sudarso 56, tel. 62265, fax 65100. A small guesthouse charging Rp25,000 s or d, including all taxes and service. Coffee and tea free, free airport service. Located between the city and the airport, with souvenir shop, travel bureau, drugstore, laundry service, taxi, doctor on call, sports facilites, and games.

Luxury
Kawanua City Hotel, Jl. Sam Ratulangi 1, tel. (0431) 52222, fax 65220. The city's only three-star hotel, in the center of town near the business district. With central a/c, elevators, two restaurants, lounge, travel agent, shops, large swimming pool, American breakfast, and sanitized toilet seats, this place tries very hard to be a Holiday Inn—but it's absolute robbery. The service is appalling and the pool green and slimy.

Manado Sahid Hotel, Jl. Babe Palar 1, tel. 52688. This two-star hotel is a better deal than the Kawanua City; Rp35,000 s Rp40,000 d, deluxe Rp90,000 s, Rp106,000 d.

New Queen Hotel, Jl. Wakeke 12-14, tel. 64440, fax 52748. A small "big" two-star hotel, very service-oriented and efficient; Rp30,400-68,400 s, Rp38,000-Rp79,000 d, plus 21 percent service and government tax. Credit cards accepted. If booked by the tourist office at the airport, the price is Rp25,000—free airport pickup for guests. Good restaurant with bad coffee; overpriced laundry service. From the roof is a sweeping view over the whole neighborhood and the waterfront.

Manado Beach Hotel, P.O. Box 1030, Manado, tel. 67001, fax 67007. The city's first international hotel, on Tasik Ria Beach about 32 km from the city. It has 250 a/c rooms decorated in traditional style, TV and video rooms, minibars, private balconies overlooking the ocean, coffee shops, restaurants, two swimming pools, fitness center, tennis courts, squash courts, jogging track, disco, shops, banks, travel agencies, free transfer to airport, fax, massage, and taxis. Tranquil, peaceful, expensive. Rates are Rp126,000 s, Rp140,000 d and up, subject to 15.5 percent service and government tax.

MULUKU

TERNATE

Moderate

Wisma Alhilal, Jl. Monunutu 2/32, tel. (0921) 21404. A good deal with outstanding meals, very helpful staff. Rooms cost Rp10,000-20,000

Wisma Sejahtera, Jl. Lawamena 21. A family-style accommodation with small, comfortable and homey rooms, prices similar to the Alhilal.

Hotel Nirwana, Jl. Pahlawan Revolusi 58, tel. 21787. Down near the harbor; Rp20,000 with meals.

Hotel Indah, Jl. Bosouri 3, tel. 21334. In the middle of Ternate, has no private bathrooms but is

quite good value at Rp20,000. The a/c rooms are almost twice the price.

Angin Mamiri, Jl. Babulah 17, tel. 21245. Offers Rp10,000-15,000 rooms; plus higher-priced a/c rooms. Meals cost extra, Rp5000 pp lunch or dinner.

AMBON

Moderate

Penginapan Beta, Jl. Wim Reawaru 114, tel. 3463. The best value in town. Run by a Protestant family, the top floor rooms have a cool balcony and easy access to the breezy roof. Even the cheapest rooms have mandi inside. Next door is the Hotel Hero with rates from Rp30,000; no tax or service charge.

Hotel Sela, Jl. A. Rhebok. This family-style hotel has rooms with *kamar mandi*—a clean, comfortable place on a quiet street.

Hotel Eleonoor, Jl. A. Rhebok 30, tel. 2834. Next door to the Chinese Protestant church and across the street from Hotel Sela, is also clean and comfortable. A family-style place on a semi-busy street; comfortable, nice breakfast.

Hotel Rezfanny, Jl. Wim Reawaru 115, tel. 42300. Has drab upstairs rooms, but better, slicker rooms downstairs with *mandi* inside, a/c, and sitting area. Barely drinkable coffee. Be sure to light your mosquito coil. Very near the governor's office and Dinas Pariwisata.

Wisma Game, Jl. Jen. A. Yani, tel. 3525. A small, very clean, family-run hotel near the Garuda office. Price includes breakfast (toast), free tea, sandals and towel. The proprietor, Mr. Kasturian, speaks Dutch.

Lelisa Beach Resort, Jl. Raya Namalatu, tel. 51990 or 51989. On the beach 14 km from the city. Rates are Rp45,000 for rooms with a/c, hot water; Rp65,000 for rooms with a/c, hot water, TV, refrigerator. Prices do not include meals; restaurant on site. Ibu Wanda Latumahina is very friendly and speaks both English and Dutch. If you don't wish to spend the night, you're free to vist the resort to swim, relax, and spend the day.

Luxury

Mutiara, Jl. Pattimura 90, tel. (0911) 3075 or 3076. Of all Ambon's hotels, the Mutiara comes closest to international standards—its 12 a/c rooms cost Rp25,500 s, Rp35,000 d with inside mandi, video, and minibar. Some rooms have private terraces.

Anggrek, Jl. A. Yani, tel. 2139. An old colonial hotel in a residential district with pleasant porches and a central location. It has some new a/c rooms, but the rest are shabby. Good meals included in the price.

Hotel Amboina, Jl. Kapt. Ulupaha 5, tel. 41725 or 3354. A one-star hotel, supposedly the best in Ambon. It's probably the best base for a businessperson; reasonably good restaurant, right in the town center. Telex, room service, restaurant, erratic TV, all credit cards accepted. Prices range from Rp60,000 per night for very basic a/c singles to Rp120,000 for clean double rooms with large bathrooms. Travelers arriving at the airport are sometimes offered a 15 percent discount to stay here; 20 percent discount for stays of more than one night.

Wisata, Jl. Mutiara SK 3-15, tel. 3293 or 3567. A close, tight, cozy place right on the waterfront. Rooms with private bath, TV, hot water, a/c, and fridge cost Rp27,500 s, Rp30,000 d. Run by Mr. Yunan, who was born in Dobo. He speaks a number of languages and is quite sharp and informative. Very good food in the clean dining room. No credit cards accepted. Not a great value despite the automatic 10 percent discount.

KALIMANTAN

BALIKPAPAN

Budget

Wisma Aida, Jl. D.I. Penjaitan 50, tel. 21006. Fancy front but unprepossessing interior; inexpensive rooms are small but clean, with fan. Lies a few kilometers from city center (take bus no. 5).

Hotel Sederhana, Jl. A. Yani 290. The frequent choice of travelers on a budget. Located at next to

Bioskop Gelora on the waterfront, it has a/c rooms; cheaper rooms are in the *penginapan* of the same name in the same building. Rooms here cost Rp15,000-40,000 depending on facilities. Other cheapies around town such as the Penginapan Royal won't take foreigners—too much paperwork.

Moderate

Gajah Mada, Jl. Sudirman 14, tel. (0542) 34634, fax 34636. The best budget to midpriced hotel, with economy rooms from Rp25,000 to Rp30,000 and a/c standards from Rp50,000 to Rp60,000. Popular with travelers and tour groups watching their *rupiah*; a decent Padang restaurant is attached. Recommended.

Tirta Plaza, Jl. D.I. Panjaitan 51-52, tel. 22324 or 22132. An American-style hotel with swimming pool; it also has bungalows for Rp45,000. Cheaper rates on the weekends.

Luxury

Blue Sky Hotel, Jl. Jen. Suprapto 1, tel. 35845, fax 24094. Friendly, with excellent food and entertainment. Rooms run from Rp80,000 (standard room, weekend) to Rp150,000 (deluxe, weekday). Facilities include a pool, fitness center, and comfortable rooms with views of the oil fields.

Altea Benakutai Hotel, Jl. Yani, tel. 31896, fax 31823. Balikpapan's original international-class hotel, with a five-star rating and 216-rooms, which caters to oil workers and group tourists; rooms cost Rp294,000-756,000.

Dusit Hotel, on the road to the airport. Even more luxurious than the Altea, with all possible amenities plus a much more efficient management than the rather disorganized Altea. The Dusit opened in early 1994.

BANJARMASIN

Budget

Borneo Homestay, Jl. Pos 87, tel. (0511) 66545. Most budget travelers head straight for this homestay. Owned and operated by Johansyah and Nurlina Yasin, a pair of young, helpful attorneys. Both are experts in travel and will help with ticketing, local tours, and trekking in the Loksado district. Rooms are extremely basic, but there's a pleasant veranda overlooking the river.

Diamond Homestay. Operated by the managers of Adi Angkasa Travel on Jl. Hasanuddin 27. Not as well situated as the Borneo Homestay but conveniently located near the boat docks, and quite acceptable. The charge is Rp10,000.

Moderate
Hotel Beauty, Jl. Haryono M.T. 176, tel. 4493. One of the best moderately priced hotels. Rooms feature fans, shared bathrooms, and *warung* close by.

Hotel Sabrina, at Jl. Bank Rakyat 21, tel. 54442. Centrally located and reasonably clean; rooms cost Rp18,000-25,000 with fan and Rp32,000-38,000 a/c.

Luxury
Barito Palace Hotel, Jl. Haryono 16, tel. 67300, fax 52240. A luxurious, urban hotel which offers an attractive pool, several restaurants, and rooms for Rp158,000-210,000.

Kalimantan Hotel, Jl. Lambung Mangkurat, tel. 66818, fax 67345. The best in town. Facilities include pool, fitness center, adjacent shopping center, and a towering block of 180 classy rooms for Rp158,000-315,000.

Maramin Hotel, Jl. Lambung Mangkurat 32, tel. 68944, fax 53350. Near the Jl. Samudera intersection. It poses as a five-star hotel, but should be avoided; truly awful rooms for Rp65,000-100,000.

NUSATENGGARA

LOMBOK

Budget
Losmen Pabean, Jl. Yos Sudarso 146. If you like a city scene, try the Chinese-owned and well-run hotel which asks Rp 4500 s, Rp6600 d. A popular *losmen* with travelers, Pabean features laundry facilities and a simple breakfast. *Rumah makan* and Chinese restaurants are down the street.

Zahir Hotel, Jl. Adi Sucipto 9, tel. (0364) 34248. Run by nice people, with a breezy garden. Rates are Rp6500-10,000.

Losmen Horas, Jl. Adi Sucipto 65. A bit cramped and too close to a mosque. Rooms are Rp5000-9000.

Wisma Triguna, Jl. Koperasi 78, tel. (0364) 31705. Farther up Jl. Koperasi toward the airport, rooms are comfy and very good value at Rp7500-16,000. Here you get in-room baths, wide verandas, a flower-filled yard, and travel information and services. Each spacious room has a private bathroom. Eddy Barubara, the proprietor, will take you on tours of the island, arrange motorcycle rentals, help you climb and camp on Gunung Rinjani, provide information on Gili Air and Komodo, and let you call home collect from the *wisma.*

Moderate
Nitour Hotel, Jl. Yos Sudarso 4, tel. 23780 The best accommodation in Ampenan. Pleasant a/c rooms sit separately in a garden, with TV, hot and cold water, and private bath. Rates are Rp35,000-60,000, including breakfast. Rates decrease during the low season. There's a fine restaurant on the premises serving Indonesian, Chinese, and Western food. A car rental service is available, and a Merpati agent is located in an attached building. A delightful place.

KOMODO

Budget
PHPA Camp, Loh Liang Bay. This well-kept camp, two km north of Kampung Komodo, is located in the north part of Teluk Slawi, surrounded by open grasslands, riverbeds, old *ladang,* savannahs, and a small mangrove swamp on the bay's west end near the coast. Tourists may only stay in the PHPA camp's visitor accommodations—several large bungalows costing Rp5500 per night per person. Generator-produced electricity operates until about 2200. There's a cafeteria with an extensive menu, though it's somewhat expensive. This is the only place on the island to buy food.

FLORES

LABUHANBAJO

Budget

Mutiara Beach Hotel, across the street from the Bajo Beach Hotel. Set partly over the water, it's basic but adequate at Rp3500 s with shared *mandi* and Rp6000 d with fan and *mandi*. The restaurant has a good menu. Captained by Leonardo Kati, a reputed weasel, the hotel harbors one of Indonesia's most wonderful collection of *losmen* scalawags. Leo rents vehicles but will try to squeeze every *rupiah* out of you.

Waecicu Beach Bungalows For those who want peace, quiet, and seclusion, this is the best place to stay though it is a short boat ride away. Good beach, great sunsets, no crowds, and no noise. Rates for rooms are Rp6500 which includes three simple meals.

Hotel Gardena, near the harbor. Built in a simple beach-bungalow style, it has a pleasant setting on a hillside. Good sunsets from the small restaurant. Rooms cost Rp8000 with shared *mandi* and Rp10,000 with private *mandi*; breakfast included.

Hotel Wisata A new place, 20 minutes on foot from the harbor. White tile, clean, somewhat sterile. It's not central and has no special location, but it's pretty good value for the money. Rooms in the back are Rp7500 s and Rp10,000 d, while up front are rooms for Rp10,000 s and Rp15,000 d. Rates include fan, *mandi,* and breakfast. Small restaurant attached.

Moderate

Bajo Beach Hotel An old traveler's standby only 10 minutes walk from the harbor. Chinese-run, this tidy place has its own transportation, laundry service, tourist information, and a good restaurant. Rooms are Rp15,000 standard, Rp17,500 with fan and *mandi*; breakfast included.

New Bajo Beach Hotel & Cottages, two km south of town along the beach. Run by the same people who own the Bajo Beach Hotel, this is the premier place to stay in Labuhanbajo. Beyond the landscaped gardens are 16 rooms (four with a/c) and ten bungalows; the spacious rooms have showers and sit-down toilets. Rooms are Rp50,000 a/c and Rp30,000 with fan; bungalows run Rp20,000. All transportation around town is provided. The restaurant has a great sunset view, and a huge fish tank where you can choose your supper.

TIMOR

KUPANG

Budget

Pitoby Lodge, Jl. Kosasi, tel. 32910. Just up from the Merpati office, this the most centrally located budget accommodations with rooms from Rp5500. Some rooms have bunk beds, all have fans; some have *mandi,* others share facilities. YHA, VIP, or STA cardholders receive a 50 percent discount. In conjunction with the Pitoby Lodge is the only organized scuba diving operation on Timor.

Fatuleu Homestay, Jl. G. Fatuleu 1, tel. (0391) 31374. Private, very quiet, clean, beautiful garden, laundry service. Rooms without *mandi* are Rp7500 s and Rp10,000 d including breakfast (tea/coffee, bread, banana, even *nasi goreng* on request). Very friendly staff. Owner Jack Sine is also a tour operator and speaks English well. Recommended.

Hotel Laguna, Jl. Kelimutu 36, tel. 21348. A sprawling complex of 23 rooms run as efficiently as a Singapore budget hotel. Popular with businesspeople, the Laguna isn't a bad deal for Kupang. Rooms cost Rp7000 without *mandi* or fan and Rp12,000-18,000 with fan and *mandi*; a/c rooms run up to Rp60,000. Coffee and sweetcakes are served at 0530. The restaurant here features Javanese food.

Losmen Eden, tel. 21921. Run by ex-parliamentarian Papa Minggus, you pay Rp3000 pp. There are also bungalows and "family" rooms, but only tea and coffee for breakfast. Also a swimming pool and a bar, and tasty food is served at all hours (the best *gado-gado!*). Small fruit and vegetable market nearby, and a *warung* on the main road sells Rp800-1200 meals. There's also a great

200-year-old spring-fed pool of cool water (the "lagoon") and many shady trees, so it's not so hot as downtown. Air Nona is a quiet area to stay in, four km up the hill from the *bemo* terminal (Rp300 by *bemo*). From Air Nona, charter a *bemo* to the airport for Rp7500.

Moderate
Morning Sun Hotel, Jl. Kelimutu 11a, tel. 32268. Owned and operated by Ruth Bowes, an Australian, it has an assortment of rooms: standard fan Rp10,000-12,500, or Rp17,500-22,000 for a larger room. Air-conditioned rooms from Rp27,500 to Rp30,000. Discount on long-term stays and for Aussie government workers. Room charge includes afternoon tea and transfer to and from the airport or harbor. Beds in a bunk room for Rp4000 pp may be available; inquire.

Hotel Komodo, Jl. Kelimutu 35, tel. 31179. Recently renovated, this clean, efficiently run, multistoried hotel has laundry service but no restaurant. Standard rooms run Rp15,000-20,000, a/c rooms Rp25,000-27,000.

Hotel Flobamor, tel. 21346, Jl. Jen. Sudirman 21, is basically a business hotel. Depending upon the floor and class of room, rates are Rp30,000-80,000, with one VIP room for Rp150,000. All rooms have a/c, hot water, satellite TV, telephone, and video. Very clean, spacious, and well kept with a nice lobby and breezy outdoor restaurant. Service is excellent except for exorbitant laundry costs. A handy tour and travel agent's office is inside, as well as a gift shop and a bar/disco. The Merpati agent is next door.

Luxury
Orchid Garden Hotel, Jl. G. Fatuleu 2, tel. 33707. Located across the street from Fatuleu Homestay, this is the city's best. Full service: swimming pool, gourmet restaurant, in-house doctor, tennis courts, room service, free transfer to the airport, tour operator and ticketing agent on premises. All 60 rooms, with TV, radio, and video equipment, breakfast included, face the courtyard—standard Rp117,600, double standard Rp134,400, superior Rp155,400, and orchid suite Rp262,500.

Hotel Sasando, Jl. Kartini, tel. 22224. A luxury hotel on a parched, windy, flat plateau six km east of town. Rates: Rp84,000-126,000, plus 21 percent service and government tax. All rooms face the ocean and the sunset. Facilities include telex, tennis courts, swimming pool, restaurant, and tour agency. The Sasando's fortunes may take an upswing as the city continues to build its administrative district, called Walikota, just behind the hotel. Take a taxi to and from Kupang for Rp6000 each way.

IRIAN JAYA

WAMENA

Budget
Syahrial Jaya, Jl. Gatot Subroto 51, tel. (0967) 151. The cheapest and best *losmen* in town; Rp10,000 pp with fan and *mandi*; a/c rooms cost Rp18,000 s. Price includes breakfast. Easy to find, close to the airport runway; Sam will probably be out at the airport to greet you. The Indonesian manager, Hamzah Tanjung, is responsible and helpful. You can even arrange to clean up there, stay half a day, and leave things in the locked storage room without checking in as a guest—a big help when trekking. Sit around in the evenings with the locals and sing Dani songs.

Losmen Sri Lestari Across from the market with rooms for Rp15,000 s and Rp27,000 d. The place is sprayed every night for mosquitos.

Wio Silimo Traditional Dani Hotel A *losmen* built in the traditional style of the Dani tribe. Dani tools hang on walls. Rp5,000 for a loft, Rp10,000 s, Rp15,000 d. Generator electricity. Julius Yikma works here as a guide; he smokes like a chimney, and speaks three languages of the Baliem Valley as well as English.

Moderate
Nayak, Jl. Gatot Subroto 1, tel. 31067 or 31030. Has 15 clean, basic rooms for Rp30,000 s, Rp40,000 d. Tariff includes breakfast, service tax, and attached *mandi*.

Losmen Anggrek, Jl. Ambon 1, tel. 31242. Rents rooms for Rp30,000-40,000. Balcony overlooks the neighborhood. Clean, *mandi*-style bath, Western toilet.

Wamena Hotel, Jl. Trikora, tel. 81292. About 1.5 km from the market on the road out of town to the north, is a typical Indonesian businessman's hotel with Western toilet and cold-water *mandi*. Beware of annoying abbreviated "short sheets." Sinks, but no water. Light breakfast of marmalade and hardboiled egg.

Hotel Trendy. Right next to the Baliem Palace towards the market, tel. 31092, offers rooms for Rp22,000 s, Rp27,000 d. Ten rooms, all with bath. The air is closed and stuffy but the *ibu* is friendly. Breakfast, coffee, cold drinks, tea.

Luxury
Hotel Baliem, Jl. Thamrin, tel. 31370. The oldest luxury hotel in Wamena. Comfortable rooms run Rp35,500 s, Rp55,000 d; price includes all taxes, continental breakfast, and afternoon snack. Clean bungalows built in typical Dani style with sitting areas, Western-style bathrooms, but no hot water and weak electricity. Seventeen rooms in 11 *honnay*-shaped buildings; even the restaurant resembles a *honnay*. Very nice dining room with good breakfast and full-course meals (Rp5000). The superb map in the office shows most of the villages and rivers of the Baliem.

Baliem Palace Hotel. This small, central hotel charges Rp55,000 s, Rp65,000 d for clean, comfortable rooms. Good maps of the Baliem Valley are for sale for Rp7500. It's almost always full in the high season, even for meals.

Restaurants

WEST JAVA

JAKARTA

Indonesian
Paradiso 2001, Jl. H. Agus Salim 30. Tasty, cheap, and clean vegetarian food. It's down the small alley next to the A&W.

Indah Kuring, Jl. Wahid Hasyim 131A near Wisma Ise. The finest Javanese and Sundanese food. From the shortage of Javanese restaurants one would think the Javanese were outnumbered in their own capital.

Handayani, Jl. Abdul Muis 36E. For East Javanese cooking. Serves such typical dishes as *sop buntut* (oxtail soup).

Chinese
Bakmi Gajah Mada, Jl. Gajah Mada 92 and Jl. Melawai IV/25 in Blok M. Specializes in all kinds of delicious noodle dishes.

The Cahaya Kota, Jl. Wahid Hasyim 9, tel. (021) 353-3015. One of Jakarta's finest Chinese-Indonesian restaurants, where the capital's rich and powerful go. Matchless Chinese food and superb frog legs.

Blue Ocean, Jl. Hayam Wuruk 5, Kota. Serves high quality dim sum. Open daily 0700-1200.

Other Asian
Omar Khayam, Jl. Antara 5-7, across from the main post office. Offers an extensive menu of Indian specialties. Buffet lunch every weekday (Rp9000). Open 1200-1500 and 1830-2400.

Tokyo, corner of Jl. Jaksa and Jl. K.H. Wahid Hasyim. Frequented by Japanese businesspeople, it's costly, but you get what you pay for. Here you can get a nice meal for Rp40,000 (sushi and tempura for two). Jakarta's numerous Japanese restaurants are expensive, less so than in the West but more so than in Yogyakarta.

Korean Tower, Bank Bumi Daya Plaza (30th floor), Jl. Imam Bonjol. Great Korean food, though only the set lunch is affordable.

Seafood
Jun Nyan, Jl. Batuceper 69 off Jl. Hayamwuruk, Glodok. Very possibly the best seafood restaurant in Indonesia. Frequented by American Embassy types, its popular specialties include cracked crab with fantastic sauce, fried whole fish, boiled shrimp, squid and frog legs in black sauce, and chicken feet in soy sauce. Be sure to make a reservation; tel. (021) 364-063 or 364-434.

European

Oasis Restaurant, Jl. Raden Saleh 47, Kebayoran, tel 327-818. For the inimitable Dutch colonial *rijstaffel,* check out this lavish restaurant decked out in true Casablanca style. Closed Sunday.

George and Dragon, Jl. Kota Bumi 34, tel. 336-241. An English pub a short walk from the Sheraton. Sip a Guinness while dining on cheese with pickles or farmhouse liver pate. The place also serves Indian cuisine. The *Far Eastern Economic Review* recently reported that "clandestine information gathering activities" (translation: spying) occur in this establishment, owned by an Australian military officer.

Le Bistro, Jl. Wahid Hasyim 75, Kebayoran, tel. 390-9249. Serves excellent, expensive French food; live music.

BOGOR

Indonesian/Chinese

Asinan Bogor, Jl. Kapt. Muslihat. A good place to sample *asinan,* one of the most popular Sundanese dishes is *asinan,* a mixture of fruit, vegetables, and peanuts in a hot peanut sauce. Sundanese food is a little drier and less spicy-hot than *nasi padang;* it also tends to be cheaper.

Bogor Permai Coffee House, Jl. Jen. Sudirman 23A (near Jl. Sawojajar), tel. (0251) 2115. A spacious, modern restaurant with Chinese/Indo food upstairs and Western food downstairs; also a bakery and supermarket.

Hidangan Puti Bungsu, Jl. Kapitan Muslihat. For delicious *nasi padang.*

CENTRAL JAVA

CIREBON

Specialties

Nasi lengko is made of rice, *tempe, tahu, sambal,* lemon, cucumber, sprouts, fried crispy onions, and meat. *Nasi jamblang* consists of sour fish, beef jerky, dried cow's lung, vegetables, and *tahu goreng,* served with a specially prepared rice. Try some at Hotel Asia around 0900 when the vendors arrive. You can also buy it at the harbor and bus station.

Warung Nasi Lengko, near the Golden Cinema, and **Nasi Jamblang** on Jl. Gunung Sari feature good Cirebon-style *nasi campur* and *nasi goreng* with lots of vegetables.

Seafood

Maxim's, Jl. Bahagia 45-47. The best seafood restaurant in Cirebon. There are over 50 items on the menu; the best deals are the freshly caught crab and shrimp dishes. The old black-and-white photographs in the front lobby, snapped by the grandfather of the present owner, illustrate the history of Cirebon's *kraton.*

YOGYAKARTA

Indonesian

Cafe Lotus Garden, Jl. Prawirotaman. Just down the street from the Metro Guesthouse. Reasonable prices for generous portions, consistently good, many vegetarian dishes. The owner, Mas Untung, possesses a wealth of information about Yogyakarta—a good place to exchange notes with other travelers. Cafe Lotus Garden features Indonesian dance and *wayang kulit* three times weekly.

Pesta Perak, Jl. Tentara Rakyat Mataram 8. Features a buffet for only Rp9500 pp. Excellent food, fantastic variety, and great service.

Japanese

Yuriko, Jl. Parangtritis (near the mosque). Excellent Japanese food (Rp3500), plus Indonesian (Rp1500), Chinese, and European. Friendly owners.

SOLO

Solonese and Indonesian

Timlo Solo, Jl. Jen. Urip Sumoharjo/Mesen 106. For Solonese chicken rice soup (*nasi timlo*).

Pak Dul's, on the corner of Jl. Imam Bonjol and Jl. Ronggowarsito. An eating tent serving tasty "100 percent *halal*" rice dishes; order cold beer from the Ramayana Restaurant across the street.

Kusuma Sari Restaurant. Escape the heat in the conveniently located a/c restaurant in the heart of Solo. The food is average, but check the photo menu—curious shots of hamburgers decorated with miniature corn, and a grinning Pinokio Sundae.

Sumatran
Pasar Pon, Jl. Slamet Riyadi (near Bioskop Dhady). The best *nasi padang* restaurant in town.

Chinese
Populair, Jl. Achmad Dahlan 70. Serves very good Chinese-style meals. The *cap cai* (Rp1500) is hard to beat; enough for two.

Ramayana Restaurant, on the intersection of Jl. Imam Bonjol and Jl. Ronggowarsito. A cozy little place with well-prepared Chinese cuisine, *sate,* and cold beer.

EAST JAVA

MALANG

Indonesian
Minang Jaya, Jl. Basuki Rachmat 111, tel. (0341) 5707. Specializes in West Sumatran cuisine. Open 24 hours a day, the restaurant will provide 20 different combinations of food—a real adventure in eating. Taste some *gulai kilkil* (buffalo feet curry). Since it's better than the food you'll find out in the villages, order a packaged lunch if you're going out to the temples on a day-trip. The **Minang Agung** also serves Padang specialties in a lovely old Dutch cafe filled with antiques and comfortable wooden furniture.

Chinese
Gloria Restaurant, near the Pelangi Hotel. Good, moderately priced Chinese food.

New Hong Kong, Jl. A.R. Hakim. Near the *alun-alun,* this is Malang's best Chinese restaurant.

European
Amsterdam Restaurant, Jl. Kawi. A favorite of expats who recommend the Western dishes.

Toko Oen, just off the square near Hotel Pelangi. Serves high-quality Western, Chinese, and In-

donesian food, as well as iced drinks and great ice cream. Like an old-fashioned Dutch coffee shop, this is a real oasis with an authentic colonial atmosphere. The place even serves such anachronistic standbys as *uitsmijter* (Dutch sandwiches), *kaasstengels* (cheese sticks), *droptoffee* (licorice toffee), *kroket* (meat snacks), and *haagsehopjes* (Dutch mocha candies). Clean, spacious, good service. Open daily 0900-2030. Next door is a well-stocked bakery.

SURABAYA

Indonesian
Restoran Aquarius, Surabaya Zoo. Surprisingly good food.

Tirta Indah Garden, Jl. Mayjen Sungkono 47-A. Excellent Indonesian food.

Sari Bundo, Jl. Walikota. Padang-style food.

East Javanese
Kombes Duryat, behind Bioskop Ria. Sample East Javanese regional specialties such as *kilkil* (a hearty soup made from the hooves of goats and cows).

Soto Ambengan, Jl. Ambengan. Try the *soto madura* (Madura-style soup); *bakwan* (soup with pork balls and wonton); *semanggi* (small boiled leaves eaten with peanut sauce); and *bumbu rujak* (chicken in chili sauce).

Chinese
Kit Wan Kie, Jl. Kembang Jepun 51. Offers superb Cantonese cuisine.

Agung, Jl. Baliwerti 1. Famous for its fried pigeon and other delicacies.

Elmi Restaurant, Jl. Samudra 37, tel. (031) 333-004. Excellent food at moderate prices, with live music most evenings.

European
Chez Rose, Jl. Raya Gubeng. Features European, Japanese, and Chinese food as well as imported beef, great pastries, and homemade bread; get a good meal with drinks for two for Rp21,000.

BALI

DENPASAR

Nasi Campur
Rumah Makan Wardani, near Hotel Adi Yasa, on Jl. Judistira at Tapakgangsul, tel. (0361) 224-398. This clean and simple restaurant serves a delicious Balinese-style *nasi campur* for only Rp3000. Open only from early morning until 1300.

Warung Satriya, Jl. Kedongong 13 (off Jl. Veteran). After 1500, this *warung* serves perhaps Denpasar's best *nasi campur.*

Specialty Foodstalls and Restaurants
Puri Agung Restaurant, Natour Bali Hotel. Features a memorable *rijstaffel* (Rp15,000) as well as fixed-price meals.

Restaurant Betty, Jl. Sumatra 56. Inexpensive but first-class and not too spicy Indonesian/Javanese food in a clean environment—a popular hangout for expats.

Kikel Sapi, Jl. Sumatra. For East Javanese specialties: tasty *gado-gado, gule, and rawon.* So popular at night you may have to share a table. Open 0800-1600.

Ayam Bakar Taliwang, Jl. Tengku Umar. Serves complete dinners of extra fat and juicy Sasak-style Taliwang chicken with rice, *sambal*, vegetables, and delicious *es kelapa muda* (Rp1000). Outstanding fish *sate* with hot sauce. Particularly popular with high-placed government people.

Chinese
Restoran Gajah Mada, close to the traffic lights on Jl. Gajah Mada. The chicken dishes are beautifully prepared.

Atoom Baru, Jl. Gajah Mada 106-108, tel. 234-772. An unpretentious but excellent—and centrally located—restaurant for tasty *nasi goreng*, *cap cai*, fishball soup, and fish and vegetables with tomato sauce. A local favorite.

Hong Kong Restaurant, Jl. Gajah Mada 85, tel. 234-845, fax 235-777. Across the road from the Atoom Baru, right in front of Kumbasari Shopping Complex. Prices in this popular, air-conditioned restaurant start at Rp6000-7000; each dish can be ordered in small, medium, or large portions. Specialties include stewed seafood and bean curd, Sichuan hot and sour soup, and fried fresh carp. Nice atmosphere; good for groups.

KUTA

Indonesian/Balinese
Bakung Mini Restaurant, Jl. Bakung Sari 7. Serves up a *nasi campur* special consisting of spring rolls, mixed *sate*, fried chicken, steamed rice, eggs, *cap cai*, and shrimp crackers for only Rp7000.

Rumah Makan Taliwang Bersaudera, Jl. Imam Bonjol. Located on the right-hand side about one km up from Kentucky Fried Chicken, near the outlet where Lombok clay pots are sold. Here another style of Indonesian cuisine—authentic, spicy Lombok food—is sold. Decidedly superior cuisine to 90 percent of Kuta's restaurants. A chicken dinner with vegetables and a drink at the Taliwang will set you back about Rp7000.

Chinese and Asian
Mini Restaurant, opposite the disco on Jl. Legian. A big, lively, smoky, open, central, and crowded restaurant where you pay about Rp15,000 for a big fish that feeds two to three. Try such seafood dishes as the incomparable sweet and sour shrimp with rice, delicious crabs, or lobster. Mini is packed at night, so go early.

Sushi Bar Nelayan, where Poppies Lane I meets Jl. Legian.With the coming of the Japanese, sushi bars are on the ascendant. This small restaurant is a top buy. You get a good choice, 10-15 pieces for Rp7000-11,000.

Agung Korean House, on the first floor of the multistoried Kuta Supermarket on Jl. Bakung Sari, tel. (0361) 752-899. For Korean barbecue, seafood, *bulgogi, sam gae tang, doe jee sam kyub sal*, lobster with *yaki* sauce, and *gyaza musi*, the

European
Mama's German Restaurants, Jl. Legian, tel. 751-805. For dedicated carnivores, Mama's specializes in steaks, famous homemade sausages, and "big soups from Mama's kettle." Under German management.

Restaurant Lilla Sverige Mamma's Kottbullar, Poppies Lane II. Swedish food, including *kottbullar* (Rp3900), *jausous frestelse* (Rp3900), *lok sas med flask och kokt potatis* (also Rp3900).

Poppies Restaurant. In a delightful and romantic setting, Poppies features above average Western and Indonesian food, local Balinese specialties, seafood salad, and excellent Mexican dishes. To get a table, reserve ahead by calling 51149, or arrive early in the evening—it fills up fast.

Un's Restaurant, on a small lane off Poppies Lane I. Has an Indo/Chinese/Euro menu—excellent steaks, schnitzels, and fish, though the service isn't the best. Nice atmosphere, listenable music, comfortable chairs, big portions, good food. Expensive, but worth it.

LEGIAN

Vegetarian

Warung Kopi, Jl. Legian 427, tel. 53602. The small garden courtyard in the back of this restaurant is a great place to relax and enjoy very good food: Greek salad with real feta and olives (Rp3000), curries (Rp5000) and other vegetarian Indian dishes, Lebanese green beans, yogurt and tahini salad (Rp4000), black rice pudding (Rp2000), superb cappuccino (Rp1500). The special breakfast of fruit salad, juice, two eggs, whole-wheat toast, jam, and Balinese coffee (Rp3000) is particularly popular. Extensive variety of desserts, cakes, and chocolate mousse. Reasonable prices, nice atmosphere. Close to central Legian.

Za's Bakery and Restaurant, Jl. Legian, tel. 752-973. Known for its award-winning breakfast, brunch, seafood, and vegetarian dishes. Try the flavorful fish soup with spicy tomato base and thick slice of multigrain bread (Rp3500). Great juices, fruit, and divine yogurt, homemade jams, toasted muesli, whole-wheat bagels, croissants, raisin bread, and cheesecakes.

Western

Swiss Pub and Restaurant, behind the Kuta Palace Hotel on Jl. Pura Bagus Taruna, tel. 751-735. A Swiss oasis in the middle of Indonesia. Run by a Balinese woman and her Swiss husband, Jon Zurcher; they import wine from France, steak from New Zealand, and bratwurst sausages and cheese from Switzerland. Asia buffets every Saturday, plus daily *rijstaffel*. Try the smoked fish (Rp5000), banana flambe (Rp2200), and superb omelettes. Jon, who also serves as the official Swiss Consul, can be recognized by his pipe and bare feet. He eschews shoes even when climbing volcanos, and will personally lead treks to places you'd never go alone. Ask to see his photo albums.

Legian Snacks, Jl. Padma Utara. Good, inexpensive Aussie delicacies like Toad in the Hole and baked beans on toast are available here as well as high-quality meals, cold drinks, low prices, always packed. The specialty is Aussie food, with some Indonesian and Chinese dishes. Especially good for breakfast.

A traditional English self-service buffet brunch (Rp7000) is served every day between 1100-1300 at The Bounty on Jl. Legian. On the Bounty's upper deck English dishes like steak and kidney pie are served; drink in the Captain's Bar. Nearby is Mama's, Jl. Legian 354, specializing in German food—*schweine braten mit rotkohl, fassbier, gulaschsuppe, hahnchen mit pommes frites*.

Japanese

Kurumaya, Jl. Padma 1, tel. 752-111. In central Legian. Savor teppanyaki, tempura, shabu-shabu, and other traditional Japanese cuisine. Open 1800-2300.

Goa 2001 Restaurant, just beyond Legian toward Seminyak. A popular eatery with Indian dishes and a sit-down sushi bar. Also Indonesian, Italian, and German food. Limited menu, but what's there is adequate to good. Tasty pumpkin soup. Meals with drink average Rp10,000-12,000. A warm-up place before the discos open; most of the Beautiful People lounge around listening to great music while downing exotic drinks from a three-page-long drink menu. The magnificent building has with vaulted ceiling of ribbed bamboo and interlocking thatch.

LOVINA

Buffets

Rambutan Restaurant, Kalibukbuk. This open-air restaurant presents a *legong* and Balinese Banquet at 1930 every Sunday and Wednesday night featuring professional dancers performing traditional dances. Cost is Rp6000. Competing restaurants try to outdo each other by hosting huge buffets on alternating evenings, and they can be very good deals.

Chono's. Three nights a week they host an extravagant *rijstaffel* buffet at 1930. The meal—15 tasty dishes including rice wine, chocolate milk, peanuts, and fried *tempe*—is followed by Balinese dancing for Rp6000. Chono's also serves fresh seafood at very reasonable prices: fried calamari with garlic butter (Rp3000), grilled tuna (Rp3000), or snapper with choice of sauce (Rp3500).

Indonesian and European

Permata Restaurant, Lovina Beach Hotel, Lovina. Serves Balinese, Indonesian, Chinese and Western dishes. Specialties include *betutu bebek* (stuffed steamed duck), *babi guling, sate ayam, nasi goreng spesial,* and *gado-gado.* The pride of Permata is *nasi tumpeng,* a truly Balinese dish consisting of a mountain of rice surrounded by *sate,* vegetables, curries, and *betutu.* The restaurant's beachfront gazebo, flanked by a garden and fishpond, offers a great spot to watch the sunset.

Warung Made, on the main road. Offers a set menu with a choice of courses and great dessert, all for Rp10,000. Great salads; prices very competitive. Classical music and acoustic guitar add to the relaxing atmosphere. Happy hour discounts on food and drink. Nice *brem.*

Arya's, on the south side of the main road, tel. (0362) 61797. One of Lovina's hands-down favorites where you'll find imaginative pasta dishes, a grilled tuna fish dinner (Rp4000), a selection of vegetarian meals, and the best homemade desserts in Lovina. Service can be so-so; its strength is its breakfast with multigrain bread baked on the premises, homemade jams, muesli, and porridge.

Flower Garden Restaurant, next to Arya's. Offers items from a set menu for Rp7500-Rp9500 in intimate surroundings. Some of the dishes are good, but portions are sometimes skimpy. If Made herself is cooking, count on a superb meal—dishes like guacamole and potato skins, cream of prawn soup, or tuna wrapped in bamboo leaf. Sample Made's Bali wine at your peril. Balinese dancing starts around 2000.

CANDIDASA

Seafood

Arie's Restaurant, in the western edge of town. One of the best for budget Western, Balinese, and Chinese food. The fish dinners are good value; also try the *gado-gado* and the fish curry with vegetables. Family-run.

Pandan Restaurant. The first and still one of the best restaurants in Candidasa is the candle-lit Pandan situated right on the beach—fantastic grilled fish with vegetable salad. The buffet dinner (Rp9000, with free beer) is highly recommended.

European

TJ's, Water Garden Cottages, tel./fax 0361 35540. The best place for Western food. Homemade bread, stuffed baked potatoes, lots of salads, delectable grilled fish, and a clean, lovely and authentic Balinese-style *nasi campur* with *urab* and not much oil. Also a popular place for cakes and expresso.

Chez Lily. Candidasa's premier gourmet restaurant. Excellent and unusual food, reasonable prices, slow service. Open 0800-2000.

Mandara Giri Pizzeria, east of the village (on the left). The resort's best Italian restaurant with extremely good, inexpensive food—crab with cognac, pizza with seafood, outstanding spaghetti and lasagna.

AMLAPURA

Rumah Makan Surabaya, Jl. Kesatrian. A little gem for really cheap, high-quality *soto ayam, cap cai goreng, es campur,* hot *gado-gado,* and wonderful *es jus nipis,* all Rp1000-2000. Open 0900-2100, and crowded every night.

SUMATRA

MEDAN

Indonesian
Garuda, Jl. Pemuda 20C-D, tel. 327-692.
Very good Padang-style food (a *nasi campur* costs about Rp1500). The fruit juices are a knockout.

Family, JL. Brig. Jen Katamso. Another good place for Minang food.

European
Tip Top Restaurant, Jl. Jen. A. Yani 92, tel. (061) 24442. Specializes in Western food and *nasi padang*. Quite good fish and meat dishes, delicious ice cream and cakes. This attractive sidewalk cafe is a nice place to sit day or night and take in the street life while sipping a cold beer.

Lyn's Cafe and Restaurant, next door to the Tip Top. An expat watering hole with probably the city's best Western meat dishes, including chateaubriand steak and spaghetti Bolognese.

Seafood
Surya Sea Food, Jl. Imam Bonjol 8, tel. 323-433. Great seafood.

Columbia, Jl. Putri Hijau 8J-K, tel. 526-374. Medan's best seafood.

Chinese
Bali Plaza Restaurant, Jl. Kumango 1A, tel. (061) 514-852. The best Chinese banquet cuisine Medan has to offer. Only the freshest ingredients are used. You're treated like royalty: hostesses light your cigarettes, continually fill your glass with beer, ladle soup for you. Fast service. Try the shrimp hot plate, fried chicken, soups, and desserts. Outrageous Shanghai Pancake—three people have trouble finishing it.

Polonia Restaurant, Polonia Hotel, Jl. Sudirman 14, tel. 325-300. An outstanding dining experience where meals are served up to 2300. Stick to the Chinese menu; prices are moderate to expensive.

Cafe De Marati, Jl. Gatot Subroto, tel. 321-751. Another good Chinese restaurant.

Ethnic and Vegetarian
Koh-I-Noor Indian Restaurant, Jl. Mesjid 21, tel. (061) 513-953, Kesawan District. Heartily recommended is this hospitable and moderately priced restaurant near the post office (Jl. Mesjid runs parallel with Jl. A. Yani). Sample North Indian curries and tandoori chicken. The owners are kind and hospitable and fluent in English.

Yoshiko Yokohama, Danau Toba International Hotel, Jl. Imam Bonjol, tel. 327-000. For Japanese food. Rather expensive.

Restaurant Vegetarian Indonesia, Jl. Gandhi 63A, tel. 526-812. Medan is blessed with an uncommonly good vegetarian restaurant run run by people from a nearby Buddhist temple. They speak no English and have no English menu but provide lots of photographs of their varied and delicious fare.

PALEMBANG

Pasar Malam. Parallel with Jl. Jen. Sudirman, the city's main street, is Jl. Sajangan, which turns into an open-air market at night with foodstalls, fruit stands, and *sate* and snack vendors.

Indonesian
Sari Bundo, on the corner of Jl. Kapt. A. Rivai and Jl. Jen. Sudirman. A notable Padang-style restaurant.

Mahkota Indah, 24 Ilir Jl. Letkol. A good restaurant.

Iskandar 243, tel. 312-236. This upstairs restaurant serves authentic Palembang dishes. Menu changes daily. Central location.

PADANG

Padang Style
Pagi Sore, Jl. Pondok 143. Another place to sample Padang-style cuisine. The famous *nasi padang* is a flavorful blend of fresh spices and, often, coconut cream. The best way is to let them serve you in the traditional manner: a waiter arrives at your table carrying up to 30 saucers of food strung out on both arms. Choose what you want; you only pay for what you eat. A huge meal should cost Rp3000-6000.

Simpang Raya, Jl. Bundo Kendang. This good *nasi padang* restaurant is just up the street from Hotel Machudum—cheaper, cleaner, and tastier than the "tourist" *nasi padang* restaurant, the Roda Baru in the *pasar.*

Chinese
Phoenix, Jl. Niaga 138, The most expensive and the best of Padang's Chinese restaurants where a superb meal and beer for three people will cost around Rp30,000.

BUKITTINGGI

The Market
Pasar Atas is piled high with regional snacks. At night, vendors dispense *sayak* (a fruit and vegetable dish with sharp sauce), *apam,* and roasted peanuts, and *sate.* Night stalls sell grilled corn-on-the-cob, *gulai* soup, and noodle dishes. A must is a lunch in one of the *nasi kapan* stalls halfway between the upper and lower markets. Open 0900-1800. Sit down and one of the ladies will give you a plate of rice heaped with about six different Padang-style veggies and whatever other side dishes you point out. Thankfully, no tourist menus—a great experience and very reasonable.

Indonesian
Roda Group Restaurant, Pasar Atas, Blok C-155. Excellent *martabak, dadih campur,* fruit salad, and juices, Padang food (fantastic curries, *rendang,* smoked eels right out of the ricefields, some of the tastiest *soto ayam),* sweet-and-sour vegetables—the menu even comes with a map. Get a table by the window and look out on the market.

Chinese and European
Mona Lisa, Jl. A. Yani 58. Offers above-average Chinese dishes—good value with efficient service. Classic menu misprint: Greenpeace Soup—perhaps it should be served with Rainbow Warrior trout.

Mexico, Jl. A. Yani 134. Very good food. Jalan A. Yani has half a dozen tourist restaurants like Mexico with western menus, serving everything from guacamole to pepper steak, with blaring rock music and local would-be cool guys hanging out in bamboo chairs.

SULAWESI

UJUNG PANDANG

Street Stalls
Numerous stalls set up between 1600 and 2400 all along Makassar Bay south of the Makassar Golden Hotel on Jl. Penghubur. Enjoy enormous grilled king prawns, cuttlefish, rice, soup, fresh ketchups, cold beer. The seafood is fresh and tasty, bursting with wholesome juiciness and served piping hot from the grill.

Makassarese
Asia Baru, Jl. Salahutu 2. Serves excellent grilled fish, shellfish, and *sate* in a tacky but unforgettable atmosphere. Here you get real *king* prawns. The price of a whole fish depends on the size, but expect to pay around Rp10,000-12,000.

Empang, Jl. Siau 7 (in the harbor area). A good value for traditional Makassarese food. Try the delicious *pulu mara,* boiled fish in spiced sauce.

Chinese
Ujung Pandang, Jl. Irian 42, tel. (0411) 7193 or 7688. Specializes in barbecued/grilled fish, crabs, and prawns. Open 0900-2300.

Oriental, within a short walk of the Ujung Pandang. Perhaps the best Chinese food in the city. Pedicab drivers know where it is.

Surya Supercrab, Jl. Nusakambangan 16. One of the finest crab, fish, and prawn restaurants in South Sulawesi. Very clean, no air-conditioning.

Hong Kong, Jl. Timor 69, tel. 315-246. A small, cheap place for Chinese food. Sample the huge plate of big, perfectly prepared prawns in butter and garlic (Rp4000). Also available are scrumptious, very large fish (Rp5000) in ginger sauce with chilies. Top notch food.

RANTEPAO

Indonesian and European
Warung Murni, Jl. Sesean (near the mosque). A local travelers' hangout that serves good *nasi campur* (Rp2000).

Rima I, Jl. Mappanyuki. A popular and reasonable eatery north of town center. with a complete menu from breakfast (great pancakes) to full-course dinners (really nice salad with tomatoes and garlic).

Pondok Ikan, near Toraja Misiliana Hotel. A restaurant on stilts in the middle of a lake filled with croaking frogs. Splendid location.

Alios Mambo. An excellent and very reasonable dinner; also fat sandwiches wrapped for traveling.

Sapurato Padang. The only local restaurant where you can consume Padang dishes—excellent quality and low-priced meals prepared by cooks who learned their trade in Bukittinggi.

MANADO

Pasar Swalayan
A gigantic modern a/c grocery store, across the street from Pasar 45, that sells just about everything. The second floor has an Indonesian restaurant and the expensive **California Spicy Chicken** —other than the fantastic lemon ice tea, not worth the money. On the third floor is the **Jumbo Restaurant**, serving Western and Indonesian dishes.

Minahasan/Indonesian
Selera Minahasa, Jl. Dotulolang Lasut. Minahasan food tends to be hot and spicy. Try here the local dishes—fruitbats, field mice, and dog.

Tinoor Jaya, Jl. Sam Ratulangi. Another, reasonably-priced Minahasan restaurant.

Penginapan Jakarta Jaya, Jl. Hasanuddin. The place to try really delicious *ikan mas.*

Hotel Minahasa, Jl. Sam Ratulangi 199, tel. (0431) 62559. Food and service are also quite good—the Rp5000 per person meal can actually feed two people. Order ahead of time.

Seafood
Manado Seaside Cottages and Restaurant, Malalayang (south of the city). An open-air, fresh seafood restaurant. Go for the sunset; you can stay here in one of seven nice cottages.

Klabat Indah, Jl. Sam Ratulangi 211. A reliable choice for seafood; the *cumi-cumi* dishes are outstanding.

Fiesta Ria Restaurant, Jl. Sam Ratulangi. Next door to the supermarket by the same name, this is another fine Chinese restaurant.

Javanese
Surabaya, Jl. Sam Ratulangi, tel. (0431) 52317.

Kalasan, Jl. Sudirman 9, tel. 3253. Known for its "special chicken."

NUSATENGGARA

LOMBOK

Chinese
Pabean, Jl. Yos Sudarso. A very good Chinese restaurant. Strong on seafood, but also feature some Western dishes.

Cirebon, Jl. Yos Sudarso. Chinese food, with a complete, well-priced menu.

Indonesian
Kiki, Indonesian and Western food. Located on a second-floor veranda setting overlooking Ampenan's main intersection.

FLORES

LABUHANBAJO

Indonesian and European
Bajo Beach Hotel. The hotel restaurant has a good reputation.

Sunset Restaurant. Not much in the way of fancy facilities, but tasty food. Perched over the bay.

Rudi's Restaurant. A simple, bamboo-walled eatery next to the post office that serves surprisingly delicious dishes—there's usually a daily special.

Minang Indah. Padang food.

TIMOR

KUPANG

Indonesian
Murah, directly in front of Hemiliki. Basic and inexpensive Indonesian food.

Pantai Timor, Timor Beach Hotel (where Jl. Garuda meets Jl. Sumatera). Specializes in seafood.

Bundo Kanduang. Only a five-minute walk from Hotel Flobamor, this is a big *nasi padang* restaurant.

Istana Garden, Jl. Tim Tim. An outstanding restaurant, out of town on the left just before the turnoff to the airport. It also has a bar, disco, and live music.

Chinese
Hemiliki Restaurant, Jl. Sukarno. Specializes in Chinese-style seafood dishes. Expensive but delicious. Serves one of the best *nasi goreng* in eastern Indonesia. Friendly, relaxing setting; open 0800-1500 and 1800-2230.

KALIMANTAN

BALIKPAPAN

Chinese
Atomic Cafe. A Chinese restaurant popular with foreigners. Known for its delicious chili crayfish.

New Shangrila, Jl. Sutoyo. Balikpapan's finest Chinese seafood. Extensive menu and reasonable prices. Immensely popular, so arrive early.

Seafood
Bondy Restaurant, Jl. Sutoyo. Seafood specialties in the rear open-air courtyard.

Blue Sky Restaurant, Blue Sky Hotel. Serves decent seafood, especially abalone. Popular with expatriates.

European
Barunawati, near the harbor. The place to go if you're hungry for reasonably priced sirloin.

Mirama, Mirama Hotel. Indonesian, Chinese, and European fare.

Indonesian
Minang Saiyo, Jl. Gajah Mada 45. Padang-style food.

BANJARMASIN

Indonesian
Simpang Tiga, Jl. Veteran. Good, cheap food.

International, Jl. Veteran. Decent food fairly cheap.

Kobana Padang Restaurant, Jl. Hasanuddin 19. Reasonable *nasi padang* and quick service. Another Kobana Padang restaurant is on Jl. Samudera.

Prambanan, Jl. Haryono. Javanese menu offering inexpensive meals including *udang bakar* and *ayam panggang*. Big color TV and nice atmosphere.

Chinese
Blue Ocean, Jl. Brig. Jen Katamso 44. Delicious Chinese food.

Phoenix, Jl. A. Yani (near the state hospital). Great Chinese food.

Shinta, Jl. Lambung Mangkurat. The city's elite Chinese restaurant; high prices.

Banjarese
Simpang Ampat, Jl. Simpang Ampat. Banjarese food such as *sop banjar* (Rp1000) and *sayur asem*.

Depot Makan Kaganangan and **Cendrawasih**, Jl. Samudera. These twin restaurants are real culinary delights. Both serve wonderful Banjarese specialties in a genuine atmosphere. Try *ikan saluangan* (small crispy fish), *es dewet* (a drink made from rice and coconut milk), baked river fish, huge *udang* with a musky sauce, fresh greens, and a delicate vegetable soup—pig out for under Rp10,000. These two restaurants are the best in town.

MALUKU

TERNATE

Maluku/Indonesian
Anugerah, Jl. Busouri (across from the *bemo* station). Serves meals for about Rp1000.

Gamalama, Jl. Pahlawan Revolusi. Inexpensive meals. Specializes in *coto ternate*.

Nasi Padang
Jaya, Jl. Busouri. Padang-style food.

Roda Baru, Jl. Pahlawan Revolusi. Padang-style food.

Chinese
Garuda Restaurant, Jl. Babulah (opposite the *bioskop)* Chinese food.

Fujiama, Jl. Pahlawan Revolusi (next to the post office). The swankiest and priciest restaurant in town.

AMBON

Indonesian and European
Halim Restaurant, Jl. Sultan Hairun SK 3/37, tel. (0911) 97126. Beside the governor's office, this place has a full menu: crab soup; the best *mie goreng;* also known for its ice cream. Nice open-air sitting area.

Adbulalie Coffee Shop and Restaurant, Hotel Abdulalie. Sirloin steak, spaghetti, all kinds of soup, and ice cream—a popular place with the city's affluent.

Restoran Kakatoe, Jl. Perintah. Offers a wide variety of European food: salad with fried chicken in garlic butter Rp4500, pizza topped with minced beef and chili peppers Rp7500, Indian-style prawns Rp10,000.

Tip Top, Jl. Sultan Hairun (next door to Halim). Good food, popular with Australians.

Restaurant Sakura, next to the Tip Top. For genuine Javanese food and Yogya-style *ayam goreng kalasan.*

Madurese
RM Ai, Jl. Sultan Babulah, Muslim quarter. A wonderful Madurese eatery. *Sate* smoke wafts through crowded, noisy rooms. Both are open 0700-0100. Near Hotel Abdulalie.

RM Madura, Jl. Sultan Babulah, Muslim quarter. Feast on a full range of genuine Islamic-Indonesian dishes such as *gado-gado* with super fresh veggies (Rp1000), perfect *soto ay madura* (Rp1100), and a selection of ice juices.

Chinese
New Garden Restaurant, Jl. Pahlawan Revolusi. Ambon's best Chinese restaurant—crowded even on Monday nights. Consume classical Mandarin fare, while an organ and vocalist perform for your dining pleasure. A fun place.

IRIAN JAYA

JAYAPURA

Indonesian and European
Kebon Siri, in front of the Irian Plaza Hotel. *Ikan bakar* (baked fish) and other seafood.

Satya House, next to the Irian Plaza. Clean and jaunty, with reasonable food at reasonable prices.

Hawaii Restaurant, near the waterfront and the IMBI cinema. Serves *soto ayam* for Rp15,000, fish and shrimp for Rp17,000, and Rp5000-6000 *nasi* dishes.

Mandala Restaurant, Jl. Percetakan, on the city side of *Kantor Gubernor.* Less expensive than the Hawaii. Located right on the waterfront, with a/c and a good view over the harbor.

Simpang Tigo, Jl. Percetakan. Japapura's best Padang-style restaurant—big, well-ventilated, and central.

Jaya Grill, Jl. Percetakan. Known for its popular Chinese and European food, with a scenic view of the harbor.

WAMENA

European and Asian

Shinta Prima. Ask for the local specialty, *udang asam manis saus*—fresh Baliem River crawfish the size of lobsters for Rp1700 apiece.

Bougainiville Restaurant. Chinese-run, with ordinary food and the decor of an Iowa barbecue joint. *Sate ayam, nasi putih,* etc. The proprietor provides pickup and dropoff service to and from anywhere in town.

Mas Budi's, Jl. Trikora 116, tel. (0967) 31214. Great for Javanese food. The *mie kuah* is delicious, as is the *nasi goreng, mie bakso, cap cai, udang goreng,* fried fish, and *es jerish.* The best traveler's hangout in town.

Warung Sari Rasa, across from the market. Excellent *mie goreng* dishes.

Flower's Coffee Shop. The best place for breakfast, new and clean, with good coffee.

Tourist Offices

Tourist offices go by the name of *Bapparda, Dipparda* and *Kanwil Depparpostel,* or you can simply ask for the *kantor pariwisata* (tourist office). In large provincial capitals these offices are usually found in or near the governor's office (*kantor gubernor* or *gubernoran*). In the smaller cities the *kantor pariwisata* is very often situated in the best hotel or the biggest travel agency in town; if not, they will know where it is. In small towns, the Department of Education and Culture (*Kantor Pendidikan dan Kebudayaan*) is the next best place to go for tourist information. Within Indonesia itself, regional offices publish excellent booklets and pamphlets like the *East Java Visitors Guide Book* issued by the East Java Government Department of Tourism, the *Bali Tourist Guide* (free from hotels) and the *Bali Path Finder,* issued by the Ubud Tourist Office (Central Bali).

Useful Addresses

SELECTED DIPLOMATIC OFFICES IN INDONESIA

Australia: 15 Jl. M.H. Thamrin, tel. (021) 323-109

Belgium: Wisma BCA, 15th floor, Jl. Jend Sudirman Kav 22-23, tel. (021) 578-0510

Denmark: Wisma Metropolitan, 16th floor, 29 Jl. Jend. Sudirman, Jakarta Selatan, tel. (021) 516-565

France: 22 Jl Lembang, Jakarta, tel. (021) 365-301

Germany: 217 Jl. S. Parman, Medan, tel. (061) 324-073

Great Britain: 75 Jl. M.H. Thamrin, Jakarta, tel. (021) 330-904

Japan: 24 Jl. M.H. Thamrin, Jakarta, tel. (021) 324-308

Malaysia: 6 Jl. Dr. Cipto, Medan, tel. (061) 517-150

Netherlands: Royal Netherlands Embassy, Jl. H.R. Rasuna Said Kav. S-3, Kuningan, tel. (021) 511-515

New Zealand: 41 Jl. Diponegoro, Menteng, Jakarta, P.O. Box 2439 DKT

Singapore: 3 Jl. Tengku Daud, Medan. tel. (061) 513-134

Sweden: 2 Jl. Hang Jebat, Medan, tel. (061), 511-017

Switzerland: Swiss Restaurant, Legian Kelod Kuta, P.O. Box 2035, Kuta 80361, Denpasar, tel. (0361) 51735

United States of America: 5 Jl. Merdeka Selatan, Jakarta, tel. (021) 360-360

SELECTED INDONESIAN CONSULATES ABROAD

AUSTRALIA

Indonesian Consulate General, Beulah Park S>A., Adelaide 6067, tel. (08) 318-108

Consulate of the Republic of Indonesia, 22, Coronation Drive, Stuart Park, Darwin NT 0801, tel. (089) 819-352

Indonesian Consulate, Judd Street, South Perth, Western Australia 6151, tel. (09) 367-1178

Indonesian Consulate General, 236-238 Marcubra Road, Marcubra, New South Wales 2035, tel. (09) 367-1178

BELGIUM

Indonesian Consulate General, Suikerul 5 Bus No. 9, 2000 Antwerp, tel. (031) 3225-6136

CANADA

Indonesian Consulate, 425 University Avenue 9th floor, Toronto, Ontario M5G 1T6, tel. (416) 591-6461

Indonesian Consulate, 1455 W. Georgia Street, 2nd floor, Vancouver, B.C. V6G 2T3, tel. (604) 682-8855

FRANCE

Consulate D'Indonesie, 25 Boulevard Carmagnole, 13008 Marseille, tel. 9171-3435

GERMANY

Indonesian Consulate General, Eplanade 7-9, 0-1100 Berlin, tel. (030) 472-2002

Indonesian Consulate General. Berliner Alle 2. Post Fach 9140. Duesseldorf. tel. (0211) 353-081

Indonesian Consulate. Widermayer Strasse 24d-8000, Muenchen 22, tel. (089) 294-609

HONG KONG

Indonesian Consulate General, 127-129 Leighton Road, 6-8 Koswick St. Entrance, tel. (5) 2890-4421

MALAYSIA

Indonesian Consulate, 467 Jalan Burma, P.O. Box 502, 10350 Penang, tel. (04) 374-686

SPAIN

Indonesian Consulate General, Rambia Estudios 119, Apartado 18, Barcelona-2, tel. 317-1900

UNITED STATES OF AMERICA

Indonesian Consulate General, Two Illinois Center, 233 North Michigan Ave. Suite 1422, Chicago, IL 60601, tel. (312) 938-0101

Indonesian Consulate, Pri Tower, 733 Bishop Street, P.O. Box 3379, Honolulu, HI 96842, tel. (808) 524-4300

Indonesian Consulate General, 3457 Wilshire Blvd. Los Angeles, CA 90010, tel. (213) 383-5126

Indonesian Consulate General, 5 East 68th Street, New York, NY 10021, tel. (212) 879-0600

Consulate of the Republic of Indonesia, 1111 Columbus Avenue, San Francisco, CA 94133, tel. (415) 474-9571

Please send all comments, corrections,
additions, amendments and critiques to:

The Guidebook Company Ltd.,
Ground Floor, 2 Lower Kai Yuen Lane,
North Point, Hong Kong
E-mail: odyssey@asiaonline.net

Index